The Nature
of the Environment

Second Edition
ANDREW GOUDIE

BLACKWELL
Oxford UK & Cambridge USA

© Andrew Goudie 1984; 1989

First edition 1984
Reprinted 1985, 1987, 1988
Second edition 1989
Reprinted 1990, 1992

Blackwell Publishers
108 Cowley Road, Oxford, OX4 1JF, UK

Three Cambridge Center
Cambridge, Massachusetts 02142, USA

British Library Cataloguing in Publication Data

Goudie, Andrew
    The nature of the environment. – 2nd ed.
    1. Physical geographical features
    I. Title
    910′.02
ISBN 0–631–16128–7 Pbk.

Library of Congress Cataloging in Publication Data

Goudie, Andrew.
    The nature of the environment / Andrew Goudie. – 2nd
        ed.
        p.   cm.
    Bibliography: p.
    Includes index.
    ISBN 0–631–16128–7 (pbk)
    1. Physical geography.   I. Title.
GB54.5.068 1989
910′.02–dc19   88–14524
                                                                                    CIP

Frontispiece A montane forest ecosystem on the slopes of a volcano in the Mount Bosavi National Park, Papua New Guinea

Typeset by Graphicraft Typesetters Ltd., Hong Kong
Printed in Great Britain by Butler & Tanner Ltd, Frome.

Martin Banns

DONATION

£12.95
Don.
DOPS
(Gon)

0631161287

Contents

Preface

First Edition

The content of courses in physical geography has changed markedly in recent years for three main reasons. First, there has been a desire to make physical geography more relevant to human affairs, to integrate it more closely with human geography, to become more concerned with natural hazards, to investigate environmental problems and to assess the human impact on environment change. Second, geography as a whole has become involved with process, measurement and numerical analysis. Third and most important, near-revolutionary developments have taken place in the subject matter of physical geography – notably in ecology, hydrology, plate tectonics and our knowledge of the Pleistocene.

All these changes mean that many general textbooks in physical geography are ceasing to have the utility they once had, and new books are needed. This book is intended as such a contribution.

In chapters 1 and 2 we cover developments in such matters as plate tectonics and climatic change, as well as background information on global patterns of natural phenomena. One aim of the book is to stress the way in which the components of the environment are integrated at different scales. Accordingly, the next four chapters deal with the four main world zones (polar, mid-latitude, desert and tropical), describing their features, showing how the different components of the environment are interrelated and explaining their problems, hazards and some of the modifications wrought by man. Part III deals with two rather special environments that occur in any one of the four main zones – mountains and coasts – but the same approach is followed as in the previous four chapters. Part IV moves from major environments to a consideration of some major classes of phenomena (e.g. rivers), and once again interrelationships are explored and human implications assessed.

The overall purpose of the book, therefore, is to impart modern information on the human environment at various scales from the global to the local; to integrate the study of geomorphology, climatology, hydrology, pedology and biogeography; and to consider the ways in which we ourselves both mould and are moulded by our landscape and environment. It is hoped that this approach will encourage readers to move on to books covering aspects of landscape and environment and their relationships to plants, animals and mankind in greater depth and detail than space allows here. To that end, I have included a guide to further reading.

To avoid the disturbance that results when the text is broken up by detailed referencing, I have refrained from providing such documentation. This means that I cannot give the acknowledgement I would like to the work and ideas of other authors, to whom I am greatly in debt.

I am grateful to those publishers and authors who have allowed me to reproduce figures published elsewhere, and to the following for comments on earlier drafts: Dr M. A. Summerfield (now of the University of Edinburgh); Professor S. Gregory; Professor E. Derbyshire; David Wright; Dr B. J. Knapp; Eleanor M. Rawling; David F. Horsfall; Gordon Smith and Dr Heather Viles.

November 1983

Second Edition

For this second edition, I have expanded sections deserving greater coverage, improved some of the plates and figures, updated the Guide to Further Reading and added material of topical interest (e.g., the threat of worldwide sea-level rise, the ozone crisis, El Niño, etc.). In an attempt to make the book even more valuable for student use, questions and exercises have been added, and I am grateful to Dr Nick Middleton and Mr Mike Corbett for assistance in preparing them.

A.S.G.
August 1988

Acknowledgements

The author and the publisher are grateful to the following for permission to redraw and reproduce figures: *Scientific American* for (1.11) reproduced from R. S. Dietz, 'Geosynclines, mountains and continent building', *Scientific American, 226(3),* 1972, p. 37, copyright © March 1972 by Scientific American, Inc., all rights reserved; Butterworth & Co. (Publishers), Ltd. for (2.13) reproduced from P. A. Furley and W. W. Newey, *Geography of the biosphere* (1983), figure 4.22; George Allen & Unwin for (2.14) reproduced from A. S. Collinson, *Introduction to world vegetation* (1977), figure 57. Curtis Brown Group Ltd. for (3.2) reproduced from R. J. Rice, *Fundamentals of geomorphology* (Longman, 1977), figure 11.6, copyright © R. J. Rice 1977. International Glaciological Society for (3.3) redrawn from J. Nye, *Journal of glaciology,* 2, 1952, figure 8; Univeristy of California Press for (3.4) reproduced from Larry W. Price, *Mountains and man: a study of process and environment* (1981), figure 5.15; Curtis Brown Group Ltd. for (3.13) reproduced from R. J. Rice *Fundamentals of geomorphology* (Longman, 1977), figures 13.5 and 13.6, copyright © R. J. Rice 1977; *Canadian geotechnical journal* for (3.18) reproduced from J. R. Mackay, *Canadian geotechnical journal,* 7, 1970, figure 6.6; Macmillan for (4.1a) reproduced from M. D. Newson and J. Hanwell, *Systematic physical geography* (1982), figure 2.10, by permission of Macmillan, London and Basingstoke; Longman for (4.4) reproduced from A. Henderson-Sellers and P. J. Robinson, *Contemporary Climatology* (1986), figure 5.30, reproduced from H. Critchfield, *General climatology* (1983), figure 5.3, © Prentice Hall, based on A. N. Strahler, *Physical geography* (1951), figure 23.4, © John Wiley & Sons, Inc.; Allen and Unwin for (4.5) reproduced from I. D. White, D. N. Mattershead and S. J. Harrison, *Environmental Systems: an introductory text* (1984), figure 8.10; Cambridge University Press for (4.6) reproduced from E. M. Bridges, *World Soils* (1970), figure 5.6; George Allen & Unwin and the *Journal of meteorology* for (4.7) reproduced from A. H. Perry, *Environmental hazards in the British Isles* (1981), figures 2.10 and 2.11, and from G. T. Meaden, 'Tornadoes in Britain, their intensities and distribution in space and time,' *Journal of meteorology,* 1, 1976; George Allen & Unwin for (4.8) reproduced from A. H. Perry, *Environmental hazards in the British Isles* (1981), figure 3.5; George Allen & Unwin and the Controller of Her Majesty's Stationery Office for (4.11) reproduced from A. H. Perry, *Environmental hazards in the British Isles* (1981), figure 5.2, and from J. Glasspoole and H. Rowsell, 'Absolute droughts and partial droughts over the British Isles 1906–1940', *Meteorological magazine,* 76, 1947; Longman and *Madoqua* for (5.4) reproduced from G. N. Louw and M. Seely, *Ecology of desert organisms* (1982), figures 3.2, 3.8 and 4.11, and from J. E. W. Dixon and G. N. Louw, *Madoqua,* 11, 1978, figures 5 and 4; John Wiley & Sons Ltd. for (6.1) and (6.2) reproduced from S. Nieuwolt, *Tropical climatology: an introduction to the climates of law latitudes* (1977), figures 6.4 and 6.5, copyright © S. Nieuwolt, 1977; Academic Press Inc. (London) Ltd. for (6.4) reproduced with permission from D. R Harris (ed.), *Human ecology in savanna environments* (1980), figure 2, copyright © Academic Press Inc. (London) Ltd.; Blackwell Scientific Publications Ltd for (6.6) reproduced from M. Begon, J. L. Harper and C. R. Townsend, *Ecology, Individuals, Populations and communities,*

(1986), figure 22.14; Harper & Row, Publishers, Inc. for (6.7) reproduced from Peter Haggett (ed.), *Geography: a modern synthesis*, third edition, figure 8.4, 'Land rotation and population density', p. 173, copyright © 1979 by Peter Haggett; Academic Press Inc. (London) Ltd. for (6.9) reproduced with permission from D. R. Harris (ed.), *Human ecology in savanna environments* (1980), figure 4, copyright © Academic Press Inc., (London) Ltd.; Longman and Butterworth & Co. (Publishers), Ltd. for (6.10) reproduced from J. Davies, *Geographical variation in coastal development* (Longman, 1980), figures 43, 45 and 46, and from P. A. Furley and W. W. Newey, *Geography of the biosphere* (Butterworth, 1983), figure 11.11; Prentice-Hall, Inc. for (6.11) reproduced from Stokes, Judson and Picard, *Introduction to geology: physical and historical*, © 1978, p. 311, reprinted by permission of Prentice-Hall, Inc., Englewood Cliffs, N. J.; Springer-Verlag for (7.5b) reproduced from H. Walter, *Vegetation of the earth*, Heidelberg Science Library, volume 15, 1973, figure 15; Indiana University Press for (7.6) reproduced from L. W. Saan in H. E. Wright and W. H. Osburn (eds), *Arctic and alpine environments* (1967); Cambridge University Press for (8.4) reproduced from R. J. Small, *The study of landforms* (1970), figure 184; John Wiley & Sons Inc. for (8.8) reproduced from A. N. Strahler and A. H. Strahler, *Modern physical geography* (1978), figure 22.31 copyright © A. N. Strahler and A. H. Strahler, 1978; I. G. Simmons for (9.1) reproduced from I. G. Simmons, *Biogeographical processes* (Allen & Unwin, 1982), figure 2.3; Macmillan for (9.2) reproduced from *Ecology of populations* by A. S. Boughey; (1986), p. 102, copyright © 1968 by A. S. Boughey; Holt, Rinehart and Winston, CBS College Publishing for (9.3) adapted from *Fundamentals of ecology*, third edition, by Eugene P. Odum, copyright © 1971 by W. B. Saunders College; Chapman & Hall for (9.5) modified from M. Gorman, *Island ecology* (1979); *Scientific American* for (9.7) reproduced from J. Harlan, *Scientific American*, 235, 1976, pp. 92–93, copyright © 1976 by *Scientific American*, Inc., all rights reserved; Methuen & Co. for (9.8) reproduced from C. Elton, *Ecology invasions by animals and plants* (1958), p. 22; Nature Conservancy Council for (9.11) reproduced from its *Summary of Objec-*
tives and Strategy, (1984), p. 7; Oxford University Press, Inc. for (10.6) reproduced from *Putnam's geology*, third edition, by Peter W. Birkeland and Edwin E. Larson, copyright © 1964, 1971, 1978 by Oxford University Press, Inc.; Cambridge University Press for (11.1) reproduced from M. A. Carson and M. Kirkby, *Hillslope form and process* (1972), figure 5.2; Oxford University Press for (11.6) reproduced from M. J. Selby, *Hillslope materials and processes* (1982), figure 7.29; Duckworth for (12.1) reproduced from I. Fenwick and B. J. Knapp, *Soil process and response* (1982), figures 6.28 and 6.29; John Wiley & Sons Ltd. for (12.4) modified from D. I. Smith and T. C. Atkinson, 'Process, landforms and climate in limestone regions', in E. Derbyshire (ed.), *Geomorphology and climate* (1976), copyright © John Wiley & Sons Ltd., 1976; Longman for (13.1) reproduced from A. Henderson-Sellers and P. J. Robinson, *Contemporary Climatology*, (1986), figure 3.8a; Prentice-Hall, Inc. for (13.2) reproduced from Frederick K. Lutgens, Edward J. Tarbuck, *The Atmosphere: an introduction to meteorology*, © 1979, pp. 103, 105, reprinted by permission of Prentice-Hall, Inc., Englewood Cliffs, N. J.; Longman for (13.3) reproduced from A. Henderson-Sellers and P. J. Robinson, *Contemporary Climatology*, (1986), figure 3.20; K. Gilman and M. D. Newson for (13.8) reproduced from K. Gilman and M. D. Newson, *Soil pipes and pipeflow – a hydrological study in upland Wales* (Geo Books, 1980), figure 17; Methuen & Co. for (13.11) modified from J. C. Rodda, 'The flood hydrograph', in R. J. Chorley (ed.), *Water, earth and man* (1967), figure 9.12; Cambridge University Press for (13.14) reproduced from H. C. Pereira, *Land use and water resources* (1973), figure 8; Methuen & Co. for (14.3) reproduced from K. S. Richards, *Rivers: forms and processes in alluvial channels* (1982), figure 2.3; W. H. Freeman and Company for (14.9) reproduced from figures 7.43 and 7.44 of *Earth*, third edition, by F. Press and R. Siever. W. H. Freeman and Company, copyright © 1982; Oxford University Press and Cambridge University Press for (14.12), reproduced from I. Statham, *Earth surface sediment transport* (OUP, 1977), figure 6.14, and from D. I. Smith and P. Stopp, *The river basin* (CUP, 1978), figure 14.10; International Association of Hydrological Sciences for

(14.13) reproduced from D. Walling and A. H. A. Kleo, 'Sediment yields of rivers in areas of low precipitation: a global view', IAHS Publication 128, 1979, figure 3; Pergamon Press for (15.1) reproduced from P. Brimblecombe in *Atmospheric environment*, 11, 1977, figure 1; W. R. D. Sewell for (15.2) reproduced from S. Chagnon in W. R. D. Sewell (ed.), *Modifying the weather: a social assessment* (University of Victoria, 1973), figure 1.5; John Wiley & Sons Ltd. for (15.4) reproduced from K. S. Richards and Wood, in K. J. Gregory (ed.), *River channel changes* (1977), figure 24.6, copyright © John Wiley & Sons Ltd., 1977; The University Press of Virginia for (15.5) reproduced from A. Gameson and A. Wheeler in J. Carins, K. L. Dickson and E. E. Hendricks (eds), *Recovery and restoration of damaged ecosystems* (1977), figure 4.

The author and the publisher are grateful to the following for permission to reproduce plates: Aerofilms 8.8; Australian Information Service, London 2.4; Daisy Blow/ICCE 10.4; Mark Boulton/ICCE Part I title illustration; British Geological Survey 2.7, 4.6; Cambridge University Collection, copyright reserved 4.5, 8.1, 8.4; J. Allan Cash 1.1, 3.3; Centralian Advocate 5.1; John Cleare/Mountain Camera 7.2, 7.4, 10.1, 11.8; Eros Data 1.4; William Felger/Grant Heilman 1.2; Geoslides 6.4; © Greenpeace/Midgley Part V title illustration; Grant Heilman 1.7, 7.3, 10.9; Eric Kay 1.6, 10.5, 10.10, 10.11, 10.12, 14.4; Douglas Kirkland (Contact/Colorific) 10.6; Mansell Collection 6.8; Professor Geoffrey J. Martin 11.5, 11.7; Colin Monteath, Hedgehog House, New Zealand 3.10a, 3.10b; Marion and Tony Morrison 6.1, 6.2, 6.6, 6.7; National Portrait Gallery, London 2.3; National Publicity Studios, New Zealand 14.1; Nature Conservancy Council 8.3; Malcolm Newdick 15.1; Oxfam/Mike Goldwater 6.3; Planet Earth Pictures/E.C.G. Lemon Part II title illustration; Popperfoto 2.4 (bottom, left), 3.6, 8.2, 9.3, 10.2, 10.3, 10.7, 13.5; Nigel Press 5.11, 14.3; Royal Geographical Society 11.6; Scottish Tourist Board 1.5; K. Shone 13.1; Soil Survey of England and Wales 2.2; Swiss National Tourist Office 3.1; Roger Tutt 4.8; University of Dundee 2.1; University Museum of Oxford 9.6; A. L. Washburn (from *Geocryology*, A. L. Washburn 1979, Edward Arnold), 3.8, 3.9; Bradford Washburn, Boston Museum of Science 3.2, 3.7; Wessex Water 4.9; Gerry Wooldridge 12.8; WWF Part III title illustration; WWF/Dr. Thomas Schultze-Westrum frontispiece; WWF/Charles Vaucher Part IV title illustration; WWF/Gerard Vienne/François Bel 9.5. All other plates were provided by the author.

PART I
The Global Framework

1 Global Geological Background

1.1 The ancient earth

Our solar system consists of planets such as the earth, moons, asteroids, comets, meteorites, dust and gas – and a central star – the sun. We do not know exactly how the solar system formed, though the most favoured theory is that condensation took place from a great revolving gas cloud in space, which gradually contracted under gravity. This made the central mass hot enough for thermonuclear reactions to set in, and so a new star was formed – the sun.

Although we may not be sure *how* the solar system originated, we are rather more certain about *when* it originated. Dates for the oldest earth rocks, the oldest moon rocks and some stony meteorites all suggest that the solar system is about 4600 million years old. This is an almost inconceivable time span, especially when we think that our own species has inhabited the earth for only a minute fraction of that time – probably around 2–3 million years.

The world we know today thus has an enormous and complicated history, and to understand the present configuration of the major elements of our planet – the oceans and the continents – we need to look at this history.

1.2 Core, mantle and crust

When it first formed, the earth must have been a molten mass. As it gradually cooled it became differentiated into a series of concentric layers. In the interior of the earth (figure 1.1) we have a layer called the *core*, the outer parts of which

have the properties of a liquid and the inner parts of which have the properties of a solid. We know that it is very dense, and that it is probably composed largely of iron, with lesser amounts of other elements such as nickel. We also know that

Figure 1.1 The structure of the earth: (a) the major zones (b) the outer layers.

Opposite The weathering and erosion of closely bedded sedimentary rocks has produced the distinctive 'pancake rock' formations on the west coast of the South Island of New Zealand.

it has very high temperatures – probably of the order of 5500°C – and very high pressures.

The middle layer of the earth is called the *mantle*. This is a thick layer (*c*.2800 km) composed of material in the solid state. It consists of 'heavy rock' including peridotite (composed largely of the silicate minerals olivine and pyroxene), dunite (pure olivine) and eclogite (a dense form of basalt). Temperatures within the mantle range from 5000°C near the core to 1300°C just below the crust. There are two main parts of the mantle. One part is so hot that is semi-molten and deformable; this is called the *asthenosphere*. It is overlain by a more rigid layer called the *lithosphere*.

The outer layer of the earth, called the *crust*, is very much thinner, generally being between 6 and 70 km thick, and is very much less dense than the underlying mantle, from which it has been derived by complex processes operating over many millions of years. The surface of separation between crust and mantle is called the *Mohorovičić Discontinuity* (after a Yugoslavian seismologist), but is often simplified to *Moho*. The crust occurs as two types: continental and oceanic. The continental crust (known as *sial*) is not very dense (averaging 2.7 gm cm^{-3} compared with 3.0–3.3 for oceanic crust and 3.4 for the upper mantle), but it tends to be relatively thicker (averaging 35–40 km, and reaching 60–70 km under high mountain chains) than the oceanic crust (called *sima*), which for its part averages only about 5–6 km in thickness. The continental crust has a varied and complicated composition, though it tends to be granitic above and basaltic beneath. The crust of the ocean basins consists simply of basaltic rocks – the granite is absent.

One particularly fascinating and important discovery of recent years has been that the ocean floors (and underlying oceanic crust) are relatively young. Some parts of the continental crust in Greenland and southern Africa are older than 3500 million years, whereas the oceanic crust is nowhere older than 250 million years.

1.3   The nature of the ocean floors

Viewed from space, one of the most striking features of the earth is how large a proportion of it is covered by the waters of the oceans. Only about 29 per cent of the earth's surface is composed of dry land – the rest is ocean. If we could remove all the water from the ocean basins some other remarkable facts would be revealed: first, the ocean floors are extremely complicated in their relief; second, that relief is characterised by some extraordinary mountains and enormous valleys or trenches.

Seaward from the coast there is generally a gently sloping platform that is called the *continental shelf* (figure 1.2), with a water depth of no more than about 180 m. In some parts of the world this shelf is very extensive, notably off China, Canada, northern Australia and western Europe (figure 1.3). Elsewhere, for example off the western coast of South America, it is very narrow, and deep water is reached very quickly as one moves off shore. The seaward edge of the

Figure 1.2 A diagrammatic cross-section illustrating some of the main features of the geomorphology of the oceans.

continental shelf is marked by the *continental slope*; this adjoins the *continental rise*, which runs down to the *abyssal plains*. Continental slopes and rises throughout the world are cut by deep valleys called *submarine canyons*. These are generally a few hundred metres deep and several kilometres wide, usually with a V-shaped cross-section. They are probably created by the erosional effects of *turbidity currents* — powerful sediment-laden currents that sweep off the continental slope — though in some areas of powerful downwarping they may have originated as fluvial valleys.

The abyssal plains lie at an average depth of about 5 km, but they are broken by a series of mountains. Some of these crests may be tall enough to rise above the ocean level as islands; the ones that do not break the surface are either drowned peaks (*seamounts*) or have had their tops planed off (*guyots*). Whatever their form, they all have a volcanic origin.

There is often a central ridge structure in an ocean (figure 1.4(a)) that divides the basin into two major compartments. This is especially clearly demonstrated in the Atlantic; in the Pacific the East Pacific Rise is off-centre. These *mid-oceanic ridges* are 2–4 km in height, up to 4000 km wide, and form a nearly continuous submarine mountain range over 40 000 km in length. They sometimes break the ocean surface to give islands and groups of islands like Iceland and Tristan da Cunha. Precisely in the centre of the ridge, at its highest point, there may be a trenchlike feature called the *axial rift*, the form of which (figure 1.2) tempts one to imagine that perhaps the crust is being pulled apart at this point. (Whether it is or not is something we shall shortly turn to.) The ridges are broken and repeatedly offset by innumerable fractures called *faults*.

Undoubtedly, these oceanic ridges are the most imposing relief feature on the face of the earth. One such ridge runs all the way down the Atlantic Ocean, turns east and enters the Indian Ocean, where one branch of it penetrates Africa and the other continues eastwards between Australia and Antarctica before swinging across the South

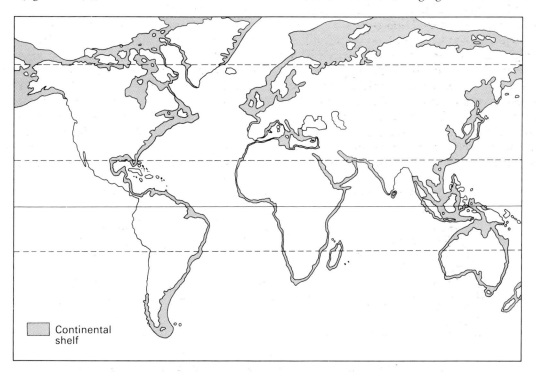

Continental shelf

Figure 1.3 The distribution of continental shelves. Note their relatively greater extent in high latitudes of the northern hemisphere including around the British Isles. Large expanses of the continental shelves became dry land when world sea levels were depressed during the glacial phases of the last Ice Age (Pleistocene).

Figure 1.4(a)   The distribution of mid-ocean ridges – submarine mountains formed of basalt.

Pacific, eventually penetrating North America at the head of the Gulf of California.

Finally, the ocean floors, and especially the floor of the Pacific Ocean, are characterised by deep, furrow-like *trenches*, hundreds of kilometres long, tens of kilometres wide and reaching to depths in excess of 7 km. They are often flanked by volcanic islands, and may sometimes lie close to major continental mountain chains with volcanic activity (figure 1.4(b)). The deepest place on earth lies in one of these trenches: it is the Nero Deep in the Pacific's Mariana Trench, where the greatest depth below sea level so far determined is 11 033 m. A trench always runs parallel to the edge of a continent or a line of islands, and it tends to have an asymmetric V-shaped cross-section. The steep side of the V always borders the continent or island arc, and the gentler slope leads out to the opean sea.

1.4   The surface of the land

Basically, the land surface of the earth is characterised by two main categories of surface. On the one hand there are the active belts of mountain-building, and on the other there are the more inactive regions of old rocks. The former

are formed either by *volcanism* or by the breaking and bending of the earth's crust by the forces of *tectonic activity*. Volcanism involves the accumulation of volcanic rock by the extrusion of molten material from within the earth, which is termed *magma*. Many high mountain ranges consist wholly or in part of chains of volcanoes built by lava or ash. In many cases tectonism and volcanism have combined to produce a particular mountain range.

The zones where active mountain-building takes place are rather narrow, and most of them lie along continental margins. They include major chains such as the European Alps and the world's highest range, the Himalayas. These chains are linked in arc-shaped groups to form the two main mountain belts. One of these, the Eurasian-Melanesian belt, begins in the Atlas Mountains of North Africa and runs through southern Europe to Turkey, Iran, the Himalayas and on into south-east Asia. In Indonesia it joins the second belt – the circum-Pacific belt – and runs up into the western Pacific. Here the mountain arcs lie well offshore from the continent of Asia and take the form of *island arcs* (figure 1.4(b)), running through the Philippines, Japan, the Kuriles and the Aleutians. In North and South America, in

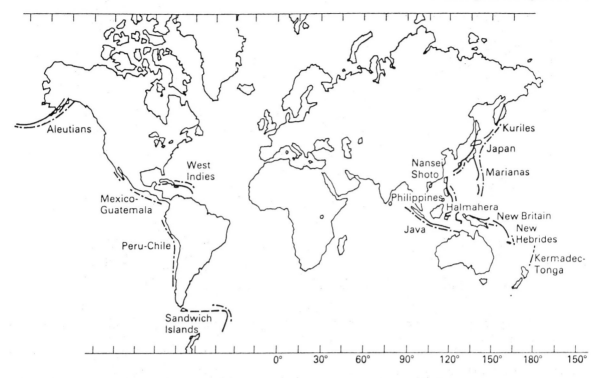

Figure 1.4(b) The distribution of ocean trenches (solid line) and island arcs (dashed line).

contrast, this mountain belt is largely on the continents, and includes the Cordilleran ranges in North America and the Andes in South America.

The zones of active mountain-building are therefore very localised in their distribution. The remainder of the continental crust is composed of less active regions where the basement rocks are much older. These *continental shields* are quite extensive (figure 1.5). For the most part they comprise areas of low hills and plateau beneath which lie igneous and metamorphic rocks. The shields may contain one or more areas of extremely ancient granitic rocks called *cratons*, which have been essentially undisturbed for at least 2400 million years. The old rocks may be covered by younger sedimentary layers, which accumulated when the shields subsided and were inundated by shallow seas.

The ancient shields are very extensive in Greenland, north-eastern Canada, eastern South America, much of Africa, peninsular India, western Australia and parts of Antarctica.

Another characteristic of these inactive areas is old mountain roots. These are formed largely of sedimentary rocks that were intensely deformed by mountain-building episodes in the past, and frequently were changed by great heat and pressure into metamorphic rocks. Such is the antiquity of these mountain-building phases that extensive erosion has since occurred, so that only the roots of the mountain remain, as chains of long, narrow ridges rising less than a few thousand metres above sea level.

1.5 Earthquakes

We have already seen that there are certain large-scale features that characterise the earth's surface – notably, the ocean ridges and the mountain chains. When we look at the pattern of earthquakes (figure 1.6) we see that they too are highly localised. A major group of earthquakes has occurred along a line formed by the mid-ocean ridges, while another group follows the world's two major mountain chains. As earthquakes represent zones in which the earth's crust is moving

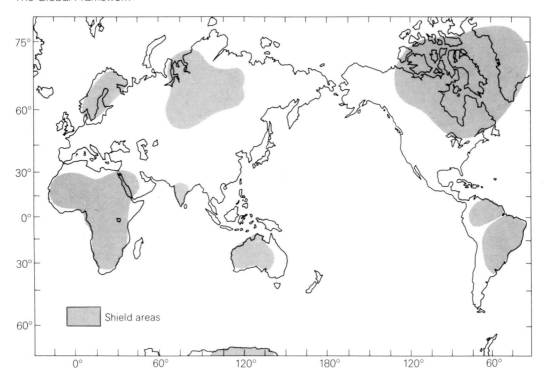

Figure 1.5 The distribution of the major shield areas of the earth, representing materials cooled from the earliest molten surface of the planet.

and is under stress (see section 10.4 for a further discussion), they give an indication of those parts of the earth where crustal activity is intense. The big question is, Why does the distribution of earthquakes, mountain ranges and mid-ocean ridges show the distinctive pattern that it does? Before answering that, however, we should consider another important aspect – the shape that the continents take.

1.6   The shape of the continents

If one looks at a map or globe of the world, one of the most striking features is the remarkable way in which, if they were to be pushed up against each other, South America and Africa would fit. This operation can be taken a step further; without too much difficulty, southern Australia can be made to fit onto Antarctica, and so forth, until one giant continent can be assembled like a jigsaw (figure 1.7). Furthermore, geologists have investigated the rocks that occur in, for example, Brazil and southwest Africa, and

find that they are much the same in both age and type. In both regions there are shield areas in which the rocks are older than 2 billion years, separated by sharp boundaries from 550 million year old rocks. When the two continents are placed in their positions prior to drift, both the rocks and their boundaries correlate well. The structural grain of the continents also matches. Furthermore, from about 550 million to about 100 million years ago, when the two continents were together, there were the same sequences of erosion, glaciation, flooding, sedimentation, coal formation, and volcanic activity. The past distribution of certain plants and animals indicates the same thing. For instance, *Mesosaurus* is a small reptile of the Permian Period (*c.*250 million years ago) which is known only from South Africa and southern Brazil; and *Glossopteris* is a fossil leaf abundant in many deposits of the same age in South Africa, South America, Madagascar, India and Australia.

There is also what is sometimes called 'wrong-latitude' evidence. Various rocks and fossils that

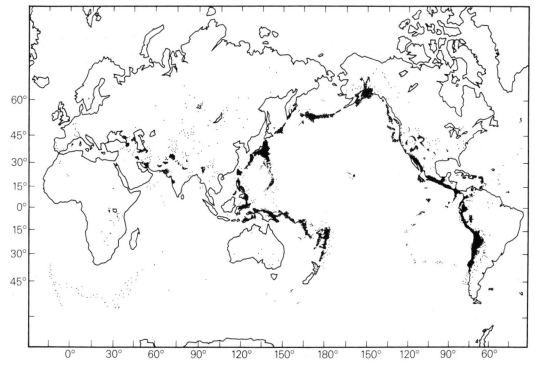

Figure 1.6 The distribution of earthquakes (1957–67).

Figure 1.7 An attempt to reconstruct the positions of the continents before continental drift had disrupted Gondwanaland, based on both geological evidence and the best computer 'fit' of continental outlines.

were thought to require rather special climatic conditions for their development were found at latitudes for which such conditions seemed impossible. For example, coal was found in rocks under the icy wastes of Antarctica; yet coal is believed to form in warm subtropical conditions like those of the present-day Florida Everglades. Conversely, evidence was found in central Africa and in lowland India of huge ice sheets which today are restricted to high latitudes. Clearly, it was not easy to reconcile observations of this kind with the present pattern of climatic belts, and so one solution was to suggest that the continents had moved, and had occupied different latitudes at different times.

These considerations have suggested that some areas that are now close together, such as North Africa and southern Europe, had once been far apart, while continents now separated by a wide ocean, such as Australia and Antarctica or Africa and America, were at one time united.

Thus we must conclude that the continents as we know them today have not been immovable, but that their shapes and positions have evolved over time. They are the drifting fragments derived from the break-up of an ancient supercontinent, called Pangaea. (The word comes from the Greek, meaning 'all land'.) The process that caused this break-up is termed *continental drift*.

Pangaea began to disintegrate about 200 million years ago, and initially split into two supercontinents, Laurasia in the north and Gondwanaland in the south. By about 180 million years ago Gondwanaland had begun to break up into South America-Africa, Australia-Antarctica, and India. The initial opening up of the South Atlantic between South America and Africa began about 135 million years ago and India began a rapid journey towards Asia, with which it was to collide about 30 million years ago. Australia and Antarctica began to separate about 45 million years ago, while Europe and North America broke away from each other some 5 to 10 million years later.

1.7   Wandering continents

In recent years the evidence to support the ancient theory of continental drift has become much more substantial. In particular, geologists have found support for the idea by studies of the past magnetism of the earth (*palaeomagnetism*) and by investigating the ocean floors.

The palaeomagnetic evidence can be explained as follows. The movement of material in the liquid outer portion of the earth's core produces a magnetic field that encompasses the earth. Molten lava, liquid igneous rocks and some water-lain sedimentary rocks all contain substances, especially iron, that respond to magnetism. As they solidify, the grains of susceptible material in the rocks orient themselves towards the magnetic pole that existed at the time of their deposition. The earth's magnetic field sometimes reverses itself, so that the north and south magnetic poles exchange places. Geologically speaking, the reversal takes place quickly and then remains stable for the order of about half a million years. The direction of the stable field is imprinted into new rocks that are formed. In the early 1960s geologists mapped the magnetic directions implanted on rocks in the ocean floor off Iceland and found a remarkable zebra-like pattern, with some rocks being magnetised in one direction and some in the other.

The explanation for this fossil pattern of magnetisation seems to be that, as lava that has emerged through fissures in the mid-ocean ridge in the vicinity of the axial rift solidifies on the sea floor, it is magnetised in the direction, north and south, of the earth's prevailing magnetic field. The crust retains, like a tape-recording, a magnetic pattern identical on either side of the ridge. In other words, this demonstrates that material rising from the earth's interior at the mid-ocean ridges slowly spreads across the sea floor.

This was the first real evidence for *sea-floor spreading*, though in the 1950s geophysicists had used palaeomagnetic techniques to determine palaeo-latitudes and thereby to add strength to arguments in favour of continental drift. The speed with which sea-floor spreading takes place can be gauged by palaeomagnetism. The largest spreading velocity, 18.3 cm yr^{-1}, occurs between the Pacific and Nazca plates. Elsewhere the rates are rather less, being for example, about 3 cm yr^{-1} along the Mid-Atlantic ridge.

More evidence was to follow, for as it became possible to drill holes into the ocean floor so it became possible to date sub-oceanic rocks by radioactive means. These dates revealed some further interesting patterns that complemented those provided by palaeomagnetism. First, it was clear that most of the ocean basins were covered by comparatively young rocks – rocks less than 200 million years old. Second, as samples were studied from cross-sections of the oceans, the rocks became younger as the mid-ocean ridges were approached. This led to the suggestion that the earth's crust is produced by upwelling magma that is extruded along the mid-ocean ridges, and then moves laterally from the ridge, to be replaced by new liquid magma. This is why the zebra-stripe pattern is produced, why the ocean rocks are so young, and why they become younger towards the ridges.

1.8   The question of plates

In the 1960s a new concept of the outer layers of the earth developed that was to tie in with the idea of sea-floor spreading. It was postulated that the earth's crust and the upper part of the mantle (the rigid part called the lithosphere) consist of a set of rigid plates (figure 1.8), which rest on the weaker and deformable asthenosphere and underlie oceans, continents or a combination of the two. Seven major plates and four or five minor plates are recognised, together with eight or nine

Figure 1.8 The world's major plates, indicating their names, their boundaries, zones of collision, zones of subduction and certain major geomorphological phenomena. The rates of sea-floor spreading and of plate convergence (both in cm yr^{-1}) are given. Note the very high rate of spreading in the Pacific.

'platelets'. They appear to average about 100 km in thickness though they vary from 60 to 300 km, and the larger ones have areas of 65 million square kilometres! These plates move, and *plate tectonics* is the name given to the study of the way these plates move and interact.

Many of the large-scale features of the earth's surface, such as most volcanoes and mountain ranges, are associated with the boundaries between the plates. Some plates spread apart along *divergent junctions*, typified by the axial ridge rift at the crest of the mid-Atlantic ridge (figure 1.9(a)). This particular feature results from the contact between the American plate on the one hand and the Eurasian and African plates on the other. Sea-floor spreading takes place along such a boundary as the void between the receding plates is filled by melted, mobile material that rises from the interior of the earth. The material solidifies in the crack, and the plates grow as they separate. The Atlantic Ocean did not exist 150

million years ago, and it seems to have opened out by this process, leading to the disruption of the ancient supercontinent of Pangaea.

The process of divergence is most prevalent in the ocean basins, but there are two major zones of spreading among the continents, one in Africa and the other in Asia. The best developed of these is the African zone (figure 1.10), which extends from the Red Sea as a series of rifts through the East African highlands. These rifts are the site of some major lake basins, including Lake Malawi, Lake Tanganikya and Lake Kivu.

In the Asian continent the site of spreading is in Siberia, where there is a rift system of which the deeper parts are occupied by Lake Baikal, and where there has been some Pleistocene volcanic activity.

These continental rifts are major features of the earth's surface; they are many tens of kilometres long, 10–50 km wide and with a central strip of crust downthrown by 1–5 km. They have under-

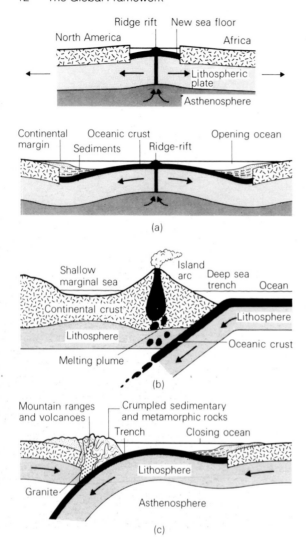

(a)

(b)

(c)

Figure 1.9 The oceans and their development. (a) The oceans developed through mid-ocean rifting. The trailing edges of the receding continents received a great deal of sediment from the land. (b) When plates collide the thinner, denser oceanic plate tends to sink under the thicker, lighter continental plate, forming an island arc of volcanoes and a deep oceanic trench. (c) As the process continues, orogenesis (mountain-building) takes place. Rocks from the ocean floor are uplifted and crumpled, and granite batholiths are intruded.

Figure 1.10 The Great Rift Valleys of East Africa comprise a zone where divergence is taking place in the earth's crust. Where it joins the Red Sea and the Gulf of Aden, this divergence is taking place about a triple junction – the Afar Triangle. This may represent the first stage in the development of an ocean. The rifts are shaded.

gone a gradual extension of a few kilometres during the last 10–30 million years, and may be considered to be incipient plate boundaries.

The rate of divergence either side of the oceanic axial rift does much to explain the nature and distribution of islands and seamounts. Along slowly spreading zones, such as those typical of the Atlantic, volcanic material tends to accumulate relatively close to the locus of spreading, so that there is a well defined mid-oceanic ridge, with relatively massive mountainous islands like the Azores. However, where, as in the case of the Pacific, the rate of spreading is quite rapid, growing volcanic structures are moved large distances from the zone of origin, where they eventually sink and become dormant. The reason for such

Plate 1.1 The splitting of plates creates tensions in the earth's crust which can lead to the development of rift valleys. The world's largest feature of this type runs through Kenya in East Africa.

sinking is that oceanic crust contracts and becomes more dense as it cools. Thus, if one looks at a map of the floor of the Pacific one notes that there is a very large number of seamounts, and that some of them – guyots – have flat tops because they were planed off by wave action before they sank. Both the seamounts and the guyots have provided platforms on which the many coral reefs, so characteristic of the warmer parts of the Pacific, have grown.

Plainly, however, if plates separate in one place then, unless the earth is expanding, they must converge somewhere else. This they do at *convergent junctions*, and the zone of contact is one that is dominated by crumpled mountain ranges, volcanoes, earthquakes and ocean trenches. At the collision point one plate normally plunges beneath the other, and the material of the submerging plate is gradually reincorporated into the upper mantle and crust. The area where the material is lost is called the *subduction zone*. As the oceanic plate plunges beneath the continental plate with which it has collided, parts of it begin to melt and form magma (figure 1.9(b)). Some of this reaches the surface as lava erupting from volcanic vents. Furthermore, as an oceanic plate is subducted under its neighbour, plunging down at an angle of between 30° and 60° into the interior of the earth (figure 1.9(c)), the surface of the crust is drawn down to produce one of the ocean trenches, and the movement is in a series of jerks, which produce earthquakes.

The third type of boundary is called a *transform* or *transcurrent boundary*. This exists where two plates do not come directly into collision but slide past each other along a fault. This type of situation is termed a *conservative zone*, in that plate movement is mainly parallel to the boundary, and therefore crust is neither created nor destroyed. The most famous example of such a boundary is the San Andreas Fault in California, which separates the northward-moving Pacific Plate from the North American Plate. This is a zone of intense earthquake activity, for the movement along the faults is irregular rather than a smooth process of gradual creep.

The process whereby many mountains are built can be interpreted in terms of plate movement. It starts with the formation of an ocean by sea-floor spreading. Thick muds and silts eroded from the land accumulate on the continental slopes alongside thinner limestones and sands on the continental shelves. After perhaps 100 or 200 million years, a trench forms on one side of the ocean and the oceanic crust is subducted under the continent. This may be followed by the consumption of the sinking crust, leading to the formation of a chain of volcanoes called an *island arc* (figure 1.9(b)). After a further period the island arc itself gets swept into the continent, and finally the ocean becomes closed and the continents collide. When this happens the sediments of the island arc, together with those of the continental margin, are caught as if in a vice, and so folding and overthrusting takes place in a zone of crumpling. Furthermore, molten igneous rock, generated as the oceanic crust melts in the depths, rises into the crust and so promotes *uplift*. In this way some of the great fold mountains are formed (figure 1.9(c)).

The formation of island arcs is thus a frequent part of the story of mountain-building. These arcs at present are largely restricted to the Pacific, where they occur around the periphery in a zone known as 'the ring of fire'. They are composed of silica-rich lavas called *andesites*, and include some of the world's most destructive volcanoes. Elsewhere, island arcs may have become incorporated into the continents; for example, the great Karakoram Mountains in northern Pakistan are composed of silica-rich lava, and are thought to be the remains of an island arc that was squeezed into the Eurasian Plate as the Indian Plate moved northwards. This is the explanation for the fact that the summit of Mount Rakaposhi (7788 m), one of the highest mountains in the world, is formed of oceanic crust material.

Some of the old mountain roots that characterise those portions of the earth's surface that are not currently very active, such as the Aravalli Mountains of India, the Urals of Siberia or the Appalachians of the eastern United States, may represent earlier phases of plate movement than do the present zones of active young fold mountains. As we have already noted, much of the continental crust is old, and may therefore have been subjected to more than one phase of plate collision or plate divergence.

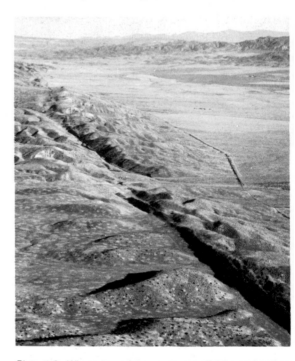

Plate 1.2 Where two plates move parallel to each other, major faults like the San Andreas Fault in California cut across the landscape.

Plate 1.3 Mount Rakaposhi in Pakistan, one of the highest mountains in the world, is formed of oceanic crust material that was thrust up when the Indian Plate collided with the Eurasian Plate. Intense uplift has created 'the steepest place on earth'.

This is illustrated for the Appalachians in figure 1.11. They may have formed by a period of rifting ((a) and (b)), which gradually led on to a period of collision and subduction (c) and to the formation of the mountains (d). Another cycle of rifting followed (e) which split up the mountain zone and led to the opening of the Atlantic Ocean (f). Meanwhile, considerable erosion had led to severe truncation of the continental terrain, producing the Appalachians we know today.

The rocks and geological structures of the British Isles show evidence that such cycles of orogenic activity may have occured more than once. Indeed, the gradual addition of new orogenic belts of varying rock type, produced by varying intensities of mountain-building, give Britain its enormous diversity of scenery. The Pre-

Plate 1.4 A Landsat satellite image shows the great fold structures which underlie the old mountain chain of the Appalachians in the eastern United States. Their relief has been greatly planed off by erosion.

Figure 1.11 (a) The development of the Appalachian Mountains and related systems in the United States by a process of rifting of a lithospheric plate into two plates, North America and Africa; (b) the development of geosynclinal and continental shelf sediments after a period of rifting had taken place; (c) and (d) period of igneous intrusion and deformation producing the structure seen today in the Appalachians; (e) the development of the mid-Atlantic rift; (f) continued rifting producing the modern Atlantic basin.

cambrian rocks of the Outer Hebrides and adjacent parts of north-western Scotland represent the edge of an ancient continent, and in the *Caledonian* orogenic cycle (*c.*400 million years ago) very considerable folding and faulting occurred, producing, for example, the fault-bounded Scottish Central Valley and initiating the Great Glen Fault further north. In a later cycle, the *Hercynian*

(*c.*250 million years ago), igneous activity produced the granite batholith that underlies many of the moorlands of the south-west peninsula of England in Devon and Cornwall; volcanic activity occurred in the Central Valley of Scotland; and a sill – the Great Whin Sill – was introduced into the domed-up northern Pennines. During the *Alpine* cycle, which followed the collision between Africa and Europe, the Alps themselves were formed. This produced ripples in southern England, producing, for example, the dome of rocks that form the backbone of the Weald. Since the Alpine orogeny, the opening up of the Atlantic produced some rifting that created volcanic activity in north-western Scotland and in Antrim. At the coast the lavas form prominent cliffs, and the hexagonal columns produced by the cooling of the basalt are striking features of the Isle of Staffa and of the Giant's Causeway in Northern Ireland.

World coastlines can also be classified and explained in plate tectonic terms. On coasts where two plates converge – *collision coasts* – structural lineations tend to be parallel to the shore. They are relatively straight with high, tectonically mobile hinterlands, and they are fronted by relatively narrow continental shelves. They suffer from earthquakes and volcanic activity, and the earthquakes sometimes generate catastrophic waves called *tsunamis*. The steep, tectonically active hinterland may well be a zone of intense erosion, in which case there will be a considerable amount of sediment deposited along the coast. The existence of mountain-building may mean that there are a series of fossil beaches at high altitudes above the present ones.

The second type of coastline is the *trailing edge* coast, and it can be subdivided into two categories: Afro- and Amero-. This distinction is fundamental because of its affect on global patterns of fluvial sedimentation. Where the coast on one side of the continent is a collision coast, as in South America, the high, tectonically active rim (in that particular case the Andes) yields a large sediment load to rivers flowing towards the opposite, trailing-edge, coast. Where both coasts are the trailing-edge type this factor does not operate; clear examples of this are provided by the coasts of Africa, where rivers like the Congo and Niger carry relatively small loads in comparison with the Amazon and Mississippi. A major consequence of this is that Amero-trailing-edge coasts are lower-lying, have more extensive sedimentary plains, and possess wider continental shelves. Large deltas may form, the weight of which may cause local subsidence of the earth's crust. Generally, however, these coastlines are tectonically very stable.

We can now see why the continents have the arrangement and shapes they have, why the oceans are dominated by their ridges, why the locations of volcanoes and earthquakes are as they are; and we can also understand how mountain ranges form. The theory of plate tectonics

Plate 1.5   The magnificent Isle of Staffa on the west coast of Scotland is composed of basaltic lava which was produced as rifting accompanied the opening up of the Atlantic Ocean.

offers an all-embracing explanation, and it has revolutionised thinking about large-scale geomorphology. There are, however, some apparent exceptions. For example, the Hawaiian Islands are great volcanoes, and yet they occur not at the boundary of a plate, as do most volcanoes, but in the *middle* of a plate. In spite of this, they may still help to explain the theory of crustal motion. Indeed there are some 10 000 central vent volcanoes within the Pacific, some of which have risen above sea level to form volcanic islands but most having remained submerged as seamounts. Many are members of linear chains of oceanic volcanoes that increase in age from one end to the other. The most dramatic example is the Hawaiian-Emperor chain, which consists of 107 islands and seamounts that stretch for about 6000 km across the Ocean. The members of this chain get progressively younger as the currently active volcanic island at one end, the island of Hawaii itself, is approached. One theory for this is that for some unknown reason there could be a local 'hot spot' beneath the Pacific Ocean, a point at which magma from the asthenosphere or lower mantle is "burning" its way up through the lithosphere. It is postulated that the crust is moving from an ocean ridge south-east of Hawaii towards a trench that lies north-westwards. The south-eastern chain of the islands is currently over the hot spot and is the scene of volcanic activity and earthquakes. The formation of the islands to the north-west occurred long ago when that part of the crust was over the hot spot. They have since moved away from the spot and volcanic activity has ceased (figure 1.12). Still further to the north-west is a chain of underwater seamounts – the remnants of volcanic activity that took place even further back in time.

1.9   Microplates and exotic terranes

If one examines the rocks along the west side of much of Alaska, Canada and the United States for a width of several hundreds of kilometres, they appear to comprise a mosaic of hundreds of very distinctive segments, the boundaries of which are quite sharp. Adjoining segments may also contain distinct fossil types, indicating that they were probably formed at different latitudes. Some of these so-called 'exotic terranes' are fragments of continent, others relicts of island arcs,

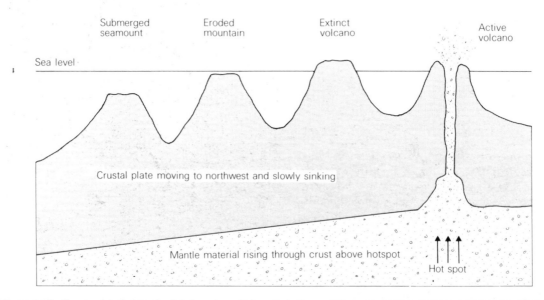

Figure 1.12   Some volcanic islands develop above hot spots in the earth's crust. As the plate moves laterally above the hot spot, so the position of active volcanic activity changes. Away from the spot the volcanoes become less active, more eroded (sometimes to give flat-topped guyots), and eventually suffer subsidence to become submarine mountains, or submerged seamounts.

still others are oceanic plateaux, pieces of oceanic ridges, or of sedimentary platforms.

Recent palaeomagnetic studies have shown that some of these exotic terranes have travelled some thousands of kilometers, and the conclusion has now been reached that these various terranes had once been scattered throughout much of the Pacific Ocean and had been driven towards North America by sea-floor spreading. Once they reached North America they were compressed, uplifted, and tilted as part of the normal processes of deformation and mountain-building at convergent plate boundaries. These segments, which range from small outcrops of a few kilometres square to larger areas with an extent of many thousands of square kilometres, are also called *microplates*.

1.10   The earth's rock types

Now that we have considered the major relief patterns both on land and under the oceans, we can turn to a consideration of the materials that make up the earth's surface. Once again we can relate the formation of the major types to the theory of plate tectonics.

Rocks are normally divided into three main types or groups: igneous, metamorphic and sedimentary (figure 1.13).

Igneous rocks

Igneous rocks are composed of mineral crystals that form during the cooling of molten magma. The cooling may take place underground, in which case the products are described as *intrusive* or plutonic; or it may take place at the surface to give *extrusive*, or volcanic, rocks. If the cooling takes place rapidly, as it might at the surface, glassy and fine-grained rocks form; however, slower cooling, which tends to take place at depth, allows bigger crystals to form. Moreover, different crystals may separate out at different temperatures. In these ways a great variety of igneous rock types are formed.

The intrusive types occur in different types of rock body (figure 1.14). When continental crust is deeply melted on a plate margin, it arises in the course of time as enormous dome-like masses called *batholiths*. These are composed of granite.

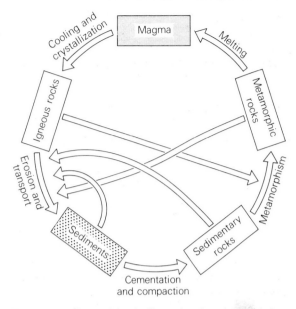

Figure 1.13   The rock cycle, illustrating the relationship between the three main rock types: igneous, metamorphic and sedimentary.

Plate 1.6   Granite is a major type of intrusive igneous rock. This weathered example from Glen Rosa, on the Isle of Arran, Scotland, is composed of coarse crystals produced by slow cooling of magma.

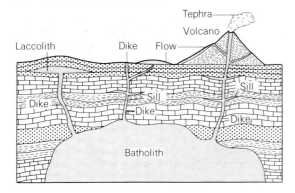

Figure 1.14 Some of the main types of igneous rock mass, showing the difference between extrusive and intrusive types. The batholiths may result from the emplacement of magma during mountain-building caused by plate collision.

Some of the magma may be intruded into steep fractures as thin sheets called *dykes*, from which magma may be spread laterally along the *strata* or layers of the rock into which it is being intruded to give flat-lying *sills* and blister-like *laccoliths*.

Magma that succeeds in reaching the surface as an extrusive rock is called *lava*. The most common form is *basalt*. This is a rock that flows freely and so forms extensive, nearly horizontal, sheets. Volcanoes with such runny basalt lava are produced chiefly in areas where the earth's crust is splitting apart, as for example along the mid-ocean ridges.

With such fluid magma, gas is easily released and eruptions are non-explosive *effusions*, sometimes of great volume and extent. More viscous types of magma impede the release of dissolved gas, which may therefore sometimes cause an explosion which throws out clouds of *tephra*. A higher silica content in a magma increases its viscosity, and thus the *andesitic* volcanoes typical of destructive plate margins are characteristically explosive in their activity.

Metamorphic rocks

Rocks that have had their textures, structures and mineral composition changed by intense heat and/or pressure, are called metamorphic rocks. They are a highly important component of the great continental shields and of the basement rocks beneath stable platforms.

They can form in a variety of ways. One group forms in the roots of ancient orogenic belts under the intense forces that are created when tectonic plates collide. This process is termed *regional metamorphism*. Other types are produced when magma is intruded into a host rock, for the temperature of the magma will be greatly in excess of the rock through which it is intruded, or upon which it is extruded. Changes may be brought about by partial melting (*contact metamorphism*), by superheating of water and by increased pressures (*dynamic metamorphism*).

In some cases the degree of change is relatively modest, and the original rocks may do little more than become more compact. This is called *low-grade metamorphism*. In *high-grade metamorphism*, on the other hand, the original characteristics of the rock may be totally transformed so that such phenomena as bedding planes, fossils, etc. are completely obliterated. Minerals may segregate, forming alternating layers of light and dark minerals, as with the metamorphism of old igneous rocks, like granite, which are thereby converted to gneiss. Often, however, it is sedimentary rocks that are changed: limestone becomes marble and mudstone becomes slate. A good example of this type of situation is provided by the granite batholith of the Dartmoor area in south-west England. The batholith is encircled by a band, often called an *aureole* of metamorphosed sedimentary rocks.

Sedimentary rocks

These rocks are formed from the destruction of earlier rocks. Weathering, erosion, transport and deposition carry material from one part of the world to another and lay it down as sediments: *marine sedimentary rocks* are deposited under the sea, and *terrestrial* ones on land.

Most sedimentary rocks are described as fragmental or *clastic*, and are formed of particles derived from earlier rocks, which have become converted into a harder substance by the process of *lithification*. Thus, gravels become *conglomerates*; angular scree fragments become *breccia*; sands become sandstones; and muds are transformed into mudstones or shales. Other sedimentary rocks are chemical precipitates, such as the limestones that develop on warm continental shelves; while others, like coal, are organic, being made out of the fossil remains of animals or plants.

The conversion of a sediment into a sedimentary rock is achieved by a variety of processes. Of great importance is compaction, for as layers and layers of sediment accumulate, they exert pressures on the layers below. This compression squeezes out air and water from between the individual constituent particles, and distorts and flattens the particles themselves so that they interlock with each other. Another important process is cementation. Groundwater, seeping through the sediment may deposit the minerals that it carries in solution, such as calcite, and may in due course unite the whole into a solid mass.

Altogether, sedimentary rocks cover more than two-thirds of the earth's surface and provide the main record of past environments, shifting coastlines and changing climates. Because they often contain fossils, they provide a record of changes in the nature and pattern of plant and animal life, and they have also supplied the principal means of establishing the divisions of geological time.

1.11   The subdivisions of the earth's history

Geologists divide up the 4600 million years of the earth's geological history into major eras and periods, as shown in table 1.1. The earliest era is called the Precambrian – a long, complex and

Plate 1.7   Spectacularly eroded sedimentary rocks at Sunset Point in Bryce Canyon National Park, Utah, in the United States. The layering demonstrated here is characteristic of this rock type.

poorly understood phase. During it there were periods of mountain-building and at least one ice age. It was a time when the lithosphere, atmosphere and hydrosphere first developed, and the first organisms appeared. Life was, however, essentially primitive, consisting of simple plants like algae. Many of the rocks of the world's great shield areas date back to this time.

In the succeeding Palaeozoic Era life evolved and became more complex. The first land plants appeared in the Silurian Period, the first animals with backbones (called vertebrates) appeared in the Ordovician, and towards the end of the era amphibians were replaced by reptiles as the main land animals. Successive closures of ancient oceans resulted in the welding together of continental masses to form one supercontinent of Pangaea.

In the Mesozoic Era life was dominated by the dinosaurs and the gymnosperms (naked seed plants), the climate was basically warm and equable, and the progressive break-up of Pangaea occurred. In the Cenozoic Era the climate deterio-

rated, sea-floor spreading has continued, and we have had the Ice Age of Quaternary times.

It was during the latter part of the Cenozoic era, at a time broadly coincident with the coming of this Quaternary Ice Age that humans first made their appearance on the face of the earth. The earliest remains, which date back to around two or three million years, are found in the Great Rift Valley of East Africa. As human populations have spread over the face of the earth, expanded their populations, and developed their level of technology, so their role in modifying the face of the earth has increased progressively. The growth in recent decades has been especially spectacular. As the Worldwatch Institute put it in their *State of the World Report for 1987*:

Between 1950 and 1986, human numbers doubled to 5 billion, expanding as much during these 36 years as during the preceding few million. Per capita income also roughly doubled, pushing the gross world product over $13 trillion. Within a generation, the global output of goods and services quadrupled. A variety of technological advances aided this expansion, but none

Table 1.1   The history of the earth, with subdivisions of time and the main events

Era	Period		Millions of years BP	Main events
Cenozoic	Quaternary	Holocene	0.01	Early civilizations
		Pleistocene	2	Emergence of man
		Pliocene	7	Start of Ice Age
		Miocene	26	
	Tertiary	Oligocene	38	Start of main Himalayan folding
		Eocene	54	
		Palaeocene	65	Extinction of dinosaurs
Mesozoic	Cretaceous		136	Main fragmentation of Pangaea; transgression of sea over land
	Jurassic		190	Start of fragmentation of Pangaea
	Triassic		225	Worldwide regression of sea from land
Palaeozoic	Permian		280	Formation of Pangaea
	Carboniferous	Pennsylvanian	315	
		Mississippian	345	
	Devonian		395	Animal life takes to the land
	Silurian		440	First land plants
	Ordovician		500	Vertebrates appear
	Cambrian		570	Major transgression of sea over continents
Precambrian				First multicellular organism
	Proterozoic			
			2500	
	Archaean		?3000	Free oxygen in atmosphere
			?3500	First unicellular organisms
			3780	Age of oldest known terrestrial rocks
			(4,500)	Formation of earth

compare with the growth in fossil fuel use. Between 1950 and 1986, world fossil fuel consumption increased fourfold, paralleling the growth in the global economy.

1.12 Conclusions

Some of the major characteristics of the face of the earth can only be understood through an analysis of the present nature of its geological character, and by appreciating how this character has evolved over many millions of years. The other great influence on global patterns is the energy that we receive from the sun. This is the theme of the next chapter.

2 Global Climatic Background

2.1 A vertical profile through the atmosphere

Just as we started our consideration of global geology with a vertical section through the earth's interior, so we shall start this consideration of global climate by taking a vertical section through the earth's atmosphere (figure 2.1). The atmosphere consists of a mixture of gases, largely nitrogen and oxygen, that surround the earth to a height of many kilometres. Held to the earth by gravitational attraction, this envelope of air is densest at sea level and thins rapidly upward. This is because air is compressible; therefore near the earth's surface it is much more dense than in higher layers. At sea level the pressure averages

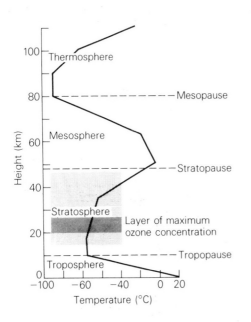

Figure 2.1 The vertical structure of the atmosphere in relation to temperature.

about 1013 millibars, while at 5000 m it is only 550 mb. This general trend is demonstrated in figure 7.1(b).

As pressure changes with altitude, so also does temperature, and the atmosphere is divided into layers on this basis. The lowermost layer, in which most of our weather is produced, is the *troposphere*. As we ascend through it the temperature falls at a rate of about 6.4°C per 1000 m – a rate that is called the *environmental temperature lapse rate*. However, this rate changes abruptly once a certain threshold is reached, and the level at which this change occurs is called the *tropopause*. The altitude of the tropopause varies according to season, but tends to be highest over the equator (*c.*17 km) and lowest over the poles (*c.*10 km). Above the tropopause is a zone called the *stratosphere*, in which the temperature gradually rises, attaining a value of about 0°C at about 50 km. This zone contains a layer of ozone (O_2) which acts as a filter for some of the burning ultraviolet radiation from the sun. As we ascend still further a temperature decrease sets in, and the point at which this change takes place is called the *stratopause*. Temperature declines to as little as – 80°C in the next zone, the *mesosphere*, until a further reversal in trend takes place at the *mesopause* (*c.*80 km above the surface), and brings us into the heat of the *thermosphere*.

Of these layers, the one that is of the greatest importance, in that it is the scene of most climate and weather phenomena, is the troposphere.

2.2 Global climate

Along with geology, climate is the prime control of the physical environment, affecting soils, vegetation, animals (including man) and the op-

Figure 2.2   (a) The albedo of the earth's surface. The fraction of the total radiation from the sun that is reflected by a surface is called its *albedo*. The albedo for the earth as a whole, called the *planetary albedo*, is about 35 per cent. The albedo varies for different surface types. Note also that the angle at which the sun's rays strike a water surface greatly affects the albedo value.

eration of geomorphological processes such as ice and wind. The prime control of climate is the heat given out by the sun. Some of this heat creates the energy for the *atmospheric heat engine* which controls the nature of pressure, wind and climatic belts. However, some of the incoming energy never reaches the earth, being absorbed by gases like carbon dioxide (CO_2), dust and water droplets in the atmosphere. Some is reflected back by clouds, and some from the surface of the earth. In all, about 30 per cent is reflected, and the degree of reflection is called the *albedo*. Albedo values range from over 80 per cent for fresh snow to less than 10 per cent in some forested areas (figure 2.2(a)).

The sun's heat reaches the earth by radiation, conduction and convection. By *radiation* solar energy travels through the vacuum of space from the sun to the earth in the form of electromagnetic waves and heats the earth's surface. By *conduction*, air in the thin layer of the atmosphere in contact with the earth is heated directly by the earth's hot surface. By *convection* the heated surface air expands and, being lighter than the air above, rises to be replaced by cooler air.

In the absence of cloud cover, the amount of energy that actually reaches the surface is dependent on the angle of the sun and the duration of daylight. These in turn, of course, depend on latitude. This means that the sun's heat reaches the low latitudes nearer the Equator in excess of that reaching high latitudes, largely because of the higher angle of the incident rays in low latitudes (figure 2.2(b)). The elevation of the sun is never great in high latitudes, even in mid-summer, while in the polar regions beyond the

Arctic and Antarctic Circles, the sun in winter lies below the horizon for considerable periods. However, within low latitudes cloud cover is an important control of the actual amount of solar energy received at the earth's surface; for the heavy cloud of the equatorial zone, especially over land masses, reduces the total annual receipt of solar radiation by as much as 50 per cent. In contrast, the great subtropical deserts experience very little reduction in solar radiation because they are cloudless for much of the year.

If our planet did not rotate and were uniformly covered with one material, the atmosphere would circulate in response to the latitudinal differences in the heat generated from the incoming solar

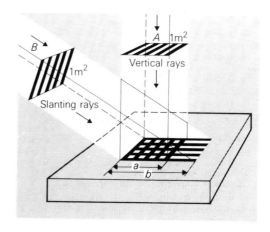

Figure 2.2   (b) The angle of the sun's rays determines the intensity of insolation on the ground. The energy of vertical rays (*A*) is concentrated in square *a*, but the same energy in the slanting rays (*B*) is spread over a rectangle, *b*. This is one of the prime reasons why more heat is received in low latitudes than at high.

radiation. The fundamental force that causes air to move is the difference in air pressure from place to place, and this in turn is due to differences in temperature. Hot air is less dense than cold air, and so it tends to rise, thereby causing a reduction in pressure. Descending air, on the other hand increases the pressure. Air will move from areas of high pressure to areas of low pressure, with the speed of movement being related to the pressure gradient. The steeper the pressure gradient, as represented by the closeness of the isobars, the higher will be the velocity.

Relating this to a rotation-free earth, it can be seen that the equatorial regions are zones of intense heating, rising air and low pressures. In the absence of rotation high pressure would develop over the Poles, where heating is weakest. There would thus be a pressure gradient between the Equator and the Poles, and a gigantic convectional system would form (figure 2.4(a)), in which the equatorial low would be fed with air from the polar highs. Thus at the surface air would flow towards the Equator, while aloft it would flow towards the Poles.

In reality, our earth *does* rotate, and furthermore it is not uniformly covered with one material. This introduces a degree of complexity. If we first look at the low latitudes, we find that the global air circulation does indeed behave much like the simple *convection cell model*. Heated air rises near the Equator and begins its journey towards the Poles. However, its progress is hindered by three obstacles. First, as it rises it no longer has a thick blanket of other air above it, and so it begins to lose much of its heat to space. At the same time, it is further from its principal source of heat energy, the warm earth surface; it gradually loses heat and becomes more dense. Second, because of the shape of the earth, air will converge as it moves poleward; at the Equator the earth has a diameter of about 40 000 km, but its east-west measurement shrinks as the Poles are approached. Third, because of an influence called the *Coriolis Effect*, which is caused by the rotation of the earth, air travelling poleward is deflected to the east.

The Coriolis Effect takes the form of an apparent deflection of a freely moving object or fluid to the right in the Northern Hemisphere and to the left in the Southern Hemisphere. For conveni-

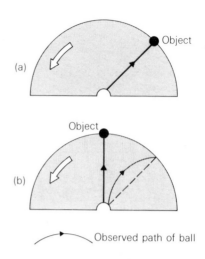

Figure 2.3 Diagrammatic illustration of the Coriolis Force. For explanation see text.

ence, scientists have introduced the concept of a fictitious force to relate, mathematically, the size of the deflection to latitude. This Coriolis Force can best be understood by imagining a person standing at the centre of a rotating disc (figure 2.3) facing an object at the rim (part (a)). When he or she throws a ball directly at the object, the ball travels in a straight line and misses it, because the object has rotated further to the left. But to the thrower, who is rotating with the object, the ball appears to have moved in a curved path *away from* the object (part (b)). Similarly, because of the earth's rotation, winds flowing from high to low pressure are always deflected.

The combination of cooling, compression/convergence and deflection means that, by the time the poleward-moving air has reached about 30° from the Equator it has already subsided. Therefore, a convectional cell does exist, called the Hadley cell, but it does not have the same latitudinal extent that one would have anticipated from the simple model developed on a non-rotating earth. The result of this is that there is a zone of high pressure characterised by subsiding air at about 30° N and S (figure 2.4(b)). This zone dominates the most important and persistent global wind systems: the trade winds, which blow on the equatorward side, and the westerly winds, which blow on the polar side. The trade winds cover in all about one-half of the earth's surface and converge towards the equatorial low-pressure zone, called the *Intertropical Convergence Zone* (ITCZ).

Between the subtropical high-pressure belt and about 60° latitude is the belt of prevailing westerly winds. In the Northern Hemisphere they are to a certain degree disrupted by land masses; but in the Southern Hemisphere between 40° and 60° S there is an almost unbroken belt of ocean, which enables the westerlies to gather great strength and persistence. The westerlies circulate around a zone of lower pressure called the *polar low*, and involve the entire depth of the troposphere. Especially in the Northern Hemisphere, the uniform flow of the upper-air westerlies is disturbed by the formation of large undulations called *Rossby*

waves. These develop along a zone called the *polar front*, which marks the contact between cold polar air, forming the troposphere on the poleward side, and warm tropical air which surrounds the globe on the equatorward side. It is a zone of great instability, along which many atmospheric disturbances are generated. Associated with the Rossby waves and the polar front is a narrow zone of very high wind speed (on average, *c*.125 km h^{-1} in winter) called a *jet stream*, which lies at the level of the tropopause. The westerlies, the Rossby waves and the polar front jet stream are responsible for a great deal of exchange of heat and energy between high latitudes and low.

The mid-latitude jet stream – the polar front jet

Figure 2.4 The general circulation of the atmosphere: (a) the atmospheric circulation pattern that would develop on a non-rotating planet; (b) the true atmospheric circulation shown schematically in a vertical section from polar regions to the Equator.

– sometimes splits into two and is not continuous round the globe. Several other jet streams are also known to exist. For instance, an almost permanent jet exists over the subtropics centred at latitude 25° N. This westerly jet is located about 13 km above the surface in the region where the Hadley cell and the middle latitude (or Ferrel) cell meet. Another jet flows from west to east at about 15 km over northern India in the summer months when the ITCZ has shifted northwards. Another jet circles the Arctic during the cold polar night at 25–30 km above the surface.

The Rossby waves in the westerlies change their shape to give different patterns (figure 2.5), and once a particular pattern is established it may be persistent. Especially in the Northern Hemisphere, the pattern is related in part to the distribution of land and sea, and to the position of high land. A ridge tends to develop over eastern North America and over the Eurasian continent, particularly in winter. The main stationary waves are located at 70° W and 150° E, related to the

Pate 2.1   A NOAA-7 satellite image of western Europe and the eastern Atlantic. The large white whirl is a rain-bearing depression which approached Britain on 17 September 1983.

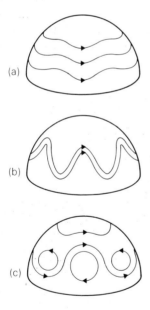

Figure 2.5   The waves in the high-level westerlies of the Northern Hemisphere take on different configurations which are extremely important in terms of surface weather conditions. In the high-index case (a) they have little north–south movement and give changeable weather. The low-index case produces lows (b), and may develop further (c) until the waves break up into a stationary 'blocking' cellular pattern which can produce more extended spells of either good or bad weather.

positions of the Rocky Mountains and the Tibetan Plateau, respectively. In all, there are normally between three and six of the waves around the middle latitudes.

The waves sometimes cover only a small latitudinal zone, with the bulk of the movement of air being from the west. This situation is called a *high zonal index*, and is associated with strong and persistent winds that produce mild, wet winters in western Europe. A *low zonal index* develops when the simple pattern of waves and troughs breaks down to give a series of cells. This can disrupt the passage of the rain-bearing depressions and lead to blocking anticyclones, which can be very persistent and can result in long spells of settled or unsettled weather. The great British drought of 1976 and the hot summer of 1983 were the result of a blocking anticyclone that lasted a long time.

We can thus summarise the nature of the atmosphere's general circulation. Briefly, it consists of three distinct but collaborative cells. In low latitudes is the so-called *Hadley cell*, with heat near the Equator being transferred from low to high altitudes by great convective activity. Polewards to approximately 30° of latitude is a zone of subsidence throughout all but the lowest kilometre or two of the troposphere. At the surface, trade winds complete the cell, flowing from the north-east in the Northern Hemisphere and from the south-east in the Southern Hemisphere. The Trades converge along the ITCZ. In middle latitudes there is a *Ferrel cell*, with westerlies prevailing at all levels in the troposphere, and with weather dominated by transitory depressions and anticyclones. In polar regions, radiative cooling causes air in contact with the earth's surface to contract, which creates subsidence of air in the lower tropopause and an anticyclonic tendency. Surface air that flows away from the Poles is deflected by the Coriolis Effect to become easterlies, but the features associated with this *polar cell* are rather indistinct and intermittent.

2.3 World patterns of precipitation

The nature of the general circulation and the arrangement of the oceans and the continents lead to certain general patterns in the distribution of precipitation (rain, snow, etc.) over the face of the earth (figure 2.6(a) and (b)). In the equatorial belt rainfall levels are high, often exceeding 2000 mm per annum. The prevailingly warm temperatures and high moisture content of the air lead to abundant convectional rainfall over areas such as the Amazon Basin of South America, the Congo Basin of Africa and the archipelago of south-east Asia. Narrow coastal belts of high rainfall extend further polewards along the eastern sides of continents as far as 25−30° from the Equator. These are the coasts where the trade winds blow off the oceans and, encountering coastal hill ranges, produce heavy relief rainfall. By contrast, in the vast belts of deserts that lie approximately along the tropics the rainfall may be as little as 20−100 mm, and will occur in the vicinity of the subtropical high-pressure cells, where subsiding rather than rising air is dominant. They are especially well developed on the west coasts of the contin-

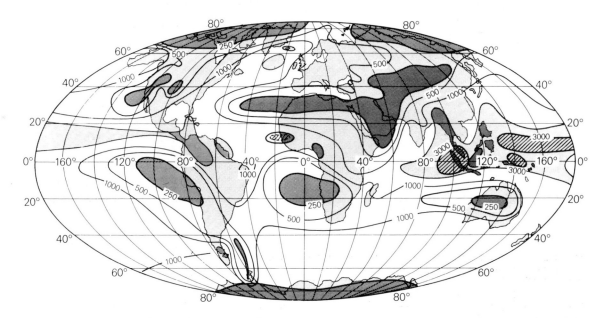

Figure 2.6 World patterns of precipitation (a) The distribution of precipitation throughout the world in mm per year: dark shading shows precipitation below 250 mm, light shading shows areas with precipitation above 2000 mm, and the diagonal shading shows areas above 3000 mm.

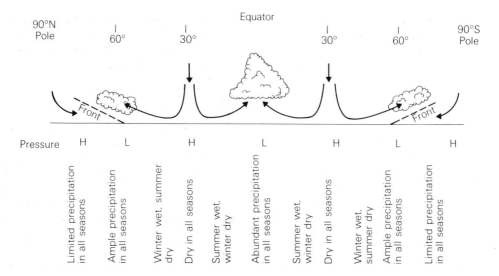

Figure 2.6(b) Schematic zonation of rainfall belts in vertical cross section from Pole to Pole.

Figure 2.6(c) World precipitation variability.

ents, where the presence of cold ocean currents favours desert development (see section 5.2). Further northwards, in the continental interiors of Asia and North America, dryness results largely from remoteness from ocean sources of moisture.

In the mid-latitude belt, especially on west coasts between the latitudes of 35° and 65°, there is another belt of high precipitation in the region of prevailing westerly winds. Where the coasts are mountainous and the air is forced to rise, precipitation can exceed 2000 mm, as in the south island of New Zealand, Norway, southern Chile and British Columbia. In the Arctic and polar regions the air is so cold that it cannot contain much moisture, so low precipitation conditions return. Except on the west coast belts, annual precipitation poleward of 60° is under 300 mm.

From the point of view of man, however, it is not only rainfall quantity that is important; one also has to consider the reliability or variability of the rainfall from year to year (figure 2.6(c)). Once again, it is possible to see clear global patterns. The most striking feature is the very high variability of rainfall in the world's driest areas. Note particularly the great belt of variable rainfall that runs through from north-west Africa to the Middle East and central Asia, and the smaller zones in south-western Africa (the Namib), central Australia, north-east Brazil, western South America, the south-west United States and northern Mexico. In the central Sahara the variability may exceed 100 per cent. By contrast, other parts of the world are fortunate in having more reliable and consistent levels of precipitation, which saves them from the worst effects of runs of dry years and droughts. In western Europe the variability

may be as little as 10 per cent, and another zone of markedly consistent rainfall is to the east of the Great Lakes in North America. In general, the humid tropics also have low rainfall variability.

2.4 World patterns of temperature

Because of the way in which radiation receipts from the sun vary with latitude, temperatures tend to decrease from the Equator towards the Poles (figure 2.7(a)). Moreover, in the equatorial regions the receipt of insolation is fairly uniform throughout the year so that temperatures are uniformly high. Because of their proximity to oceans, which act as a moderating influence, coastal areas also tend to have rather limited temperature ranges over the year. The annual range (figure 2.7(b)) is moderately large on land areas in the zone of the subtropical high-pressure cells, and because of the frequent absence of cloud cover, maximum temperatures in summer can be very high – higher even than those in the equatorial zone. Large land masses in the sub-Arctic and Arctic zones develop areas of extremely low temperatures in winter but in the summer temperatures can rise to quite high levels, so that

Figure 2.7(a)   World patterns of temperature: surface temperatures for July (°C), expressed as those at sea level.

Figure 2.7(b) World patterns of temperature: annual range of air temperatures (°C), showing differences between the means for January and July. Note the particularly high differences in the interior of eastern Asia.

over eastern Siberia and northern Canada the annual temperature range may exceed 45°C. Areas of perpetual ice and snow such as the great ice caps of Greenland and the Antarctic are always intensely cold. Temperatures vary greatly with season in the mid-latitude and sub-Arctic zones, because of the annual march of the sun. Thus, in North America the 15°C *isotherm* (a line drawn to connect all points having the same temperature) lies over Florida in January and near Hudson Bay in July.

The lands and the oceans are very different in the way in which they take up and give out heat. Heat moves into the land by conduction, and as a result only the upper few metres of the land exchange much heat with the atmosphere on an annual basis. Moreover, land materials generally have low heat capacities. For these reasons the heat taken in by the soil in the warm summer is quickly lost in the ensuing cool season. By contrast, heat moves into the oceans by convection and is thus carried to much greater depths than

on land. Moreover, water has a high heat capacity, and hence tends to give up its heat much more slowly than the land does. Oceans therefore tend to have a moderating influence on temperatures, so that land areas in winter are typically much colder than the oceans, whereas in the summer they are much warmer. Thus in the interior of continents temperature ranges over the year tend to be higher than they are near oceans.

These differences in heat storage result in pressure differences in the atmosphere. The large land masses, such as Eurasia, tend to have very high pressures in winter and low pressures in summer. This affects the direction of the major wind belts and contributes, for example, to the wind reversal that is such a feature of the monsoonal lands of Asia (see section 6.5).

2.5 The major climatic zones

By combining the patterns of temperature, precipitation and evapotranspiration, one can construct a series of major world climatic zones – zones that will form the basis of Part II below, and are important for understanding the world patterns of such phenomena as soils and vegetation.

The *humid tropical zone* surrounds the Equator and extends discontinuously about 10°N of it. Mean daily temperature approximates 25–27°C, and the diurnal variation exceeds the modest annual variation. Precipitation totals vary greatly according to such factors as relief, but are frequently in excess of 2000 mm per annum. One of the outstanding features of this zone is the relative lack of seasonality.

A *semi-arid tropical zone* extends from the humid tropics, and the further one moves away from the Equator, the more seasonal becomes the climate because of the migration of the overhead sun. Rainfall and temperature reach their maxima in the warm wet season when the sun is at its zenith; a dry season then prevails for some months when the sun moves into the opposite hemisphere. Polewards from this zone, and extending to as much as 30° N and S, is the *arid tropical zone*, containing the great hot deserts such as the Sahara. This is a zone of subsiding air, with sporadic rainfall in time and space, high diurnal temperature ranges and limited cloud cover and high radiation levels. Evapotranspiration greatly exceeds precipitation so that there is a severe water deficit.

This zone is gradually replaced by a belt with more humid conditions, called the *semi-arid subtropical zone*. The subsiding dry air of the tropics predominates in summer, while in winter low pressure brings rain and lowered temperatures. These areas thus show very marked seasonal contrasts, and are often described as being of 'Mediterranean' type, though they show great variability in type according to distance from the sea.

At about 50° N and 45° S, the impact of the dry, subsiding air is replaced almost totally by the effects of the polar front, the westerlies and various low-pressure cells. In oceanic areas with a marked maritime influence, such as the British Isles, the annual temperature regime is not great – in the case of the Scilly Isles off the south-west peninsula of England it is only 8°C. This *humid temperate zone* has mild winters, cool summers and year-round rainfall. Away from the maritime influence the precipitation level decreases; there is more snow in winter, and summer thunderstorm activity is frequent. The annual range of temperature increases, and in the far interior may reach as much as 40–50°C. This zone is generally called the semi-arid temperate zone, but in extreme continental situations the precipitation level becomes so small that an *arid steppe* climate develops.

Moving yet further towards the poles is the *boreal zone*, though because of the lack of land in the southern hemisphere in the latitudes 55°–60° S it is only well developed to any great degree across northern North America, Scandinavia and the USSR. Summers are cool and moist, but very low temperatures occur in the winter. Edmonton in Canada, for example, which can be taken as a representative station, has a July mean of around 15°C and a January mean of as little as −8°C.

The most poleward of our zones is the *Arctic zone*, where the effects of the seasons is intense. For three months of the year there may be 20 hours of darkness each day, and for another three there may be 20 hours of daylight. Precipitation levels are generally rather small, and the mean annual temperatures may be low enough for the subsoil to be permanently frozen (a state called *permafrost*).

2.6 The hydrological cycle

When they talk about the *hydrological cycle* (see chapter 13 for a fuller discussion), scientists refer to the process whereby water comes to the earth from the atmosphere through precipitation and eventually returns to the atmosphere by evaporation. The largest amounts of water in the whole cycle (figure 2.8) are those involved in direct evaporation from the sea to the atmosphere and in precipitation back to the sea. Evaporation from the land surface, and the transpiration of water from plants, combine with precipitation of water on to the land to play a quantitatively smaller (but from the human point of view, important) part in the cycle. The precipitation from the land that is not lost by evaporation runs off the surface in the form of streams and rivers.

The great bulk of the world's water is in the oceans – around 97 per cent. For that reason,

Figure 2.8 The world hydrological cycle: (a) the main components; (b) freshwater and salt water proportions; (c) the latitudinal variation in evaporation, precipitation and runoff.

(a)

(b)

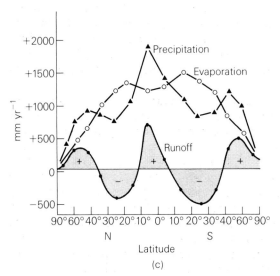

(c)

most of the world's water is salty. Of the 3 per cent of fresh water, about 75 per cent is locked up in the ice caps and glaciers, and much of the rest is present below ground in the rocks as *groundwater*. Only a minute proportion is present at any one time in the rivers (0.03 per cent), and in the lakes (0.3 per cent).

On a global basis, certain patterns emerge (figure 2.8(c)). Three major zones with an excess of moisture generate substantial stream runoff, while there are two zones where evapotranspiration is so greatly in excess of precipitation that there is a severe moisture deficit.

2.7 Ocean currents

Ocean currents are controlled by, and contribute to, global climatic conditions. On the one hand they aid in the exchange of heat between low and high latitudes, and modify extremes of climate. On the other, they are set in motion largely by the prevailing surface winds associated with the atmospheric general circulation. The transference of energy from wind to ocean water is achieved by the frictional drag of the air blowing over the water surface. As with winds, the Coriolis Effect affects the direction of water movement. Temperature differences (figure 2.9(a)) also affect currents through their influence on density. Thus, for example, the chilled surface water of the high-latitude seas will sink to the ocean floor, spreading equatorwards, and displacing upward the less dense, warmer water.

If we look at a map of surface currents (figure 2.9(c)) certain major features become apparent. Given the importance that we have attached to the subtropical high-pressure zones in the atmosphere, it is perhaps not surprising that in the oceans these are the locations of some major circular movements, called *gyres* (figure 2.9(b)). To the equatorward side of these great whirls is an *equatorial current* that flows westwards and marks the belt of the trade winds. The equatorial currents are separated by an *equatorial counter-current*.

Poleward of these subtropical gyres is a zone that comes under the influence of the westerlies, and here we have a current type called a *west-wind drift*. This is especially well developed in the Southern Hemisphere, extending between latitudes 30° and 70° S.

In low latitudes, the equatorial current turns poleward on encountering the coastlines on the west sides of the oceans, and thus forms a warm current that parallels the coast. Examples of this include the Gulf Stream off North America, the Brazilian Current off Brazil, and the Kuroshio Current off Japan. Such coastlines have higher-than-average water temperatures.

West-wind drifts tend towards the east sides of continents, and may turn either polewards or equatorwards. The poleward movement is illustrated by the North Atlantic Drift which warms the British Isles, Norway and even the far north-west of the USSR, enabling navigation into the Arctic port of Murmansk all the year round. Equatorward flow produces cool currents along the eastern shores of the oceans, such as the Humboldt (Peruvian) Current off South America, the Benguela Current off southern Africa, the Canaries Current off West Africa and the California Current off the western United States. These have an important bearing on the location of some of the world's deserts (see section 5.2).

Finally, in the Northern Hemisphere cold water flows from the largely land-locked polar sea along the west side of the large straits connecting the Arctic Ocean with the Pacific and the Atlantic. Running southwards from the Bering Strait is the cold Kamchatka Current; along the western coast of Canada from western Greenland is the Labrador Current; and between Iceland and Greenland is the Greenland Current.

The oceans are basically cold. The water is warm only at the surface, and becomes progressively colder with depth (figure 2.10). Only 8 per cent of the ocean water is warmer than 10°C, and more than a half is colder than 2.3°C. This helps to explain the very considerable effect that oceans have on climate. With respect to temperature the ocean, when viewed in cross-section, presents a three-layered structure. At low latitudes throughout the year, and in mid-latitudes in the summer, a warm surface layer develops, which because of the mixing effects of wave action may be as much as 500 m thick. In equatorial regions it may have a temperature in excess of 25°C, but this rapidly declines poleward.

Below this layer temperatures drop rapidly, creating a second layer called the *thermocline*. Beneath this there is cold deep water, temperatures of which range from 0 to 5°C. In high latitudes the three-layer structure is replaced by a single layer of cold water, which, because it is denser than warm water, 'flows' at depth towards the tropics.

In certain configurations of the coastline, the trend of the currents and the direction of the offshore winds, cold water may move upwards to the surface by a process called *upwelling*. This is a common feature on the west coasts of continents, notably off Peru, Oregon, the western Sahara and south-western Africa. Upwelling creates a narrow strip of ocean water of low temperature that is uncharacteristic of that latitude as a whole. Because the surface waters are being constantly replenished with nutrients from below, such areas are zones of great fertility, thus support-

(a)

(b)

(c)

Figure 2.9 Some of the main features of the oceanic circulation: (a) annual mean sea surface temperature over the world (°C); (b) schematic view of the wind-driven circulation of the oceans, with a clockwise gyre in the Northern Hemisphere and a counterclockwise gyre in the Southern Hemisphere. A countercurrent separates the two gyres, and is located between the region of the north-east and south-west tradewinds; (c) the actual circulation of the oceans illustrating the main currents.

Figure 2.10 The main temperature characteristics of the ocean in profile.

ing huge fish populations. By contrast, the Sargasso Sea, which lies in the tropical north Atlantic in the centre of the subtropical high-pressure zone, is a marine desert, in which nutrients cannot be so readily replenished. The warm surface water is markedly less dense than the cooler water beneath and thus forms a stable layer. Because of this, once the nutrients are used up they are not replaced from below (see also section 9.3).

Overall, however, it has to be said that, in comparison with land areas, the oceans are not, in biological terms, very productive. Whereas the *net primary productivity* (NPP – the rate of production of organic matter) of the oceans averages $155 \, g \, m^{-2} \, yr^{-1}$, the comparable figure for the continents is 782. This is a topic we shall return to in our consideration of the major world vegetation types (see section 4.7).

The oceans have a huge heat storage capacity and so have a very fundamental influence on world climates. Should the nature of the ocean temperatures change, then there will be consequential changes of weather patterns on land. Such atmosphere-ocean interactions have become a major research focus in recent years.

The most interesting illustration of atmosphere-ocean interactions is provided by the *El Niño phenomenon*. Although the term originally referred to a local warm current that runs southward along the coast of Ecuador in the eastern Pacific around the Christmas season (hence, 'The Child'), it has now become employed to describe much larger scale warmings of the eastern equatorial Pacific that last for one or two years and occur in intervals ranging from 2 to 10 years.

The relationship between El Niño and global climate needs to be seen in the context of its atmospheric counterparts, the *Walker Circulation* and the *Southern Oscillation*. Under 'normal'

conditions the nature of the Walker Circulation, one of the most important components of the global atmospheric system, is as shown in figure 2.11, with a great longitudinal cell readily observable across the Pacific. Near the coast of South America the winds blow offshore, causing upwelling and the subsequent cold, nutrient rich, offshore waters. However, under El Niño conditions, the circulation pattern is reversed and this causes water temperatures off the coast of South America in the equatorial belt to rise substantially. This see-saw in atmospheric conditions is called the Southern Oscillation.

The oscillation seems to have significance beyond the Pacific coast of equatorial South America, where the presence of warm water may be associated with anomalously high rainfalls over Peru and Ecuador, and with fish mortality in the sea. Recent studies have shown that at times of El Niño numerous persistent climatic anomalies occur elsewhere on Earth, such as droughts in Australia, Indonesia and north-east Brazil, severe winters in the USA and Japan, and cyclones in the central Pacific. The oceanic circulation plays the role of a flywheel in the climate system and is responsible for the extraordinary persistence of the atmospheric anomalies from month to month and even from season to season.

2.8 The world's great soil orders

Having discussed the global patterns of precipitation, temperature, wind, evapotranspiration and ocean waters, we now move to a consideration of the global patterns of another important component of man's environment – the soil.

When a rock is first exposed at the earth's surface by erosion, it becomes subjected to the action of atmospheric and biologic agents. Mechanical weathering by frost and other such processes achieves the first stages in soil formation by fragmenting the rock. Chemical weathering gradually changes the minerals of the rock, and some of the easily soluble components thus released are removed into streams by being *leached* out of the surface layers, while others may be involved in the nourishment of invading micro-organisms. As time passes, these increase in bulk, in complexity of life form and in their effect on the soil mantle, and eventually an organic rich

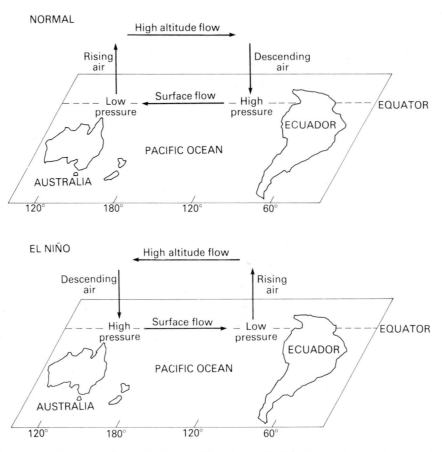

Figure 2.11 The nature of the 'normal' and El Niño conditions in the Pacific Ocean, showing the changing nature of the Walker Circulation.

layer may form at the surface. A soil may therefore be defined as an aggregate of many individual physical, chemical and biological processes that can be classified into various types, which gradually lead to the development of distinct layers or horizons by additions, removals, transfers and transformations of materials and energy. Most notable additions are organic matter and gases; removals involve salts and carbonates; transfers are of humus and sesquioxides; and transformations occur of, for example, primary minerals to secondary clays. All these processes take place in various combinations more or less simultaneously, the balance between them governing the nature of the soil profile.

Thus, within the soil numerous processes go on continuously as matter is transferred from one horizon to another, is added to the soil from above and is lost to plant roots from below. Such processes (which are discussed in greater detail in chapter 12) depend in part upon climatic conditions, so that at a gross scale certain patterns of soil development can be identified.

Soils that develop in areas of low precipitation, where rates of evaporation are high, have a water deficit for much of the time and undergo a process called *calcification*. When rain does fall it is sufficient to penetrate the upper soil layer, dissolve some calcium and percolate downwards. However, there is insufficient rainfall to leach the soil effectively, and soon the available water is evaporated or absorbed, leading to the deposition of the calcium carbonate.

In cool, moister climates, soil development tends to be influenced by *podsolization*. Under such circumstances the water supply is more

Plate 2.2 A typical podzol showing marked horizon development. Beneath a shallow upper organic layer, there is a light-coloured leached silica horizon. The dark band is the iron-cemented B horizon.

ample, so that the rainfall is sufficient to leach soluble materials quite thoroughly from the upper horizons, leaving only the rather inert silica behind. The leaching is assisted and accelerated by the presence of organic matter from the upper humus layer, and the minerals are transferred downwards to accumulate in the B horizon as an iron-cemented layer called an ironpan (section 12.2).

The hot wet regions of the tropics undergo *lateritization*. High rainfall and high temperatures combine to promote intense chemical weathering; high temperatures promote bacterial action, and organic matter is rapidly destroyed so that only a very limited humus layer is developed. These soils are often red in colour, and are dominated by large quantities of iron and aluminium sesquioxides.

Processes such as these help to account for the major differences in soils between major climatic

zones. The US Department of Agriculture has identified ten main soil *orders*, and their classification is called the Comprehensive Soil Classification System (CSCS) or, alternatively, *The Seventh Approximation*. We can appreciate their distribution and character by taking an hypothetical continent from the Northern Hemisphere (figure 2.12).

In the south-east region of this hypothetical continent, hot moist conditions produce lateritization processes and lead to *oxisols*. In the dry hot south-west are the *aridisols*, which are affected by calcification processes. In the cool and cold north podsolization occurs, producing *spodosols*. *Mollisols* are located in intermediate positions between dry and moist climates, in areas of grassland vegetation. They display some calcification, but in addition possess a dark humus-rich upper layer. On the moist side of the mollisols lie the *alfisols*, located between arid and subhumid soils on one side and more humid ultisols on the other. These are soils that are subject to neither calcification or podsolization, nor do they show an horizon where oxidation has occurred; however, they do have a lower horizon of clay accumulation. *Ultisols* develop where there is a pronounced summer wet season and a water-deficient dry season. They

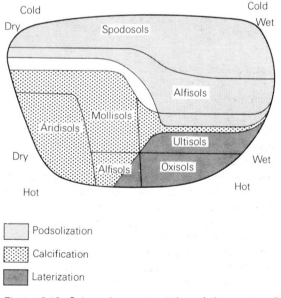

Figure 2.12 Schematic representation of the great soil orders on an hypothetical continent in the Northern Hemisphere.

Table 2.1　US Department of Agriculture soil classification – the Seventh Approximation (1975)

Order	Sub-order	Characteristics/environment
Alfisols (soils with an argillic horizon and moderate to high base content)	Aqualfs	Gleying features
	Boralfs	Others in cold climates
	Udalfs	Others in humid climates (including most leached brown soils)
	Ustalfs	Others in sub-humid climates
	Xeralfs	Others in sub-arid climates
Aridisols (desert and semi-desert soils)	Argids	With argillic horizon (i.e. zone of clay accumulation)
	Orthids	Other soils of dry areas
Entisols (immature usually azonal soils)	Aquents	Gleying features
	Arents	Artificially disturbed
	Fluvents	Alluvial deposits
	Psamments	Sandy or loamy sand textures
	Orthents	Other entisols
Histosols	Fibrists	Plant remains very little decomposed
	Folists	Freely draining histosols
	Hemists	Plant remains not recognisable because of decomposition; found in depressions
	Saprists	Plant remains totally decomposed (black)
Inceptisols (moderately developed soils, not in other orders)	Andepts	Volcanic ash
	Aquepts	Gleying features
	Plaggepts	Man-made surface horizon
	Tropepts	Tropical climates
	Umbrepts	Umbric epipedon (i.e. dark-coloured surface horizon of low base status); hills and mountains
	Ochrepts	Other inceptisols (including most brown earths) of mid–high latitudes
Mollisols (soils with a dark A horizon and high base status, e.g. chernozems, rendzinas)	Albolls	With argillic and albic horizons
	Aquolls	Gleying features
	Rendolls	Highly calcareous materials
	Borolls	Others in cold climates
	Udolls	Others in humid climates
	Ustolls	Others in sub-humid climates
	Xerolls	Others in sub-arid climates
Oxisols (soils with an oxic horizon or with plinthite near surface)	Aquox	Gleying features
	Humox	With a humose A horizon
	Torrox	Oxisols of arid climates
	Orthox	Others in equatorial climates
	Ustox	Others in sub-humid climates
Spodosols (soils with accumulation of free sesquioxides and/or organic carbon, e.g. podzols)	Aquods	Gleying features
	Ferrods	Much iron in spodic horizon
	Humods	Little iron in spodic horizon
	Orthods	Both iron and humus accumulation
Ultisols (soils with an argillic horizon, but low base content)	Aquults	Gleying features
	Humults	With a humose A horizon
	Udults	Others in humid climates
	Ustults	Others in sub-humid climates
	Xerults	Others in sub-arid climate
Vertisols (cracking clay soils with turbulence in profile)	Torrerts	Usually dry (cracks open for 300 days per year)
	Uderts	Usually moist (cracks open and close several times per year)
	Usterts	Cracks remain open 90 days per year (in monsoon climates)
	Xererts	Cracks remain open 60 days per year

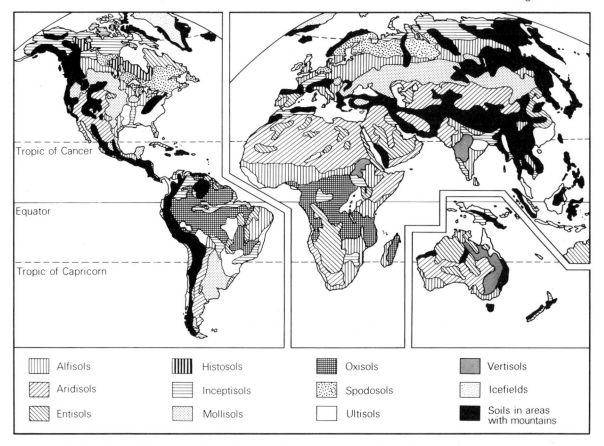

	Alfisols		Histosols		Oxisols		Vertisols
	Aridisols		Inceptisols		Spodosols		Icefields
	Entisols		Mollisols		Ultisols		Soils in areas with mountains

Figure 2.13 The global distribution of the main world soil orders according to the Seventh Approximation.

are quite deeply weathered and are transitional towards oxisols, often displaying the characteristic reddish-yellow colouration in the B horizon owing to the concentration of iron oxides.

The other four main soil orders are less clearly associated with any particular climatic regime. *Entisols* are soils that either have not existed long enough to develop mature horizonation (i.e., they are *recent*) or lie on parent materials, such as quartz dune sand, that do not readily evolve into horizons. *Inceptisols* include soils formed on the alluvium deposited by major rivers. *Vertisols* are clayey soils characterised by deep, wide cracks in the dry season. These cracks close up in the wet season when the available moisture increases causing the clays to swell, but before it does so a portion of the surface material has washed into the cracks: it becomes in*v*erted. Finally, *histosols* are primarily organic matter rather than mineral

soils and occur in bogs, moors or as peat accumulations where waterlogging is prevalent.

Thus, the Seventh Approximation has ten soil orders (table 2.1 and figure 2.13), and although the terminology may at first sight appear forbidding and bewildering, it is relatively easy to understand once the principles of its construction have been grasped. The name of each order is based on syllables that are intended to convey the major attributes of that class, and we have already seen the origin of the terms entisol and vertisol. To construct class names at the sub-order level we take two formative elements: the first indicating the characteristics of the soil or its environment (such as *aqu*, indicating wetness – see table 2.2), and the second being a suffix derived from the name of the order. Thus we could have the sub-order *Aquox*, being an oxisol with gleying features indicative of wetness.

Table 2.2 Formative elements in names of sub-orders of Seventh Approximation

Formative element	Meaning
alb	Presence of albic horizon (a bleached eluvial horizon)
and	Ando-like (i.e. volcanic ash materials)
aqu	Characteristics associated with wetness
ar	Mixed or cultivated horizon
arg	Presence of argillic horizon (a horizon with illuvial clay)
bor	Of cool climates
ferr	Presence of iron
fibr	Fibrous
fluv	Floodplain
fol	Presence of leaves
hem	Presence of well-decomposed organic matter
hum	Presence of horizon of organic enrichment
ochr	Presence of ochric epipedon (a light-coloured surface horizon)
orth	The common ones
plagg	Presence of a plaggen epipedon (a man-made surface 50 cm thick)
psamm	Sandy texture
rend	Rendzina-like
sapr	Presence of totally humified organic matter
torr	Usually dry
trop	Continually warm
ud	Of humid climates
umbr	Presence of umbric epipedon (a dark-coloured surface horizon)
ust	Of dry climates, usually hot in summer
xer	With annual dry season

2.9 Climatic geomorphology: the influence of climate, soil and vegetation

Although we started this part of the book by considering the pattern of major world land forms (shields, ocean ridges, etc.) in terms of plate tectonics and global geology, it is also undoubtedly true that the nature of land forms may, at a global scale, owe much also to the nature of the climate in the area, and to the influence that climate has through its effect on the nature of soil and vegetation. Because of this, attempts have been made by various climatic geomorphologists to delimit *morphogenetic regions*. The concept behind this is the theory that, under a certain set of climatic conditions, particular geomorphological processes will predominate; these will give to the landscape of a region characteristics that will set it apart from those of other areas developed under different climatic conditions. Because of the frequency and nature of climatic changes, it is necessary to consider the influence not only of present climates, but also of past climates.

One classification attempt has been that of Büdel, a German geomorphologist. His regionalisation scheme is illustrated in table 2.3. For comparison, table 2.4 sets out a more recent scheme – that of Wilson, an American geomorphologist. Whichever scheme is adopted, it is evident that climate does control the distribution of certain important phenomena and processes, including glaciation, permafrost, coral reef growth, dune formation, frost weathering and wind erosion. These are topics that we shall consider further in Part II.

2.10 Major vegetation types

Just as it is possible to classify and map major climatic types, so it is possible to classify and map the main types of vegetation on the face of the earth. At a very gross scale, the distribution of vegetation types is closely related to the distribution of climatic types, and one of the classic ideas of biogeography was that if an area of land – bare of vegetation because of some event like a volcanic eruption – became colonised by vegetation, there would be a gradual *succession* of vegetation changes until the optimum for the conditions, known as the *climatic climax community*, established itself (see chapter 9).

Table 2.3   Büdel's morphogenetic zones of the world

Zone	Present climate	Past climate	Active processes (fossil ones in brackets)	Landforms
(1) Of glaciers	Glacial	Glacial	Glaciation	Glacial
(2) Of pronounced valley formation	Polar, tundra	Glacial, polar, tundra	Frost, mechanical weathering, stream erosion (Glaciation)	Box valleys, patterned ground, etc.
(3) Of extra-tropical valley formation	Continental, cool temperate	Polar, tundra continental	Stream erosion (Frost processes, glaciation)	Valleys
(4) Of subtropical pediment and valley formation	Subtropical (warm; wet or dry)	Continental, subtropical	Pediment[a] formation (Stream erosion)	Planation surfaces and valleys
(5) Of tropical planation surface formation	Tropical (hot; wet, or wet–dry)	Subtropical, tropical	Planation, chemical weathering	Planation surfaces and laterite[b]

[a] A pediment is a low-angle, concave rock surface at the base of a high-angle slope.
[b] Laterite is an iron-rich and/or aluminium-rich crust characteristic of a tropical region and caused by rock weathering.

Table 2.4   Wilson's morphogenetic systems of the world

System	Dominant geomorphological processes	Landscape characteristics
(1) Glacial	Glaciation, snow action (nivation), wind action	Glacial scour, alpine topography, moraines, kames, eskers, etc.
(2) Periglacial	Frost action, solifluction	Patterned ground, outwash plains, solifluction lobes, etc.
(3) Arid	Desiccation; wind action; running water	Dunes, salt pans, deflation basins, etc.
(4) Semi-arid (sub-arid)	Running water, rapid mass movements, mechanical weathering	Pediments, fans, badlands, angular slopes with coarse debris
(5) Humid temperate	Running water, chemical weathering, creep (and other mass movements)	Smooth slopes, soil-covered; ridges and valleys; extensive stream deposits
(6) Selva	Chemical weathering, mass movements; running water	Steep slopes, knife-edge ridges, deep soils (laterites included); coral reefs

There is no doubt that climate does affect plant growth. In a broad sense, meagre rainfall results in desert vegetation, light rainfall causes grassland and abundant rainfall produces forest. Likewise, temperature plays a large part in accounting for the differences between, by way of example, tropical rainforest and the coniferous forests of higher latitudes. Low temperatures tend to result in lower plant growth and smaller size, and frosts can be lethal to certain species. Many plants cannot make active growth if the temperature is below 6°C, and for most of the species of a temperate deciduous forest there must be at least six months with temperatures above such a minimum.

On the other hand, any simple relationship between climate and vegetation type may be obscured by differences in such factors as soil type, the activity of fires and the actions of man. The problem of mapping the major zones is compounded by the fact that their delimitation will inevitably be arbitrary, for there are very few clear-cut lines in nature. There is also the perennial problem of whether the zones should be small in number, simple in type – and thus probably overgeneralised – or whether one should go for more categories – but then inevitably cause a lack of clarity.

Bearing these problems in mind, one can see that the map of vegetation types (figure 2.14) is remarkably similar to our map of major climatic types, and this is brought out further in table 2.5.

The rate at which vegetative matter is produced, together with the actual amount of vegeta-

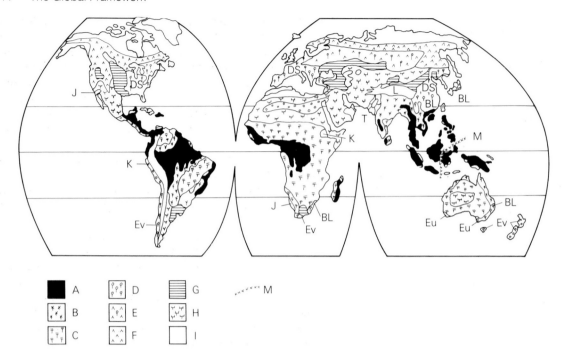

Figure 2.14 Generalised distribution of the world's vegetation types: A, tropical rainforest; B, tropical seasonal forest; C, savannas; D, temperate forest including deciduous summer forest (DS), evergreen mixed forest (Ev), broad-leaved evergreen forest (Bl), Eucalyptus forest (Eu), and southern pine forest of the USA (Pi); E, mixed boreal and deciduous forest of the Northern Hemisphere; F, boreal forest (including west coast forest of the USA); G, temperate grasslands; H, arid and semi-arid vegetation; I, tundra; J, true desert with intermittent grass cover; K, montane vegetation of the Andes and Abyssinian (Ethiopian) highlands which includes major formations of tropical montane forest; L, alpine vegetation of central Asia with extensive grassland areas; M, Wallace's line.

Table 2.5   The relationship between climatic zone and vegetation type

Climate	Vegetation
Humid tropical zone	Rainforest, with mangroves on coasts
Semi-arid seasonal tropics	Savanna
Arid tropics	Desert scrub, or vegetationless
'Mediterranean'	Evergreen woodlands and shrubs
Humid temperate (maritime)	Temperate deciduous forest
Cool temperate (continental)	Temperate grasslands, steppe, etc.
Boreal zone	Coniferous and birch forests
Arctic zone	Tundra, shallow-rooted shrubs

tive material that exists in a particular area (the *biomass*), also show broad patterns that are related to climate. In desert areas and in the tundra biomass levels are very low; they are intermediate in the boreal forests and mid-latitude deciduous forests, and reach their highest levels in the humid tropical rainforest. These differences in the production of organic matter (table 2.6) have great importance in terms of soil development and rock weathering in different parts of the world.

Altitude modifies the general distribution pattern, and introduces local complexity (figure 2.15). Unless the relief is very slight, each altitudinal zone will afford suitable conditions for the appearance of plants in general characteristic of a zone or zones in higher latitudes; subtropical plants will occur here and there in tropical regions, temperate plants will occur in both tropical and subtropical zones, and so on. The effect of altitude is discussed further in chapter 7.

Table 2.6 Net primary production (NPP) and biomass of major world vegetation types.

	Mean Net primary productivity $(g\ m^{-2}yr^{-1})$	Mean Biomass $(t\ ha^{-1})$
Tropical rainforest	2200	450
Tropical seasonal forest	1600	350
Temperate evergreen forest	1300	350
Temperate deciduous forest	1200	300
Boreal forest	800	200
Savanna	900	40
Temperate grassland	600	16
Tundra and alpine	140	6
Desert and semi-desert shrub	90	7
Extreme desert, rock, sand	3	2

2.11   Floral realms

From the time in the distant geological past when plants spread rapidly around the world until the present, the plant cover has never ceased to evolve. Mutations have emerged continuously, and their survival and establishment has depended on ecological circumstances at the time of their appearance. Climates have changed; continents have shifted, isolating some plant groups and joining others; new mountain barriers have developed; and sea level has varied, creating or destroying land-bridges between continents. For these reasons the world today does not have a uniform flora, but we can none the less detect areas where there is some coherence in the distribution pattern of particular species. These can be generalised into maps – maps of *flora* and not of vegetation types. The distinction between the two is an important one: the flora of an area is the sum total of all the plant species in it; vegetation is the kind of plant cover in that area. Thus, although two floral regions may be similar in their vegetation, because for example, they are both areas of tropical rainforest, they do not necessarily have much in common botanically or share more than a few genera.

An example of a floral regionalisation is shown in figure 2.16(a), and it has certain broad similarities to a map of the faunal realms, a topic we shall turn to shortly. Although there can be many small regions (in this example, 37), they can be lumped into six major groups called *kingdoms*: Holarctic, Palaeotropical, Neotropical, Cape, Australian and Antarctic.

2.12   Faunal realms

Finally, in this study of present global patterns we must take a look at the distribution patterns of the world's animals, and try to subdivide the world into zoogeographical regions or realms (figure 2.16(b)). Of the various attempts that

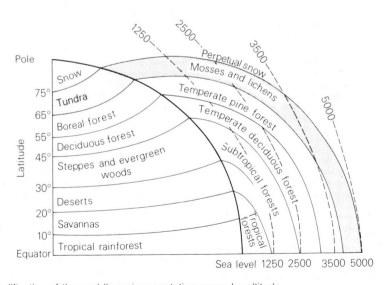

Figure 2.15   The modification of the world's major vegetation zones by altitude.

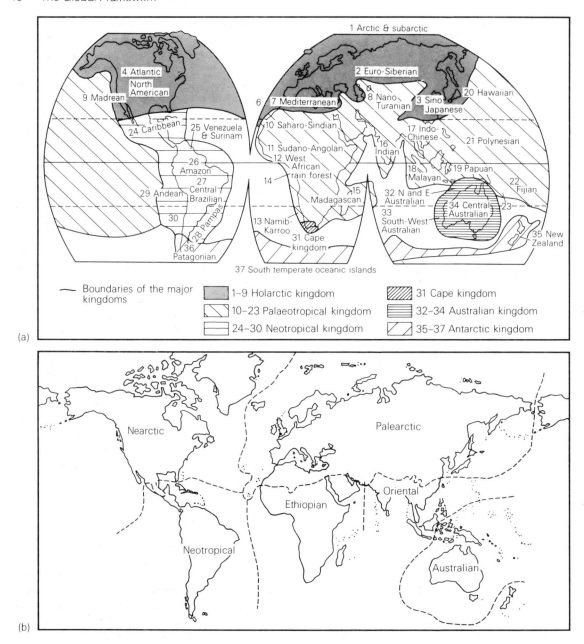

Figure 2.16 The major floral and faunal realms of the world: (a) flora; (b) fauna.

have been made to do this, the most famous is that of a contemporary of Charles Darwin, A. R. Wallace. In the late nineteenth century Wallace established six major regions, to which he gave special names as they do not correspond very precisely with political or cultural areas. They are still widely accepted as useful, though subdivisions and amalgamations have been made from time to time. Some scientists have considered the Neotropical and Australian regions to be zoologically so different from the rest of the world, and from one another, as to rank as regions equivalent to the remaining four put together. In this classification there are three realms: Neogea

Plate 2.3 One of the greatest zoo-geographers of all time was A. R. Wallace, who divided the world up into a series of faunal realms or regions. He noted the considerable differences between the fauna of Australia and of Asia, and the boundary between these two faunal areas is normally called Wallace's Line.

(Neotropical), Notogea (Australian), and Arctogea (the rest of the world). Another proposal is that Palearctic and Nearctic do not merit separate regional status, and should thus be combined into one region – the Holarctic. As with all schemes of regionalisation and classification, some people are 'lumpers' and some are 'splitters'.

The important point, however, is that there are major differences in the nature of the species of animal found in different parts of the world. This reflects many factors, including present and past climates, the absence or presence of former land connections between continents, the operation of continental drift and the differential operation of evolution in different parts of the world. For example, the fauna of Australia may have been similar at one time to that in other parts of the world, because it was part of the great supercontinent of Pangaea or Gondwanaland; but for

some considerable time, it has been isolated by a zone of deep water from Asia, and so exchanges have been limited, and evolution has been able to take place in comparative isolation, producing some unique species that are adapted to the particular environmental conditions of that continent. It is for these sorts of reasons that the Australian fauna is so special. Apart from bats, there are only nine families of mammals, and eight of these are unique. The dominant mammal fauna is marsupial; it is made up of six families, none of which occurs in the New World, where are found the only other living marsupials. The remaining two families of Australian mammals belong to a separate sub-class of mammals, Monotremata. They are those bizarre egg-laying beasts, the duckbilled platypuses and the spiny anteaters.

Since we have developed the means of long-distance travel, particularly across the oceans, we have greatly modified the distribution of animal species. In some cases people have been the un-witting cause of the introduction of foreign species to an area, as for example when cats and rats escaped from ships that visited tropical islands. At other times they have deliberately introduced particular species – for sport, for economic gain or out of nostalgia – and as a consequence some species, like the trout, have a vastly greater distribution than they would have had without our assistance.

2.13 Climatic change

As we have already seen, our knowledge of how the world works and why it is as it is, has been revolutionised in the last couple of decades by the concept of plate tectonics. Over much the same period another major transformation in ideas has also taken place – again owing much to discoveries on the ocean floors, and again having a bearing on the history of the earth: our ideas about climatic changes over the last few millions of years have been revolutionised.

It has become increasingly apparent that world environments have been subject to frequent and massive changes during the course of the latest period of geological time – the Quaternary. Even in the last 20 000 years the area of the earth covered by glaciers has been reduced to one-third

Plate 2.4   Australia has many endemic species of fauna, including marsupials. Isolation has enabled the evolution of such strange beasts as the koala bear (bottom, left), the kangaroo (bottom, right), and the platypus (below).

what it was at the glacial maximum; the waters thereby released have raised ocean levels by over a hundred metres; the land, unburdened from the weight of overlying ice, has locally risen by several hundred metres; vegetation belts have swung through the equivalent of tens of degrees of latitude; permanently frozen ground and tundra conditions have retreated from extensive areas of Europe; the rainforests have expanded; desert sand fields have advanced and retreated; inland lakes have flooded and shrunk; and many of the world's finest mammals have become extinct. Thus on the one hand the major patterns of climate, ocean currents, fauna, flora, landforms and soils that we have been examining are not very long-lived, and on the other they owe much to the happenings of the last few million years.

The changes of climate, and the other environmental changes that they produced, have occurred over a wide range of time scales (figure 2.17).

Figure 2.17 The climate of the world has varied by many different time scales over the last billion years: (a) by decade; (b) by century; (c) by millennia; (d) by tens of millennia; (e) by hundreds of millennia; (f) by era.

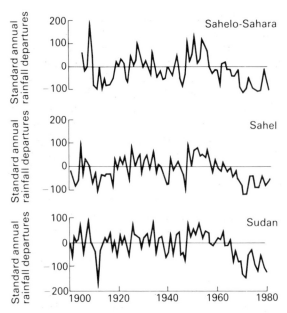

Figure 2.18 Standard annual rainfall departures for three Sub-Saharan zones in Africa in the twentieth century. Note the especially dry conditions that have existed since the mid-1960s.

The shorter-term changes include such events as the period of warming that took place in the first decades of the twentieth century, the years of low rainfall and high temperatures which contributed to the formation of the 'Dust Bowl' in the High Plains of the United States in the 1930s, and the run of very dry years since the 1960s that have caused such human misery to the people of the Sahel and Ethiopia in sub-Saharan Africa. The extremely serious climatic deterioration that has afflicted this zone since about 1968 is illustrated by the rainfall data shown in figure 2.18.

But changes lasting hundreds of years were also characteristic of the last 10 000 years (a time often called the Holocene (see table 1.1), including a period of glacial advance between about 1500 and 1850 called the 'Little Ice Age'. This cold event has been identified all over the world, and besides causing glaciers to extend down their valleys, it also caused the retreat of settlement in marginal areas of highland Europe and Iceland, and there seems to have been a period of severe avalanching, landsliding, rock falls and flooding in countries like Norway and Switzerland. There were other phases of glacial expansion within the

Holocene, events to which the name, *Neoglacial*, is now normally applied. By contrast, there were also certain phases within the Holocene when conditions were rather warmer than they are today. For example, from about AD 750–1300 there was a period of marked glacial retreat, and this is called 'The Little Optimum' or 'Medieval Warm Epoch'. It was a time when the climate of England was sufficiently mild to permit vine cultivation and wine manufacture as far north as York. A more extended period, 'The Climatic Optimum' or 'Altithermal' witnessed the spread of relatively warm conditions in the earlier millennia of the Holocene, and temperatures may have been 1–3°C higher on average than they are today.

The fluctuations within the Pleistocene (the portion of the Quaternary that preceded the Holocene) consisted of major cold phases (called *glacials*) and warm phases (called *interglacials*). The Pleistocene itself consisted of a group of glacial and interglacial events that lasted in total around two or so million years. Such major phases of ice age activity seem to have been separated by around 250 million years.

Realisation that the world had undergone an ice age over the last few millions of years goes back to the 1820s, but it is only in recent decades that the real nature of the changes has become appreciated and that accurate dates have been applied to them. These changes have taken place partly because of the availability of techniques like radiocarbon and potassium argon dating, which postdate the Second World War, and partly because it is now possible to retrieve cores of sediment from the ocean floors. Before these cores were accessible, the evidence for glaciation was obtained from glacial deposits on land, deposits that were repeatedly being destroyed by subsequent glaciation and erosion. By contrast, the oceans have been a more stable environment where the record of deposition has been much less subject to disturbance. Indeed, the problem of estimating the number of glaciations from evidence on the land has been likened in complexity to estimating the number of times that a blackboard has been erased; while using the evidence provided by layers of sediment in ocean cores has been likened to finding the number of times that a wall has been painted.

During the glacials the ice caps of the world were greatly expanded. In North America the Laurentide Ice Sheet came down to as far south as 38° or 39° N, and another huge sheet, the Scandinavian Ice Sheet, covered much of western Europe, including a large part of the British Isles. The European Alps formed another major centre of ice. Thus today large areas in the mid-latitudes show the imprint of glacial erosion and glacial deposition. On the periphery of the great ice sheets, which in areas like Hudson Bay may have been around 3300 m thick, there were, particularly in Europe, great areas of open tundra, which were frequently underlain by permafrost (figure 2.20). Today, continuous permafrost is restricted by the mean annual isotherm of −5°C to areas like Novaya Zemlya and the northern parts of Siberia; but during the glacials it underlay much of Britain south of the ice sheets, and was also widespread down to the latitude of Biarritz in western France. The forests that form the natural vegetation of so much of western Europe today were largely replaced by cold, rather dry tundra and steppe.

During the interglacials the conditions were broadly similar to those that exist today, though from time to time they may have been slightly warmer. What is of interest, however, is that the deep sea cores suggest that over the last few million years temperatures have been as warm as today for only about 10 per cent of the time. In other words, present conditions are essentially untypical and short-lived.

For many years it was believed that the climatic changes associated with the glacials and interglacials also affected lower latitudes, and that during glacials wetter conditions existed in the tropics, causing lakes to reach high levels and rivers to flow in areas that are now arid. Such humid phases were called *pluvials* and the warm dry phases between them were called *interpluvials*. It was widely believed that the humid tropics were little affected by the changes of climate that transformed higher latitudes.

There is indeed much evidence that at certain times in the past there has been more water available in desert areas; huge lakes, for example, filled the now largely dry basins of the south-west United States. However, there is also evidence that in other areas the period of the glacials were

Plate 2.5 A. Penck and E. Brückner were responsible, in the first decade of the present century, for producing one of the most important sequences of glacials and interglacials in the Bavarian valleys: Günz, Mindel, Riss and Würm.

In a sense, over the period of the Pleistocene, the ocean floors have been like a dustbin into which layers of sediments and dead organisms have been poured. By looking at these layers it is possible to reconstruct the history of the world's climate in detail.

Prior to the availability of such techniques there was wide support for the idea of four major Pleistocene glaciations. This we call the *Penck and Brückner model* (figure 2.19(a)), after the scientists who propounded it while working in the Bavarian foreland of central Europe. Now, however, following the work of scientists like Emiliani, since the 1950s we know that the situation has been much more complex and that there have been multiple glaciations over the last 2 million years (figure 2.19(b)).

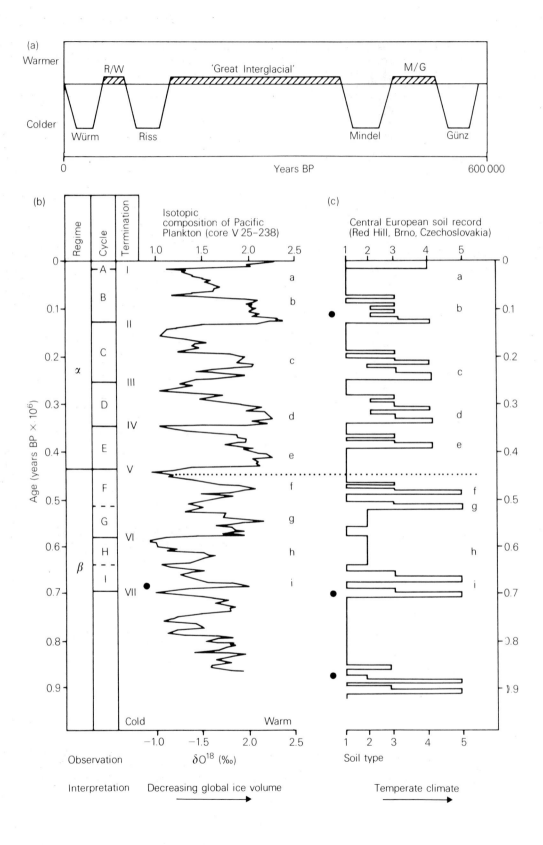

(a)

Warmer

R/W   'Great Interglacial'   M/G

Colder

Würm   Riss   Mindel   Günz

0   Years BP   600 000

(b)

Regime

Cycle

Termination

Isotopic
composition of Pacific
Plankton (core V 25–238)

1.0   1.5   2.0   2.5

(c)

Central European soil record
(Red Hill, Brno, Czechoslovakia)

1   2   3   4   5

Age (years BP × 10⁶)

A   I   a   a
B   b   b
0.1   II
C   c   c
0.2   III
D   d   d
0.3
E   IV   e   e
0.4 α
     V   f   f
F
0.5   g   g
G
0.6 VI   h   h
H
     I   i   i
0.7 β VII
0.8
0.9

Cold   Warm

−1.0   −1.5   2.0   2.5   1   2   3   4   5

Observation   δO¹⁸ (‰)   Soil type

Interpretation   Decreasing global ice volume →   Temperate climate →

Figure 2.19 Models of glacial history in the Pleistocene: (a) the classic four-fold glaciation model of Penck and Brückner; (b) the sequence derived from the evidence of deep sea cores; (c) the changes represented in soil profiles developed in loess sequences in Czechoslovakia. Note how (b) and (c) indicate a greater frequency of change than (a), with multiple glaciations.

times not of increased humidity, but of reduced precipitation. The most spectacular evidence for this is the great expansion that took place in the distribution of sand dunes in low latitudes. Dunes cannot develop to any great degree in continental interiors unless the vegetation cover is sufficiently sparse to permit sand movement by the wind. If the rainfall is much over about 150 mm per annum this is not possible. Studies of air photographs and satellite imagery indicate clearly that degraded ancient dunes, now covered in forest or savanna, are widespread in areas that are now quite moist (perhaps with rainfalls of the order of 750–1500 mm). (See plate 2.6.) Today about 10 per cent of the land area between 30° N and 30° S is covered by active sand deserts. At the time of

the last great glacial advance, about 18 000 years ago, they probably characterised almost 50 per cent of the land area in those latitudes (figure

☰ Sea	▦ Mountain tundra meadows
☰ Proglacial lake	▦ Forest mainly coniferous
☐ Polar desert	▥ Tundra and forest tundra
▨ Proglacial forest steppe and steppe	☐ Ice
---- Present coastline	0 ⊢——————⊣ 1000 km

(a)

(b)

Figure 2.20 Europe in the Ice Age. (a) A reconstruction of Europe during the maximum of the last glacial phase (c. 18 000 years BP). Note the great extent of ice over Britain and Scandinavia. (b) A comparison of the vegetation conditions of Europe across a north–south transect in an interglacial (top), and a glacial (bottom). Notice the absence of trees during a glacial cold phase.

Plate 2.6   The stripes running from right to left across this Landsat image of Zambia, central Africa, are old fossil dunes that were formed, probably in the Pleistocene, under a formerly more arid climate. Note that in the top right portion of the image some of the tributaries of the Zambezi River show similar alignment.

2.21). In between, tropical rainforests and adjacent savannas were reduced to a narrow corridor, and were much less extensive then they are today.

2.14 Causes of long-term climatic change

As we have already seen, climate has undergone changes over a variety of different time-scales and

(a) Today

(b) 18 000 BP

Ice-caps   Sand dune areas

Figure 2.21 Because of greater aridity over large parts of low latitudes at or just after the time of the maximum extent of the last glacial episode, the extent of sand dunes 18 000 years ago (b) was very much greater than it is today.

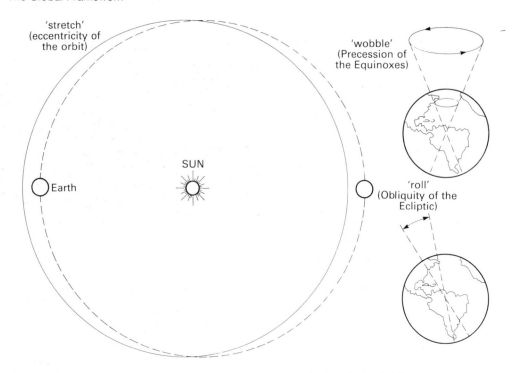

Figure 2.22   The three types of fluctuation in earth geometry involved in the Milankovitch hypothesis.

with a varying degree of intensity. An intriguing question is to ask why such changes have taken place.

At a very long time scale it is evident that the changing configurations and positions of the continents and oceans, together with the uplift of mountain chains, will have had a major effect on world climate. Such geological causes of change have been described in chapter 1. Another geological change that can affect world climates is volcanic activity. A prolonged period of severe eruptions could inject large amounts of dust into the upper atmosphere. This might decrease the quantity of solar radiation reaching the earth's surface, and so cause a phase of cooling.

It is also possible that the output of solar radiation from the Sun varies through time, possibly in a cyclic manner. There is some good evidence for sunspot activity (an indication of radiation conditions) having a cyclic pattern, with eleven and twenty-two-year cycles being ones particularly noted. Substantial proof of longer term cycles is less certain.

What has become more certain in recent years,

however, is that the amount of radiation received at the earth's surface through time has varied as a consequence of the ever changing position of the earth with respect to the sun. This is the so-called *astronomical theory of climatic change*, which is also sometimes termed the *Milankovitch hypothesis*. The basis of this idea is that there are three ways in which the earth's position varies, and that these variations take place in a regular and predictable way through time (figure 2.22).

First, the earth's orbit around the sun is not a perfect circle but an ellipse. The degree to which this ellipticity varies determines the length of the seasons, and the effect is referred to as the *eccentricity of the orbit*. Over a period of about 96 000 years the shape of the orbit varies from almost circular to strongly elliptical.

Second, the tilt of the earth's axis of rotation varies, a mechanism called the *obliquity of the ecliptic*. This means, that over a period of about 40 000 years the positions of the Tropics shift slightly.

Thirdly, there is a mechanism called the *precession of the equinoxes* which is based on the fact that the time of year at which the earth is nearest the sun varies. The reason is that the earth wobbles like a top and swivels its axis round. This process has a cycle length of about 21 000 years.

Evidence in support of the Milankovitch hypothesis comes from cores that have been drilled through undisturbed ocean sediments which have accumulated over many thousands of years. Fluctuations in climate, as determined from the nature of their chemistry and their fossil content, tie in closely with the Milankovitch cycles.

Once this astronomical mechanism leads to a reduction in temperature, the effects may be intensified by some *positive feedback processes*. For example, as temperature cools, the summer melting of the Arctic ice cap will be delayed and reduced. Because the ice survives for longer, and because this ice has a high albedo, much incoming solar radiation is reflected back to space. This in turn produces reduced heating of the surface, which enables the ice caps to survive even longer, which increases reflection further, which reduces temperature, and so forth.

2.15   Sea-level changes

The climato-vegetational changes of the Quaternary era were equalled in importance only by the world-wide changes in sea level that took place, though these themselves were caused partially by climatic factors. The sea-level changes are significant because they have affected the configuration of coastlines, the size and existence of islands, the migration of plants, animals and man and the

Plate 2.7   Sea level changes have been an important feature of the Pleistocene and Holocene. Higher sea levels the represented by raised beaches, like this example from Cornwall, south-west England.

degree of deposition and erosion carried out by rivers in response to a fluctuating base level.

The most important cause of world-wide, or *eustatic*, sea-level change in the Pleistocene was *glacio-eustasy* (see section 3.8). When the ice sheets were three times as voluminous as today, a very large quantity of water was stored up in them, and thus there was less water in the oceans. Calculations differ as to the exact quantity of change that would take place, but sea levels may well have dropped between 100 and 170 m (figure 2.23), thereby exposing most of the

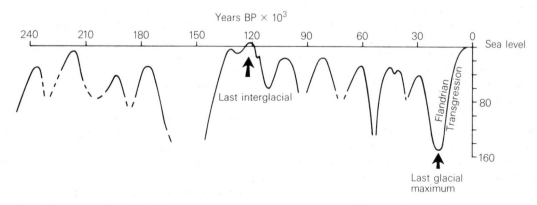

Figure 2.23   The nature of world sea-level change over the last quarter of a million years.

Figure 2.24 The nature of world sea-level change during the Flandrian Transgression of the Holocene.

world's continental shelves as dry land. If, on the other hand, the two remaining major polar ice caps were to melt, sea level would probably rise by 66 m above its present position. The ice caps may have been slightly smaller during interglacials than they are today, and this may have caused sea levels to be a few metres higher than now, producing *raised beaches* in some coastal areas. In the Holocene, sea level rose very quickly (figure 2.24), especially between 11 000 and 6000 years ago; it flooded the North Sea, broke the land link between Britain and Ireland and flooded many river valleys to give features like the indented coastline of south-west England, with its winding inlets, called *rias*. This transgression is often called the *Flandrian Transgression*.

Other world-wide changes of sea level have been caused by *orogenesis* (mountain-building), associated with plate movement. This, together with the sea-floor spreading, can change the volume of the oceans, and through that worldwide sea levels. An increase of only 1 per cent in the area of the oceans would lower sea level by around 40 m. The spreading of the ocean basins since the last major stand of high interglacial sea levels some 120 000 years ago may have lowered world sea level by as much as 8 m.

2.16   Conclusions

In these first two chapters we have seen that the most important large-scale patterns on the face of the earth are controlled either by geological or by climatic factors. It is evident that certain phenomena, such as soils, vegetation, ocean currents, landforms and hydrology, show global patterns that are related in their distribution to the major climatic zones. Part II will involve a consideration of the physical geography of some of the world's most important zones: polar regions, periglacial regions, temperate regions, arid regions and the tropics.

PART II
Major World Zones

3 Polar Regions

3.1 Polar climates

Enduring cold typifies the climate of high latitudes. For six months at the North and South Poles the sun is out of sight entirely. For another six it is constantly above the horizon, but as it is never very high solar radiation is weak. The sun's rays are too oblique to be genuinely effective. Moreover, much of the solar energy is either reflected by the snow and ice or involved in melting snow and evaporating meltwater, so that neither the land surface nor the air adjacent to it becomes warm. At the Arctic and Antarctic Circles (latitude 66½°) the daily period of sunlight varies from 24 hours at the time of the summer solstice to zero hours at the winter solstice.

The equatorward boundary of polar climates is generally taken as the line where the mean temperature of the warmest month is no more than 10°C. This line broadly corresponds with the poleward limit of tree growth. In the Northern Hemisphere the threshold isotherm swings well poleward of the Arctic Circle over most of Asia and Alaska, coincides reasonably well with that parallel over lowland Europe, and lies to the south of it over much of Greenland and eastern North America. In the Southern Hemisphere the only extensive area of land with polar climates is the ice-covered Antarctic continent. Because its single land mass is centred near the South Pole and surrounded by extensive oceans with relatively uniform temperatures, the Antarctic possesses much greater uniformity and simplicity of climate than the Arctic.

Both areas are major sources of chill air; this tends at all times to move equatorward, converging in mid-latitudes with warmer air from the subtropical anticyclones and thereby playing a primary role in the generation of mid-latitude disturbances along the zones of contact between cold and warm air.

Polar climates can be subdivided into two types: *ice-cap climates* and *tundra climates*.

In the case of the former, the average temperatures of all months are below freezing (0°C) so that vegetation growth is impossible, and a permanent ice-and-snow cover prevails. At the South Pole the warmest month (December) has a temperature of −28°C and the three coldest (July, August, September) a temperature of −59°C. At Vostok, in the interior of Antarctica and at a height of 3500 m, the average August temperature is no less than −68°C and the thermometer has been known to drop to nearly −90°C. Information about precipitation is limited, but it is generally believed to be scanty in amount; for the low temperatures, the low specific humidity and the extreme stability of the air, as indicated by persistent strong temperature inversions, inhibit snowfall. At Eismitte in interior Greenland the annual precipitation is equivalent to only 80−100 mm of water, while the whole Antarctic continent receives on average less than 150 mm of water annually.

The tundra class of climate, which is confined almost exclusively to the Northern Hemisphere, is intermediate between the ice-cap climate of perpetual snow and ice, and the climate of the middle-latitudes. This belt lies between the 0°C warmest-month isotherm on its polar side and

Opposite Scientist and seals amid the snow and ice of the Antarctic.

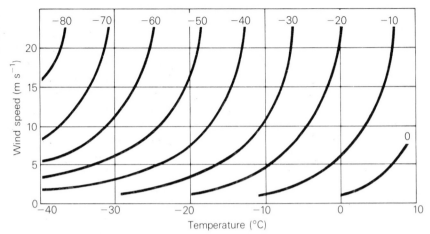

Figure 3.1 Wind chill. The numbers of the slanting lines indicate the effective temperature in °C of air at a given temperature and wind speed.

the 10°C warmest-month isotherm on its equatorward side.

Usually only a few months have average temperatures above freezing, and frosts may occur at any time. The continuous but weak summer sun may free the land of its snow cover for a few months and cause the upper layers of the soil to thaw, but the subsoil remains frozen from year to year as *permafrost* (section 3.10). Precipitation does occur, usually in summer, but is generally low, in the range 75–450 mm per annum. In some maritime regions, such as the Aleutian Islands between Alaska and Siberia, precipitation may be higher, attaining 1500 mm per year, and precipitation levels may also increase as one moves equatorwards.

The extreme cold of high-latitude and high-altitude areas creates problems for humans, but such problems are greatly accentuated when the extreme cold is accompanied by high wind velocities. This produces a phenomenon called *wind chill*. On a cold but calm day, warm human skin heats the air next to it, which in turn passes heat to the next layer and so on until the heat is carried away from the body. This is not a particularly efficient way to lose heat, because the conductivity of air is low. Therefore calm air feels relatively warm. A wind, however, *pulls* heated air away from the surface. Cold air replaces skin-warmed air, and the faster the air moves the more heat is taken from the body. This makes it feel much colder than the thermometer reading, as is demonstrated in figure 3.1.

Table 3.1   Some adaptations of Arctic vegetation to polar climates

Adaptation	Effect
Prostrate shrub	Insulation between snow, warmer micro-climate; less wind
Cushion plants	Warm micro-climate and less wind
Annuals rare	Growing season too short for full cycle
Herbaceous perennials common	Large underground root structure; storage of food over winter
Reproduction often by rhizomes, bulbs or layering	Avoids reliance on completing flower to seed cycle
Pre-formed flower buds	Maximises time for seed production
Growth at low positive temperatures	Maximises length of growing season
Optimum photosynthesis rate at lower temperatures than most plants	Maximises length of growing season
Frost resistance	True of flowers, fruits and seeds
Longevity	Suitable for 'opportunist' life style; e.g., lichens may live for several thousand years
Drought resistance	Suitable for rock surfaces or arid climates

Source: modified after D. Sugden, *Arctic and Antarctic* (Oxford: Basil Blackwell, 1982), table 5.1.

3.2   Vegetation and wildlife

Because of the climatic definition we employed earlier, polar regions lie beyond the limit of real trees. Indeed, the area and its vegetation are described by the Finnish word *tundra*, meaning 'barren land'. In reality, however, some plants have adapted to the extreme conditions of the tundra (table 3.1). They belong to five main groups: lichens, mosses, grasses and grass-like herbs, cushion plants and low shrubs. Nearly all of them are perennials, for climatic conditions provide too short a growing season for an annual's life-cycle to be completed. They spring into life for just a few months in summer, remaining dormant for up to ten months per year. Most manage to achieve only a very low annual growth rate, partly because of low temperatures and partly because of the high winds. Wind chill is just as discouraging for plants as it is for man – indeed, the reduction of wind speed near the ground is one of the reasons for the widespread development of dwarf vegetation. Plant growth is further hampered by the fact that Arctic soils are also relatively infertile; they tend to lack nitrogen, one of the most important of plant nutrients. Tundra plants also have to face being covered with snow for extended periods; they have to endure very severe frosts; and they have to withstand the disturbance of the soil by permafrost.

Some scientists divide tundra plants into two main types. The first is the *fell field community*, where the vegetation is so scantily developed that the ground is never covered with a complete sward. Rock surfaces have lichens and some cushion plants such as moss campion (*Silene acaulis*) and various saxifrages. The second type consists of the *tundra communities*. In the sward shrub-heath tundra there are creeping willows, dwarf birch and berry-bearing members of the *Vaccinium* family, interspersed with Arctic heather (*Cassiope*) and a carpet of mosses and lichens such as *Cladonia*. In other areas there may be grassland tundra with a great development of sphagnum moss and cotton grass (*Eriophorum*). The grass and sedges often occur as tussocks. Finally, there may be willow and alder thickets, especially where abundant summer moisture is available, as along stream banks and below some snow patches.

In Antarctica, because of the almost universal lack of vegetated ground, there are virtually no truly land animals or birds – the life is very largely marine, with some beasts, notably penguins and seals, venturing on to the land when conditions permit. However, in the northern polar regions there is a much richer land fauna, though it is still a relatively poor range of species compared with more favourable climatic zones. For example, it has been calculated that of 8600 bird species in the world only 70 breed in the Arctic, while of 3200 mammals in the world only 23 occur north of the tree-line. There are no reptiles. Some individual faunal species may, however, occur in large numbers e.g. mosquitoes, lemmings and caribou.

Polar animals have adapted themselves to extreme cold and fluctuations in temperature (table 3.2). One way of doing this is to grow fur (as for example, with the polar fox and the musk ox) or

Table 3.2   Faunal adaptations to polar climate

Stress	Consequence
Severe climate	Low number of species Low mean densities
Low temperature	High quality fur insulation Increased metabolic rates
Snow	Life below snow patch for smaller animals Large herbivores favour soft/thin snow
Short summer	Birds migrate Breeding cycle compressed Large clutch/litter size

Source: after D. Sugden, *Arctic and Antarctic* (Oxford: Basil Blackwell, 1982), table 5.3.

feathers. Sometimes the fur may have certain characteristics that add to its insulational properties. For instance, the hair of the caribou is thicker at the tip than at the base, thus entrapping air which assists in insulation; it also contains many air cells within the hair stem. Another form of adaptation is to hibernate during the coldest months, though where ground temperatures are very low even this is not possible. Most of the Arctic insects spend the winter in a larval or even egg form. The third form of adaptation is to migrate during the coldest months to areas where food may be available. Birds are especially prone to do this, though some of the larger mammals may also migrate (generally in search of a winter food supply), notably the caribou.

3.3 Glacier types

The earth is at present in an ice age, and around 10 per cent of its surface is covered by glaciers. Moreover, over the past few million years the extent of such ice has been frequently much more expanded than now, covering around one-third of the earth's surface (see section 2.13). Glaciers are therefore important both because they cover substantial parts of the earth's surface and because they have left their imprint on the land they formerly covered.

The biggest glaciers are called *ice sheets*. These have a flattened dome-like cross-section and are hundreds of kilometres in width. The most famous ice sheets, because of their size, are those of the two polar regions – Antarctica and Greenland. During the cold, glacial phases of the last ice age, which took place during the Pleistocene, there were also two other enormous ice sheets, one over Scandinavia and Britain, and another, called the Laurentide Sheet, over much of North America. Those dome-shaped masses with a smaller area, less than about 50 000 km^2, are called *ice caps*. We can summarise these *non-valley glaciers* as follows.

Ice sheet	more than 50 000 km^2, with a flattened dome, which buries underlying relief
Ice cap	a small ice sheet with an area less than 50 000 km^2, but which still buries the landscape
Ice dome	the central part of an ice cap or ice sheet
Outlet glacier or ice	a stream of ice that drains part of an ice sheet or ice cap, and which often passes through confining mountains
Ice shelf	a thick, floating ice sheet which is attached to a coast
Ice field	a relatively flat and extensive mass of ice

The other main class of glacier is the *valley glacier*. These 'rivers of ice' occupy basins or valleys

Plate 3.1 The largest valley glacier in Europe is the Aletsch Glacier in Switzerland. Its snout extends down to an altitude of around 1500 m above sea level. The stripe down the centre of the glacier is a medial moraine composed of till.

in upland areas, and can be further subdivided into miscellaneous types as follows:

Valley glacier	a body of ice that moves down a valley under the influence of gravity and is bounded by cliffs
Cirque glacier	a small ice body that occupies an armchair-shaped hollow in mountains which has been cut into bedrock; the hollows are sometimes also called cwms or corries
Niche glacier	a small upland ice body resting upon a sloping rock face or in a shallow hollow that the glacier itself has modified only slightly
Diffluent glacier	a valley glacier that diverges from a trunk glacier and crosses a drainage divide through a diffluence col
Piedmont glacier	a glacier that leaves its confining rock walls and spreads out to form an expanded foot glacier; formed on a lowland or at a mountain foot

Large valley glaciers in the Karakoram Mountains in the western Himalayas may be 60 km or more long, while small niche and cirque glaciers may extend only a few hundreds of metres.

3.4 The formation of glacier ice

When snow crystals fall they have an open, featherlike appearance, and therefore a low density. This is why it is generally reckoned that 100 mm of snow is equivalent to only 10 mm of rainfall. However, if the snow crystals are compacted by the weight of overlying snow, or if they are partially melted, they are converted to a mass of partially consolidated ice crystals, with interconnected air spaces between them. Such material is called *firn* or *nevé*, and as it develops further it becomes denser and denser until most of the air spaces are eliminated and pure ice develops. In the lower-latitude glaciers this process of transformation may take a few years, whereas in colder areas, such as central Antarctica, the transition may take a few thousands of years. Most glaciers are composed of the ice produced from

snow that has been modified in this way, but on some glaciers refrozen meltwater can make up much of the mass. Either way, if the climate and relief of an area are favourable, sufficient ice may accumulate so that, under the influence of gravity, the mass begins to move and thereby becomes a glacier.

The existence and development of a glacier depends on the simple fact that in its accumulation area snowfall is greater than thaw. In cold regions a winter snowfall of 1 m may be enough to keep a glacier going, whereas in a warmer area 8–10 m would be needed. The altitude below which glaciers cannot form (*the glaciation level*) depends on the balance between snowfall and thaw and also on temperature. Temperatures in turn largely depend on latitude and altitude above sea level, precipitation, the nature of winds and the distance from the sea. Thus the glaciation level is low in polar regions and high in the tropics, low in coastal areas, and high in continental interiors. For instance, in the Antarctic the glaciation level is at sea level, whereas in the European Alps it is at 2600 m in the west and as much as 3200 m in the east (where it is drier and the accumulation of snow on the glaciers is smaller).

3.5 How glaciers move

That glaciers flow is made evident by a consideration of their velocity characteristics. A glacier's surface velocity is highest near the centre line and diminishes towards the sides, where friction against the rock will bring it close to zero. Velocity also tends to decrease with depth, especially in the lower parts near the bed (figure 3.2).

Although at first it is difficult to understand how a seemingly rigid mass of ice can propel itself, glaciers do move, and while they do not progress with anything like the same speed as a river, their movement is none the less easily measured, and is sometimes appreciable. Some glaciers occasionally surge, and may for short periods reach speeds of 5 m per *hour* or more, but most move at only a fraction of that speed, say 50 m per year.

The movement of the glacier takes place in three main ways: by *sliding* over bedrock, by internal deformation (*creep*) of the ice, and by alternate *compression and extension* of the ice

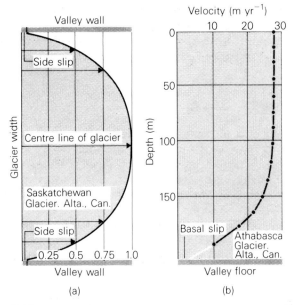

Figure 3.2 Velocity measurements of glaciers: (a) the surface velocity of a glacier in plan view; the movement is expressed as a proportion of the maximum velocity along the centre line of the glacier; (b) velocity changes with depth.

mass in response to changes in the bedrock surface below the ice. The first of these processes – sliding over the base – is relatively easy to envisage. Ice normally forms from water at a temperature of 0°C, but the temperature at which water freezes is reduced under pressure, and as a glacier moves it will exert pressure and therefore some melting may take place at its base. For this and other reasons a thin film of water may exist between the glacier and the bedrock. This film reduces friction and hence allows the glacier to slide. Plainly, such a film of water is more likely to occur in glaciers whose temperature is close to their melting point (the so-called 'warm' glaciers) than in glaciers of extremely cold areas.

Basal slip is an important cause of movement. Expressed as a percentage of the total movement, the amount of slip in temperate glaciers has been found to vary from 10 to 75 per cent with a mean value of around 50 per cent. The presence of a water film at the base of the glacier is an important requisite, and at least a portion of the movement probably takes place by the refreezing (*regelation*) of water around small irregularities in the bedrock floor. This occurs because there is increased pressure on the upstream side of any protruberance, which leads to local melting along that area. The water then flows to the downstream side, where it refreezes under conditions of diminished pressure.

Ice is brittle and plastic at the same time. Hit it with a hammer and it will crack like a piece of brittle glass; leave a horizontal bar of ice supported at only one end and it will, given time, deform plastically under its own weight. In the case of glacier ice the deformation, or creep, will take place under the action of gravity, depending on the stresses involved – the weight of the overlying ice column and the slope of the upper ice surface. Thus the rate of plastic deformation will increase with increasing surface slope. Temperature also plays a role, for cold ice moves less readily than ice that is close to melting point, rather in the same way as oil is more viscous at low temperatures. Other things being equal, therefore, a thick steep glacier in the temperate zone will flow faster than a thin, flat ice cap in a polar area.

Under some conditions compression and extension take place because the ice cannot deform sufficiently quickly to the stress within the ice. As a result ice fractures, and movement takes place along a plane. *Tensional fractures*, where the ice on either side of the fracture is separated, are exemplified by crevasses in the upper layers of the glacier. *Shear fractures* occur where thrusting takes place along a slip plane or fault (figure 3.3 and section 3.6).

Alpine glaciers have generally been recorded as moving at velocities between 20 and 200 m per year, but may accelerate to rates in excess of 1000 m per year down the steeper slopes. Some of the fastest rates are found on outlet glaciers of the polar ice sheets, where velocities as high as 7000 m per year have been recorded.

As mentioned above, some glaciers are prone to *surging*, or flowing for short periods at rates of over 10 km per year. Glaciers in the Himalayas and the United States are known to have moved at rates over 300 m per day at the height of a surge. They seem to do this because of an instability that is induced when snowfall that collects in the accumulation zone is not transmitted down valley efficiently. Instead there is a prolonged storage of surplus snow and ice which causes the glacier to grow in bulk to unstable proportions. The glacier surface steepens until it is out of equilibrium. Once some critical threshold is reached, and possibly with the help of a trigger such as an earthquake, the glacier begins to surge. Some glaciers seem to to this with some regularity, perhaps every 30 to 100 years. Such surges can be dangerous: the advancing ice front may cause damage to farms; large quantities of melt-water may be released causing floods; and if the surging glacier enters the sea dangerous icebergs may create hazards for shipping. Also, a surging glacier coming from a side valley may block a major through-flowing river and thereby cause the formation of a major natural lake behind its dam; should this dam fail, a great wall of water may surge down valley causing loss of life and damage to property. This is an especially severe problem in parts of the Karakoram Mountains in Pakistan.

3.6 Glacial erosion

The Victorian writer John Ruskin once remarked that a glacier could no more erode its valley than custard could erode a custard bowl, suggesting that glaciers tend to lie rather impotently in their valleys, that the valleys were there before the glaciers, and that ice is softer than rock just as custard is softer than the sides of a dish. Glaciers

Plate 3.2 In some mountainous areas glaciers are prone to surge at exceptional speeds. Glaciers that have this characteristic, such as the Susitna Glacier, Alaska, have highly deformed moraines.

do indeed often lie in pre-existing valleys, and ice is indeed softer than rock, but glaciers are by no means impotent agents of erosion. Recent studies of the quantities of material being carried away by glacial meltwater streams indicate that erosion in a glaciated catchment may frequently be equivalent to a ground surface lowering of 2000–3000 mm per thousand years, perhaps ten times the norm for ordinary fluvial catchments without glaciers. How then is this high rate of denudation achieved?

First of all, glaciers can in some respects be likened to a conveyor belt. If a rockfall puts a vast amount of coarse debris on to a glacier surface, for example, or if frost shattering sends down a mass of angular rock fragments on to the glacier surface, it can then be transported, almost whatever its size, down valley. The range of debris size that can normally be carried by a river is much more limited. Second, beneath glaciers there is often a very considerable flow of meltwater. This may flow under pressure through tunnels in the ice at great speed, and may be charged with coarse debris from the bed of the glacier. Such subglacial streams are highly effective at wearing down the bedrock beneath a glacier. Third, although glacier ice itself might not cause marked erosion of a rock surface by *abrasion*, when it carries coarse debris at its base some abrasion can occur. This grinding process has been observed directly by digging tunnels into glaciers, but there is other evidence for it: rock beneath glaciers may be *striated* or scratched (just as wood may be scratched by sandpaper), and much of the debris in glaciers is ground down to a fine mixture of silt and clay called *rock flour*.

Glaciers also cause erosion by means of *plucking*. If the bedrock beneath the glacier has been weathered in preglacial times, or if the rock is full of joints, the glacier can detach large particles of rock. As this process goes on, moreover, some of the underlying joints in the rock may open up still more as the overburden of dense rock above them is removed by the glacier. This is a process called *pressure release*.

In order to account for the irregular erosion at the base of a glacier by which deep basins and intervening bars may be formed, variation in the nature of glacier flow down valley needs to be considered. Particularly helpful in this context is *the theory of extending and compressing flow* (section 3.5). Figure 3.3 shows the theoretical pattern of slip planes or potential shear surfaces associated with the two types of flow. Where the flow of the glaciers is accelerating (extending), a series of planes of weakness is likely to develop within the ice, curving down tangentially to the glacier bed. In contrast, in the *ablation zone*, where melting takes place, and those parts of the glacier where the flow is decelerating (compressing), the planes of weakness will tend to develop curving upward tangentially from the bed in a down-glacier direction. This type of plane becomes pronounced near the snout of the glacier and also at the base of steep slopes. The significance of this for glacial longitudinal profiles, or *long profiles*, is that in the zones of compression the ice may be expected to carry up debris from the glacier floor into the ice – thereby causing erosion. In this way basins at the base of a steep slope or ice fall, once initiated, may become self-perpetuating. Irregularities in the bed of the glacier influence the glacier flow, and in turn the different types of flow can influence the bed.

Figure 3.3 Extending and compressive flow of a glacier: (a) the two types of flow and their associated slip lines; (b) the distribution of the two types of flow down the long profile of an idealized glacier. Compressive flow tends to accentuate existing concavities.

Once irregularities in the glacier bed have appeared, therefore, they will tend to become accentuated. It is this tendency of *positive feedback* that probably accounts for so many of the differences between the long profiles of glacial valleys and those of ordinary river valleys, the former being irregular and the latter being more smoothly concave downstream.

Landforms produced by glacial erosion

As debris-laden ice grinds and plucks away the surface over which it moves, characteristic landforms are produced which give a distinctive character to glacial landscapes (figure 3.4). Of the features resulting from glacial quarrying, one of the most impressive is the *cirque*. This is a horseshoe-shaped, steep-walled, glaciated valley head. It is called a *cwm* in Wales, and a *corrie* in Scotland. In Europe and North America, where cirques occur they are nearly always orientated between north-west and south-east, and there are two reasons for this. First, north-facing slopes receive less insolation from the sun, and this helps to preserve small glaciers. Second, the main snow-bearing winds are from the west, and eddies would ensure that snow banks were preserved on the lee slopes, i.e. those facing east.

The origin of cirques is still uncertain but they may develop from an initial hollow in which a snow bank accumulated. The presence of the snow bank would increase the amount of diurnal and seasonal frost weathering caused by meltwater in the hollow, so that it would gradually be enlarged until it was big enough to hold a small glacier. This glacier would then start to cause plucking and quarrying at its head, probably as a result of the downward percolation of water and the frost-shattering of the rocks in the headwall. Another process that seems important is the rotational movement of the ice, which excavates closed basins in the floors of cirques. Should the glacier disappear such basins become the sites of small lakes (figure 3.5), which add immeasurably to the beauty of the landscape.

As cirques develop they eat back into the hill mass in which they have developed. When several cirques lie close to one another, the divide separating them may become progressively narrowed until it is reduced to a narrow, precipitous ridge called an *arête* (figure 3.6). Should the glaciers continue to whittle away at the mountain from all sides the result is the formation of a pyramidal *horn*, of which the Matterhorn in the European Alps is the most famous example.

Some of the most spectacular erosional effects of glaciation observable today are those of valley glaciation. The lower ends of spurs and ridges are blunted or truncated; the valleys assume a U-shaped configuration; they become more linear; and hollows or troughs are excavated in their floors. Many high-latitude coasts, such as those of Norway and western Scotland, are flanked by narrow troughs, called *fiords*, which differ from land-based glacial valleys in that they are submerged by the sea. Some of them are extraordi-

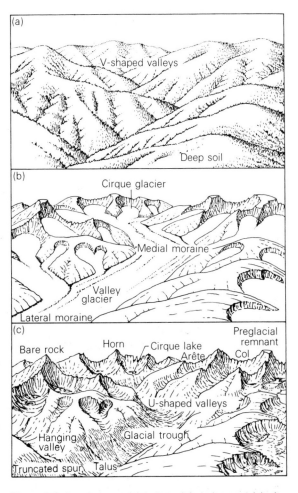

Figure 3.4 Landscapes (a) before, (b) during and (c) after glaciation.

Figure 3.5   Blea Water in the English Lake District – a typical
cirque basin. Note the approximately north-easterly orientation of the basin.

Figure 3.6   Stages in the development of horns and arêtes
by backward extension of cirques.

narily deep, and bear witness to the power of
glaciers to excavate to great depths – the maximum known depths of Greenland, Norwegian
and Chilean fiords are of the order of 1300–
1400 m, and in Antarctica fiords almost 1000 m
deeper are known. These great depths are usually
separated from the open oceans by a *sill* of solid
rock, over which the depth is only around 200 m
or so. *Fjards* are related to fiords. They are

coastal inlets associated with the glaciation of
a lowland coast, and therefore lacking the steep
walls characteristic of glacial troughs. A good
example of a fjard coast is that of the state of
Maine in the United States.

A further erosional effect of valley glaciers is
the breaching of watersheds, for when ice cannot
get away down a valley fast enough – perhaps
because its valley is blocked lower down by other
ice, or because there is a constriction – it will
overflow at the lowest available point, a process
known as *glacial diffluence*. The result of this
erosion is the creation of a *col*, or a gap in the
watershed.

A striking example of present-day diffluence is
provided by the Rimu Glacier in the Karakoram
Mountains of the Indian sub-continent (figure
3.7). The Rimu consists of three branches fed
by numerous minor glaciers draining from the
surrounding peaks. Part flows into the Yarkand,
which flows into central Asia, and part flows into
the Shayok, which eventually flows into the Indus
and thence into the Indian Ocean.

The long profile of a glacial trough is characteristically irregular: steps, basins and reversed

Plate 3.3   The Trollfjord in the Lofoten Islands in Norway
illustrates the great amount of incision that can be created by
glacial erosion in areas with heavy precipitation. Some
Norwegian fiords are over 1000 m deep.

Plate 3.4 A classic U-shaped valley with truncated spurs developed in the granite mountains of north central Portugal.

Figure 3.7 An example of glacial diffluence: the Rimu Glacier in the Karakoram Mountains (heights in metres).

gradients occur. The factors determining where pronounced deepening of the valley floor takes place have been the subject of many arguments. For example, it has been proposed that where two glaciers join there is a great increase in erosive capacity. Elsewhere it can be shown that the glaciers have plucked preferentially at areas of non-resistant and closely jointed rock. Sometimes the basins may be areas where the rock was deeply weathered by chemical action or by freeze-thaw in preglacial times. Alternatively, if the valley is for some reason laterally constricted, say by a zone of resistant rock, the glacier enlarges its cross-sectional area by eroding its floor more deeply.

Tributary valleys to the main glacial trough have their lower ends cut clean away as the spurs between them are ground back and truncated. Furthermore, the floor of a trunk glacier is deepened more effectively than those of feeders from the side or at the head, so that after a period of prolonged glaciation such valleys are left hanging high above the main trough. Such *hanging valleys* have often become the sites of waterfalls.

The development of an ice sheet tends to scour the landscape. In Canada there are vast expanses of empty territory where the Pleistocene glaciers

Plate 3.5 A glacier moving across metamorphic rocks in the Hunza Valley of northern Pakistan created this example of a *roche moutonnée*.

scoured and cleaned the land surface, removing almost all the soil and superficial deposits and exposing the joint and fracture patterns of the ancient crystaline rocks beneath. Streamlined and moulded rock ridges develop, including *roches moutonnées* (figure 3.8(a)). In parts of Scandinavia and New England these may be several kilometres long and have steepened faces of more than 100 m in height. They are interspersed with scoured hollows which may be occupied by small lakes when the ice sheet retreats. In Scotland relief that is dominated by this mixture of rock ridges and small basins is called *knock and lochan* topography.

In areas made of tough limestone, such as the carboniferous limestone landscapes of northern England and western Ireland, glacial scour has planed off the limestone, exposing bedding plane surfaces, and stripping off any overlying, superficial materials. The result is the development of bare rock surfaces, called *limestone pavements*, some of which may show distinct signs of glacial moulding. The micro-forms developed on their surfaces are the result of post-glacial solutional modification.

Another feature, known as *crag-and-tail* (figure 3.8(b)), is the result of the presence of an obstructive mass of rock, the crag, that lies in the path of oncoming ice. This mass protects softer rocks in its lee from the effects of glacial erosion, for the ice appears to have moved over and around the 'crag' leaving a gently sloping 'tail' in its lee. The best-known example of this phenomenon is in the city of Edinburgh, where Edinburgh Castle

Figure 3.8 Two glacial landforms: (a) *roche moutonnée.* (b) crag and tail.

Plate 3.6 The imposing bulk of Edinburgh Castle rests cn a resistant igneous crag that was shaped by glacial erosion.

rests on a resistant igneous plug (the crag) with its tail of limestone and sandstone sloping eastward along the line of the 'Royal Mile'.

Glacial modification on a major scale can also be achieved in low-lying areas of *scarp and dip* topography. The characteristic form of scarp to the south of the generally accepted limits of glacial advance can be seen in the Chilterns of southern England, where there is a prominent chalk escarpment with a firm crestline and a considerable degree of relief (figure 3.9). To the north of this glaciation line the from of the scarp is radically different: the typical *cuesta* (escarpment) from is replaced by a low and relatively even-crested plateau. Thus, from the Goring Gap to Ivinghoe Beacon the main scarp stands within 1.5 km of the basal outcrop of the Chalk; but further north the main escarpment is found progressively farther from the basal outcrop, and in the Breckland of East Anglia it may be removed by as much as 12–14 km. It is also greatly flattened. In effect, the ice has lowered and displaced the line of the escarpment.

Glacial erosion does appear to be highly selective, which leads us to hypothesise that within an ice sheet, which may as a whole be slow-moving, there are local streams of high velocity. In areas of high relief (as, for example, on the west coast

of Scotland) one would have suitable conditions for high velocities to occur, and where the pre-existing relief was favourable and rocks erodible, there would be fast-moving ice streams beneath the glacier that would be capable of great erosive activity.

Figure 3.9 During a major Pleistocene ice advance the chalk escarpment of eastern England was greatly modified by erosion. Compare the position of the escarpment, with regard to the position of the base of the chalk, in the zone of glaciated scarpland with that of the scarp to the south of the glacial line.

Figure 3.10 Lake Garda at the foot of the Italian Alps, with its bordering lateral and terminal moraines. It owes about 150 m of its depth to the thickness of the morainic barrier, but below that level to a maximum depth of 350 m it occupies an ice-excavated rock basin.

Glaciers produce a great deal of *meltwater*, some of which flows *on* the glacier, some within, and some over the bedrock. It often flows very swiftly; moreover, the meltwater that moves in tunnels at the base of a glacier may be subject to very great pressure, and under certain conditions it can flow uphill. Some streams may also contain large quantities of debris that may give them further erosive power. In Denmark and Germany great subglacial meltwater rivers flowing southwards towards the wasting margin of the last Scandinavian ice sheet are thought to have cut the so-called *tunnel valleys*, some of which are over 70 km long and in places over 100 m deep. Some such channels have humped sections in their long profiles, indicating that the subglacial streams accomplished much erosion while flowing uphill under great pressure.

Lakes are a widespread feature of many areas that have been glaciated, and they result from a variety of erosional and depositional causes. Some are caused by glacial overdeepening, some are the result of blockage of drainage by moraines, and others may be the result of uneven deposition and melting of till sheets. In some cases a combination of erosion and deposition may explain their development; this is the case with both the lakes at the foot of the Italian Alps (figure 3.10) and the Great Lakes in the United States. During the Ice Age some glacial lakes were huge. The North American ice sheet, round about

25 000 years ago, dammed many of the northward-draining rivers of central Canada and north-central United States to form Lake Agassiz, which, at various times inundated an area of 950 000 km².

3.7 Glacial deposits

Because glaciers are so effective at erosion and transport, they are also associated with large quantities of debris. According to its location with respect to the glacier, such debris transported by an ice mass may be divided into three main categories: *englacial* debris (which occurs within the glacier), *supraglacial* debris (which occurs on the glacier surface), and *subglacial* debris (which occurs at the base of the glacier). Deposition of the transported material is a complex process, but that fraction deposited directly from the ice is called *till*. It consists of a wide range of grain sizes, and is thus often called *boulder clay*. It also possesses very little stratification, frequently contains far travelled erratic material, tends to have *clasts* with edges and corners blunted by abrasion, and often has its larger particles showing a preferred orientation or alignment.

Traditionally, two types of till have been recognised: *lodgement till*, which is laid down subglacially when debris is released directly from the sole of the ice, and *ablation till*, which accumulates initially in a supraglacial position and is later lowered to the ground surface by undermelting. Ablation till can be further subdivided into *meltout till* and *flow till*: the former is the direct product of ablation continuing beneath a cover of detritus, while the latter consists of debris that has built up on the ice and after saturation with meltwater becomes so unstable that it flows or slumps into nearby hollows.

Till may be deposited as a series of distinctive landforms. Ridges of glacially deposited material occurring along the terminal margins of glaciers and ice sheets are called *end moraines*. Across lowland regions they may be traced for hundreds of kilometres, and those laid down by valley glaciers may be over 100 m in height. They are partly the result of debris being deposited in the ablation zone, and partly the consequence of pushing of debris by the glacier. On the sides of

Plate 3.7 Glaciers are extremely effective as transporters of debris. The Barnard Glacier in Alaska shows a whole suite of medial and lateral moraines. Note also the truncated spurs of the main valley, caused by substantial erosion.

glaciers there may be prominent ridges called *lateral* moraines.

In some areas, particularly where a glacier opens out on to a plain, the till is deposited as swarms of rounded hummocks, called *drumlins*. These sometimes occur in a regular pattern, and the term 'basket of eggs relief' is often applied to a glacial landscape of this type. Drumlins are

streamlined hills which may vary in size from only a few metres in height to over 50 m. They are commonly between 1 and 2 km in length and about 0.5 km wide. They generally lie with their long axes parallel to the inferred direction of ice movement and have an approximately elipsoid plan.

Closely related to drumlins are a whole series

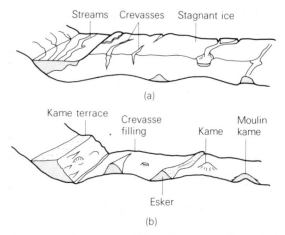

(a)

(b)

Figure 3.11   The process of formation of some fluvio-glacial landforms: (a) stagnating ice; (b) the resulting landforms.

Figure 3.12   The pattern of eskers left behind as the last ice sheet wasted in the Labrador Peninsula, Canada.

of other streamlined forms described under the broad heading of *fluted ground moraine*. Some of the largest flutes are up to 20 km long, 100 m wide and 25 m high, but they are generally much smaller than this and are found just beyond the glacial front.

There is also a series of landforms that, while not strictly speaking made of till, owe their form and origin to glacial agency. Included in this category are *kames* and *eskers*. These are the product of glacial rivers (figure 3.11). Kames are features produced at the margins of the ice and eskers are primarily forms developed beneth the ice. Kames consist of irregular undulating mounds of bedded sands and gravels that are essentially a group of alluvial cones or deltas deposited unevenly along the front of a stagnant or gradually decaying ice sheet. Some kames occur as *kame-terraces* and were formed along the trough between the glacier and the valley side, forming narrow flat-topped terrace-like ridges. Perforation or *moulin kames* are formed in hollows and perforations in decaying ice, and if they develop along major crevasses they may have an angular dog-leg form.

Eskers are elongated ridges of stratified gravel, usually thought to be the casts of streams formed either on the ice or beneath it. The largest examples may be 100 m high and extend for tens of kilometres (figure 3.12). Often they are sinuous.

Some attempts have been made to create a model of drift landform zonation. Deposition

takes place in two zones. In the zone of active ice, streamlining takes place and lodgement till and drumlins are deposited. As one moves towards the outer edge of the ice sheet, stagnant ice becomes dominant, with eskers and end moraines being deposited.

The meltwater that flows from an ice mass creates large outwash plains which are sometimes called after their Icelandic name of *sandur* (plural *sandar*). These are characterised by multi-thread channels called *braids*, by abundant coarse debris and by marked variations in discharge, including catastrophic floods.

In some cases ice may dam up a river so that a lake forms. If the ice dam persists long enough a shoreline may be formed, lacustrine sediments may develop, deltas may grow at the mouths of any inflowing streams and an overflow channel may be cut across some convenient col. The classic illustration in Britain is the parallel roads of Glen Roy in Scotland (figure 3.13(a)). As the ice gradually retreated, so lower cols were exposed, which permitted the lake to overflow at lower

(a)   (b)

Figure 3.13 Two examples of glacial lakes (a) the parallel roads of Glen Roy, Scotland. The three small sketches show the three stages in the evolution of the lake system as the main ice-mass withdrew towards the south-west. (b) Lake Harrison in the English Midlands at its maximum extent.

levels. At each lower stage a *strandline* was cut by the lake. The overflow channels may persist as important features of the landscape even when ice has disappeared completely. Similarly, in the English Midlands (figure 3.13(b)) Welsh ice ponded up the drainage of the Severn-Avon lowlands to form Lake Harrison. Its shoreline can be traced for a distance of 55 km at an elevation of around 125 m – the height of the overflow channel at Fenny Compton, by which the lake water overflowed into the Cherwell and thence into the Thames.

Another form of drainage modification is the *glacier margin channel* (see figure 3.14). These are extremely widespread in areas of slow deglaciation.

3.8 Glacier ice and sea-level change

If one visits many coasts, the evidence of sea-level change is clear to see. Where there are stranded beach deposits, marine shell beds and platforms backed by steep cliff-like slopes, one has evidence of emerged shorelines. Elsewhere there is often evidence of submerged coastal features such as the drowned mouths of river valleys (*rias*), glaciated valleys (fiords), submerged dune chains, *notches* and *benches* in submarine topography, and remnants of forests or peat layers at or below present sea level.

The fluctuations in degree of glaciation (see section 2.13) play a major role in explaining fluctuations of sea level. The expansion and contraction of ice sheets cause an alternating uptake and release of water into the world's oceans, which in turn cause alternating regressions and transgressions. Such changes are called *glacio-eustatic*. During glacial maxima, world sea level fell by the order of 100–150 m, while during interglacials sea levels would be at a level similar to, or slightly higher than, today's. If the two main existing ice caps – Greenland and Antarctia – were to melt totally, sea level would be raised a further 66 m.

Another fundamental way in which ice sheets would affect sea level is through *glacio-isostasy*. The presence of large ice masses causes a depression of the earth's crust, but when such ice masses

Figure 3.14 Diagrammatic representation showing the development during deglaciation of glacier margin hillside channels.

Table 3.3 Some facts about permafrost

Country	Area (10⁶ km²)	Percentage of total area of state
USSR	11.0	49.7
Mongolian People's Republic	0.8	
China (without Tibet)	0.4	
Tibet	1.5	
Alaska, USA	1.5	80
Canada	5.7	
Greenland	1.6	
Antarctica	13.5	
TOTAL	36.0	24% of total land area of the world

melt the crust rises by way of compensation. The present polar ice caps are big enough to cause considerable isostatic depression, so that interior Greenland, for instance, has a bedrock surface that is at or below present sea level. If the several thousands of metres of ice above this bedrock were to melt, geophysicists estimate that the bedrock surface would slowly rise to form a plateau about 1000 m above sea level. In the areas that were covered by Pleistocene ice but have since been released from its weight, the degree of isostatic uplift in post-glacial times (c. the last 11 000 years only) has been considerable: 300 m in both North America and Scandinavia.

3.9 Permafrost

Having considered the importance of glacier ice in the environment, we must now consider a no less important form of ice – *permafrost*. This is perennially frozen ground. It underlies approximately one-fifth to one-quarter of the land surface of the earth (table 3.3), with large areas in the Soviet Union, Canada and Alaska and other major occurrences in Greenland, Spitzbergen and northern Scandinavia (figure 3.15). Permafrost also exists offshore, particularly in the Beaufort Sea of the Western Arctic and in the Laptev and East Siberian Seas of the Soviet Union, and at high elevations in mid-latitudes, such as the Rocky Mountains of North America and the interior plateaux of central Asia. It occurs not only in the tundra and polar desert environments poleward of the tree-line, but also in extensive areas

Figure 3.15 The distribution of the main permafrost types in the Northern Hemisphere.

of the boreal forest and forest–tundra environments.

Above the layer of permanently frozen ground there is usually a layer of soil in which temperature conditions vary seasonally, so that thawing

Figure 3.16 Vertical distribution of permafrost and active zones in longitudinal transects through (a) Eurasia and (b) North America.

Plate 3.8 In permafrost areas susceptible sediments may be broken up into polygonal patterns by ice wedges. When such wedges melt, the tapering structures shown in this photograph are produced. Relict examples of such wedges can be found in southern England, and are indicative of the former much greater extent of permafrost during the Pleistocene Ice Age.

occurs when temperatures rise sufficiently in summer but freeze in winter or on cold nights. This zone of freeze-thaw processes is called the *active layer*. It varies in thickness, ranging from a depth of 5 m where unprotected by vegetation to typical values of 15 cm in peat.

Conventionally, two main belts of permafrost are identified. The first is the zone of *continuous permafrost* (figure 3.15): in this area permafrost is present at all localities except for localised thawed zones, or *taliks*, existing beneath lakes, river channels and other large water bodies which do not freeze to their bottoms in winter. In the *discontinuous permafrost* zone small scattered unfrozen areas appear (figure 3.16).

Maximum known depths of permafrost reach 1400–1450 m in the northern USSR and 700 m in the north of Canada, regions of intense winter cold, short cool summers, minimal vegetation and limited snowfall. In general, the thickness decreases equatorwards. Sporadic permafrost tends to occur between the −1°C and −4°C mean

annual air temperature isotherms, while continuous permafrost tends to occur to the north of the −7°C to −8°C isotherm.

3.10 Ground ice

The ice that occurs in the ground in permafrost areas takes on a variety of forms. Sometimes it may occur as *massive ice*, tens of metres thick. Elsewhere it may occur as *ice wedges*; these tend to occur as polygonal crack patterns, with the wedges being about 1.0–1.5 m across at the surface and extending as tapering wedges 3.0 or more metres into the ground. The average dimensions of the polygons range from 15 to 40 m. They are

Plate 3.9 The build-up of ice can create small ice-cored hills called pingos. This particularly large example from northern Canada is starting to collapse.

thought to form because, when soils are cooled to below −15°C to −20°C, there is a shrinkage of the volume of ice held within the soil and this leads to the development of cracks and fissures in the frozen ground. In the following spring moisture collects in these fissures and freezes, preventing the crack from closing when the ground expands as the temperature rises. It is believed that this process is self-perpetuating, since the wedge of ice provides a plane of weakness which is reopened under stress the following year, allowing the deposition of a further layer of ice.

Another form of ground ice is described by an Eskimo word – *pingo*. Pingos are ice-cored hills that have been domed up from beneath by ice growth. They vary from a few metres to over 60 m in height and are up to 300 m in diameter. Normally two types have been recognised. *Open-system pingos* occur in areas of thin or discontinuous permafrost where surface water can penetrate into the ground and continue to circulate in the unfrozen sediments beneath the permafrost. When this water rises towards the ground surface, it freezes to form localised bodies of ice which force the overlying sediments upwards. *Closed-system pingos*, on the other hand, are much more characteristic of low-lying areas with continuous permafrost and are brought about by the local downward growth of permafrost into a previously unfrozen zone.

3.11   Thermokarst

The term *thermokarst* is used to describe irregular, hummocky terrain often studded with small water-filled depressions created by the melting of ground ice. This terrain appears similar to the sinkhole topography of limestone regions, but despite the apparent similarity of topography it should be made clear that thermokarst is not a variety of *karst*: the latter is a term applicable to limestone areas where the dominant process is a *chemical* one – solution (see section 12.5). Underlying the development of thermokarst is a *physical* process – ground ice melting in permafrost regions.

The development of thermokarst is primarily the result of the disruption of the permafrost and an increase in the depth of the active layer. We can illustrate this by a simple example (figure 3.17). In stage 1 we have an undisturbed tundra soil which has an active layer 45 cm thick. Beneath this is frozen ground which is supersaturated: it yields, on thawing, 50 per cent excess water and 50 per cent saturated soil. In stage 2 some of the upper ground surface is removed (say 15 cm), together with its insulating vegetation, and as a result, under the bare ground conditions, the active layer equilibrium thickness

1–3 = Stages before, immediately after, and subsequent to, disturbance

Figure 3.17 Diagram illustrating how disturbance of high-ice-content terrain can lead to permanent ground subsidence.

might increase to 60 cm. As only 30 cm of the active layer remains, 60 cm of the permafrost must thaw before the active layer can thicken to 60 cm (since 30 cm of water will be released). Thus in stage 3 the surface subsides 30 cm because of the thermal melting associated with the degrading permafrost, to give an overall depression of 45 cm.

There are many reasons why thermal equilibrium and subsequent permafrost degradation might take place: climate might change; there might be a forest fire; erosion might remove the upper soil layer; or humans might strip off the vegetation during the building of a road or other structure, or warm the permafrost by building a house or constructing a pipeline. Thus, although some thermokarst is natural, human intervention in a permafrost area can cause subsidence to occur. Such subsidence can be very dangerous for engineering structures.

3.12   Ice segregation and frost heaving

When the water in a soil starts to freeze, there is a tendency for unfrozen water within the soil to migrate towards where the freezing is taking place. This has two consequences: freezing takes place unevenly in the soil, leading to the formation of *ice segregations*; and freezing of the soil leads to local heaving of the ground surface because of the localised migration of water and its subsequent expansion upon freezing – there is a volume expansion of approximately 9 per cent when water turns into ice.

Like thermokarst development, frost heaving is a major problem that the engineer has to face in the development of permafrost areas. *Differential frost heave* is a particularly serious engineering problem. Structures are frequently built on piles in many of the world's environments, but in periglacial areas the piles are subject to heave by frost processes. This is especially true in those areas of discontinuous permafrost where the active layer is thick. In parts of Alaska many bridges show the effects of heave (figure 3.18). It is not uncommon for a thawed zone to occur beneath the river channel, so that piles inserted in the stream bed itself are subjected to minimal frost heave. Likewise, piles inserted into the permafrost on either side of the river are relatively

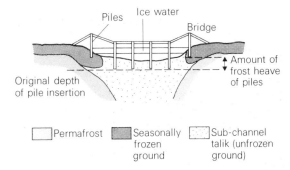

Figure 3.18 Diagrammatic illustration of how frost-heaving of piles inserted in the layer of seasonally frozen ground can result in bridge deformation.

unaffected, since the freezing of the piles to the permafrost provides a resistance to the upward heaving of the seasonally frozen zone. In between these two zones, the piles are located in the zone of seasonal freezing, with the result that up-arching of both ends of the bridge may occur.

Within periglacial areas, the seriousness of frost heave and freeze-thaw processes varies with climatic conditions and material types (figure 3.19). The most hazardous zone is that in which summer temperatures are high enough for thaw to take place but winter temperatures are low enough for freezing to occur to a great depth. In very cold areas where there is very little summer thaw the problem is less, and in relatively mild areas where the degree of winter freezing is reduced the problem is also diminished. Sands and gravels are relatively immune to the worst aspects of frost heave, whereas sediments with a large content of silts and clays are highly susceptible.

One of the prime consequences of frost action in the soil is the development of soil and vegetation patterns. On flat ground, circles, nets and polygons with dimensions several metres across may develop; on moderate slopes, steps; and on steeper slopes, stripes. Six main causes for the development of such patterned ground have been recognised:

(a) the upward movement of stones by freeze–thaw activity;
(b) differential heaving produced by the effect of alternate freezing and thawing on sediments of different grain size;

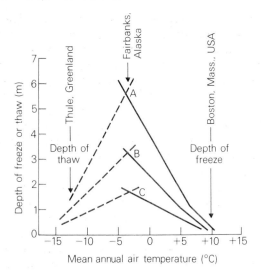

Figure 3.19 The amount of freeze and thaw penetration in relation to mean annual temperature. In very cold areas (e.g. Thule, Greenland), the amount of *thaw* is highly restricted, whereas in warmer areas (e.g. Boston) the amount of *freezing* is limited. It is the zone in between (exemplified by Fairbanks, Alaska) in which the amount of freeze–thaw activity is greatest, and the associated risks most severe. The risk varies according to the nature of the materials. A is the relationship for highly susceptible materials, B is the relationship for average conditions, and C is the relationship for less susceptible materials.

(c) solifluction (a type of soil movement on slopes) (section 3.14);

(d) pressure effects such as those produced by the down-freezing of the active layer in the autumn;

(e) contraction effects;

(f) the effect of peat and vegetational cover on the rapidity of freezing and thawing.

3.13   Frost shattering and soil formation

In areas where frosts are frequent, alternations of freezing and thawing are an effective cause of rock breakdown so long as moisture is present. The breakdown is not the result of a chemical change in the constituents of the rock, as would be brought about by *chemical weathering*, but is a mechanical breakdown – a type of weathering called *physical weathering*.

Frost leads to mechanical breakdown in two main ways. The first method depends on the fact

that when water freezes at 0°C it expands by about 9 per cent. This creates pressures, calculated to be around 2100 kg cm^{-2}, that are higher than the tensile strength of rock (generally less than 250 kg cm^{-2}).

The second method results from the fact that when water freezes in rock or soil the ice attracts small particles of water that have not frozen from the adjoining pores and capillaries. Nuclei of ice crystal growth are thus established, and some workers believe that this mode of ice crystal growth is a more potent shattering agent than the change in volume that occurs when water becomes ice.

The rate at which frost shattering occurs depends on many factors. One of the most important controls is the presence of moisture; laboratory experiments have shown that the amount of disintegration in rocks supplied with abundant moisture is much greater than that in similar rocks containing less moisture. For this reason, dry tundra areas and cold deserts may undergo less extreme frost weathering than moister environments. A second major factor is the frequency and magnitude of temperature changes, although much controversy surrounds this subject. There is still doubt as to whether rapid freezing of moisture in rocks during, say, a daily cycle of freeze-thaw, is more effective than slow freezing (during, say, a seasonal cycle of freeze-thaw), and whether intense cold during the period of freezing is more potent than temperatures just a few degrees below freezing. In general, laboratory experiments tend to show that the number of freeze-thaw cycles is more important than their intensity. This would tend to suggest that those areas with high moisture availability and many daily cycles of freezing and thawing in the course of a year would be most prone to the effects of frost weathering. This in turn indicates that in extremely cold polar areas there may be less frost shattering than in environments where daily freeze-thaw cycles are more frequent (e.g. Iceland, or low-latitude – high-altitude areas such as the Himalayas).

The nature of the rock type is also a vital factor. Working from both laboratory experimentation and field observation, geologists have ranked rock types in their order of susceptibility. Rocks such as tough quartzites and igneous rocks tend to be most resistant, while shales, sandstones and porous chalk tend to be least resistant.

In many periglacial environments of both past and present, extensive upland surfaces of angular rocks and boulders (called *blockfields*) are a dramatic exemplification of the role of frost. Other associated features include large *screes*, and angular, frost-riven *tors* (section 4.16).

Although little has so far been said specifically about the soils of tundra areas, in effect many of the main processes that form them, together with many of their characteristics, have already been described. It is obvious that the presence of permafrost, the development of an active layer, the operation of *solifluction*, frost weathering and frost heaving, the existence of low evapotranspiration rates, the development of a limited plant cover and the tendency for summer waterlogging all combine to make the soils of tundra regions highly distinctive. The waterlogging tends to promote *gleying* (section 12.2); the frost heaving tends to disturb what might be called 'normal' soil layer development; and low rates of organic decomposition may lead to the accumulation of peat.

3.14 Slope processes, avalanches and river regimes

Slope processes of mass wasting occur with great power in the periglacial environment. There are various reasons for this. First, the presence of permafrost provides a barrier to the downward infiltration of water into the ground, thereby inducing high pressures in the soil pores in the surface layers. Second, the layer above the permafrost, the active layer, is extremely moist and highly unstable. Third, the permafrost acts as a lubricated surface over which the materials of the active layer can flow. Fourth, the process of frost heave tends to cause a downhill movement of material under the influence of gravity.

For these reasons, hillside slopes tend to be characterised by instability, and *slope failure* is frequent, posing problems for buildings and other engineering structures. On exposed cliff faces blocks may be detached by frost weathering, while on more gentle slopes there are frequent flows of debris and soil. Indeed, many people

regard *solifluction* – the slow flowing from higher to lower ground of masses of waste saturated with water – as one of the most widespread processes of soil movement in periglacial regions. This process can operate over low-angle slopes (as low as 1°) and tends to involve movement of the upper 50 cm of the soil at rates of around 0.5–5.0 cm per year. It tends to create a series of *lobes* on slopes, resulting in a landscape that bears some resemblance to the wrinkled hide of an aged elephant.

Another feature of some periglacial slopes is the development of *cambering*. Where there is a jointed rock, like a limestone, overlying clay, as there is along the Cotswold Escarpment in the English Midlands, joints and bedding planes would have been opened up by frost wedging during the Ice Age. Moreover, thawing of the underlying clays would have made them very mobile, so that they would have been squeezed outwards by the weight of the overlying caprock of limestone, which in turn would sag at the edges and be cracked apart. Large masses would slip down the hillside.

One special form of mass movement that is common in areas of snow and ice is the *avalanche*. These occur especially in areas of steep slopes – generally above about 22° – but their momentum may carry them on to lower slopes, particularly if they are channelled into a gully. Northerly and western slopes (in the Northern Hemisphere) are especially dangerous, for the lack of sun causes the snow to stabilise less readily.

There are various different types of avalanche (figure 3.20), but the two most important are the airborne dry-snow avalanches and the flowing wet-snow avalanches. In the first of these the devastation is largely the result of the associated shock waves, which are powerful enough to decimate mature forests and collapse buildings. A wave of snow-free air precedes the actual avalanche, and within the avalanche itself there are violent internal gusts that can travel at speeds in excess of 300 km per hour. In the case of the flowing wet-snow avalanches it is the sheer weight of the snow that causes the devastation. One destructive avalanche in the Italian Alps in 1885 comprised no less than 2.5 million tonnes of snow and its energy was equivalent to about

Plate 3.10b A slab avalanche of dry snow in the Southern Alps of New Zealand.

300 million horsepower (a powerful ocean liner, for comparison, generates about 150 000 horsepower). The power of such avalanches may be augmented by some of the boulders and other debris that they pick up in the course of their movement.

Rivers in periglacial areas have very distinctive *runoff regimes* that reflect the importance of the

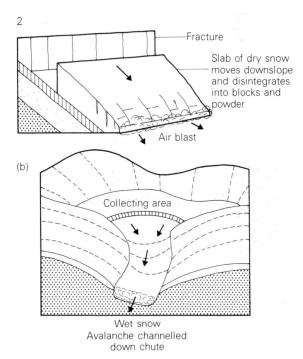

Figure 3.20 Snow avalanches. (a) The dry snow type. A new fall of snow adds extra weight to the top layer of snow. The extra pressure causes it to start moving over an underlying layer that was deposited in an earlier snow fall. As the slab moves over the earlier layer it fragments under the force of gravity. Some damage will be caused by the air blast that precedes it. (b) The wet snow type of avalanche. Snow accumulates in a collecting area and when meteorological conditions are suitable it starts to flow down a pre-existing channel or chute.

Plate 3.10a Avalanches pose a major natural hazard in periglacial areas and occur in a variety of forms. Here we have an example of a powdery dry snow avalanche in the Himalayas.

(a)

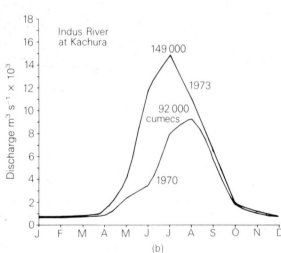

(b)

Figure 3.21 (a) The seasonal runoff regimes for periglacial rivers in North America (b) the seasonal runoff regime for the Indus, which derives the bulk of its flow from mountains of the Karakorams and Himalayas. The melting of snow and glacier ice in the warm summer months produces this highly seasonal regime. Although the size of the peak flow varies from year to year, the peak always occurs between June and August.

short summer melting season (figure 3.21). Snow and ice tend to melt rapidly in the early summer (late June or early July in the case of the Canadian Arctic), and as the summer progresses and

there is less snow to melt, the runoff steadily decreases. This type of regime is described as *nival*. However, in those types of river basin where permanent snow or ice fields occur, melting goes on throughout the summer months whenever it is warm enough. Peak runoff under these conditions is often delayed until late July or early August. Such regimes are often called *proglacial*. In some proglacial streams a potentially hazardous event is the occurrence of a *jökulhlaupe* – a large-magnitude, localised flood surge caused by the bursting of ice dams along the margins of the ice.

3.15 Environmental problems and hazards for tundra development

We have already seen that the tundra environment has certain characteristics that have to be dealt with if humans are to undertake successful development of the area, as in Siberia, Alaska and elsewhere. These can be listed as follows.

Avalanches near steep slopes
Slope instability associated with solifluction
Rockfalls caused by frost action
Thermokarst subsidence – both natural and induced by people
Ground heaving (e.g. pingo growth, frost boils)
Spring snow melt floods
Glacier burst and glacier damming floods
Ice jams on rivers
Icings
Frost heave of piles
Freezing of public utilities (e.g. sewers, waterpipes)
Lack of water in winter for effluent disposal
Wind chill
Very short growing season
Lack of sunlight in winter months
Severe snowfalls
Bitterly low temperatures
Icebergs and pack ice offshore
Infertile soils
Bogs, etc., creating transport problems

Some of these hazards, such as avalanches and floods, can be avoided by building settlements in locations that are not prone to them. Other problems can be overcome by appropriate engineering solutions. Thus, thermokarst subsidence pro-

Plate 3.11 Many mountains in periglacial areas like the high Sierra Nevadas in California are furrowed by chutes which act as preferred routes for avalanches and may be enlarged by them. It is advisable not to locate buildings or other engineering structures at the bases of such chutes.

duced by the heat given out by buildings or pipelines can be lessened by building them on an insulating pad of gravel or on piles above the ground. Alternatively, in the case of thermokarst subsidence produced by vegetation disturbance, great care can be taken to limit this by keeping vehicles to narrow strips rather than allowing them to range widely over the countryside. Public utilities such as sewers and water mains can be placed in specially designed and insulated boxes that run above ground on supports, and are called *utilidors*. *Icings*, which are sheet-like masses of water that form at the surface in winter when water issues from the ground, can be a major hazard to motorways, but they can be evaded by, for example, avoiding the creation of road cuttings from the walls of which water seepage might occur.

Floating sea ice poses major problems for coastal development, navigation and the exploitation of ocean resources. A distinction can be made between *sea ice*, formed by direct freezing of ocean water at temperatures below −2°C, and *icebergs* and *ice islands*, which are bodies of land ice broken free from glaciers and ice shelves. Sea ice is relatively thin (generally less than 5 m), and when it completely covers the sea surface is called *pack ice*. However, wind and current action may break the pack ice up into individual *ice floes* separated by narrow strips of open water called *leads*. Where ice floes are brought together by winds, they buckle and turn upward into a chaotic landscape of rugged pressure ridges that make travel difficult. Icebergs, formed by the calving of blocks of glacier ice, drift under the influence of ocean currents in a partly submerged form. Large, tabular examples are called ice islands, and these may be enormous − 30 km across and 60 m or more thick.

With care, these fragile and sometimes dangerous tundra environments, with their easily disrupted permafrost and their slow-growing plants, can be developed; but it requires a deep and sympathetic appreciation of their character.

4 The Mid-latitudes

4.1 The westerlies

The world's mid-latitudes are dominated by upper winds that blow from the west. They encircle the globe with a series of large waves more than 2000 km across called *Rossby waves*. These waves affect the interface between the colder air masses of high latitudes and the warmer air masses of low latitudes. While they may be accentuated by the disturbing effect of mountain barriers like the Rockies, they are inherent features of a rotating fluid system which has a thermal gradient applied to it. In the Northern Hemisphere, at any one time, the pre-dominent number of Rossby waves is five. Within these westerlies there is a narrow band of high-velocity winds, called the *jet stream*, which flow at speeds of up to 300 km h^{-1} at altitudes between 9000 and 15 000 m.

The character of the Rossby waves is important in affecting mid-latitude weather because surface weather sytems, such as depressions (areas of low atmospheric pressure) and anticyclones (areas of high pressure), are related to them. As figure 4.1(a) indicates, the soaring and diving action of the upper waves pulls air columns upwards and downwards, producing low-pressure and high pressure-systems respectively.

Figure 4.1 Rossby waves and their relationship to surface weather conditions. (a) The relationship between waves in the upper air and areas of high and low pressure near the surface. (b) The different configurations of the Rossby waves as they affect the development of blocking anticyclones, etc.

The shape of the waves can vary considerably (figure 4.1(b)), for the essentially west-east trajectory can be deformed so that the troughs and ridges become accentuated, ultimately splitting up into a cellular pattern with pronounced meridional (north-south) flow at certain longitudes. The deep, relatively permanent *blocking anticyclones*, which may exist in association with increased meridional flow, act as a barrier to the travelling eddies of low pressure, and so can have an important effect on weather. In England the very cold winter of 1963 and the extraordinarily severe drought of 1976 (see section 4.17) were brought about by blocking anticyclones.

4.2 Cyclones and anticyclones

Much of the unsettled, windy, cloudy, wet weather of the mid-latitudes is associated with the development of low-pressure systems called *depressions* or *cyclones*. The convergence of air towards the centre of the low-pressure zone is accompanied by uplift and subsequent cooling of air, which in turn produce cloudiness and precipitation. By contrast, much of the settled, fair, sunny weather in these latitudes is associated with anticyclones, in which the air subsides and spreads outwards, causing warming.

These mid-latitude cyclones depend for their development on the coming together of large bodies of air of contrasting physical properties. Such bodies of air are called *air masses*. Air masses differ widely in temperature (from very warm to very cold), and in moisture content (from very dry to very moist). The boundaries between air masses in the mid-latitudes are relatively sharply defined, and are called *fronts*. The character of the air masses depends on where they come from (obviously, equatorial air will be very different from polar air) and the type of surface over which they developed (maritime air will have very different moisture characteristics from continental air).

Many of the day-to-day changes in mid-latitude weather are associated with the formation and movement of fronts. Masses of cold polar air meet warm moist tropical air along the *polar front*. Instead of mixing and diffusing freely, these two very different air masses remain clearly

defined; but they interact along the polar front in great spiralling cyclonic whorls.

We can now follow the stages in the development of such a whorl (figure 4.2). At the start of the cycle (stage A), the polar front is a relatively smooth boundary along which air is moving in two different directions. At stage B a wave begins to form, and cold air is turned in a southerly direction and warm air in a northerly direction, so each invades the domain of the other. In stage C the wave disturbance along the polar front has intensified and deepened; while cold air is now actively pushing southwards along a *cold front*, warm air is actively moving north-eastward along a *warm front*. In stage D the cold front has overtaken the warm front, reducing the zone of warm air to a narrow sector and producing an *occuluded front*. Eventually (stage E) the warm air is forced off the ground, isolating it from the source region of warm air to the south. The source of moisture and energy is thus cut off, the cyclonic storm gradually dies out, and the polar front is re-established more or less as it was at the beginning of the cycle in stage A.

The cold front, produced where cold air is invading the warm air zone, is a zone where the colder air mass, being the denser, remains in contact with the ground and forces the warmer air mass to rise over it. The warm air tends to rise about 1 km vertically for every 40 km of horizontal distance. Cold fronts are associated with phenomena such as thunderstorms, which are created as unstable warm air is lifted.

In the case of a warm front, warm air is moving into a region of colder air. Once again, the dense cold air remains in contact with the ground, forcing the warm air mass to rise. The slope is generally less steep than for that of a cold front, and is generally between 1 in 80 and 1 in 200.

The type of weather associated with the passage of a cyclone and its different types of front is shown in figure 4.3.

4.3 Air masses

Because the development of fronts is intimately connected with the differences between air masses, it is necessary to consider air masses further at this point. First, a definition: 'Air masses are large bodies of air in which conditions of temperature and humidity are remarkably uniform over distances of about 1000 km.' They form because, if air remains over a part of the earth's surface with little movement for about three to five days, it tends to take on certain characteristics related

to the amount of radiation and evaporation there is in the area. These in turn affect the air's temperature and humidity. The areas where the mass of air remains stationary for such a period are called *source areas* (figure 4.4), and they are associated closely with the large, slow-moving high-pressure (anticyclonic) belts of the subtropics and of high latitudes. Thus one can distinguish six main types of source region: those that dominate temperature characteristics (polar air (P) and tropical air (T)) and those that dominate humidity characteristics (continental air (c) and maritime air (m)) (table 4.1).

Britain stands in a region where four source regions are important, and this means that its climate is subjected to a wide range of influences that help to explain its inherent variability over quite short time spans. *Maritime tropical air* (mT) is the major type of air that Britain receives from

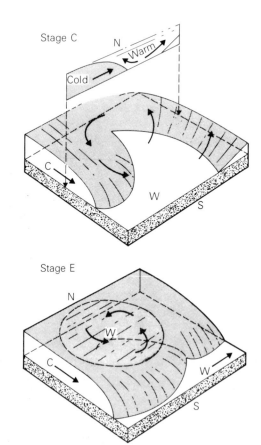

Figure 4.2   Stages in the development of a mid-latitude frontal depression.

Figure 4.3   Weather conditions associated with the passage of a mid-latitude frontal depression: (a) cold front; (b) warm front; (c) weather prior to occlusion; (d) occluded front; (e) weather associated with occluded front. For a definition of the different cloud genera see table 13.1.

Figure 4.4 Global distribution of air mass source regions. The main types are classified in table 4.1.

Table 4.1 Classification of air masses

Major group	Subgroup	Source regions	Properties at source
Polar (P)	Maritime Polar (mP)	Oceans poleward of approx. 50°	Cool, rather damp, unstable
	Continental Polar (cP)	Continents in vicinity of Arctic Circle; Antarctica	Cold and dry, very stable
	Arctic (A) or Antarctic (AA)	Polar regions	Cold, dry, stable
Tropical (T)	Maritime Tropical (mT)	Trade wind belt and subtropical oceans	Moist and warm, stability variable: stable on east side of oceans, rather unstable on west
	Continental Tropical (cT)	Low latitude deserts, chiefly Sahara and Australian deserts	Hot and very dry, unstable
	Maritime Equatorial (mE)	Equatorial oceans	Warm, moist, generally slightly stable

the tropics. It originates in the oceanic subtropical high-pressure belts, and tends to be warm and humid. In summer, surface heating of this warm, moist air may promote instability and thunderstorm formation. *Continental tropical air* (cT)

originates over the great Sahara desert, but it very rarely reaches Britain in its original dry, hot, dusty form, since its high temperature and low relative humidity encourage moisture to be evaporated into it as soon as it crosses the oceans.

Maritime polar air (mP) reaches Britain after crossing the North Atlantic, and when it travels in a northerly direction it brings heavy clouds and rain. *Continental polar air* (cP) forms over Siberia and northern Scandinavia. In winter it brings intensely cold weather, though it tends to be very dry and stable. When it crosses the North Sea it picks up some moisture, and may bring cloudy and drizzly weather.

4.4   Cool temperate climates

The cool temperate climates can be differentiated from the warm temperate climates by one main characteristic: they possess a real cold season that retards or inhibits active plant growth and places a check on agricultural activity. The severity of the cold season increases from west to east, for winter warmth and rain come from the west, and this means that the relative position of land and sea are more important than latitude in this zone.

The depressions of the westerlies influence climate throughout the year in this zone rather than primarily in the winter, as is the case in the warm temperate regions, though they tend to be repelled by the high pressures that develop over the cold continents in winter. It is therefore useful to make a distinction between maritime and continental types of climate. The areas under maritime or oceanic influence (table 4.2) tend to have a smaller annual range of temperature; a higher

humidity and rainfall; a relatively evenly distributed rainfall with a tendency towards a winter maximum; a rather imperceptible gradation of the seasons with frequent relapses from, for example, spring into winter or autumn into summer; and rapidly fluctuating weather associated with the passage of fronts and anticyclones.

The importance of degree of continentality is brought out very clearly in figure 4.5. This diagram shows the annual temperature regimes for five stations all of which are at approximately 52° N. As one moves eastward, away from the moderating influence of the Atlantic Ocean, the sever-

Figure 4.5 Annual temperature regimes for five stations along latitude 52° N with mean monthly temperatures corrected to sea level.

Table 4.2   Representative climatic data, cool temperate climates

	Year	J	F	M	A	M	J	J	A	S	O	N	D
Cool temperate oceanic climate													
Portland, Oregon, USA (45° N)													
Temperature (°C)	12	4	6	8	11	14	16	19	19	16	12	8	5
Precipitation (mm)	1112	170	140	122	79	59	40	15	15	48	84	165	175
Hokitika, New Zealand (42° S)													
Temperature (°C)	12	16	16	15	13	10	8	7	8	10	12	13	14
Precipitation (mm)	2949	249	186	247	234	249	247	229	239	234	299	269	269
Cool temperatate continental climate													
New York City (41° N)													
Temperature (°C)	11	−1	−1	4	9	16	21	23	22	19	13	7	1
Precipitation (mm)	1067	84	84	86	84	86	86	105	110	86	86	86	84
Moscow (56° N)													
Temperature (°C)	4	−11	−9	−5	3	12	17	19	17	11	4	−2	−8
Precipitation (mm)	536	28	25	30	38	48	51	71	74	56	35	40	38

ity of the winter cold becomes greater, as does the intensity of the summer heat. The equability of the climate enjoyed in the western parts of Ireland contrasts starkly with the extremes of climate endured in the eastern USSR.

4.5   Western margin warm temperate climates (the Mediterranean type)

The area that comes under the influence both of the westerlies and the trade winds, according to season, is a zone of climatic transition. This warm temperate or subtropical zone derives its summer influences from the east and its winter influences from the west; summer is therefore continental on western margins and maritime on the eastern; winter, conversely, is maritime on western margins and continental on eastern. Clearly, therefore, eastern or western marginal situation must be a fundamental criterion for the subdivision of warm temperate climates.

The western margin type of climate is often termed 'Mediterranean', although it occurs in locations other than the Mediterranean basin, notably California, Chile, the Cape area of South Africa and western Australia. While there are differences both between and within these different areas, this climatic type has certain essential ingredients: a winter incidence of rainfall and a more or less complete summer drought; hot summers and mild winters; and a high amount of sunshine, especially in summer.

The annual temperature range is greater here than in the tropics, especially when one moves away from maritime influences, and the daily range of temperature is also considerable, especially in the dry summer months (table 4.3). Rainfall levels (produced mainly by the passage of westerly depressions in the winter months) tend to be between 350 and 900 mm per year. Westward-facing shores backed by mountain ranges may have rather high totals. Some of the mountains of Dalmatia in Yugoslavia receive over 4500 mm, making them one of the wettest spots in Europe. The length of the wet and dry seasons tends to vary with latitude. Polewards, the rainy season lengthens at each end until the dry season can no longer be said to exist, and one enters the zone of the cool temperate climate. Tunis, on the south side of the Mediterranean, has five months with less than 25 mm of rain, while Genoa, just to the south of the Alps in Italy, has none. Equatorwards, the winter rains begin later and later and cease earlier and earlier until one is in effect in the zone of the trade-wind deserts (see chapter 5).

One of the most interesting climatic features of the Mediterranean lands is the occurrence of a number of local winds of distinctive character. These are associated with the movement of depressions. A moving depression involves air masses originating both on its poleward and its equatorward side, and therefore both cold and warm winds may result. Polar air masses associ-

Table 4.2   Representative climatic data, warm temperate climates

	Year	J	F	M	A	M	J	J	A	S	O	N	D
	Warm temperate western margin (Mediterranean type)												
Haifa, Israel (33° N)													
Temperature (°C)	22	14	14	16	19	23	25	28	28	27	24	21	16
Precipitation (mm)	595	180	145	23	18	3	0	0	0	0	13	69	170
Perth, Australia (32° S)													
Temperature (°C)	18	23	23	22	19	16	14	13	13	14	16	18	22
Precipitation (mm)	861	8	13	18	40	125	175	165	145	84	54	20	15
	Warm temperate eastern margin												
Charleston, South Carolina (33° N)													
Temperature (°C)	19	10	11	14	18	23	26	28	27	25	20	14	11
Precipitation (mm)	1202	76	79	84	61	84	130	157	165	132	94	64	81
Sydney, Australia (33° S)													
Temperature (°C)	17	22	22	21	18	15	12	11	13	15	17	19	21
Precipitation (mm)	1212	91	112	125	137	130	122	127	76	74	74	71	71

ated with depressions may cause cold winds to burst into normally milder areas, especially if topographic conditions are favourable. In the Mediterranean the *bora* of Yugoslavia and the *mistral* of the south of France blow from the winter high-pressure areas over continental Europe, moving with great ferocity when channelled between uplands. The mistral, for example, is often channelled down the Rhône Valley between the Alps and Massif Central. Comparable winds elsewhere include the *norte* and *papagayo* in Mexico, the *pampero* in the Argentine, and the southerly *burster* in New South Wales, Australia.

A depression moving eastwards along the Mediterranean basin may sometimes lead to an outbreak of hot air from the Sahara. The *gibli* in Tunisia and Libya, the *leveche* in Spain, the *scirocco* in Italy and the *khamsin* in Egypt are notable examples of such depressions. They are often hot, dusty and excessively dry, though sometimes, if they have crossed the sea, they may become very humid and unpleasantly sticky.

Both the very cold winds and the very hot winds may have most unfortunate effects on crops in this region.

4.6 Eastern margin warm temperate climates

On the eastern sides of the continents the transition between the trade wind and westerly circulations is represented by a type of climate that, while generally sharing the mild winters and hot summers of the Mediterranean climates, differs fundamentally in the amount and distribution of precipitation. Because they are on shore, the trade winds that bring summer drought to western margins are here rain-bearing; the westerlies that bring cyclonic rain to western margins are here continental; and depressions are less vigorous. Winter rain is thus relatively less than in the zones with a Mediterranean climate, but summer rains are relatively generous, and tropical cyclones may bring severe storms. Areas with this type of climate include Argentina, Uruguay and south Brazil, the south-east coast of South Africa, the Gulf-Atlantic states of the United States and south China. Rainfall is reasonably well distributed (table 4.3), winters are mild, and summers, because of high temperatures and high humidity, can be rather oppressive.

Plate 4.1 In high latitudes or high altitude situations in mid-latitudes one of the major vegetation types is the boreal forest, dominated by evergreen conifers. This example comes from the Front Range of the Rocky Mountains in Colorado, USA.

4.7 Boreal forest

To the equatorward side of the tundra zone, summer temperatures gradually rise and trees begin to become an important component of the flora. Evergreen conifers start to thrive, and they have certain adaptations suited for survival: provided water is available, they can photosynthesise all the year round; the needles are a type of leaf that helps the trees to resist drought either when water is locked up in the form of ice or when strong winds increase transpiration rates; and the shape of the crowns helps them to shed snow so that branches are not snapped off by the weight. Large trees up to 40 m high form a fairly continous *stand* that permits relatively little light to penetrate to the ground, so that a lower layer of trees is uncommon. None the less, there is usually a fairly continuous ground cover made up of lichens, mosses, low shrubs such as crowberry, and bog-moss like *Sphagnum*. Which of these occurs depends on local conditions of drainage and light.

Spruces (*Picea*) are the dominant tree, but firs (*Abies*), pines (*Pinus*) and larches (*Larix*) may also be important. On the boundary with the tundra, birch scrub may form an important belt of vegetation, while in the Rocky Mountains the deciduous aspen (*Populus tremuloides*) occurs at the tree-line between the alpine grass and herb communities and the evergreens.

The boreal forest is quite productive (see section 2.7) – generally producing about 800 g $m^{-2}yr^{-1}$ of vegetable matter (compared with up to 1200 for the deciduous forest of mid-latitudes). Because of the generally low temperatures, organic matter decays rather slowly, so that litter tends to accumulate as a thick layer on the forest floor. From time to time this litter may be consumed by, and provide fuel for, forest fires.

4.8   Deciduous forests

Equatorwards of the boreal forest comes a forest type in which growth is seasonal; for the trees are deciduous, losing their leaves in the winter. The deciduous habit of the main trees can be seen as a form of dormancy, which is a response to the low winter temperatures and the freezing of water. The dominant trees are 40–50 m in height, and their leaves tend to be broad. They are sometimes hosts for climbers such as ivy (*Hedera helix*), and epiphytes such as mosses, lichens and algae grow on the trunks. Dominance by two or three species is common, and single-species stands are often found. The dominant trees are typically oaks (*Quercus*), elms (*Ulmus*), limes (*Tilia*), beeches (*Fagus*), chestnuts (*Castanea*), maples (*Acer*) and hickories (*Carya*). The species density of trees never reaches the levels found in the tropics, the maximum bring about 8 species per acre in Europe and 40 in North America.

Where light penetrates the canopy formed by these dominants a shrub layer may form, and its species may include hazel (*Corylus*), holly (*Ilex*) and members of the *Rosaceae* (such as hawthorn).

4.9   Mid-latitude grasslands

In the continental interiors of the mid-latitudes, especially where a rainfall total of 300–500 mm occurs, there are some extensive areas of grassland. They have many names (*steppe* in Eurasia, *prairie* in North America, *pampas* in Argentina, *veld* in South Africa, etc.). Much of this grassland has in the last two centuries been heavily modified by human activity – ploughed up for wheat or grazed with cattle and sheep – but it is still far from clear whether these grasslands are by origin man-made, or are a natural response of plants to certain environmental pressures in this particular environment. It used to be fairly generally thought that prairies were essentially a climatic phenomenon, and botanists tended to believe that, under the prevailing conditions of soil and climate, the invasion and establishment of trees was greatly hindered by the presence of a dense sod. High evapotranspiration levels were thought to give a competitive advantage to herbaceous plants with shallow, densely ramifying root systems, capable of completing their life-cycles rapidly.

However, various lines of evidence have been used to suggest that trees can survive, and indeed flourish, in these areas. Trees planted in plantations or groves have been successful even during drought years. Furthermore, along escarpments and other abrupt breaks in topography trees are often found in an otherwise treeless area. One possible explanation for this is that fire, whether natural or man-made, is more effective on flat-level surfaces, where there are higher wind speeds and no barriers to its movement, than along escarpments and the like. What may well have been underestimated by some earlier workers is the ability of early and primitive man to use fire – to clear land for agriculture, to improve grazing by removing dead grass and encouraging new growth, to drive wild animals, etc. Many additional fires may have been accidental. Natural fires caused by lightning may also have played a role in denuding flat areas of tree cover, as may intense grazing by wild animals such as bison.

4.10   Mediterranean evergreen woodland

The warm temperate Mediterranean climate belt, at least in the moister areas, was probably originally covered mainly by open woodlands consisting primarily of various types of evergeen oaks, though there were also some conifer forests, with pines, firs, cypresses and cedars.

However, where rainfall conditions are less favourable, and/or where human activity has degraded the natural forest through grazing, burning and cutting, the forest appears to degenerate into a low scrub (the *mallee* of Australia, the *garrigue* and *maquis* of southern Europe and the *chaparral* of California). The dominants in this form of vegetation are low trees and shrubs, usually about 3–4 m high. In the Mediterranean proper they include the wild olive (*Quercus ilex*), pines, a strawberry tree (*Arbutus unedo*) and some heathy shrubs such as *Erica*, *Ulex* and *Genista*.

4.11 Soils of cool temperate climates

In areas with cool temperate climates there are four main soil types that have a wide distribution: podzols, brown earths, leached soils and grey soils. There are, of course, many divergences from these zonal types, depending on the interplay of parent material, vegetation type, soil drainage, maturity and other such factors; but what they have in common is the fact that in such cool climates there is sufficient precipitation to maintain an overall downward leaching of any soluble soil constituents. In very general terms, the podzols are typical of the boreal forest; brown earths and grey-brown podzolic soils are normally associated with the deciduous forest; and the grey soils are representative of the transition zone between forest and grassland (steppe).

Podzols (figure 4.6(a)(i)) are characterised by the presence, just below the surface, of an ashy-coloured horizon. In the Northern Hemisphere they are generally regarded as being found in a circumpolar belt approximately from the Arctic Circle southwards to the latitude of the Great Lakes in North America and to about 50° N in Europe. They develop best on permeable gravels and sands. Podzols are soils in which a redistribution of the soil constituents has taken place through the action of downward-percolating rainwater, which contains decomposition products derived from the thick surface organic layer. This transports iron downwards, and it may accumulate in the B horizon as an iron-enriched layer called an *ironpan* or *hardpan*.

Brown earths and related soils derived much of their character from their association with the deciduous forests. With the annual leaf fall of the deciduous trees and the contribution from the smaller shrubs, herbs and grasses, the litter produced is more varied than that of the coniferous forest. It also has a higher nutritive status and

is more easily digested by the many soil-living fauna. Thus there is an efficient breakdown of litter, and the humus is incorporated into the soil by the action of earthworms. The brown earth profile frequently lacks the superficial horizons of organic material associated with the podzols, but leaching is still important and the upper horizons are normally neutral to slightly acid, carbonates having been largely leached away (figure 4.6(a)(v)).

The *grey soils* (figure 4.6(a)(ii)) tend to form in continental environments and are found between the podzols and the chernozems. Rainfall levels tend to be modest so that leaching is not as complete as it is in the brown earth zone, and some calcification occurs in the B horizon. A major feature of these soils is the accumulation of clay, derived from the upper horizons, in the B horizon.

4.12 Soils of warm temperate climates

In the Mediterranean region of climate the length of the summer drought is the most important zonal factor in soil formation. Increasing length of drought produces a sequence of soils ranging from brown earths (figure 4.6(a)(vi)), developing in a leaching environment with less than one month of summer drought, through red and brown Mediterranean soils (figure 4.6(a)(iii)) to cinnamon soils (figure 4.6(a)(vii)), where five or six months of drought leads to some soil calcification.

Brown Mediterranean soils developed under the original mixed Mediterranean forest dominated by oaks and pines. They are characterised by a brown colour, a friable humus-rich A horizon and a denser and less friable B horizon. In the lower horizons of these soils clays and complexes of iron and silica are deposited to give the characteristic rich red colour. The *red Mediterranean soils* have resulted in some cases from the development of soils on the eroded remains of the brown Mediterranean soils. Other red soils are formed upon the relic clays resulting from limestone weathering. Where a longer summer drought is experienced, the characteristics of the soil gradually become more typical of semi-arid areas: a light, yellowish-brown soil results, called a *cinnamon soil*. The A horizon is moderately rich

(a)

(b)

(i) Diagrammatic profile of a humus–iron podzol

L　Mor or moder
F
H
A　Thin mixed mineral and organic horizon, strongly acid
Ea　Eluvial horizon bleached, depleted of iron, strongly acid
Bh　Black-coloured illuvial horizon
Bfe　enriched with organic matter with indurated horizon below enriched with iron
Bs　Orange-brown illuvial horizon enriched with iron, strongly acid
C　Parent material: little altered sands and gravels or sandstone

(v) Diagrammatic profile of an acid brown soil

L+F　Moder or acid mull humus
A　Mixed mineral and organic horizon, strongly acid
A/　Transitional horizon, probably
(B)　depleted by leaching
(B)　Weathered horizon without appreciable enrichment with colloidal material discerned by slight differences of structure and colour
C　Little altered sandstone, siltstone or glacial sand

(ii) Diagrammatic profile of a grey forest soil

L　Mull humus
A　Mixed mineral and organic horizon, slightly acid
Eb　Eluvial horizon depleted of clay and some organic matter. Ped faces coated with grey powdering of silica remaining in situ
Bt　Illuvial horizon enriched with clay and humus, slightly acid tongues of grey penetrate down fissures
C　Parent material, little altered loess or loess-like loam

(vi) Diagrammatic profile of a brown Mediterranean soil

A　Mull humus
Eb　Eluvial horizon which has lost clay, slightly acid
Bt/ir　Illuvial horizons which are
Bir/C　enriched with clay and iron and have become red-coloured
C　Limestone or calcareous marl

(iii) Diagrammatic profile of a red Mediterranean soil and terra rossa

A　Thin mull humus forming in eroded remains
Bt　of B horizon
Bir/C　Illuvial horizons which are enriched with clay and iron and have become red-coloured
C　Limestone or calcareous marls

(vii) Diagrammatic profile of a cinnamon soil

A　Mull humus. Mixed organic mineral horizon, neutral or
Eb　slightly acid
Bca　Undifferentiated B horizon, increasing clay content with depth, calcareous
C　Slightly calcareous clay parent material

(iv) Diagrammatic profile of a red-yellow podzolic soil

L+F
A　Acid mineral and organic horizon
Eb　Lighter coloured acid eluvial horizon thicker in yellow soils
B　Red or brownish-red horizon rich in clay which increases with depth. Iron more hydrated in yellow soils
C　Parent material formed from wide range of geological materials

(viii) Diagrammatic profile of a chernozem

A　Mull humus incorporated to considerable depth by earthworms, neutral or slightly acid
　　Krotovinas (burrows) of vertebrate animals
Cca　Parent material of loess or loess-like loams, concentration of $CaCO_3$ in Cca horizon but depth varies
C　according to amount of leaching

L　Undecomposed litter

F　Partially decomposed litter

H　Well decomposed humus layer, low in mineral matter

A or Ap　Acid incorporated humus

A or Ap　Neutral or calcareous, incorporated humus

Ea or A_2　Bleached horizon of podzolized soils

Eb or A_2　Eluvial horizon depleted of clay and/or sesquioxides

(B)　Weathered horizon without appreciable enrichment in colloidal material

B　Undifferentiated illuvial horizon

Bt　Horizon containing illuviated clay (textural B horizon)

Bh　Horizon of maximum humus deposition in podzolized soils

Bfe　Horizon of maximum iron deposition in podzolized soils

Bs　Sesquioxide-enriched horizon of temperate soils

Bir　Sesquioxide-enriched horizon of tropical soils

C　Calcareous parent material

C　Non-calcareous parent material

Eag　Bleached, gleyed horizon of podzolized soils

Ebg　Bleached, gleyed horizon of gley soils

Bg　Illuvial horizon with strong gleying features

Cg　Parent material with strong features of gleying

Bca or Cca　Horizons enriched with calcium carbonate

Figure 4.6　(a) Some characteristic soil profiles from mid-latitudes; (b) Some of the abbreviations used to describe different horizon characteristics.

in organic matter, calcium carbonate concretions occur below about 30 cm in drier localities, and clay content increases from the lower part of the A horizon downwards through the profile.

The soils of the warm temperate east margin climates are typically *red and yellow podzolic soils* (figure 4.6(a)(iv)), and as they occur between the major areas of podzolisation (poleward) and ferrallitization (equatorward), evidence of both processes is present. The moist climate throughout the year is conducive to leaching, so that the surface horizons tend to be acid. The clay content increases with depth, partly by translocation of clay down the profile and partly because of clay mineral formation *in situ*. The red and yellow colours of these soils indicate different degrees of iron oxide hydration, with the red soils developing under drier conditions and the yellow developing where moister conditions prevail.

In the warm temperate continental interiors occurs one of the world's most famous zonal soil types; the *chernozem*, or black earths (figure 4.6(a)(viii)). They are a feature of the Russian steppes and the prairies of the United States and Canada. Many of them have developed on great expanses of aeolian silts, called *loess*, which were laid down on the margins of the greatly expanded Pleistocene ice sheets by winds transporting fine material from areas of moraine and outwash (see section 4.14). The chernozem soils are associated with grassland vegetation. Under the prevailing climatic conditions of this zone, grass growth is vigorous in the spring and early summer, but the drought of late summer and the frosts of the winter arrest the process of decomposition. Consequently, losses of organic material are minimised. The loess parent material also provides a source of calcium carbonate. There is a rich soil fauna, including miscellaneous burrowing animals, that cause some mixing in the soil profile. There is a deep, humus-enriched A horizon, while lower down there is a concentration of calcium carbonate caused by mild leaching from above followed by re-evaporation in the warm summers. In drier areas the soils may be less rich in organic matter and are called *chestnut soils*.

Plate 4.2   In the Breckland of East Anglia, near Thetford, stripes of heather (*Calluna*) are one type of patterned ground that is a relict feature of extreme periglacial conditions during the late Pleistocene. Active examples of such features may be found in Alaska today.

4.13   The impact of climatic change on the landscape

As we saw in chapter 2, the last couple of million years have been marked by very frequent and extreme changes in climate. For much of this time, the world has had a climatic zonation that is very different from what we see today, and this is especially true when we look at the mid-latitudes, for during the colder phases of the Pleistocene they were greatly affected by the expansion of both permafrost and glaciers. Many mid-latitude landscapes, sediments and soils still show, often to a marked degree, the imprint of these changes.

In North America a great sheet of ice was more or less continuous from Atlantic to Pacific, and was composed of two main bodies: the Cordilleran glaciers associated with the coastal ranges and the Rockies, and the great Laurentide ice sheet. At its maximum, the ice extended to approx-

Plate 4.4 In a great belt from western Europe through the Soviet Union to China there is loess – wind blown silts that were derived by deflation from outwash streams from great ice caps, or by deflation of desert surfaces. This example in Soviet Central Asia (the Tajik SSR) reaches a thickness of almost 200 m and forms imposing cliffs.

Plate 4.3 During the late Pleistocene the Stiperstones of Shropshire were just on the margins of a great ice sheet. Severe frost weathering caused quartzite rocks to be shattered. The debris formed blockstreams, some of which are sorted into periglacial patterns of stripes and polygons.

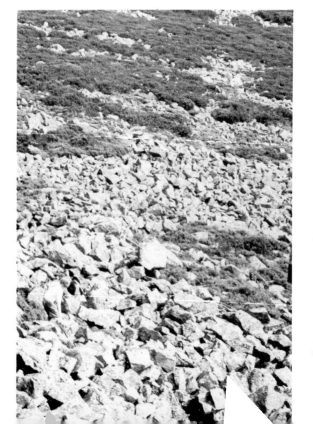

imately the present positions of St Louis, Missouri, and Kansas City. In the British Isles there were ice sheets that varied in their extent during different glacials, but merged with those of Scandinavia. At its maximum the ice extended as far south as Essex, Oxfordshire and the northern coast of the southwest peninsula. In Europe the alpine glaciers formed a great sheet that may have been over 1500 m thick in places, and reached down to altitudes as low as 500 m on the north side of the Alps and 100 m on the south side. There was also a great sheet that covered Scandinavia and reached into the North European Plain. This sheet may have been over 3000 m thick. Another extended ice sheet occurred in Siberia. Other major Pleistocene ice sheets developed in Argentina, Tasmania and New Zealand.

As a consequence of these great glacial expansions, many mid-latitude areas show all the imprints that glaciers can create in a landscape (see section 3.6). The mountains of upland Britain show many of the classic features of glacial erosion (U-shaped valleys, amphitheatrical cirques, lakes, hanging valleys, *roches moutonnées*, drainage diversions, etc.), while British lowland areas like East Anglia show a mantle of till and outwash deposits.

Beyond the limits of the great Pleistocene ice sheets, particularly in Europe, there were great areas of open tundra. These areas were frequently underlain by permafrost, and we can find evidence for its presence in Britain in the form of fossil ice-wedge polygons and pingos. In East Anglia, Kent, the Severn and Avon Valleys and parts of Devon there are wide expanses of patterned ground of various types that result from tundra conditions and probably only the extreme tip of the south-west peninsula was unaffected. Permafrost was also important in Europe; although there is still some dispute as to its precise maximum extent, it appears that only the south and central Balkans, peninsular Italy, the Iberian Peninsula and south-west France were unaffected. The degree of change has been substantiated by the study of pollen remains in old peat deposits. Much of the area, of course, was covered by cold steppe and tundra vegetation, rather than by the forests that are the natural vegetation of Europe during interglacial conditions.

4.14 Loess sheets

One of the great features of much of the mid-latitudes is the development of major sheets of silty sediment, of primarily windblown origin, called *loess*. Over vast areas (at least 1.6×10^6 km^2 in North America and 1.8×10^6 km^2 in Europe), loess blankets pre-existing relief, and in China it has been recorded as reaching a thickness in excess of 350 m. In the Missouri Valley of Kansas in the United States the loess may be 30 m thick, in Argentina it reaches 100 m, in New Zealand it reaches 18 m, in the Rhine Valley 30 m and in the southern Soviet state of Tajikistan it approaches 200 m. The maximum depth of loess in Britain is only a couple of metres.

The distribution of loess throughout the world suggests that much of its was derived by deflation (removal by wind) of fine material from the great outwash plains that lay equatorward of the great Pleistocene ice sheets, though in some areas it

may have been derived from deflation from desert basins – indeed, there is considerable controversy as to which source is the most important. In any case, there is no doubt that loess has been a most important parent material for soils, especially chernozems; that it has provided light soils that could be readily ploughed by early farmers in Europe; and that, if subjected to erosion by water, it can form some dramatic badlands types of scenery and contribute large amounts of sediment to rivers like the Yellow River in China.

4.15 Dry valleys and mis-fit streams

One of the most striking features of the geomorphology of much of lowland England, especially on limestone, chalk and sandstone, is the presence of dry valleys and mis-fit streams. *Mis-fit streams* are streams that are smaller (often by a ratio of about 10:1) than the valleys in which they flow, the meanders of the present streams being very much smaller than the meanders made by the valleys as a whole. Some of the streams of the Cotswold dip-slope have very small discharges at present, for example, but they occur in valleys with extremely large meanders, which appear to be quite out of proportion to the streams they contain. They are in a sense dry valleys that have not quite dried up.

There is no common consensus as to the causes of valley meander, mis-fit stream and dry valley development. Some of the main hypotheses that have been postulated are listed below. They can be categorised into uniformitarian hypotheses (those requiring no major changes of climate or base level, but merely the operation of normal processes through time), marine hypotheses (related to base-level changes), and palaeoclimatic hypotheses (associated primarily with the major climatic changes of the Pleistocene).

Uniformitarian Superimposition from a cover of impermeable rock or sediments
Joint enlargement by solution over time
Cutting down of major through-flowing streams
Reduction of precipitation in catchment area and fall of groundwater levels arising from scarp retreat
Cavern collapse
River capture
Rare events of extreme magnitude

Plate 4.5 The chalklands of southern England, including the White Horse hill on the Berkshire Downs near Uffington, certain many dry valleys. This oblique air photograph shows a valley called The Manger. The furrows on the right side of the valley have an uncertain origin, but may have been cut by Ice Age avalanches.

Marine Failure of streams to adjust to a falling
  Pleistocene sea level and associated fall of
    groundwater levels
  Tidal scour in association with former estuar-
    ine conditions

Palaeoclimatic Overflow from proglacial lakes
  Glacial scour
  Erosion by glacial meltwater
  Reduced evaporation caused by lower tempera-
    tures
  Spring snow-melt under periglacial conditions
  Runoff from impermeable permafrost

The uniformitarian hypotheses cannot be dismissed, though many workers claim that most
dry valleys are the product of cold phases of the
Pleistocene. Some dry valleys do appear to head
back into areas of impermeable rocks that overlie
rocks like limestone, and in such cases it is

entirely possible that the former were superimposed from a cover of clay, grit or some such
impermeable stratum that has since been removed
by erosion. Likewise, it is apparent that in a limestone area, as time goes on, the joints in the limestone will be progressively widened by solution so
that the rock mass becomes more and more permeable, thereby reducing the volume of surface
stream flow. In the same way, with the passage of
time a master stream may cut down preferentially
to the others and thereby abstract some of the
water from their basins, thus making them go
dry. The retreat of an escarpment through time is
another factor that could reduce the catchment
area of a stream, and it might also cause a reduction in groundwater levels (the Chandler–Fagg
hypothesis). The collapse of underground caverns
or the capture of one river by another (see section
10.12) could cause localised examples of dry

Plate 4.6 The great Cheddar Gorge of the Mendip Hills in England is a dry valley cut into Carboniferous limestone. It was probably largely shaped under periglacial conditions, though its lower course may be flooded by extreme storms like that of 1968.

valleys, though it would scarcely account for a widespread pattern. We must remember that occasional extreme rainfall can sometimes cause so-called dry valleys to flow, as was the case with the great storm on the Mendips in Britain in 1968 which caused substantial flow down Cheddar Gorge.

None of the theories so far mentioned is based on an assumption of a change in sea level or a change of climate. However, most workers invoke some such major change to account for the development of dry valleys and mis-fit streams. Some geomorphologists, for example, have maintained that in the early Pleistocene there was a high stand of sea level at around 180 m in parts of south-east England, and that at that time groundwater levels would have been high, so that streams might have flowed on the chalk. As the sea retreated, however, the groundwater level

might also have fallen, causing some of the valleys to go dry. Tidal scour may have played a role in widening some of these valleys.

The most popular theories, however, have involved changes of climate in the Pleistocene, for as we have seen, many parts of the mid-latitudes were subjected to a rigorous glacial or periglacial climate in the Pleistocene glacial phases. Large lakes were ponded up in certain areas by the glaciers, and overflow from such lakes could have carved some channels that are now dry. Some of the valleys might even have been scoured by glaciers themselves, or by meltwater running from them. Most importantly, however, cold climatic conditions would have caused low evaporation rates so that runoff could be a greater proportion of rainfall; much of the precipitation would have fallen in the winter months as snow, and when this melted in the summer thaw period rapid runoff would have occurred; and the presence of an impermeable permafrost layer would have enabled surface flow on rocks like limestone which are normally too pervious to permit it. Frost weathering might have broken some of the rocks up and rendered them more susceptible to fluvial erosion.

Some field evidence supports the idea that periglacial conditions may have been responsible, possibly in combination with some of the other hypotheses, for dry valley formation in south-east England. Many of the dry valleys are fronted by a fan of debris, called *coombe rock* or head, which is thought to be frost-shattered debris moved by solifluction. In some dry valleys on the chalk downs in Wiltshire and Dorset the coombe rock may contain extremely large boulders of Tertiary sandstones (called *sarsens*) which occur as block-streams, and once again solifluction is thought to have been the cause of their movement. Moreover, many of the dry valleys in the Chilterns do not seem to be related very strongly in their direction to the joints in the chalk, and this may be because they were fashioned by periglacial torrents working on rock that was impregnated with

permafrost. Some of them also display marked slope asymmetry. Under periglacial conditions, the aspect of a slope may have a considerable influence on its form and development, for some slopes exposed to greater sunlight will be more subject to freeze-thaw and solifluction processes, and this will influence the steepness of the valley side slopes.

4.16 Tors

Another landform that has often been attributed to periglacial times is the *tor*, an upstanding mass of rock or boulders that rises above more gentle slopes around. Such features are not restricted to periglacial areas – they are, for example, often developed on sandstone and granite outcrops in low latitudes – but frost action may be one of the

Plate 4.7 There are many examples of tors in Britain, and they have developed on a wide range of rock types. The Stiperstones in Shropshire (below) are composed of quartzite, the Pennine tors (right) are often formed of gritstone, and the Dartmoor Tors (below right) of granite. Frost weathering and solifluction may have contributed to their development.

many processes that favours their development. Certainly, many workers believe that the granite tors of Dartmoor, the gritstone tors of the Pennines or the quartzite tors of the Stiperstones in Shropshire are relict features that are inactive today.

One school of thought interprets mid-latitude tors as essentially angular landforms produced by frost shattering, with the weathered debris being transported away from the remaining more resistant masses by solifluction. These tors tend to be known as *palaeo-arctic tors*. Under this hypothesis, the tors are the remnants of a frost-riven bedrock outcrop surrounded by a low-angle terrace (called an altiplanation terrace) across which the frost-shattered material is removed by solifluction and other mass movment processes. On Dartmoor, the presence of great spreads of angular debris (called clitter), arranged in stripe and polygonal patterns and extending very long distances over quite gentle slopes, lends support to this idea.

However, a second school of thought argues that tors are prepared by deep weathering along joints to produce rounded subsurface core-stones (*wool-sacks*) under warm, humid conditions in the Tertiary. It is maintained that these are exhumed by the stripping of the weathered bedrock or *regolith* (called 'growan' on Dartmoor) by solifluction. Such tors are regarded as being *palaeo-tropical forms*, analogous, but on a smaller scale, to the inselbergs and koppies of tropical regions (see section 6.12).

4.17 Natural hazards in the UK

Having considered the main characteristics of the present and past environments and landscapes of mid-latitudes, let us now move to a consideration of the natural hazards that afflict people within one particular mid-latitude environment, the British Isles:

Storms
  Gales
  Convective storms
    Hail
    Thunderstorms
    Tornadoes
Snow, frost and cold
Floods
  Inland

  Coastal
Droughts
Fog
Air pollution
Water pollution
Land pollution
Heavy metals
Noise
Seismicity
Geomorphological hazards
  Mass movements
  Subsidence
  Coast erosion
Biological hazards
  Human health
  Plant and animal disease (e.g., Dutch elm; foot and mouth)
  Botanical infestations

As the above list shows, although this area is normally thought to be favoured with a relatively equable climate and very limited tectonic activity, there is none the less a wide range of natural events (sometimes exacerbated by man) that prove hazardous.

The first class of hazard is the storm. Because Britain lies within the belt of westerly depressions and from time to time comes under the influence of disturbances with steep pressure gradients, gales can be strong and frequent, especially in the coastal fringes of northern Ireland and western and northern Scotland, and at altitudes above about 700 m. A gale (in which the mean wind speed attains a speed of 34 knots or more over any period of ten consecutive minutes during the day) occurs on over 50 days in the year in parts of the Shetlands but on only 0.1 days in Kew (Surrey). These gales cause considerable damage during the course of the year, and on average nearly a quarter of a million buildings are damaged. In addition crops are damaged, transport services delayed and sailors drowned.

The most notable and vicious storm in living memory was the disastrous one which struck southern and eastern England in the early hours of October 16, 1987. It killed nineteen people, blew down fifteen million trees, brought down almost 5000 km of telephone lines, and deprived hundreds of thousands of homes of their electricity. The damage was caused by a mid-latitude depression which intensified over the Bay of Bis-

Plate 4.8 On October 16 1987, large areas of south-east England were afflicted by a ferocious storm, which caused much damage to buildings and trees. At Brasted Chart a majority of the trees on the estate were felled.

cay with great abruptness. Its particular power may have been caused by a particularly large temperature difference existing at that time in north-west Europe. The pressure dropped to 959 millibars, and the intensely concentrated low pressure system brought winds of great fury. Between 5 a.m. and 6 a.m. the Dover coastguards registered wind speeds averaged over 10 minutes of 85 mph, (c.136 km hr^{-1}) and elsewhere extreme gusts occurred, which proved particularly damaging to trees. The trees suffered badly not only because of this gusting, however, but because they were less securely anchored than usual because of the waterlogged nature of the ground, and because they had not yet shed their leaves they presented a large resistance to the wind.

The British Isles are also influenced by various types of convective storm (figure 4.7). Hailstorms do not reach the intensity or frequency of those in some other parts of the world, though in 1846 large hailstones are reported to have smashed 7000 panes of glass in the House of Commons! Of more significance is lightning associated with thunderstorms, which kills on average about 12 people each year, and may disrupt electricity supplies. Thunderstorms are especially frequent over London, and the building of the city may have increased their incidence (see section 15.1).

A third type of storm encountered in the British Isles is the tornado. This is an intense whirl of a small diameter, with a reduction in pressure of 100–300 mb within a few metres of the centre and with wind speeds that may exceed 200 knots. Prerequisites for tornadoes are warm moist air at the surface underlying cold dry air aloft, giving conditions of potential instability and leading to strong persistent vertical currents. They are most common in the English Midlands, especially from May to July, and while they do not attain the significance that they have in the interior of the United States, they do from time to time cause severe, but highly localised damage.

The second class of hazard is that associated with snow (figure 4.8), frost and cold. Severe winters occur when Atlantic depressions are prevented from moving from south-west to north-

Number of days with thunderstorms

□ under 3	▦ 12–15	■ Most frequent	□ Very infrequent
▥ 3–6	▦ 15–18	▤ Frequent	
▤ 6–9	■ 18–21	▥ Scarce occurrences	
▥ 9–12		▧ Infrequent	

Figure 4.7 Some natural hazards in the UK: (a) distribution of days with thunderstorms (1955–64); (b) the incidence of damaging hailstorms; (c) the distribution of severe tornadoes for 10 000 km² areas.

east on their normal tracks through the gap between Scotland and Iceland by the establishment of high pressure in the Greenland-Scandinavia region. Such anticyclones, called *blocking highs*, deposit, or *advect*, very cold air of continental origin over the British Isles, and these bitterly cold air masses are but slightly modified by their passage over the North Sea. Most heavy snowfalls are associated with warm fronts or warm occlusions, the majority of which move from (or are situated in) the south, south-west or west of the area where the snow falls (figure 4.9). Another important synoptic situation for heavy snowfalls is the presence of polar lows or troughs in northerly airstreams. Among the consequences of severe winter weather are high fuel costs, the laying off of outdoor workers,

Figure 4.8 Mean number of days with snow lying at 0900 hrs each winter over the period 1941–70.

(a)   (b)

Figure 4.9 Meteorological conditions giving heavy snowfalls over Britain in 1962/63. (a) On 30 December a wave depression had moved northwards from Biscay to a position south of Ireland, having become partially occluded with the warm occlusion moving very slowly northwards in the Channel region. A cold easterly airstream covered most of the British Isles. The front remained quasi-stationary in the Channel region before (b) moving northwards to northern England by 4 January.

Warm front   Occluded front   L = low pressure

Cold front   —1000— Isobars (mb)   H = high pressure

damage to crops and flocks, damage to plumbing and disruption of transport services. In the winter of 1979, for example, insurance companies paid out £70 million in claims for damage to property, at least 49 people were killed by severe weather, and at one time more than 150 000 km of road were blocked.

The third type of hazard is that associated with flooding (see section 14.12), which can be subdivided into those occurring on the coast and those occurring inland. Inland floods occur when meteorological conditions produce intense precipitation, prolonged precipitation or rapid snowmelt, acting either singly or in combination. Although the lower evaporation rates of the winter months cause heavier saturation of river catchments after heavy rainfall, much of the most severe flooding occurs in the summer months because of extremely localised, short-duration convective precipitation often associated with thunderstorms. The effects may be magnified by *orographic lifting* (section 13.2) or by the presence of a major urban area (see section 15.1). A wide variety of weather conditions, or synoptic situations, can produce the deep convection and the unstable atmosphere necessary to allow heavy, thundery summer rainfall, but frequently it is small, rather shallow depressions moving from the Bay of Biscay up the English Channel or across southern England that are responsible (figure 4.10). Snow-melt floods occur after severe winters when substantial quantities of snow are rapidly melted by the influx of warm moist air.

Coastal flooding is a serious problem, especially along the low-lying areas of eastern England. The worst event in recent history was the flooding of 1953, when over 800 km^2 were inundated by seawater, over 300 people were killed, and damage was estimated to have cost £30–50 million. It was caused by a North Sea storm surge which

Figure 4.10 A synoptic chart for conditions of very heavy rainfall in England on 15 September 1968.

occurred when strong north-westerly and northerly winds drove water southwards into the increasingly narrow confines of the southern North Sea. The strong winds were associated with a large and intense depression, and mean wind speeds of 70 knots with gusts of 100 knots were observed along the east coast of Scotland. In addition, river levels were high and were further ponded up by high tides pushing up the estuaries. Because south-east England is subsiding and world sea levels are rising, the coastal flood risk is becoming more serious. It is for this reason that a large flood barrier across the Thames at Woolwich, has recently been constructed.

Our fourth type of hazard – paradoxically, after our discussion of flooding – is drought. In Britain *absolute droughts* are defined as a period of at least 15 consecutive days when there is no day with 0.25 mm or more of rain, and a map of their distribution shows that southern England is the area most prone to them (figure 4.11(a)). The worst drought on record was in 1975–76, and as figure 4.11(b) shows, rainfall was less than 60 per

0   160 km

(a)   (b)

Figure 4.11 Drought conditions in Britain: (a) the regional distribution of mean annual absolute drought; (b) the distribution of rainfall, May 1975–August 1976 (the great drought) as a percentage of the 1916–50 mean.

cent of average over a wide area from Yorkshire in the north to the Isle of Wight in the south.

Such periods of drought are associated with the presence of one of two types of persistent anticyclonic systems:

(a) north-eastward extensions of the Azores high across southern England;
(b) persistent or repetitive blocking anticyclones centred near to or over Britain: the normal westerly flow with its travelling depressions is diverted north, and also sometimes south, of the high-pressure cell.

Why such anticyclonic patterns should become established in certain areas, and for such long periods, is still a matter of discussion, but it may be that unusual seawater temperatures over the Atlantic play a role. Droughts may have numerous consequences, including a reduction in agricultural productivity, a shortage of water for municipal and industrial use, an increase in the severity of fires in grassland and woodland areas, and subsidence and cracking of buildings caused by the shrinkage of clay substrata. In 1976 between £50 million and £60 million were paid out in insurance claims for 20 000 properties damaged by this process.

The final type of meteorological hazard to be considered is fog. This occurs with meteorological conditions that are conducive to the cooling of air below its dew point (table 4.4). Radiation fog tends to occur during anticyclonic spells when winds are light. Visibility is worst around dawn, when temperatures are at their lowest, and is caused by intense cooling under clear skies. This produces low-level inversions of temperatures. The temperature of the air increases with height up to several hundred metres above the ground, so that the lower atmosphere is very stable and little mixing occurs. In areas of industrial pollution, and in areas where topographic conditions favour the development of a frost hollow, the fog is not easily dispersed. *Advection fog* occurs when warm air is cooled, either by its passage over a cool sea or by passage over a cold (often snow-covered) land surface.

Plate 4.9 Severe droughts can occur in the UK. In the most severe drought on record, in the summer of 1976, this reservoir at Sutton Bingham almost dried up. High temperatures and low levels of rainfall, caused by the existence of a persistent blocking anticyclone, brought on the drought.

Table 4.4 Summary of fog characteristics in Britain

Type of fog	Season	Areas affected	Mode of formation	Mode of dispersal
Radiation fog	October–March	Inland areas, especially low-lying, moist ground	Cooling due to radiation from the ground on clear nights when the wind is light	Dispersed by the sun's radiation or by increased wind
Advection fog (a) over land	Winter or spring	Often widespread inland	Cooling of warm air by passage over cold ground	Dispersed by a change in air mass or by gradual warming of the ground
(b) over sea and coastline	Spring and early summer	Sea and coasts, may penetrate a few miles	Cooling of warm air by passage over cold sea	Dispersed by a change in air mass and may be cleared on coast by the sun's heating
Frontal fog	All seasons	High ground	Lowering of the cloud base along the line of the front	Dispersed as the front moves and brings a change of air mass
Smoke fog (smog)	Winter	Near industrial areas and large conurbations	Similar to radiation fog	Dispersed by wind increase or by convection

Source: A. H. Perry, *Environmental Hazards in the British Isles* (London: Allen & Unwin), 1981

Fog is one type of hazard that may be rendered more serious by human activity. A fog caused by a combination of favourable meteorological conditions and particulate emissions by industry may therefore be called a *quasi-natural hazard*. Such fogs are a type of pollution, and together with the other forms they may be injurious to human health.

The seismic hazard of earthquake activity is not one of major significance in Britain, though the building of sensitive structures such as nuclear power stations requires that they be accorded some attention. Earthquakes do occur (figure 4.12), notably in a rather diffuse area stretching from South Wales through Herefordshire into the north Midlands, and in the vicinity of the Great Glen and Highland Boundary Faults. The largest-intensity earthquake known in Britain occurred in the Colchester area in Essex in 1884 and damaged more than 12 000 buildings.

A far more important geomorphological hazard is that involving various types of mass movement. For instance, the landslide at Mam Tor has disrupted the main road from Manchester to Sheffield for some years; 147 people were killed by the debris flow at Aberfan in South Wales in 1966; the railway from Folkestone to Dover has been cut; large slabs of cliff line have

Figure 4.12 The epicentres of known earthquakes in Great Britain.

Plate 4.10 Even in England, slope instability can occasionally cause serious problems for transport. In this example, the main road from Manchester eastwards through the Peak District to Sheffield has been disrupted by landslipping at Mam Tor, 'the shivering mountain'.

subsided in areas such as the Isle of Wight and the Charmouth area of Dorset; and peat bog bursts have affected many highland areas.

Another form of geomorphological hazard,

partly induced by human activity, is land subsidence. For example, coal mining, salt extraction and the draining of peaty areas have caused the ground surface to be lowered, sometimes catastrophically. Soil erosion is a hazard on light sandy soils, as in the Breckland of East Anglia, and the presence of groynes and sea walls along much of the coastline is a testimony to the seriousness of coast erosion. Once again, the role of man in causing and intensifying the nature of the hazard is important.

The final natural hazards that we need to consider are those that can be termed 'biological hazards'. These can include the health hazards posed for people by certain components of the environment. Many recent studies have shown that certain diseases are not uniformly distributed over the country; for example, it is becoming apparent that some types of cancer may be associated with the presence of especially high concentrations of certain rare metals in the ground, and that the incidence of some types of cardiovascular disease may be increased in areas where the water supplies are hard (i.e., rich in salts such as calcium carbonate). Also coming under the heading of biological hazards are diseases that affect plants and animals. For example, since the 1960s an aggressive strain of Dutch elm disease has killed more than 11 million trees, transforming the rural landscape. Our increasingly mobile society means that biological hazards involving the introduction of various pathogens may become an increasingly serious problem.

5 Deserts

5.1 Introduction

The deserts of the world (figure 5.1) are areas in which there is a great deficit of water, predominantly because they receive only meagre amounts of precipitation. Whereas even the driest parts of Britain have around 500 mm of rainfall per year, there are many desert weather stations that normally record less than one-tenth of that figure. In some years they may even record no rainfall at all.

It is this shortage of moisture, often worsened by high temperatures, that determines many of the characteristics of the soils, the vegetation, the animals, the landforms and the human activities of such an area. Thus modern systems for defining aridity tend to be based on the concept of the *water balance* – the relationship that exists in a given area between the input of water in the form of precipitation (P), the losses arising from evaporation and transpiration by plants (*evapotranspiration*) (E_t), and any changes in storage (soil moisture, groundwater, etc.). By definition, in arid regions there is an overall deficit in water balance over a year, and the size of that deficit determines the degree of aridity. The actual amount of evapotranspiration (AE_t) that occurs will vary according to whether there is any water to evaporate, so climatologists have devised the concept of *potential evapotranspiration* (PE_t), which is a measure of the evapotranspiration that would take place from a standardised surface never short of water. The volume of PE_t will vary according to four climatic factors: radiation, humidity, temperature and wind. C. W. Thornthwaite developed a general moisture index based on PE_t:

When $P = PE_t$ throughout the year, the index is 0.

When $P = 0$ throughout the year, the index is -60.

When P greatly exceeds PE_t throughout the years, the index is $+100$.

Under this system, areas with values below -40 are regarded as arid, those between -20 and -40 as semi-arid, and those between 0 and -20 as subhumid. The arid category can be further subdivided into arid and extreme arid, with *extreme aridity* being defined as the condition experienced in any locality in which at least 12 consecutive months without any rainfall have been recorded, and in which there is not a regular seasonal rhythm of rainfall.

Extremely arid areas cover about 4 per cent of the earth's surface, arid about 15 per cent, and semi-arid about 14.6 per cent. Combined, these amount to almost exactly one-third of the earth's land surface area. The deserts occur in five great provinces separated by either oceans or equatorial forests. The largest of these by far includes the Sahara and a series of other deserts extending eastwards through Arabia to central Asia. The southern African province consists of the coastal Namib Desert and the Karroo and Kalahari inland dry zones. The South American dry zone is confined to two strips – the Atacama along the west coast and the Patagonian Desert along the east coast. The North American desert province occupies much of Mexico and the southwestern United States, including the Mojave and Sonoran Deserts. The fifth and final province is in Australia.

Although the water balance approach is one of the most satisfactory ways in which to subdivide desert environments, it must be remembered that there are many other factors that affect the nature of any particular desert area. Thus it is useful to draw a distinction between warm deserts and

Figure 5.1 (a) The distribution of world deserts (b) World map of rainfall variability. Note the way in which the major desert belts depicted in (a) show variability that is often in excess of 30 per cent.

those deserts that, because of either high latitude or high altitude, have winter frosts. Likewise, coastal deserts such as the Atacama and the Namib will have very different temperature regimes and humidity characteristics from the deserts of continental interiors. There are also many different landscape types, or *relief units*, in deserts; for just as the temperate regions of the world comprise such features as mountains and plains, rivers and deltas, lakes, etc., so deserts have corresponding topographic features.

On a large scale, one can divide these various relief units on the basis of their geological history into shield deserts and mountain and basin deserts. The *shield deserts*, which occur in India, Africa, Arabia and Australia and were once part of the Gondwanaland mass (see section 1.7) have much less relief than the mountain and basin deserts; because they do not suffer from extensive tectonic activity at present, ancient land surfaces have often survived over wide areas. In contrast, the *mountain and basin deserts*, such as those of the south-west USA or Iran, have much steeper relief, and because they are often undergoing present-day mountain-building they tend to have sharp fault junctions between mountains and plains. The block-faulted topography of the American south-west is an excellent example of this type. In California's Death Valley, one of the hottest and driest places on earth, high mountains rising to over 3000 m are in close juxtaposition to shimmering white salt flats that lie below sea level. The high relative relief is a major control of the types of geomorphological processes that operate.

Within desert regions of these two structural types, some areas are dominated by wind, some by water, some by erosion and some by deposition. Various major settings can be identified, each of which has distinctive landforms, surface materials and plant life. According to the classification of an Australian geomorphologist, J. A. Mabbutt, there are the following main types of desert area:

Desert uplands, where geological controls of relief are important, bedrock is exposed, and relief is high

Desert piedmonts, which are zones of transition separated from the uplands by a break of gradient but which none the less receive runoff and sediments from the uplands, and which have both depositional (e.g. alluvial fans) and erosional forms (e.g. pediments)

Stony deserts, which consist of stony plains and structural plateaux, and may have a cover of stone pavement

Desert river and floodplains (features of *desert lowlands*)

Desert lake basins, which are sumps to which the disorganised drainage progresses, and which are often salty

Sand deserts, which tend to be beyond the limits of active fluvial activity but often derive their materials by wind action removing erodible material from floodplains or lake basins; they are characterised by dunes.

5.2   What causes aridity?

Most of the world's deserts, whatever their form, derive their character from the fact that they receive little rainfall. This is because they tend to occur in zones where there is subsiding air (section 2.3), relative atmospheric stability and divergent air flows at low latitudes, associated with the presence of great high-pressure cells around latitude 30°. Such areas, as we learnt in chapter 2, are but seldom subjected to incursions of precipitation-bearing disturbances and depressions either from the Intertropical Convergence Zone of the tropics or from the belt of mid-latitude depressions associated with the circumpolar westerlies. The trade winds that blow across these arid zones are evaporating winds and because of the trade wind inversion they tend to be areas of subsidence and stability.

The subtropical highs are the major cause of aridity, though the desert zones are not always continuous around the earth at 30° – for instance, the Indian monsoon gives substantial quantities of rain over nothern India, and elsewhere the high-pressure cells are disrupted into a series of local cells, notably over the oceans, where air moving clockwise around the equatorial side of the cell brings moisture-laden air to the eastern margins of the continents in the Caribbean, Brazil and Queensland.

The rather general global tendencies produced by the subtropical highs are often reinforced by more local factors. Of these, distance from the sea (*continentality*) is a dominant one and plays a large part in the location and characteristics of the deserts of areas like central Asia. The *rain-shadow effect* produced by great mountains can create arid areas in their lee, as in Patagonia, where the southern Andes play this role. Other deserts are associated with the presence of cold ocean currents offshore. In the case of the Namib and the Atacama, for example, any winds that do blow onshore tend to do so across cold currents produced by the movement of water from high latitudes to low and associated with zones of upwelling of cold waters from the depths of the oceans. Such cool winds are stable because they are cooled from beneath. They also have a relatively small moisture-bearing capacity. In other words, they reinforce the stability produced by the dominance of subsiding air in desert areas.

5.3   Desert rainfall

The main characteristics of deserts are caused by the very low levels of rainfall, and extremely low levels of precipitation are a particular feature of some coastal deserts. For example, mean annual totals at Callao in Peru are only 30 mm, at Swakopmund in Namibia only 15 mm, and at Port Etienne in Mauritania only 35 mm. In Egypt there are stations where the mean annual precipitation only amounts to 0.5 mm. Years may go by in such areas of extreme aridity when no rain falls at all.

Another highly important characteristic of desert rainfall is that it is highly variable over time (figure 5.1(b)). This inter-annual *variability* (V) can be expressed as a simple index:

$$V(\%) = \frac{\text{the mean deviation from the average}}{\text{the average}} \times 100$$

Plate 5.1 Although generally dry, deserts can suffer from floods caused by a combination of abnormal rainfall and impermeable surfaces. In January 1984 severe disruption occurred in the arid heart of Australia, and at Marla Bore the railway was washed away.

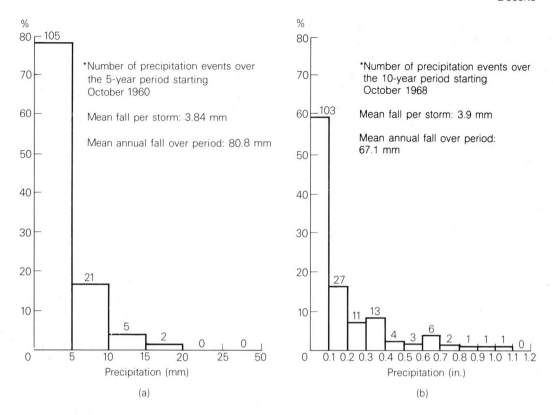

Figure 5.2 Histograms of the amount of rain falling in each rainy day for two desert locations: (a) H4, Jordan; (b) Death Valley, California. Note that in both cases the average fall per storm is less than 4 mm.

European humid temperate stations may have a variability of less than 20 per cent, whereas variability in the Sahara ranges from 80 to 150 per cent. This implies that from time to time, although mean rainfall levels are so low, there can still be individual storms of surprising size. Indeed, maximum falls in 24 hours may exceed the long-term annual precipitation values. For example, at Chicama in Peru, where the mean annual precipitation over previous years had been a paltry 4 mm, in 1925 394 mm fell in one storm. Similarly, at E1 Djem in Tunisia (mean annual precipitation 275 mm), 319 mm fell in three days in September 1969, causing severe flooding and creating great geomorphological changes.

It would, however, be wrong to give the impression that all desert rainfall occurs as storms of such ferocity and intensity. Most falls in storms of low intensity. This is brought out clearly when one considers the rainfall statistics for the Jordanian Desert in the Middle East and Death Valley in California (figure 5.2). Both these areas have very low rainfall in terms of mean annual levels (80.8 and 67.1 mm, respectively), yet on average rain falls on 26 and 17 days respectively, so that the mean rainfall event tends to be only 3–4 mm – which is much the same as for London.

In coastal deserts, with cold currents offshore, the moisture provided by fogs may augment that produced by rain. In the coastal fringes of Namibia the mean annual fog precipitation (35–45 mm) may exceed that from rain, and the fog may occur on up to 200 days in the year and extend over 100 km inland. In Peru the fogs and low cloud provide enough moisture to support a growth of vegetation.

Precipitation in arid zones, in addition to showing temporal variability, also shows considerable spatial variability. For this reason it is often described as being 'spotty'.

5.4   Desert temperatures

According to their type, deserts have a wide range of temperature conditions. Interior deserts can be subjected to extremes of temperature, both seasonally and diurnally, that are not equalled in any other climatic region, while coastal deserts tend to have relatively low seasonal and diurnal ranges.

In the case of coastal deserts, the climate is modified and moderated by the presence of cold currents and upwelling. Temperature ranges over the year are low – Callao, in the Peruvian desert, has an annual range of only 5°C. Daily ranges in such stations are also low, often around 11°C, and only about half what one would expect in the Sahara. The annual temperature values are also generally moderate (c.19°C in the Atacama, and 17°C in the Namib).

By contrast, great extremes of temperature can occur in interior deserts, with maximum shade temperatures exceeding 50°C. Temperatures in excess of 37°C may occur for many days on end in the summer months, but because of the clear skies there may be a marked reduction of temperature at night, and daily ranges of 17–22°C are normal. In the winter months in high-altitude interior deserts, frost can occur frequently.

While some deserts show great daily and seasonal ranges in air temperatures, ground surface temperatures show even greater ranges. Sand, soil and rock have been recorded as reaching temperatures as high as 82°C, and some Soviet workers have reported daily ranges as high as 75°C! Such extreme values have many implications both for rock weathering and for plant and animal life.

5.5   Past climates in deserts

During the Ice Age of the Pleistocene the world was very different from today. In high latitudes the great ice sheets were far more extensive than now, and permafrost extended into areas like southern England. Lower latitudes did not escape these changes; temperature and rainfall conditions fluctuated repeatedly, and many deserts were subjected to increased rainfall; such periods are called *pluvials*, or lacustral phases. Some de-serts have also been subjected to even greater aridity than today: such dry phases are called *interpluvials*.

There are a number of indicators in the present desert environments of higher levels of precipitation in the past: high lake levels marked by ancient shorelines around now dry, salty closed basins; expanses of fossil soils of humid type, including laterites and other types indicative of very marked chemical changes under conditions of humidity; great spreads of spring-deposited lime, called *tufa*, indicating former higher groundwater levels; vast river systems which are currently inactive and blocked by dune fields; and animal and plant remains, together with evidence of former human habitation, in areas now too dry for people to survive.

The evidence for formerly drier conditions includes the presence of degraded, stable sand dunes in areas that are now too wet for sand movement to occur (see section 2.13).

Some of the pluvial lake basins reached colossal dimensions, especially in the south-west of the United States, where faulting had created a large number of closed basins in which lakes could accumulate during periods of greater humidity. Lake Bonneville, near Salt Lake City in Utah, now has a water area of 2600–6500 km² and is highly saline – in the pluvials of the Pleistocene it had an area of 51 700 km² (almost the size of present-day Lake Michigan), and was probably relatively fresh. It was 335 m deeper than it is now.

Likewise, on the margins of the Sahara, Lake Chad underwent major changes in level: it may have been about 120 m deeper than it is now, and it extended for hundreds of kilometres north of its present limits. In central Asia there was another colossal lake, in the area of the present Aral and Caspian Seas, that covered over 1.1×10^6 km² and extended 1300 km up the Volga from its present mouth.

The dates for these more humid phases are still the subject of great discussion. In general, it appears that in the American south-west the high lake levels were broadly contemporaneous with the last major expansion of the great ice caps (around 18 000 years BP), but in areas like the margins of the Sahara and in East Africa the last major lake expansion phases (probably one of many) took place just after the start of postglacial times (around 9000 years BP).

Although climatic change of a marked degree appears to have taken place in the Pleistocene and early Holocene, it is apparent from the study of meteorological records, dating back in some cases to the middle of the last century, that appreciable fluctuations may still take place. Thus, for example, in the 1930s a period of greatly reduced rainfall and higher-than-average temperatures in the United States contributed to the extreme wind erosion and dust blowing of the 'Dust Bowl' years. Likewise, in the late 1960s and 1970s a great belt, extending from Mauritania in the west to northwest India in the east, suffered from a series of prolonged and serious droughts, with rainfall only around two-thirds of the long-term mean. This caused extensive famines and led to great pressures on the limited vegetation available for grazing animals on the desert margins. Severe land degradation and erosion ensued.

5.6 Desert vegetation and animals

One consequence of the present aridity of deserts is that the vegetation cover is generally low – a closed cover is seldom encountered. A useful measure of the degree of vegetation development in an area is its *biomass*, the total amount of living plant material above and below ground. Deserts have a low biomass, often 100 times less than that of an equivalent area of temperate forest. Water is the vital influence on plant growth, of course, and is responsible for this low biomass level. Most plant tissues die if their water content falls too low; the nutrients that feed plants are transmitted by water; water is a raw material in the vital process of photosynthesis; and water regulates the temperature of a plant by its ability to absorb heat and because water vapour lost to the atmosphere during transpiration helps to lower plant temperatures. However, water not only controls the volume of plant matter produced, it also controls the distribution of plants within an area of desert; some areas, because of their soil texture, topographic position or distance from rivers or groundwater, have virtually no water available to plants, whereas others do.

The nature of plant life in deserts is also highly dependent on the fact that they have to adapt to the prevailing aridity. There are two general classes of vegetation: *perennials*, which may be succulent and are often dwarfed and woody; and annuals or *ephemerals*, which have a short life-cycle and may form a fairly dense stand immediately after rain.

The ephemeral plants evade drought. Given a year of favourable precipitation such plants will develop vigorously and produce large numbers of flowers and fruit. This replenishes the seed content of the desert soil. The seeds then lie dormant until the next wet year, when the desert blooms again.

The perennial vegetation adjusts to the aridity by means of various avoidance mechanisms (figure 5.3). Most desert plants are probably best classified as *xerophytes*. They possess drought-resisting adaptations: transpiration is reduced by means of dense hairs covering waxy leaf surfaces, by the closure of stomata to reduce transpiration loss and by the rolling up or shedding of leaves at the beginning of the dry season. Some xerophytes, the *succulents* (including cacti), impound water in their structures. Another way of countering drought is to have a limited amount of mass above ground and to have extensive root networks below ground. It is not unusual for the roots of some desert perennials to extend downwards more than ten metres. Some plants are woody in type – an adaptation designed to prevent collapse of the plant tissue when water stress produces wilting. Another class of desert plant is the *phreatophyte*. These have adapted to the environment by the development of long tap roots which penetrate downwards until they approach the assured water supply provided by groundwater. Among these plants are the date palm, tamarisk and mesquite. They commonly grow near stream channels, springs or on the margins of lakes.

In addition to a shortage of water, many desert plants have to be able to cope with saline soil conditions. Salt-tolerant plants are called *halophytes*.

Animals also have to adapt to desert conditions (figure 5.4), and may do it through two forms of behavioural adaptation: they either escape or retreat. Escape involves such actions as *aestivation*, a condition of prolonged dormancy or torpor during which animals reduce their metabolic rate and body temperature during the hot season or during very dry spells. Seasonal migration is another form of escape, especially for large mammals or birds. The term *retreat* is applied to the short-term escape behaviour of desert animals,

and it usually assumes the pattern of a daily rhythm. Birds shelter in nests, rock overhangs, trees and dense shrubs to avoid the hottest hours of the day, while mammals like the kangaroo rat burrow underground.

Some animals have behavioural, physiological and morphological (structural) adaptations that enable them to withstand extreme conditions. For example, the ostrich, *Struthio camelus*, has plumage that is so constructed that the feathers are long but not too dense. When conditions are hot the ostrich erects them on its back, thus increasing the thickness of the barrier between solar radiation and the skin. The sparse distribution of the feathers, however, also allows considerable lateral air movement over the skin surface, thereby permitting further heat loss by convection. Furthermore, the birds orientate themselves carefully with regard to the sun and gently flap their feathersome wings to increase convective cooling.

5.7   Soils and surface materials

Arid environment soils, which are called *aridisols*, have certain general characteristics that are distinctive. Because of the low plant biomass they have a low organic content, and thus are dominantly mineral soils of an immature and skeletal type. They are also little subjected to leaching because of low precipitation levels, so that soluble salts tend to accumulate in the profile at a depth related either to the position of the water table or to the depth of moisture percolation. Such deposition forms one of the few distinct horizons in aridisols, and it occurs nearer to the surface as precipitation diminishes. Another

Figure 5.3 Some forms of adaptation of desert plants to the rigours of the environment: (a) a succulent plant, which can store a great deal of water and so can rely on near-surface roots collecting rain from sporadic precipitation events; (b) an acacia bush of a type very characteristic of desert margins, which adopts a dual strategy of having subsurface roots to collect any moisture sporadically available from rainfall, together with a very deep rooting system stretching down to permanently available groundwater in the subsoil and rock; (c) a plant with very small leaves in relation to the size of the branch (c.25 cm), thereby limiting evapotranspiration loss; (d) the thorny euphorbia of the Namib Desert in South West Africa; and (e) its equivalent in North America, the cactus.

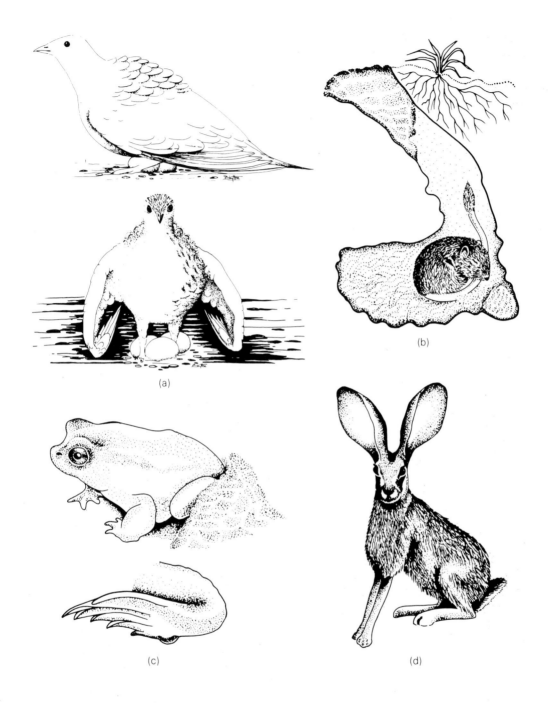

Figure 5.4   Some forms of adaptation of desert animals to the rigours of the environment. (a) The ground-nesting sandgrouse shades its eggs during the hottest hours of the day and reduces the radiation load by erecting the mantle feathers. It also faces into the wind and raises itself above the nest, thereby facilitating convective cooling of the shaded eggs. (b) The kangaroo rat burrows, thereby sheltering from predators, radiation and desiccation. (c) Using its strong feet, which have a horny projection, the spadefoot toad of the Sonoran Desert can escape to depths as great as 90 cm below the surface during unfavourable climatic conditions. (d) The enormous ears of the jack rabbit assist the animal in offloading excessive body heat.

general characteristic is that desert soils have a generally low clay content compared with humid zone soils. In general, clay formation increases with increasing rainfall.

Of these characteristics, salt accumulation is one of the most important. When groundwater is present near the surface, as in the floodplains of through-flowing rivers or in proximity to salt lakes, concentrations of salts may occur at high enough levels to be toxic to plants. Soils of this type with a saline horizon of NaCl (sodium chloride) are called *solonchaks* (white alkali soils), and those with Na_2CO_3 (sodium carbonate) are called *solonetz* (black alkali soils). High-saline contents affect plant growth in various ways. First, they affect the physical structure of the soils: a high content of sodium salts leads to a dispersal or *deflocculation* of the soil particles or aggregates, causing the soils to lose their structure so that they become relatively impervious and badly aerated. Second, there is the *osmotic effect*, which opposes the entry of water into plant roots and thus increases total moisture stress. Third, there is a straightforward nutritional effect, whereby toxicity or nutritional imbalance is caused: some salts in large quantities are poisonous.

Although much of the salt ultimately comes from natural sources (from the atmosphere, from rock weathering, from inflowing rivers, etc.) and is a normal characteristic of many desert areas, human activity has increased the extent and degree of salinity in many ways. In particular, the development of irrigation for agriculture can lead to a build-up of salt levels in the soil through the mechanism of raising groundwater, so that it is near enough to the surface for capillary rise and subsequent evaporative concentration to occur. Elsewhere over-pumping of fresh groundwater in coastal areas can permit the incursion of more saline water from the sea. The problem of induced salination arising from irrigation is severe; it has been estimated that the percentage of salt-affected and waterlogged soils in the irrigated areas of Iraq and Syria amounts to 50 per cent.

Sometimes the accumulation of soluble materials progresses so far that hard surface or subsurface crusts develop. Warm deserts have a variety of these crusts – sometimes called *duricrusts* – and they are classified according to the nature of the main chemical composition of the cement.

Calcretes, calcium carbonate crusts, are the most widely distributed, and the numerous different forms that have been described include hardened or indurated horizons some metres thick. *Silcretes* are crusts formed by the cementation of a matrix by silica in the form of opal, chalcedony or quartz. The most extensive areas of silcrete occur in southern Africa and in Australia, but they are by no means restricted to semi-arid areas, and some develop in wetter zones. *Gypcrete* crusts are composed of calcium sulphate, and while calcretes predominate in areas where precipitation ranges from 200 to 500 mm, gypcretes tend to be found in zones with between 50 and 200 mm. In still drier areas the crusts are often composed

Plate 5.2 A typical calcrete hardpan at Barberspan in South Africa. Beneath the book there is the solid crust, and beneath that there is a more friable, nodular zone. Such crusts are a feature of the soils of semi-arid areas.

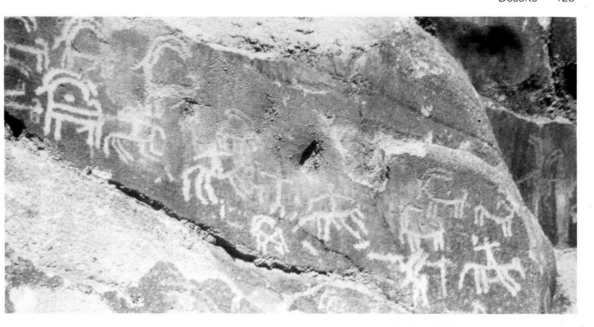

Plate 5.3 In desert areas, like the dry valleys of the Karakoram in Pakistan, rock surfaces are often covered by desert varnish. Where the dark varnish has been scratched away, as with these graffiti, the lighter underlying rock is evident.

of sodium chloride and, exceptionally – notably in the Atacama – sodium nitrate. This distribution pattern, controlled by precipitation levels, would appear to be related to the solubility of the various minerals involved, each mineral having a threshold above which the climate is wet enough to dissolve and leach the near-surface accumulations.

The processes responsible for the development of these duricrusts are as diverse as the crusts themselves. Some crusts result from salts being deposited in evaporating lakes; some develop *in situ* and involve a relative accumulation of the cementing mineral by the leaching of other minerals; some develop as a result of evaporation of groundwater in areas of high evaporation rates; some develop as a result of the evaporation of laterally moving subsurface and surface waters on features like pediments and alluvial fans; others involve the downward leaching and accumulation of soluble materials that have been brought in as dust.

Another crust, somewhat different from those just described, is the thin patina of iron and manganese oxide that covers many rock surfaces. This is called *desert varnish*.

Of the various surface types found in deserts, *stone pavements* are one of the most characteristic. These are armoured surfaces composed of rock fragments, either angular or rounded, usually one or two stones thick, set in or on matrices of finer material such as sand, silt and clay. The traditional explanation for these features is that they are a consequence of *deflation*, or the removal by wind, of fine materials from a deposit of initially mixed grain size. This would tend to leave the coarse contents as a lag or residue at the surface (figure 5.5). However, a similar result could occur from water sorting. Coarse materials could remain at the surface after raindrops had dislodged fine materials and they had been flushed away by running water in the form of sheet flow. Vertical processes may also play a role, for both freezing and thawing and wetting and drying can lead to the migration of coarse particles towards the ground surface.

5.8 Insolation and salt

Mechanical weathering, involving the disintegration of rock without any chemical change, has often been considered important in the desert en-

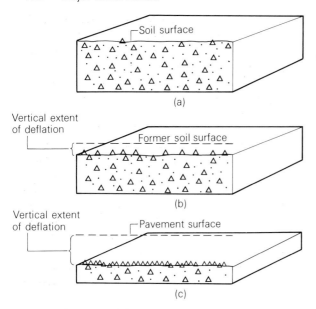

Figure 5.5 The classic deflation model of stone pavement development, with an initial alluvial sediment containing both fine and coarse materials (a) being subjected to deflation (b) until such time as the surface is lowered to such an extent (c) that a coarse gravel lag is left at the surface, the fine material having been blown away.

vironment. There are probably two main types of mechanical weathering: that produced by insolation and that produced by salt.

Insolation weathering is the rupturing of rocks and minerals primarily as a result of large daily temperature changes which lead to temperature gradients within the rock mass. Areas that are heated expand relative to the cooler portions of the rock and stresses are thereby set up. In igneous rocks, which contain many different types of mineral with different coefficients and directions of expansion, such stresses are enhanced. Moreover, the varying colours of minerals exposed at the surface will cause differential heating and cooling.

Daily temperature cycles under desert conditions may exceed 50°C, and during the heat of the day the rock surface may exceed a temperature of 80°C. However, rapid cooling takes place at night, creating, it has been thought, high tensile stresses in the rock. Desert travellers have claimed to hear rocks splitting with sounds like pistol shots in the cool evening air – certainly, split rocks are evident on many desert surfaces.

At first sight the process of insolation weathering seems a compelling and attractive mechanism of rock disintegration. However, in recent years doubt has been cast upon its effectiveness on a variety of grounds. The most persuasive basis for doubting its power was provided by experimental (albeit crude) work in the laboratory by geomorphologists like Blackwelder, Griggs and Tarr. They all found that simulated insolation produced no discernible disintegration of dry rock, but that when water was used in the cooling phase of a weathering cycle disintegration was evident. This highlighted the importance of the presence of water. Likewise, studies of ancient stone buildings and monuments in dry parts of North Africa and Arabia showed very little sign of decay except in areas, for example close to the Nile, where moisture was present. Indeed, there are many situations where there is moisture in deserts: in the Namib coastal desert rocks may be wetted by fog on as many as 100 days in the year; in parts of Israel there may be dews on 150 days in the year; and even in a very arid area like Death Valley in California there are 17 days in the year when rain falls. When water combines chemically with the more susceptible minerals in a rock they may swell, producing a sufficient increase in volume to cause the outer layers of rock to be lifted off as concentric shells – a process called *exfoliation*. Thus, some of the weathering that used to be attributed to insolation may now be attributed to chemical changes produced by moisture.

However, the importance of insolation cannot be dismissed entirely. The early experimental work had grave limitations: the blocks used were very small, they were unconfined, and the temperature cycles employed were unlike those encountered in nature. Some recent experiments using a wide range of rock types under more natural temperature cycles have revealed that some micro-cracking can take place.

One agent of mechanical weathering that has come into favour recently is *salt weathering*, for salts of various types are widespread in deserts. Low rainfall levels mean that salts are prone to accumulate rather than being dissolved and carried away in rivers. The salts include common salt ($NaCl$), sodium carbonate (Na_2CO_3), sodium sulphate (Na_2SO_4), magnesium sulphate

Plate 5.4 When fine materials are washed or blown away in deserts, stone pavements may develop, in which a coarse lag of stones mantles the ground surface. These particles in Death Valley, California, have been broken up by salt weathering.

(MgSO$_4$), gypsum (Ca$_2$SO$_4$) and (especially in the Atacama) sodium nitrate (Na$_2$NO$_3$). They break up rocks in two main ways. First, when a solution containing salts is either cooled or evaporated salt crystals will form, and pressures accompanying the *crystallisation* can be great enough to exceed the tensile strength of the rocks in which the solution was contained. Second, salt minerals expand when water is added to their crystal structure. This change of state is termed *hydration*. Some salts exist at atmospheric temperatures and humidities in the non-hydrated form, but variations in temperature or humidity may cause a phase change into the hydrated form, taking up water of crystallisation and expanding. In the case of Na$_2$SO$_4$ and Na$_2$CO$_3$ the volume expansion involved may be in excess of 300 per cent. If the salts are in the rock, the pressures generated can break the rock.

There is now plenty of laboratory and field evidence for the power of salt weathering (figure 5.6). Rapid decay of buildings in salty areas has been noted in Bahrain, Suez and the Indus Valley of Pakistan, while telegraph poles and grave

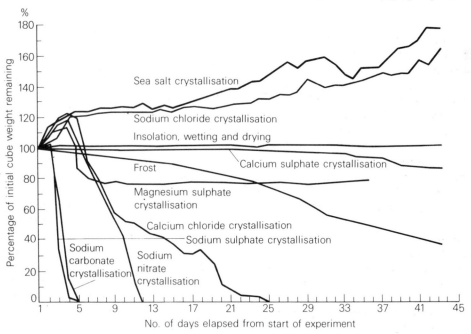

Figure 5.6 In a laboratory experiment, small cubes of rock were subjected to a variety of physical weathering processes, and their weight was recorded after each cycle. Some salts appear highly effective, especially sodium carbonate and sodium sulphate. Some samples increased in weight because of the absorption of salt, but when leached they also showed signs of disintegration.

stones in some deserts seem to act like wicks for groundwater solutions and suffer from salt crystallisation as the water evaporates. In Death Valley, California, boulders of resistant igneous rock (20–60 cm in diameter) in alluvial fans can be seen to disintegrate to dust within a few metres of reaching the salt pan.

5.9   Wind action in deserts

Because deserts are so dry and vegetation cover so limited, there is little to protect the desert surface against the action of wind, but the importance of wind in shaping desert landscapes has been subject to rapid changes of emphasis. At the end of the nineteenth century many workers who had experience in some of the new colonial territories like South West Africa attributed the formation of isolated hills (*inselbergs*) and the surrounding low-angled smooth rock-cut surfaces that surrounded them (*pediments*) to the planing action of sand-laden wind, with its supposedly high abrasional ability. This phase has been termed the phase of 'extravagant aeolation'.

In due course, however, there was a reaction against these views, partly because of an increasing body of work in the deserts of North America, with their steep slopes, active tectonics and slightly wetter conditions. Various arguments were marshalled against the proponents of widespread wind planation, and many of them are valid today. First, it was appreciated that rare rainstorms, acting on surfaces with limited vegetation cover and soils with limited infiltration capacities, could cause fluvial processes to be active. Second, the pluvials of the Pleistocene and Holocene were thought to have had an important influence on the moulding of desert surfaces. Third, it was shown that many desert surfaces were protected from the reduction of the surface by wind action, by stone pavements or crusts. Fourth, wind erosion depends on the presence of abrasive sand (which is not present everywhere), and as the sand moves at only a metre or so above the ground surface it operates only over a limited height range. Fifth, many of the features that were attributed to wind erosion either could be explained by other processes (e.g. closed basins, or inselbergs), or were of no very great

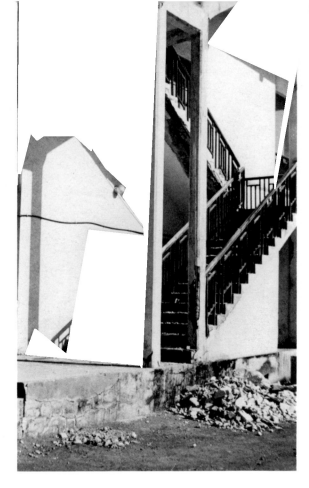

Plate 5.5   After only twelve years from the date of construction this nurse's home in Bahrain was disintegrating as a result of salt attack. The house was built in a low-lying area, so salty groundwater rose into the foundations and crystallisation occurred.

significance in the landscape (e.g. the curiously shaped rocks called *zeugen*).

None the less, where there are high winds, with plenty of abrasive sand, operating on susceptible surfaces, wind erosion may be important. Indeed, the examination of air photographs and satellite imagery has revealed that extensive areas of bedrock in many deserts have huge bowed, or *arcuate*, grooves with relative relief of more than 100 m; these run for tens of kilometres, and are aligned with the prevailing winds (see table 5.1). Such areas of groovy ground are called *yardangs*. Many desert depressions also appear to have an aeolian origin; for they have a streamlined shape, occur in lines, and have dunes on their lee sides resulting from the deposition of sands excavated

Plate 5.6 In Iran, satellite images show great parallel grooves, called yardangs or kaluts. They are caused by erosion of sediments by strong north-westerly winds. These examples are tens of kilometres long.

Table 5.1 Yardangs

Location	Lithology
Taklimakan, China	Fluvial and lacustrine sediments of Pleistocene age
Lut, Iran	Pleistocene fine-grained horizontally bedded silty clay and limey gypsiferous sand
Khash Desert, Afghanistan	Clay
Sinai	Nubian sandstone
Saudi Arabia	Caliche, Limestone
Bahrain	Aeolianite (Pleistocene), dolomite
Egypt	Eocene limestone, lake beds; Nubian sandstone
South-central Algeria	Cretaceous clays, Cambrian claystones
Borkou, Chad	Palaeozoic and lower Mesozoic sandstones and shales
Jaisalmer, India	Eocene limestones
Namib Desert	Precambrian dolomites, granites and gneisses
Rogers Lake, California	Dune sands and lake beds
Northern Peru	Weakly to moderately consolidated upper Eocene to Palaeocene sediments (shales and sandstones)
South-central Peru	Siltstones of upper Oligocene to Miocene age (Pisco formation)

by winds from the hollows. Moreover, the general association of so many hollows with deserts implies that 'normal' processes (presumably fluvial action and slope movements) are inadequate to fill them in, and that some abnormal process (presumably wind) is effective at digging them out. It should be remembered, however, that many processes can produce a hole in the ground, and that many desert depressions may be the result of hole-forming processes that inherently have very little to do with aridity, for example, tectonic processes can produce fault basins, solution can create hollows in limestone areas, animals can excavate water holes, etc..

That wind action is an important factor in creating desert landscapes is perhaps best indicated by the occurrence of *dust storms* produced by the deflation of fine materials (especially silt) from unvegetated desert surfaces. Such deflation is an insidious form of soil erosion. Dust storms

Plate 5.7 A small closed depression in the arid zone of Western Australia. The main processes responsible for its development are probably rock disintegration caused by salt weathering, followed by deflation by wind. Such hollows often have a small dune on their lee sides, called a lunette, which is composed of material deflated from the basin.

may be of sufficient intensity to reduce visibility to below 1000 m for 20–30 days in the year, and are large enough (with dimensions up to 2500–2000 km) to be seen on satellite imagery. Dust may be transported large distances: on occasions, Saharan dust has reached places as far away as Britain and Florida.

In a dust storm of average violence a cube of air (dimensions 3m × 3m × 3m) might well contain 28 g of dust suspended in it. Thus a storm 500 km × 600 km across might well be sweeping 100 000 000 t of solids along with it!

5.10 Sand deposition – dunes

Although the romantic view of deserts envisages landscapes dominated by ever-changing sand dunes, with oases, camels and men in flowing robes, only about one-third to one-quarter of the world's deserts are covered by aeolian sand, so its

role in deserts should not be exaggerated. Indeed, in the American deserts sand dunes occupy less than 1 per cent of the surface area. None the less, great *ergs*, or seas of sand, are found nowhere else on earth, and they form some of the most beautiful, repetitious and regular landforms that our planet (and, indeed, Mars) has to offer. Particularly large ergs occur in Arabia and the Sahara.

The sand that makes up dune fields is a result of wind winnowing grains of an easily transported size from alluvial plains, from lake shores, from sea shores and from weathered rock like sandstone and granite. When wind velocity exceeds the threshold velocity required to initiate sand grain movement (generally this is about 20 km h^{-1}), the grains begin to roll along the ground, but after a short distance this gives rise to a bounding or jumping action called *saltation*. Grains are taken up a small distance into the airstream (often only a matter of a few centimetres) and then fall back to the ground in a fairly flat trajectory. The descending grains dislodge further particles and thereby the process of saltation is maintained across country. The saltating grains (which generally have a diameter between 0.15 and 0.25 mm) lift larger grains (with diameters generally in the range of 0.25–2.00 mm), which move forward by *surface creep*. The smallest grains (<0.15 mm) may be carried high up into the air in *suspension*.

Dunes form because saltating grains tend to accumulate preferentially on sand-covered areas rather than on adjoining sand-free surfaces. This seems to result from the check to a strong wind through intensified sand movement over a sand surface and from the lower rate of sand movement where saltating grains 'splash' into loose sand compared with that over firm ground.

The geometric forms of deposition of sand as dunes are very varied (figure 5.7) and depend on the supply of sand, the nature of the wind regime, the extent of vegetation cover and the shape of the ground surface. As these conditions vary from desert to desert, the relative importance of different dune types also varies (table 5.2).

One class of dune is that formed by the interference of an obstacle, such as a hill, with wind and sand movement. Where the wind velocity is checked by the hill sand will be deposited sometimes to the lee and sometimes to windward. Large shrubs can have a similar effect on wind flow, leading to the formation of *nebkhas* (figure 5.7(a)(i)). Some obstacle or topographic dunes develop in the lee of desert depressions and such crescentic features are called *lunettes* (figure 5.7(a)(ii)). Most dunes, however, do not require an obstacle, whether hill, shrub, depression or dead camel. Indeed, the most regular dune forms develop on the most regular surfaces.

Probably the best known and most common basic dune form results from winds having a single dominant direction and the dune being oriented with its axis at right angles to the wind direction. Such dunes range from small crescent-

Plate 5.8 In February 1983 the inhabitants of Melbourne, Australia, were made aware of the importance of dust storms in arid environments. In some desert areas 'black blizzards' such as these reduce visibility to a matter of metres on as many as 20 to 30 days in the year.

Plate 5.9 Sand dunes have a great variety of forms. One common type is the linear dune or seif. These features, which in the case of the Namib examples shown here, in South West Africa, may be several hundreds of metres high, can run parallel for tens of kilometres. The Namib dunes have a more barchanoid form near the coast (on the left of the Landsat satellite image). Their northern and eastern boundary is marked by the Kuiseb River.

Table 5.2 Relative importance of major dune types in the world's deserts

	Thar (%)	Takla Makan (%)	Namib (%)	Kalahari (%)	Saudi Arabia (%)	Ala Shan (%)	South Sahara (%)	North Sahara (%)	North-east Sahara (%)	West Sahara (%)	Average (%)
Linear dunes (total)	13.96	22.12	32.55	85.55	49.81	1.44	24.08	22.84	17.01	35.49	30.54
Simple and compound	13.96	18.91	18.50	85.85	26.24	1.44	24.08	5.74	2.41	35.49	23.26
Feathered	—	—	—	—	4.36	—	—	3.56	1.13	—	0.91
With crescentic superimposed	—	3.21	—	—	—	—	—	4.02	7.32	—	1.46
With stars superimposed	—	—	14.34	—	19.21	—	—	9.52	6.15	—	4.92
Crescentic (total)	54.29	36.91	11.80	0.59	14.91	27.01	28.37	33.34	14.53	19.17	24.09
Single barchanoid ridges	8.96	3.21	11.80	—	0.59	8.62	4.08	0.06	—	0.65	3.80
Megabarchans	—	—	—	—	—	—	—	7.18	1.98	—	0.92
Complex barchanoid ridges	16.65	33.70	—	—	14.32	18.39	24.29	26.10	12.55	18.52	16.45
Parabolics	28.68	—	—	0.59	—	—	—	—	—	—	2.93
Star dunes	—	—	9.92	—	5.34	2.87	—	7.92	23.92	—	5.00
Dome dunes	—	7.40	—	—	—	0.86	—	—	0.80	—	0.90
Sheets and streaks	31.75	33.56	45.44	13.56	23.24	67.82	47.54	35.92	39.25	45.34	38.34
Undifferentiated	—	—	—	—	6.71	—	—	—	4.50	—	1.12

shaped types (*barchans*) (figure 5.7(g)) through parallel rows of *barchanoid ridges* to essentially straight ridges known as *transverse dunes* (figure 5.7(j)). These dunes are all characterised by slip faces in one direction and represent unidirectional wind movement. Barchan dunes occur where sand supply is limited and transverse dunes where sand is abundant. *Dome* dunes normally show no obvious slip face and are circular or elliptical in plan view (figure 5.7(d)). They may result from strong winds that truncate the top and flatten the lee slopes of a barchan.

Figure 5.7 (above and over) Some of the main types of dune form encountered in the world's deserts: (a) obstacle or topographic dunes: (i) a small dune or nebkha in the low-velocity area to the lee of a shrub; (ii) a crescentic lunette formed to the lee of a small desert depression (playa); (iii) wind-shadow dunes formed in the lee of some hills; (iv) a dune formed to the windward of a hill; (v) dune development in the proximity of a plateau; (b) linear dunes, or seifs. The arrows show probable dominant winds; (c) star dunes. The arrows show effective wind directions; (d) dome dunes; (e) reversing dunes. Arrows show wind directions; (f) parabolic dunes. Arrow shows prevailing wind direction; (g) barchan dunes. Arrow shows prevailing wind direction; (h) barchanoid ridge. Arrow shows prevailing wind direction; (j) transverse dune. Arrow shows prevailing wind direction.

(f)

(g)

(h)

(j)

A class of dune in which the form owes much to the presence of a limited vegetation cover or some soil moisture is the *parabolic dune* (figure 5.7(f)). These are hairpin-shaped with the nose pointing downwind. They may occur in clusters creating rake-like forms.

Linear dunes, or *seifs*, are straightish ridges with slip faces on both sides that run more or less parallel to the wind (figure 5.7(b)). They are commonly 5–30 m high and occur as evenly spaced ridges 200–500 m apart. The ridges may extend for tens, or even hundreds, of kilometres and link together in tuning-fork-shaped junctions that almost invariably point downwind. They occur in areas where there is a seasonal or diurnal change in wind direction.

The regularity in form of many longitudinal dunes is also attributed to some regularity in the patterns of turbulence in the wind. It is possible that parallel corkscrew-type threads of flow within the trade winds, called *helical-roll vortices*, play a role (see figure 5.8).

If the winds come from many different direc-

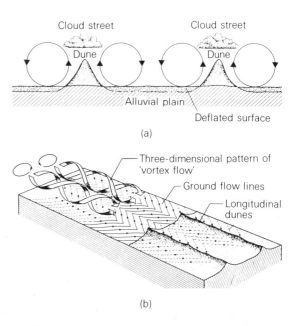

(a)

(b)

Figure 5.8 (above)   An interpretation of linear dune development in terms of the nature of air flow: (a) a two-dimensional illustration of roll vortices and associated dunes, deflational plains and cloud streets; (b) a three-dimensional illustration of the type of vortices in the trade winds which could produce regularly spaced and parallel longitudinal dunes.

tions, *star dunes* (or *rhourds*), with arms extending radially from a central peak, occur (figure 5.7(c)). These are up to 150 m high and between 1 and 2 km across. Intermediate in character between the star dune and a transverse ridge is the *reversing dune*, which characteristically forms where two winds from nearly opposite directions are balanced with respect to strength and direction (figure 5.7(e)).

Although we have discussed the major dune forms individually, in many situations it is apparent how one dune type can grade into or develop from another. The crescentic barchan can, by moving into an area with a different wind regime or sand supply, become deformed into a longitudinal *seif*. Likewise, the hairpin-shaped parabolic dune can gradually be elongated until a blowout occurs so that two longitudinal dunes are developed.

Even at the greatest scale of investigation – on a continental scale – dunes show a remarkable regularity of pattern. They tend to occur as a *wheel-round* or swirl in an anti-clockwise direction related to dominant continental wind patterns (figure 5.9).

5.11   The work of rivers

Although we have discussed the role of wind erosion and deposition in the arid environment at some length, present and past river action is also important in moulding desert landscapes. As we noted earlier, although rainfall quantities may be low overall, substantial falls may occur from time to time. Moreover, many desert surfaces have a number of characteristics that enable them to generate considerable runoff from quite low rainfall intensities. First, the limited vegetation cover provides little organic litter on the surface to absorb water. Second, the sparseness of vegetation means that humus levels in the soil are low, and this, combined with the minimal disturbance by plant roots and a greatly reduced soil fauna, makes the soil dense and compact in texture. Third, as there is virtually no plant cover to intercept the rainfall, rain is able to beat down on the soil surface with maximum force; and fine particles, unbound by vegetation, are redistributed by splash to lodge in pore-spaces and to create a puddled soil surface of reduced permeability. Stu-

Plate 5.10   The linear dunes of the inland Kalahari Desert in South West Africa are smaller than those of the Namib. They are often only a few tens of metres high. The road follows a depression between two parallel ridges.

Plate 5.11 This Landsat image of Algeria, North Africa, shows a large field of star dunes. The frame is about 180 km acros.

Figure 5.9 Regional patterns of dune trends to illustrate the characteristic wheel-round form: (a) Southern Africa; (b) Australia; (c) Arabia. See p. 128.

be subjected to large flows of water and sediment. Such flows, as one might expect from the character of desert rainfall, are sporadic in time and space. In the Sahara there is an average of one flood a year in the semi-arid parts, but in the more arid core some of the wadis may go ten years without carrying water. It is also common for any one stream to carry discharge along only a portion of its course, and floods often peter out because of losses from seepage and evaporation. When these streams flow they carry a considerable sediment load and can pose problems to roads – the flow may erode the road, while the sediment may clog culverts and the like.

A useful measure of geomorphological activity is sediment yield per unit area over a period of time (figure 5.10). This can be determined by such means as recording the quantity of sediment accumulation in reservoirs or measuring the amount of material carried by rivers. Studies suggest that in deserts, as rainfall rises from zero, yields of sediment increase rapidly because more and more runoff becomes available to move sediment; and yet there is still plenty of bare ground susceptible to rainwash erosion. However, as the amount of vegetation cover increases, sediment yields start to decline. Thus, while in extreme deserts sediment yields are very small, in semi-

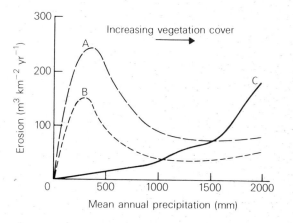

Figure 5.10 Sediment yield in relation to mean annual precipitation. A represents rates of erosion in high-relief situations. B represents rates of erosion in lower-relief situations, C represents rates of limestone solution. Rates of erosion appear to be at a maximum under semi-arid conditions, whereas rates of solution become high only under conditions of much more substantial rainfall.

dies in various areas have shown that, where such crusted and impermeable soils exist, the infiltration rate is only a few millimetres per hour, so that a rainfall rate in excess of this is likely to produce overland flow.

Desert stream channels or valleys are called *wadis*, and while they are normally dry they can arid areas they may be among the highest in the world. Moreover, many streams are so full of sediment that there are frequent occurrences of mudflows, in which solid matter may account for between 25 and 75 per cent of the flow. Such large sediment concentrations are important in the formation of alluvial fans, and can lead to rapid sedimentation behind engineering structures such as dams.

On desert margins, disturbance or removal of the vegetation cover by human activity can markedly increase the background natural rates of sediment yield. A study in Tanzania showed that soil loss was virtually nil under ungrazed thicket or grass but rose to 78 t ha^{-1} under millet, and to almost 146 t ha^{-1} under bare fallow (figure 5.11). There was a comparable increase in the amount of water lost by runoff, for water infiltration was far less under bare fallow conditions.

Because of the high runoff and sediment yields

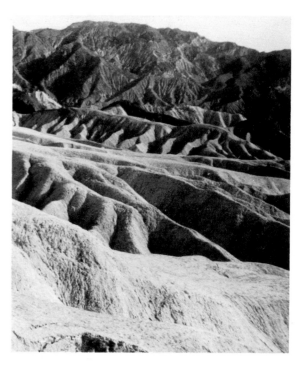

Plate 5.12 Even in the depths of Death Valley, California (mean annual rainfall only about 70 mm), the imprint of fluvial processes is clearly visible in this heavily dissected landscape. Some desert areas have exceptionally high drainage densities.

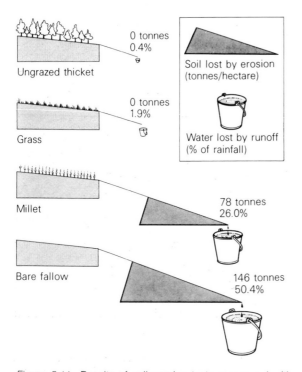

Figure 5.11 Results of soil erosion tests on ground with different vegetation covers in a semi-arid part of Tanzania. The grass-covered plots had little loss of soil and water, whereas rates of soil loss and runoff from bare fallow ground were very high.

from some desert surfaces, the imprint of water is often made clear through the development of a considerable degree of dissection or drainage density. On erodible rocks and sediments *badlands* may develop that have *drainage densities* (the total length of drainage line per unit area) between 10 and 20 times the average under humid climates. In parts of arid North America densities may be as high as 350 km km^{-2} compared with 2–8 km km^{-2} over most of Britain. However, in sandy areas in deserts, where surface conditions give a high infiltration rate and hence little runoff, drainage density will be low.

Drainage systems are not always very highly integrated. Much of the drainage, because of high evaporation or high infiltration losses into alluvial fans or aeolian materials, does not reach the sea, and because of the existence of closed basins (see section 5.9), much of the drainage may be *endoreic* (i.e. centripetal, flowing towards the centre). None the less, some desert rivers, including many of those that are of most use to man, such as the Nile, Tigris–Euphrates and Indus, have their sources outside the desert realm, and such *allogenic* or *exogenous* rivers may be through flowing and perennial.

A characteristic feature of desert drainage systems are *alluvial fans* (see figure 5.12(a)). These are cones of sediment that occur between the mountain front and a low-lying plain. Their size is variable – small ones may have a radius of only a few tens of metres while the large ones may be more than 20 km across and 300 m thick at the apex. They form where rivers emerge from their confined upper mountainous courses. At such a point the river can spread out, dissipating energy and decreasing its velocity, so that deposition of sediment occurs. They form most easily where there is a sharp juxtaposition of mountain and lowland, and for this some tectonic activity may be required, as in the basin and range province of the western United States. Moreover, fans derived from easily eroded rocks (such as shales) are larger than those derived from resistant rocks (such as quartzites). The types of flow that deposit the material comprising the fans vary from simple streamflows to highly viscous mud and debris flows. Because of the variability of flow regime and the variable nature of the material comprising the fans, they are subject to rapid changes in character, with channels shifting laterally over a wide area and alternately cutting and filling themselves. This presents problems for the establishment of transport links and buildings on fan surfaces.

5.12 Desert slopes

Slope profiles in arid areas, being little obscured by vegetation, are visually more dramatic than those of most humid regions and many workers have commented on their apparent angularity. Their form can be analysed in terms of an idealised slope profile (see figure 5.12(b)) with four components: an upper convexity (the waxing slope), a cliff (free face), a straight segment (constant slope), and a basal concavity (pediment). The pediment (see figure 5.12(c)) and the constant slope are often separated by an abrupt break of slope. The pediments may coalesce and cover extensive areas (called *pediplains*), and from them may rise isolated residual outliers

Figure 5.12 Some slope forms encountered in the desert environment: (a) an alluvial fan formed at the mountain front where a river (wadi) leaves a canyon; (b) the four main slope components of some arid profiles; (c) pediments and pediment passes around inselbergs in the Sacaton Mountains, Arizona.

called *buttes*, which possess one or both of the steep slope components.

The pediments consist of a gently sloping rock-cut surface, generally at an angle of between 1° and 7°, with a few lines of concentrated drainage and a thin veneer of rock detritus. An early explanation for them was that they were formed by sheets of water of high velocity (called *sheetfloods*) which planed down the surface. Such sheetfloods have been described from time to time, but the hypothesis suffers from the perennial problem of the chicken and the egg. Which came first, the pediment or the sheetflood? A second hypothesis sees pediments as having been shaped by lateral planation; that is, it is envisaged that streams flowing from the mountain front on to the plains would swing from side to side and gradually erode the surface. However, this explanation fails to account for pediments that directly abut the mountain front away from such swinging channels. A third hypothesis involves the role of surface and subsurface weathering. This is likely to be accentuated at the junction

Plate 5.14   Steep slopes developed by erosion of the Brule rocks of the Badlands of South Dakota, USA.

Plate 5.13   One of the classic landform assemblages of a desert area such as the Mojave Desert in California is the formation of pediments. There is a very sharp break in slope between them and the mountain front behind. Note the sparse vegetation cover.

between the mountain front and the plain because of the natural concentration of water there through percolation. The weathering will produce fine-grained material that can be removed, in the absence of a vegetation cover, by sheetfloods, wind and other processes.

Rising above the pediments there are often isolated steep-sided hills called *inselbergs*, formed as a result of gradual slope retreat produced by weathering and erosion at the break of slope. They occur in a wide variety of rock types including coarse sandstones (e.g. Ayers Rock in Australia) and granites. While not restricted to desert areas, such inselbergs, which may be over 600 m high, are spectacular landscape features in many deserts.

Whether desert slopes develop by parallel retreat to give pediplains and steep-sided residuals or evolve by gradual slope decline through time depends very much on rock type. This was demonstrated very clearly by a study that S. A. Schumm made in semi-arid Dakota, in the United States. In that area there are two sedimentary rock types occurring under identical climatic conditions, the Brule and the Chadron. The Brule had steep (44°) straight slopes, and erosion had produced outliers with a similar slope profile. By contrast, the Chadron had rounded slopes with broad interfluves, and residuals had lower slope angles than the scarp from which they had become detached by erosion. The explanation for this can be seen in terms of the processes operating on the two different rock types. Because it had a low infiltration capacity, the Brule was characterised by surface wash and so the steep slopes were produced by stream incision. The Chadron produced a surface of clay aggregates with an open texture which had a much higher infiltration capacity, and so the creep of the clay aggregates when saturated with moisture was the main slope-forming process.

5.13 Groundwater

Because of the low rainfalls and the general absence of perennial rivers (with the exception of the great exogenous rivers like the Nile), groundwater is often especially important if arid areas are to be exploited.

Groundwater occurs underground in the rocks and sediments, in zones termed *aquifers*. Such aquifers may have been charged with water either by occasional storms or during pluvials, when arid zones were less extensive than now, or because they extend into presently relatively humid areas. In permeable rocks like the Nubian sandstone of the Sahara, large quantities of water may be involved, and if the arrangement of the strata is favourable artesian flow may occur (see section 13.7). Sand dunes and wadi gravels, both being highly permeable, may also be useful sources of groundwater. Indeed, this is the explanation for some oases in the middle of an erg. When it rains the water infiltrates rapidly into the dune sand and, provided the underlying platform is more or less impermeable, the water accumulates in a dome shape. Lateral seepage from the dunes may be sufficient to water some palm trees. In a similar manner coastal dunes along the shores of the Arabian Gulf have been favoured sites for settlement.

However, groundwater resources are neither infinite nor endlessly exploitable without certain problems. First, as some of them are fossil, having been created in pluvial phases, over-pumping may cause their rapid depletion. In parts of the high plains of Texas, water levels have fallen 50 m in 40 years. Second, some of them are too saline to be used for many purposes (see table 5.3). Third, over-pumping in coastal areas may cause saltwater from the sea to intrude. The reason for this is that freshwater has a lower density than saltwater, so that a column of seawater can support a column of freshwater; if the freshwater is pumped away too quickly, saltwater rapidly rises to replace it from beneath. Fourth, by pumping out groundwater from the pores of rocks, some subsidence of the ground surface may result, creating engineering problems. In Mexico City 7.5 m of subsidence has occurred (equivalent to a rate of $250-300$ mm yr^{-1}) and in the Central Valley of California, 8.5 m.

Groundwater resources are being exploited at an ever increasing tempo. This is partly because of the availability in the last two or three decades of new means of groundwater exploitation for

Table 5.3 Water salinity characteristics

Nature of water use	Concentration of salts (ppm TDS[a])
Sea water	35 000
Maximum potable level for man	3000
Recommended potable level for man	Less than 500–750
Domestic animals of desert	Less than 15 000; extreme 25 000
Irrigation water (assuming optimum soil and drainage conditions)	Less than 750; no salinity risk
	750–1500; restricted yields of very sensitive crops
	1500–3500; restricted yield of many crops
	3500–6500; salt-tolerant crops only
	6500–8000; restricted yield of salt-tolerant crops

[a] Total dissolved solids.

irrigation purposes. Especially notable in this context is the adoption of a technique called centre-pivot irrigation, which is achieved by pumping water up a borehole and then distributing it across the land by means of a huge revolving boom equipped with sprinklers.

5.14 Dams and reservoirs

Besides exploiting groundwater by drilling deep boreholes, man can improve water supplies in arid areas by damming rivers. Indeed, the first recorded dam was built in Egypt some 5000 years ago to enable irrigation to take place. Since then

the numbers and size of dams has increased dramatically: they control floods, reduce the threat of famine and provide electricity.

However, dams have a whole series of environmental consequences that may or may not have been anticipated (figure 5.13). They trap sediment, which leads to a reduction in the sediment load of the river downstream. This in turn, as is the case with the Aswan Dam on the Nile, may reduce the amount of flood-deposited nutrients on the fields, provide less nutrients for fish in the south-east Mediterranean Sea, and cause coast and riverbed erosion because less sediment is available to cause accretion. The weight of water

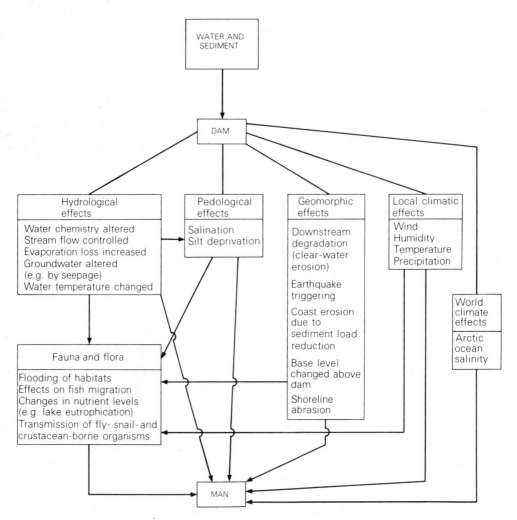

Figure 5.13 Some of the consequences of dam construction on the environment.

Plate 5.15 The round field produced by a centre-pivot irrigation system near Port Elizabeth in South Africa. Similar fields, which are often several hundreds of metres in radius, are also a major feature of land use in the western United States.

in the reservoir behind the dam may accelerate earthquake activity by depressing the earth's crust; seepage from the reservoir and from canals may cause a build-up of salinity; local climates may change; the diversion of river flow may change salinity in the seas, which in turn may affect their ice cover and affect world climate; water-borne diseases may be more widely transmitted; and the migration of fish may be disturbed.

5.15 Desertification

The problems associated with dams and reservoirs provide an indication that desert environments may be very difficult to develop without unfortunate environmental consequences. In recent years the fear has been expressed that human actions may even be leading to the spread of desert-like conditions – a process termed *desertification* or *desertisation*. Not everyone is agreed as to the cause of the spread of desert-like conditions, and the question has been asked whether this process is caused by temporary drought periods of high magnitude, is due to a longer-term climatic change towards aridity, is caused by man-induced climatic change, or is the result of human action through man's degradation of the biological environments in arid zones. Most people now believe that it is produced by a combination of increasing human and animal population levels, which causes the effects of drought years to become progressively more severe, so that the vegetation is placed under severe stress – by overgrazing, by cultivation of marginal areas, by burning shrub vegetation to increase the area of pasture, and by collection of wood for fuel. The removal of vegetation sets in train the operation of such insidious processes as deflation and water

Plate 5.16 Overgrazing by cattle and goats near Baringo in Kenya has lowered the ground surface to such an extent that tree roots have been exposed. This type of erosion is one component of the desertification problem.

Plate 5.17 Overgrazing in sandy areas, as around a well in southern Botswana, can cause dunes to become active. Virtually all ground cover has been removed by domestic animals.

erosion. These further reduce the utility of the available land.

5.16   Problems of the desert realm

Although deserts cover one-third of the earth's surface, they are generally hostile environments for man, and they are easily degraded. Some of the problems they present are as follows.

Sand encroachment on roads, etc.
Wind erosion of soils
Dust storms
Salinity
    Weathering of buildings
    Reduction of soil quality
    Restriction of plant growth
Floods
Debris flows
Siltation of dams
Dams
    Silt depletion downstream

Earthquakes
Salinity build-up
Disease transmission
Climatic change
Groundwater extraction
Subsidence
Saltwater incursion
Climate
Smog (produced by sunlight and inversion)
Extreme heat

Very low humidity

Although spectacular advances in desert utilisation may occur in some of the developed countries and the new oil-rich states of the Middle East (because they have money to invest in long-term research and in projects of dubious short-term economic value), much of the world's desert areas will remain relatively untouched wilderness areas for decades to come.

6 The Tropics

6.1 The general atmospheric circulation

The tropics do not constitute one uniform environmental type. Within the zone bounded by the Tropics of Cancer and Capricorn there is a wide range of climatic, vegetational, topographic and pedological characteristics. There are, for instance, rainforests, grasslands, mangroves, corals, mountains, plains, and while some areas teem with human populations others are almost uninhabited. They are all linked, however, by the fact that as a rule they receive much more solar radiation throughout the year than other zones.

Indeed, one of the main functions of the general atmospheric circulation in the tropics is to dissipate to other parts of the globe the surplus heat energy supplied to low latitudes by solar radiation. According to the simple cell model, proposed as early as 1735 by G. Hadley, the heated air from the equatorial regions rises; the air masses are then transported to higher latitudes by upper air currents, sometimes called the *antitrades*, which gradually slow down at about 20°–30° latitude. At that latitude subsidence of the air takes place, resulting in an area of relatively high pressure – the subtropical highs. The *Hadley cell* is closed by a massive air stream called the trade winds moving at low levels towards the Equator. The two trade wind systems coverge in an area of low pressure called either the *equatorial trough* or the Intertropical Convergence Zone (ITCZ). Although this model has certain deficiencies and is rather over-simplified, it none the less presents a reasonably accurate picture of the main air movements over the tropical oceans (see section 2.2).

During the course of a year, the ITCZ migrates north and south following the sun, though the latitudinal extent of the migration is normally only a few degrees, except for over the Indian Ocean, where it may amount to 30 degrees of latitude – an important consideration in explaining the great Indian monsoon (see section 6.5). The ITCZ is characterised by relatively low surface pressure, rising air movement and a convergence of air masses. Wind speeds are generally low and of variable direction, and are sometimes called the 'doldrums'.

6.2 Trade winds

Between the subtropical highs and the ITCZ, the low-level general circulation is dominated by strong and persistent easterly winds called the *trades*. They cover about 20° of latitude in the summer hemisphere and approximately 30° in the winter hemisphere.

Usually three distinct layers are identified in them. The general direction of the *lower trades* is east-north-east (ENE) in the Northern Hemisphere and ESE in the Southern Hemisphere, and they often show a remarkable constancy of direction. They are limited to elevations of about 500 m near the subtropical highs, but near the ITCZ they can reach levels as high as *c*.2500 m. This is therefore a shallow layer, and so the short cumulus clouds rarely produce much precipitation.

Over the lower trades lies the important *tradewind inversion layer*, in which the temperature increases with elevation at a rate of about 1°C/100m. The main effect of this inversion is that it acts as an efficient lid, which prevents all upward movements of the air and thus dampens down convectional precipitation. It disappears when convergence prevails, as near the ITCZ.

Above the inversion are the *upper trades*,

which are low-velocity westerly winds that may reach elevations between 6000 and 10 000 m.

6.3 The wet tropics

The wet tropics characterise almost 10 per cent of the earth's land area and form a discontinuous belt that typically extends 5–10 degrees of latitude into each hemisphere. They tend to have a greater latitudinal extent along the eastern side of continents (especially South America) and along some tropical coasts. This is due primarily to the windward position of these areas on the weak western side of the subtropical high, a zone dominated by neutral or stable air – western coasts often have cold offshore currents and zones of upwelling that cause precipitation levels to be low.

The wet tropics have temperatures that usually average 25°C or more each month, and have both high annual means and small annual ranges. Since these areas lie so close to the Equator, the vertical rays of the sun are always relatively close and changes in the length of daylight throughout the year are slight: hence seasonal temperature variation is minimal. Daily temperature variations greatly exceed seasonal differences, so that while annual temperature ranges in the wet tropics rarely exceed 3°C, daily temperature ranges are two to five times greater than this. The temperatures tend not to reach the very high absolute levels that may occur in some extra-tropical areas – the highest temperatures recorded in New York (40°C) are higher than those recorded in equatorial stations like Djakarta in Indonesia and Belém in Brazil.

The wet tropics generally receive from 1750 to 2500 mm of rainfall per year, though topographic differences cause considerable variability. The high rainfall levels are in part the result of thermal convection caused by the extensive heating of the zone, and of converging winds associated with the widespread ascent of warm, humid, unstable air. Completely cloudless days are rare, and cloudiness averages 50–60 per cent. On average, there are 75–100 days with thunderstorms in the course of a year, and the number of rain-days is large (e.g. Belém in Brazil has 243 a year). In some core areas like the western Amazon Basin and the innermost Congo Basin there

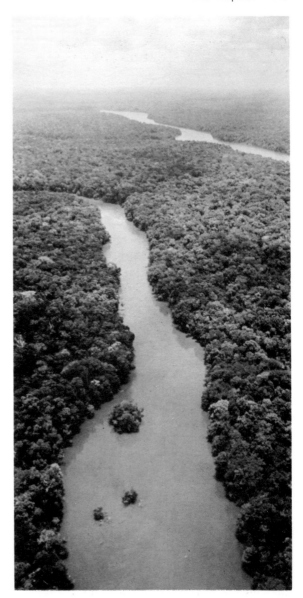

Plate 6.1 The wet tropics are characterised by rain forest. The largest area of such rain forest occurs in the Amazon basin of Brazil. The Rio Branco here threads through an almost unbroken stand.

may be no dry months at all, but more generally there is a brief dry season of one, or at most two, months' duration.

The rainfall in the tropics is of high intensity, which has great implications for landform development and soil erosion, particularly if the protective covers afforded by the canopy of the

Table 6.1 Rainfall intensity, represented as annual mean rainfall per rain-day

Table 6.1 Rainfall intensity, represented as annual mean rainfall per rain-day

	mm
Hong Kong	21.2
Djakarta (Indonesia)	13.5
Rangoon (Burma)	20.9
Calcutta (India)	15.5
Bombay (India)	22.4
Entebbe (Uganda)	12.4
Lagos (Nigeria)	14.4
Accra (Ghana)	13.6
Georgetown (Guyana)	13.3
Quito (Ecuador)	8.5
San Salvador (El Salvador)	16.1
San Juan (Puerto Rico)	10.1
MEAN	15.2

rainforest are removed (table 6.1). Annual values of rainfall per rain-day for humid temperate stations like London are between 4 and 6 mm; the mean value for the tropical stations listed is 15.2 mm, about three times as much.

6.4   Tropical seasonal climates

In between the wet tropics and the great subtropical deserts is a belt of climate where there is usually a smaller total precipitation and one that is much more seasonal than in the wet tropics. This is a zone in which the natural vegetation tends towards savanna rather than rainforest. During the course of a year, with the north–south shifting of the solar radiation belts and the consequent latitudinal displacement of pressure and wind, this belt is alternately affected by the wet ITCZ and equatorial westerlies (in summer) and by the drier parts of the trades and subtropical anticyclones (in winter).

The annual temperature range, while higher than that in the wet tropics, is still rather low and seldom exceeds 8°. During the rainy season of the summer months the diurnal range is also low, but in the dry season it is likely to be higher. Frequently the hottest months do not coincide with the time of highest sun but somewhat precede it, for during the rainy season persistent cloud cover and heavier precipitation tend to lower the air temperature (table 6.2).

It is the seasonal distribution of precipitation that makes this zone distinct, and the seasonal contrast is particularly clear in the case of those areas subject to the influence of the monsoons.

6.5   Monsoons

For centuries it has been known that in some low-latitude areas there is a summer and winter reversal of winds accompanied by a distinct seasonal change in rainfall – the wind from one direction being humid, unstable and conducive to rainfall, and from the other direction being stable and dry. South Asia has the classic example of a monsoon, or seasonal wind reversal, and it is notable for the suddenness with which the onset (*burst*) of the rainy season takes place. However, monsoons also occur elsewhere, notably on Equator-facing coasts between 5° and 25° from the Equator; they are also encountered along the Guinea coast of West Africa, the northern coast

Table 6.2 Representative climatic data, tropical climates

	Year	J	F	M	A	M	J	J	A	S	O	N	D
Tropical wet climates													
Singapore (1°18′ N)													
Temperature (°C)	27	26	27	27	27	28	27	27	27	27	27	27	27
Precipitation (mm)	2413	252	172	193	188	172	172	170	196	178	208	254	257
Belém, Amazon Valley, Brazil (1°18′ S)													
Temperature (°C)	26	25	25	25	25	26	26	26	26	26	26	26	26
Precipitation (mm)	2743	340	406	437	343	287	175	145	127	120	91	89	175
Tropical wet-and-dry climates													
Calcutta, India (23° N)													
Temperature (°C)	26	18	21	26	29	30	29	28	28	28	27	22	18
Precipitation (mm)	1494	10	28	35	51	127	284	308	292	229	110	13	5
Normanton, Australia (18° S)													
Temperature (°C)	27	30	29	29	28	26	23	22	24	27	29	31	31
Precipitation (mm)	952	277	254	155	38	8	10	5	3	3	10	45	142

of Australia, and to a degree along the Gulf Coast of the United States and the east coast of Asia.

The traditional explanation for the Indian monsoon is that it is essentially a giant land-sea breeze system caused by seasonal contrasts in temperature between the land masses and the oceans. These temperature differences, which are especially marked in the case of Asia because of its enormous mass, affect the seasonal movement of pressure and winds. Over the oceans the seasonal shifts of heat and pressure zones are rather small, in keeping with the similarly small annual temperature changes. Over land, by contrast, where temperature variations are larger, the movement of the heat and pressure zones is exaggerated. This shows up in the summer and winter movement of the ITCZ, which over India in summer occurs more than 30° away from the Equator. This extreme position is associated with the large temperatures in the continental interior, which create rising air and low pressure, thereby drawing the ITCZ away from the Equator and giving south-westerly winds.

However, this simple thermal explanation of the seasonal wind reversal needs to be supplemented by a consideration of the role of upper air conditions, for these help to explain the sudden burst and the extreme seasonal contrast that are such features of the Indian monsoon.

The breaking of the monsoon is now related to the shifting of the mid-latitude jet stream. Anticyclonic conditions and subsiding air are normally found on the earth surface a short distance equatorward of the position immediately below the jet. It has been suggested that in winter the jet runs southwards of the great topographic barrier formed by the mountains and high plateaus of Tibet and neighbouring areas. This induces a subtropical anticyclonic cell of dry subsiding air over northern-central India, and divergence of air from this centre gives the oceanward winter monsoon. However, as the winter season recedes the jet stream slowly moves northwards until it is quickly diverted to the north side of the topographic barrier.

6.6 Tropical disturbances

In comparison with disturbances of the higher latitudes (see chapter 4), those of the tropics show two major differences. First, there is an almost complete absence of the fronts so typical of the mid-latitude depressions, for in the tropics the differences in temperature between two air masses are usually so small that no clear front develops. Second, the Coriolis Force has a lower strength close to the Equator, and this means that most disturbances in very low latitudes are of shorter duration or lower intensity than those of the higher latitudes.

The main prerequisite for the formation of tropical disturbances is the presence of warm and humid air masses in which no inversion exists. This type of air is potentially unstable, and any upward movement will be reinforced by the release of large amounts of latent heat of condensation. Uplift may be caused by heating from the earth's surface (convection), and convectional cells may turn into *thunderstorms*, the smallest and most frequent form of tropical disturbance (figure 6.1). Uplift can also result from the convergence of two air masses, for when this occurs

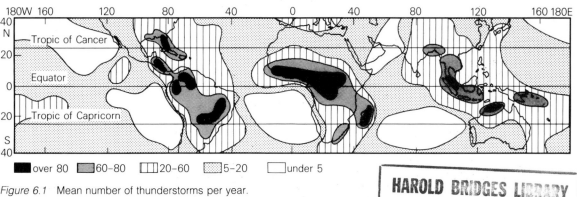

Figure 6.1   Mean number of thunderstorms per year.

there is no way for the air to go but upward, and so once again thunderstorms may occur, arranged in bands called 'linear systems'. The effects of convergence at low levels in the atmosphere will be accentuated if there is divergence aloft. An upper tropospheric high-pressure area, which creates a general outflow of air, can cause upward movement of air and instability at lower levels. Upward movements of air are also related to the topographic features of the earth's surface – for example, air may be forced upwards over mountains, hills and coastlines.

Some disturbances that occur in the tropics have their origins outside this zone, for depressions from the polar front region of mid-latitudes may occasionally venture far towards the Equator, and then regenerate when meeting warm and humid air masses.

Monsoon depressions

Another type of tropical disturbance is the monsoon depression (figure 6.2(a)). These are closed isobaric low-pressure systems with a diameter of the order of 500–1000 km. They occur at the rate of about three per month in the Asian summer monsoon, and they develop over the Bay of Bengal and, to a lesser extent, over the Arabian Sea. Convergence in the westerly monsoon current near the surface combined with divergent easterlies aloft initiate an upward air movement, which becomes intensified into a large low-pressure area because of the release of large amounts of latent heat.

Linear systems (squall lines)

Linear systems or squall lines consist of lines or bands of thunderstorms; they can be hundreds of kilometres long and 10–30 km wide. They result from convergence, for instance when local land and sea breezes from different islands meet, as they often do in south-east Asia.

Wave disturbances

The trades and the equatorial easterlies of the central Pacific develop rain-giving perturbations that are quite unlike the depressions of mid-latitudes. They take the form of wave troughs,

which are scarcely detectable in the surface pressure field, and are about half the size of a mid-latitude depression. The air in front of the trough diverges and is characterised by descen-

(a)

(b)

Figure 6.2 Some types of atmospheric perturbation in the tropics: (a) an example of a monsoon depression over the Bay of Bengal, 1000 mbar contours in decimetres for 1200 hrs GMT on 20 August 1967; the hatched area represents the zone of continuous rainfall; (b) an easterly wave in the Caribbean area; the hatched area indicates the main rainfall zone.

ding drying air, while the air behind the trough converges. This convergence creates instability, so that heavy cumulo-nimbus and cumulus clouds develop that produce moderate or heavy thundery showers. As these waves move with the easterlies they are generally called *easterly waves* (figure 6.2 (b)).

The main areas in which these waves occur are the western edges of the large ocean basins, in latitudes between 5° and 20°. They are best known in the Caribbean but also occur in the Pacific. In the former area during the late summer they come as often as every 3–5 days and in the latter, every 2–3 days. They tend to move at about 15–20 km h^{-1} and bring substantial quantities of rain. Some of them occasionally develop into the much more hazardous tropical cyclones.

Tropical cyclones

Tropical cyclones are closed low-pressure systems, generally about 650 km in diameter, which bring violent winds, torrential rainfall and thunderstorms. They usually contain a central region, the *eye*, with a diameter of some tens of kilometres and with light winds and more or less lightly clouded sky. They are given a variety of regional names, including 'hurricane' (West Indies), 'typhoon' (China Sea), 'willy willy' (Australia) and 'cyclone' (Bay of Bengal).

In order for cyclones to develop various conditions need to be fulfilled. First, there must be a plentiful supply of moisture, and for this reason distribution of cyclones is closely related to those regions where the highest sea-surface temperatures are found (i.e. the western portions of the tropical oceans in late summer), with temperatures of at least 27°C. This moisture provides the necessary latent heat to drive the storm and to provide the rainfall. Tropical cyclones tend to occur mainly within this zone (figure 6.3), and when they leave it or pass over land their violence is rapidly dissipated. They also tend to occur only in areas beyond about 5° from the Equator, because closer than that to the Equator the Coriolis parameter approaches zero. The main cyclone activity in the Northern Hemisphere is in late summer and autumn during the time of the equatorial trough's northern displacement.

Early theories of cyclone development held that convection cells generated a sudden and enormous release of latent heat to provide energy for the storm, but it is now believed that cyclones develop from pre-existing disturbances such as easterly waves. Most disturbances, however, do not lead to such cyclones, and it seems that the presence of an anticyclone in the upper troposphere is another necessary precondition. This is essential for high-level outflow, which in turn allows the development of very low pressure and high wind speeds near the surface.

Generally, tropical cyclones have a life span of about one week, and in that time they can wreak havoc because of the high winds that they bring, the high rainfall levels that they can produce (values of over 2000 mm per day have been recorded in the Philippines), and because the very low atmospheric pressures with which they are

Figure 6.3 The distribution, frequency and movement of tropical cyclones (hurricanes). Encircled numbers indicate approximate number in each area per year.

Table 6.3 Damage caused by natural hazards in Japan, 1946–70

Phenomenon	No. of events	Deaths	Houses destroyed
Typhoon	59	13 745	576 378
Extra-tropical cyclone	89	8156	65 818
Earthquake	11	5490	113 339
Landslide	5	86	143
Hail + thunderstorm	4	28	847
Heavy snow	2	242	1734
Volcanic eruption	1	12	12

Source: modified after data in J. B. Whittow, Disasters (Harmondsworth: Penguin, 1980).

associated can cause sea levels to be unusually high. The width or diameter of the destructive winds of tropical cyclones is variable. The average-sized hurricane probably produces hurricane winds (winds of more than 119 km h^{-1}) over about 160 km, but more extreme values than this are known. The 'Labor Day Hurricane' that struck the Florida Keys in the United States in 1935 probably achieved wind speeds of 320–400 km h^{-1}.

As a result of the high tidal surges, high rainfall levels and high wind velocities with which they are associated, hurricanes are one of the most serious natural hazards in low latitudes, particularly in low-lying coastal areas. A Bay of Bengal cyclone in 1970 killed somewhere between 300 000 and 1 000 000 people in Bangladesh and India – people who lived on the overcrowded and storm-prone Ganges Delta. In Japan cyclones or typhoons are the most dangerous of the natural hazards with which the population has to contend (see table 6.3), more serious even than earthquakes. Although Japan itself lies outside the tropics, many of these storms are derived from lower latitudes.

6.7 Tropical rainforest

In the wet tropics (figure 6.4) the dominant form of vegetation is the tropical rainforest – the most luxuriant of all vegetation types. There are three main formations: the American formation (which has its most massive development in the Amazon Basin), the African formation (largely in the Cameroons and the Congo Basin) and the Indo-Malaysian formations of the Far East and north-

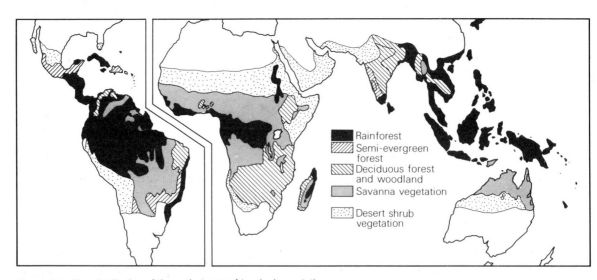

Figure 6.4 The distribution of the main types of tropical vegetation.

Plate 6.2 Some rain forest trees, like this *Ficus* from Amazonia, display enormous buttress roots.

ern Australia. Although there are differences in species between the three formations, certain features of this vegetation type are fairly general:

(a) The trees are nearly all evergreens, and the vast majority cast their old leaves and grow new ones continuously and simultaneously; they are rarely leafless.

(b) Most of the trees have leathery, dark green leaves similar in shape and size to the ones that are typical in the Laurel family. Particularly in the lower storeys of the forest leaves may have 'drip tips' – devices that may have evolved for shedding heavy rain (figure 6.5(a)).

(c) Many trees have either buttress roots or stilt roots (figure 6.5(b)). These may give stability to very tall trees, but their precise function is not always clear.

(d) The trunks of many rain forest trees bear flowers and fruit – a habit called 'cauliflory'.

(e) Climbers, including lianas, are large and numerous and some are said to attain lengths of over 200 m.

(f) The forest contains large numbers of *epiphytes*. These are plants that grow attached to the trunks, branches and even the leaves of trees, shrubs and lianas. Some epiphytes send down roots to the soil and may eventually kill the tree that originally supported them – these are called 'stranglers'.

(g) In the better illuminated areas of the forest floor there are normal herbaceous plants, but in areas of great darkness some plants called *saprophytes* manage, with the help of certain fungi, to grow without the necessity for photosynthesis.

(h) Away from clearings, river banks, etc., a shrub layer is ill-developed and the ground is almost bare of low-growing plants because of a shortage of light.

(i) The trees may exceed 60–90 m in height, but the taller trees rarely average more than *c*.50 m. They are in general taller than those in temperate forests, but they never

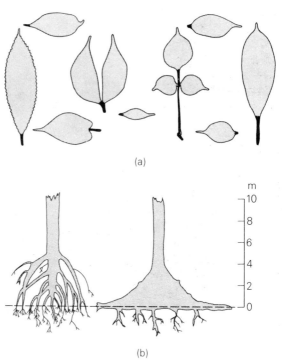

Figure 6.5 Some features of tropical plants: (a) various shapes of leaves with conspicuously differentiated drip-tips; (b) stilt roots of *Uapaca* sp. (left) and heavy buttresses of *Piptadeniastrum africanum* (right).

reach the gigantic dimensions of the Californian redwoods or the huge *eucalyptus* of Australia.

(j) In a European or North American forest the dominant trees belong to a few, or often only a single, species; whereas in the tropical rainforest there are seldom less than 40 species of tree over 10 cm in diameter per hectare, and sometimes over 100 species.

(k) Overall, the rainforest has a very diverse flora, especially in the Indo-Malaysian area. Malaysia has about 7900 species and 1500 genera of seed plants, whereas the British Isles, with an area about 2.3 times greater, has 1430 species and 628 genera.

A great increase in the diversity of species takes place from the poles to the tropics. This tendency can be traced in a wide variety of groups (figure 6.6), which include molluscs, ants, lizards and birds. The pattern can be seen, moreover, in marine, freshwater and terrestrial habitats, and both in small communities and over extensive geographical regions. A single hectare of humid tropical moist forest may, for example, contain 40–100 different species of trees, while comparable areas of deciduous forest in eastern North America may have 10–30, and coniferous forests in the far north of Canada only 1–5 tree species. There are exceptions to this general trend (e.g. arid areas or islands near the tropics may have relatively few species), but overall the great rich-

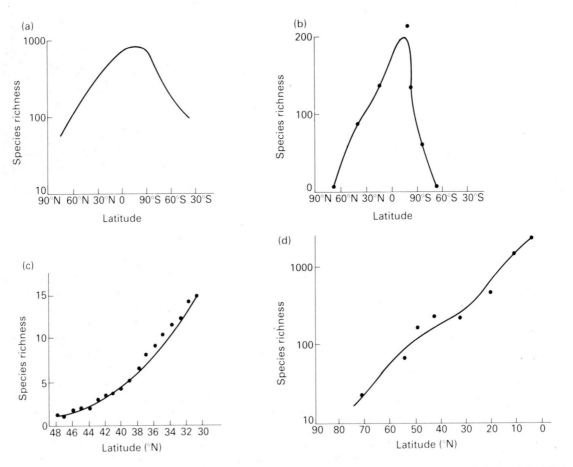

Figure 6.6 Latitudinal patterns in species richness of: (a) marine bivalve molluscs; (b) ants; (c) lizards in the United States; (d) breeding birds in North and Central America.

ness of species in the humid tropics is one of their most important characteristics, even if there is as yet no fully acceptable explanation.

The vertical structure of the tropical rainforest has been described and represented by profile diagrams in many works, but there is considerable debate as to whether it consists of distinct layers or strata. The traditional view is that there are five recognisable above-ground strata:

(a) the upper tree layer of convergent trees (> 25 m);
(b) the middle tree layer (10–25 m);
(c) the lower tree layer (5–10 m);
(d) the shrub layer;
(e) the herb layer.

However, we must remember that the rainforest canopy is constantly changing as individual trees pass through their life-cycles.

The biomass of the rainforest may be around 1100 t ha^{-1}. The huge mass of leaves carried by the trees provides a massive litter fall (11 t ha^{-1}yr^{-1}), yet soil humus reserves and surface litter accumulations are usually small except in lowland swamps or in upland (*montane*) forests (section 7.4). This is because, in general, the litter is destroyed more rapidly than it is supplied. As humus turnover is about 1 per cent per day, there is little chance of it accumulating on the surface. The litter is rapidly decomposed with the help of fungi and other micro-organisms, and its nutrients are rapidly returned by a dense shallow root network to the trees. Thus there is a huge circulation of nutrients – but they are essentially cycled within the vegetation rather than into the soil, so that many of the soils of the rainforest, in spite of the luxuriance of the vegetation they appear to support, are actually highly infertile.

Indeed, because so many of the nutrients are tied up in the vegetation rather than in the soil, the removal of the rainforest can lead to very serious impoverishment of the soil. Traditional farming systems involving slash-and-burn recognise this. The forest is cleared by burning and cutting, and this releases nutrients in the soil. But under conditions of rapid breakdown and rapid leaching combined with high rainfall, the fertility does not last long, and so the farmers move on, allowing the cleared area to become revegetated

Plate 6.3 Large areas of rain forest in countries like Nicaragua are being removed by slash-and-burn agriculturalists.

by secondary forest. In other words, there is an extended period of fallow. Unfortunately, as population pressures increase there is sometimes insufficient land available for such an extensive means of land use, and so the fallow period becomes reduced, with unfortunate long-term implications for soil fertility (figure 6.7).

Not all soils in the humid tropics, however, are so low in nutrients. On ancient, stable land surfaces, topographic stability, combined with the hot, wet climate, has led to very deep and thorough weathering and leaching of underlying rocks. Moreover, although some underlying rocks, like quartzites, may have been low in nutrients before they were so extensively weathered, there are areas where recent geological activity –

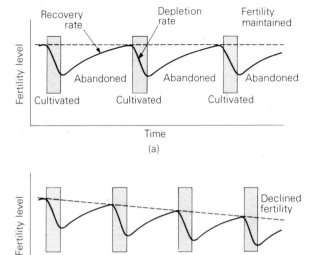

Figure 6.7 Land rotation and population density. The graphs show the relationship of soil fertility to cycles of slash-and-burn agriculture. In (a) fertility levels are maintained under the long cycles characteristic of low density populations. In (b) fertility levels are declining under the shorter cycles characteristic of increasing human population density. Notice that in both diagrams the curves of both depletion and recovery have the same slope.

volcanism, erosion or delta and alluvium deposition – has provided areas of nutrient-rich soils. Thus some of the great deltaic and volcanic areas of south-east Asia have supported dense human agricultural populations for centuries.

Population pressure is not the only cause of the removal of the rainforest: commercial ranching, logging and the like are also making increasing

inroads. Already it is estimated that something like 40 per cent of the world's rainforests have been removed, though West Africa has lost 72 per cent and south-east Asia, 63.5 per cent.

Future forest extents are difficult to assess with any degree of accuracy. The *Global 2000 Report to the President* forecasts that in the year 2000 the Amazon Forest will cover less than half the area it does now, and that the area of rainforest in Africa will be reduced by a further 28 per cent.

Because the rainforests are so immensely diverse and rich in their species, both faunal and floral, their wholesale removal will cause severe declines in numbers. The *Global 2000 Report* envisages the extinction of somewhere between 249 000 and 1 250 000 species as a result of rainforest deforestation by the turn of the century. This is around 57–66 per cent of the world total, and is a matter of widespread concern, for the value of the rainforests is immeasurable. They provide a potential source of foods, drinks, medicines, contraceptives, gums, resins, scents, colourants and pesticides, to name but some.

Another major change that results from deforestation is the physical erosion of the soil. Forest cover intercepts the intense, torrential rainfall of tropical storms and protects and binds the soil. As deforestation occurs the percentage of rainfall that becomes runoff is increased. Thus rivers become choked with sediment derived from erosion and transported by runoff and are rendered more prone to floods. An indication of how rates of tropical runoff and erosion increase after vegetation removal is given in table 6.4. The five studies from different parts of Africa indicate that under forest the annual runoff in rivers as a percentage of the mean annual rainfall is a mere 0.9

Table 6.4   Runoff and erosion under various covers of vegetation in parts of Africa

Locality	Average annual rainfall (mm)	Slope (%)	Annual runoff (%)[a] A	B	C	Erosion (t ha^{-1} yr^{-1})[a] A	B	C
Ouagadougou (Upper Volta)	850	0.5	2.5	2–32	40–60	0.1	0.6–0.8	10–20
Sefa (Senegal)	1300	1.2	1.0	21.2	39.5	0.2	7.3	21.3
Bouake (Ivory Coast)	1200	4.0	0.3	0.1–26	15–30	0.1	1–266	18–30
Abidjan (Ivory Coast)	2100	7.0	0.1	0.5–20	38	0.03	0.1–90	108–170
Mpwapwa* (Tanzania)	c.570	6.0	0.4	26.0;	50.4	0	78	146
MEAN VALUES			0.9	17.4	40.1	0.09	28.8	69.1

[a] A = forest or ungrazed thicket; B = crop; C = barren soil.

Plate 6.4 Areas that have been cleared for slash-and-burn agriculture in Sri Lanka typically have a few forest trees remaining, but large numbers of species may be being lost.

per cent, whereas under crops this rises to 17.4 per cent, and under bare soil conditions to over 40 per cent. The erosion rates go up in a comparable manner. Under forest they are minimal (0.09 ha^{-1}yr^{-1}), whereas under crops they go up by 320 times to 28.8 ha^{-1}yr^{-1}, and under bare soil conditions they go up 768 times, to 69.1 ha^{-1}yr^{-1}.

Removal of rainforest may have some more general world-wide implications, notably for world climate through its effect on atmospheric carbon dioxide levels. These levels in the atmosphere have an effect on the heat balance, since CO_2 is virtually transparent to incoming solar radiation but absorbs outgoing terrestrial infrared radiation – radiation that would otherwise escape to space and result in loss of heat from the lower atmosphere. Because of this 'greenhouse effect' one would expect increased CO_2 levels to lead to an increase in surface temperatures (figure 6.8). It is argued that tropical forests, because of their huge biomass and great areal extent, contain

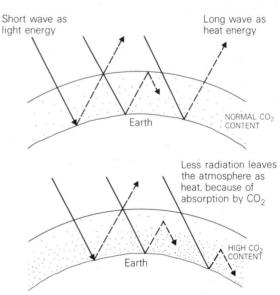

Figure 6.8 The greenhouse effect: short-wave radiation strikes the earth's surface and is transformed into long-wave radiation (heat). Since CO_2 absorbs long-wave radiation, the greater the atmospheric CO_2 content, the more heat is retained and the warmer the atmosphere becomes.

large amounts of carbon, and that if they are cut down this will be released in significant quantities into the atmosphere as CO_2. If this argument is correct, then deforestation, in combination with the release of CO_2 by the burning of fossil fuels such as oil and coal, could lead to an increase in world temperature levels of a few degrees in the next century or so, which in turn will cause some melting of ice caps and flooding of low-lying coastal areas because of the resulting rise in sea level.

6.8   Secondary forest

Because of the various pressures exerted on the rainforest by human activity increasingly large areas of the humid tropics are characterised not by true rainforest but by *secondary rainforest*. When an area of rainforest has been cleared, either for cultivation or for timber exploitation, and is then abandoned, the forest begins to re-generate; but for an extended period of years the type of forest that occurs – secondary forest – is very different in character from the virgin forest that it replaces. First, secondary forest is lower and consists of trees of smaller average dimensions than those of primary forest, although since

Plate 6.5 An area of typical savanna in Rajasthan, India. This is a semi-arid area, but much of the character of the vegetation has been changed from its natural state by grazing and wood-cutting.

it is comparatively rare that an area of primary forest is clear-felled or completely destroyed by fire, occasional trees much larger than the average are usually found scattered throughout the re-growth. Second, very young secondary forest is often remarkably regular and uniform in struc-ture; and an abundance of undergrowth, unlike in primary forests, makes it laborious to pene-trate. Third, secondary forest tends to be much poorer in species than primary, and is sometimes dominated by a single species, or a small number of species. Fourth, the dominant trees of secon-dary forest are light-demanding and intolerant of shade; most of them grow very quickly (at rates of up to 12 m in three years); and most of the trees possess efficient dispersal mechanisms (hav-ing seeds or fruits well adapted for transport by wind or animals). Fifth, because of their rapid growth the wood often has a soft texture and low density, making it less desirable for many com-mercial purposes than the hardwords of the virgin forest.

6.9   Tropical seasonal forest and savanna

As the drier season becomes more distinct, the tropical rainforest, dominated by evergreens, is gradually replaced by a forest type that is partly evergreen and partly deciduous. The tropical sea-sonal forest occurs in some of the monsoon lands of Asia, but is relatively rare in Africa, where savannas occur in close juxtapositon to the rain forest belt.

Between the perennially dry deserts of the sub-tropical high-pressure belts and the equatorial rainforests lie the world's *savannas*. They occupy about one-fourth of the world's land surface, and display great variety in form. Broadly, savannas occur in those parts of the tropics that experience a dry season of 2½ to 7½ months' duration – a season that checks plant growth. (Desert shrub vegetation occurs mainly where the number of arid months exceeds 7½).

The savannas have been defined by T. L. Hills as 'a plant formation of tropical regions, compris-ing a virtually continuous ecologically dominant stratum of more or less xeromorphic (drought tolerant) plants, of which herbaceous plants, especially grasses and sedges, are frequently the principal, and occasionally the only, components, although woody plants often of the dimension of

Figure 6.9   Some of the range of vegetation types found in the seasonal tropics: (a) semi-evergreen seasonal forest; (b) deciduous seasonal forest; (c) savanna woodland; (d) tree savanna; (e) shrub savanna; (f) grass savanna.

trees or palms generally occur and are present in varying densities'. Most savanna consists, therefore, of grassland with scattered trees, and the biomass is intermediate between that of rainforest and that of deserts. Net primary productivity of savanna averages about 1200 g m^{-2}yr^{-1}, com-

pared with 2400 for rainforest and about 200 for deserts, but there is a very wide range.

Typically, the trees in a savanna area are 6–12 m in height, strongly rooted and with flattened crowns (figure 6.9). They exhibit various drought-resisting features to cope with the long dry

Plate 6.6   A savanna dominated by palms bordering the River Uruguay in Argentina.

Plate 6.7 Along tropical coasts mangrove swamps occur. These *Rhizophora* mangroves have large stilt roots. These examples are found in northern Brazil.

season, including partial or total seasonal loss of leaves, and some of them are fire-resistant, possessing thick bark and thick bud-scales. The tree species vary greatly – in Honduras there is savanna dominated by pine trees, in Australia there are various types of eucalyptus and in Africa there is the thorny acacia, various palms and the bottle-shaped baobab (*Adansonia digitata*). The grasses are often long and reach up to 3.5 m in height, thus providing ample fuel for dry-season fires. Savannas are also characterised, where man has not decimated them, by a very diverse fauna, especially of large herbivorous mammals such as antelope, wildebeeste, zebra and giraffe, together with scavengers and predators (such as hyena and lion).

The nature and distribution of savanna owes a great deal to climate conditions, and initially scientists regarded it as a type of *climax vegetation* (see section 9.5) that occurred in those areas of the tropics in which there was an extended season of drought. However, it is now recognised that, as with many vegetation types in the world, this is a rather simplistic view, and that other factors play a role. Some workers have championed the importance of *edaphic* (soil) conditions, including poor drainage, soils that have a low water-retention capacity in the dry season, soils with a shallow profile due to the development of a laterite hard-pan, and soils with a low nutrient supply (either because they are developed on a poor parent rock such as quartzite or because the soil has undergone an extended period of leaching on an old land surface). Another highly important factor is fire. The importance of this factor in maintaining and originating some savannas is suggested by the fact, already noted, that many of the savanna trees are fire-resistant. Experiments in fire control have shown how trees can re-establish themselves when burning ceases, and there are many observations of the frequency with which, for example, African herdsmen and agriculturalists burn over much of tropical Africa and thereby maintain grassland. Some of the fires may be deliberately started, while others may be caused naturally by lightning, which on average strikes the land surface of the globe 100 000 times every day! In general, regular burning favours perennial grasses with underground stems that can regenerate after a fire has passed.

6.10   Mangrove swamps

One type of vegetation assemblage that is more or less restricted to within 30° of the Equator, because they are intolerant of frost, are the tidally submerged coastal woodlands called *mangrove swamps* (figure 6.10(a)). Mangroves are basically salt-tolerant trees that can reach 40 m in height but are generally much smaller. They occur along the borders of many tropical shores where wave action is not too intense and mud and peat are deposited, and some have stilt or prop roots to help them hold on to the shifting sediments. They may extend inland up to 60 km where there are tidal rivers, and they may also occur round the lagoons of some coral atolls.

Mangroves are most luxuriant and complex on the coasts of Malaysia and the surrounding islands, and in general mangrove vegetation in the east is taller and richer in diversity than that of western Africa and the Americas.

Mangrove swamps are important environments, being among the most productive and biologically diverse ecosystems in the world. Nutrients which are released when their leaves and twigs decompose are an important food for aquatic animals, including economically important fish species. They are also valuable as a source of timber products, and their ramifying root systems act as silt traps, thereby stabilizing shorelines and helping to maintain the quality of estuarine and coastal waters.

Mangrove swamps, in spite of their great value, are being subjected to increasing human pressures, including deforestation and reclamation for agriculture and aquaculture.

6.11   Coral reefs

An important environment which is more or less totally restricted to the intertropical zone is the *coral reef* (figure 6.10(c)). These features have fascinated scientists for over 150 years, and some of the most pertinent observations of them were made in the 1830s by Charles Darwin on the voyage of the *Beagle*. He recognised that there were three major kinds: (1) *fringing reefs*, (2) *barrier reefs*, and (3) *atolls*; and he saw that they were related to each other in a logical and gradational sequence (figure 6.11).

A *fringing reef* is one that lies close to the shore of some continent or island. Its surface forms an uneven and rather rough platform around the coast, about the level of low water, and its outer edge slopes downwards into the sea. Between the fringing reef and the land there is sometimes a small channel or *lagoon*. When the lagoon is wide and deep and the reef lies at some distance from the shore and rises from deep water it is called a *barrier reef*. An *atoll* is a reef in the form of a ring or horseshoe with a lagoon in the centre.

Darwin's theory was that the succession from one coral reef type to another could be achieved by the upward growth of coral from a sinking foundation, such as a subsiding volcano. He argued that, so long as the rate of coral growth was more rapid than the rate of sinking, there would be a progression from a fringing reef, through the barrier reef stage until, with the disappearance through subsidence of the central island, only a reef-enclosed lagoon or atoll would survive. A long time after Darwin put forward this theory, some deep bore-holes were drilled in the Pacific atolls in connection with the testing of atom bombs in the 1950s. The drill holes passed through more than 1000 m of coral before reaching the basalt substratum of the ocean floor, and indicated that the coral had been growing upward for tens of millions of years as the crust subsided at a rate of between 15 and 51 m per million years. Darwin's theory was therefore proved basically correct. There are some submarine islands (see section 1.8) called *guyots* and

Figure 6.10 (a) The distribution of mangroves is strongly controlled by temperature conditions. Broken lines enclose the total range; thick lines denote major stretches of coast dominated by tidal woodlands. (b) Cold-month sea surface isotherms for 20 °C and 26 °C. Since the fall in tropical sea surface temperatures during Pleistocene glacials was of the order of 6 deg, the double hatched area gives an approximate idea of the reduced availability of tropical water at such times. (c) The distribution of coral reefs is also strongly related to sea temperatures. The hatched area includes the zones of most prolific reef development, and almost all oceanic atolls.

Figure 6.11   Darwin's model of coral atoll formation as a result of subsidence of a volcanic island. Note the progression from fringing reef to atoll as subsidence progresses.

seamounts, in which subsidence associated with sea-floor spreading has been too speedy for coral growth to keep up.

Coral reefs are found where the ocean water temperature is not less than 21°C (see figures 6.10 (b) and (c)), where there is a firm substratum, and where the seawater is not rendered too dark by excessive amounts of river-borne sediment. They will not grow in very deep water, so a platform within 30–40 m of the surface is a necessary

Plate 6.8 Charles Darwin, the Victorian naturalist, developed one of the most important theories for coral atoll formation, based on subsidence.

prerequisite for their development. Their physical structure is dominated by the skeletons of *corals*, which are carnivorous animals living off zooplankton. However, in addition to corals there are enormous quantities of algae, some calcareous, which help to build the reefs. The size of reefs is variable. Some atolls are very large – Kwajelein in the Marshall Islands of the South Pacific is 120 km long and as much as 24 km across – but most are very much smaller, and rise only a few metres above the water. The 2000 km complex of reefs known as the Great Barrier Reef, which forms a gigantic natural breakwater off the north-east coast of Australia, is by far the greatest coral structure on earth.

Like mangrove swamps, coral reefs are extremely important habitats. Indeed, they have been called the marine version of the tropical rain forests, rivalling their terrestrial counterparts in both richness of species and biological productivity. They also have significance because they provide coastal protection, opportunities for recreation, and are potential sources of substances like

drugs. They are coming under a variety of threats, of which two of the most important are dredging, and the effects of increased siltation brought about by accelerated erosion from neighbouring land areas.

6.12   Weathering of rocks

High temperatures, large amounts of rainfall and a high biomass promote the rapid decay of many rock minerals. The speed of chemical reactions, following *Van't Hoff's temperature rule*, approximately doubles for every 10°C rise in temperature. Water is the main chemical reagent in the decay of rocks, and the large quantities of organic matter decaying on and within the soil liberate organic acids and carbon dioxide gas which play an important part in the mobilization of some of the minerals formed during the weathering process, especially iron oxide.

The prolonged action of tropical weathering, combined with relatively slow rates of surface erosion so long as the forest cover is maintained, have led to the development over susceptible rocks of considerable thickness of weathered material called *regolith*. Such *deep weathering* (figure 6.12) is characteristic of the wet tropics, and sometimes the rocks are decomposed for tens of metres, locally exceeding 125m. Deep weathering is especially effective where the rock is penetrated by a dense network of joints and is less effective where the joints are widely spaced. For this reason the *weathering front* (the boundary zone between the bedrock and the regolith) may be very uneven.

There are various different types of deep weathering profile, some of which are capped by an iron (*laterite*) or aluminium (*bauxite*) crust (duricrust). A duricrust (section 5.7) is a hard crust formation at or just below the ground surface, and of the various types found in the moister parts of the tropics probably laterites are the most extensive. They are formed because intense weathering preferentially removes silica, leaving behind the relatively insoluble residues of iron and aluminium sesquioxides. These oxides harden on exposure when vegetation is removed and produce a hard material that is resistant to weathering and erosion. Sometimes the surface is so impermeable that it has only a very limited

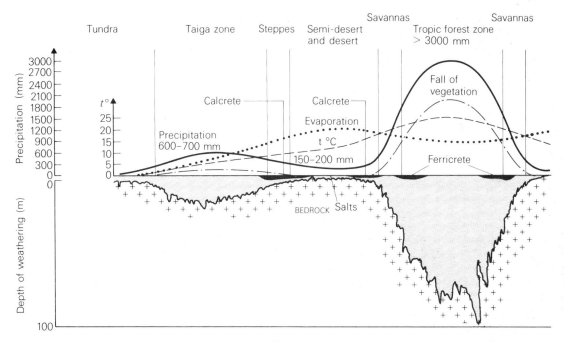

Figure 6.12 Schematic representation of the depth of weathering between the Poles and the tropics, showing the great depths of weathering that are attained in the hot, wet areas of the equatorial zone, and the moderate depths that are attained in the humid mid-latitude zone.

Plate 6.9 Intense chemical weathering of basalt in Maharashtra, India, has created laterite caprocks, which lead to the development of distinctive tabular-shaped hills.

Figure 6.13 The development of tropical plains and insel-bergs by a two-cycle process of deep weathering, followed by stripping. (a) Inselbergs are buried beneath weathered rock; depth of weathering varies according to the amount of jointing. (b) Weathered rock is stripped away, leaving fresh unweathered rock as inselbergs–bornhardts. (c) Deep weathering continues. Sub-aerial erosion attacks born-hardts, leading to formation of castle kopjes.

periods but are less weathered and generally less deep than ferralitic profiles. They occur in conjunction with areas of semi-evergreen, deciduous forest and in savannas with a pronounced dry season. The tropical podzols resemble their temperate counterparts but are very much deeper, and they develop most strikingly in unconsolidated quartz-rich parent materials such as alluvial sands. Other river valleys, deltas and swamps may have *alluvial hydromorphic soils* (inceptisols or entisols – see section 2.8), in which seasonal waterlogging may produce gley features. In flat and low-lying portions of the seasonal tropics *vertisols* may occur. These are dark clay soils which shrink and crack in dry periods and swell in wet, and which may often be derived from the weathering of base-rich parent materials such as basalt. Clay contents are high, and *montmorillonite*, a clay mineral that expands and contracts greatly according to moisture content, is widespread. The cracks may form polygonal patterns and micro-relief called *gilgai*, and building on such soils, often described as 'expansive', may create stresses in foundations that can cause structural failure.

vegetation cover. The crust often forms a distinctive capping to tabular-shaped hills.

If a change in climate or in base level causes fluvial incision into the landscape (figure 6.13) then the uneven weathering front may be exposed, leading to the exhumation of the areas of widely spaced jointing as large isolated hills called *bornhardts* or *inselbergs*. More closely spaced joints will produce smaller features called *castle kopjes*, and in rock where very close jointing leads to almost complete rock breakdown, the effect of stripping will be to reveal a pile of rounded boulders or core stones.

The soils of the humid tropics include *oxisols*. These soils, which are sometimes described as *ferrallitic*, are generally intensively weathered soils, which over long periods have evolved into deep, slightly acid profiles, with an accumulation of kaolinitic clays. They are rich in *sesquioxides*, rich in clays, distinctively bright in colour and highly leached of nutrients. *Ferruginous soils* and *tropical podzols* have also evolved over long

Plate 6.10 Areas of ancient granitic and gneissic rocks in the tropics are often studded with inselbergs or bornhardts. The Sibebe inselberg in Swaziland is composed of coarse-granite in which there are very few joints

6.13 Slope movements

Although the existence of deep weathering profiles indicates that in many areas the removal of material from slopes is slower than the rate of production of weathered material, this does not mean that mass movements are ineffective. The high intensity of rainfall, the high amounts of rainfall, the lack of much vegetation or humus on the forest floor and the impermeable nature of many clay-rich soils mean that there are probably considerable quantities of surface wash over tropical forest floors caused by rain splash.

The other very important process is *landsliding*, facilitated by the combination of rotted rock, clay soils, heavy rainfall and generally shallowly rooted trees. This has proved a particular hazard when cities like Rio de Janeiro, Hong Kong and Kuala Lumpur have expanded, causing building to spread on to steep slopes.

6.14 Some problems of the humid tropics

Although some early European travellers marvelled at the luxuriant nature of the rainforest, believing that the tropics were fertile and merely awaited commercial exploitation, development in the humid tropics is faced with some major environmental problems:

Large areas of soil infertility
Lateritisation
Erosion caused by intense storms
Slope instability associated with deeply weathered rock
Extremely enervating climate (caused by high humidity)
Rapid loss of nutrients on deforestation
Hurricanes
Active attack on wood and other organic material by termites, fungi, etc.
Flooding (both natural and following deforestation)
World climatic change (the CO_2 problem)

While it would be wrong to replace early optimism with an equal degree of pessimism, the tropics are a zone where unwise human actions can have devastating consequences. For example, some rubber plantations established in Amazonia after the First World War had a very short life. When the forest was cut down, some of the soils rapidly hardened to laterite, and others were washed away. Likewise the attempt by the British government to establish groundnut farming in East Africa just after the Second World War foundered when the soils proved to suffer marked deterioration in their structure when cultivated by heavy machinery. They also needed heavy applications of expensive fertilizer to make up for the loss of natural nutrients.

PART III

Mountain and Maritime Environments

7 Mountains

7.1 Introduction

As we saw in chapter 1, mountain ranges tend to run in long, linear belts along the margins of continents. One exceptionally long belt runs around the edge of the Pacific Ocean, while another runs from west to east along the under-belly of Eurasia. Their distribution follows closely the distributions of earthquakes, fault zones, volcanic activity, island arcs and ocean trenches. Many mountains are composed of marine sediments, which may have been metamorphosed and they often injected with volcanic material produced during the course of mountain-building.

In addition, mountainous relief results from the operation of the various forces of weathering and erosion, including rock falls, glaciation, avalanching and river transport.

Folding, faulting and volcanism are the forces that have created mountains. The key to understanding their distribution, form and composition lies in understanding the theory of plate tectonics described in chapter 1. The purpose of this chapter is not to investigate that theme further, but rather to discuss the modifications that mountains produce in the zonal patterns of such phenomena as climate and vegetation.

7.2 Mountain climates

Fundamental to an understanding of mountain climates are the changes that occur in the atmosphere with increasing altitude, especially the decrease in temperature, air density, water vapour, carbon dioxide and impurities.

Although the sun is the ultimate source of energy, very little heating of the atmosphere takes place directly from the sun. The earth's surface receives and absorbs the short-wave radiation coming from the sun and converts it to long-wave energy, and the earth itself then becomes the radiating body. The atmosphere is therefore heated directly by the earth and not by the sun. This explains why the highest temperatures usually occur next to the earth's surface and decrease outwards and upwards. Because mountains present a smaller land area at higher elevations, they are less able to warm the surrounding air.

Furthermore, the density and composition of the air control its ability to hold heat. As one ascends a mountain the pressure of the air decreases markedly (figure 7.1(b)). At sea level it is generally expressed as 760 mm of mercury. By the time one reaches elevations of around 7000 m, atmospheric pressure is less than 300 mm of mercury. This is important, because the ability of air to hold heat is a function of its molecular structure. At higher altitudes, where pressures are less, molecules are spaced further apart, so there are fewer molecules in a given volume of air to receive and hold heat. Also, with altitude the air loses much of its water vapour, carbon dioxide and suspended particulate matter (figure 7.1(a)). These too are important in determining the ability of air to hold heat. Most water vapour, for example, is concentrated in the lower levels of the atmosphere, with half of it occurring below an elevation of 1800 m.

For these reasons a change of temperature occurs with elevation (table 7.1) and this change

Opposite Among the world's greatest mountains are those of the Western Cordillera of the Americas. Although they are primarily caused by tectonic activity, the morainic lake and large debris cones indicate that much of the variety of mountain scenery is caused by the operation of powerful weathering and erosional processes. The location is the Banff National Park, Alberta, Canada.

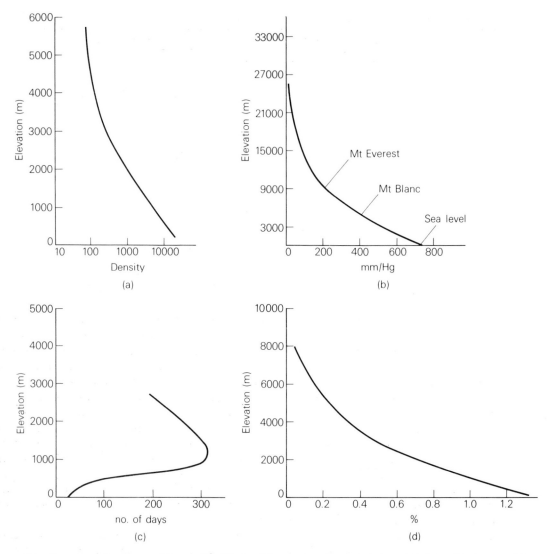

Figure 7.1 Changing climatic conditions with altitude: (a) average density of suspended particles per cubic metre; (b) atmospheric pressure; (c) number of foggy or cloudy days at different altitudes in Japan; (d) average water vapour content of air as volume percentage.

is called the *lapse rate* or vertical temperature gradient. The lapse rate varies according to many factors, but generally ranges from 1 to 2°C per 300 m.

Another major influence that mountains have on climate is through the *barrier effect*. Damming of air flows can occur if mountains are sufficiently high, with the effectiveness of the damming depending upon the depth of the air mass and the elevation of the lowest valleys or passes. When the air mass is effectively dammed, the winds are usually deflected by mountains. Moreover, large mountain ranges may be the foci of anticyclonic systems (because the mountains are a centre of cold air), and the presence of such anticyclones may cause storms to detour round the mountains. Jet streams may also split to flow round mountains (such as the Tibetan plateau), but they can rejoin to the lee of the range where they often intensify and produce storms. The tornadoes and

Table 7.1   Temperature conditions with elevation in the eastern Alps

Elevation (m)	Mean air temperature (°C)				Annual number of		
	January	July	Year	Annual range	Frost-free days	Frost alternation days	Continuous frost days
200	− 1.4	19.5	9.0	20.9	272	67	26
400	− 2.5	18.3	8.0	20.8	267	97	1
600	− 3.5	17.1	7.1	20.6	250	78	37
800	− 3.9	16.0	6.4	19.9	234	91	40
1000	− 3.9	14.8	5.7	18.7	226	86	53
1200	− 3.9	13.6	4.9	17.5	218	84	63
1400	− 4.1	12.4	4.0	16.5	211	81	73
1600	− 4.9	11.2	2.8	16.1	203	78	84
1800	− 6.1	9.9	1.6	16.0	190	76	99
2000	− 7.1	8.7	0.4	15.8	178	73	114
2200	− 8.2	7.2	−0.8	15.4	163	71	131
2400	− 9.2	5.9	−2.0	15.1	146	68	151
2600	−10.3	4.6	−3.3	14.9	125	66	174
2800	−11.3	3.2	−4.5	14.5	101	64	200
3000	−12.4	1.8	−5.7	14.2	71	62	232

Source: R. Geiger, *The Climate near the Ground* (Cambridge, Mass. Harvard University Press, 1965), p. 444.

violent squall lines that form in the American mid-west and create such havoc may also result from the great contrasts in air masses that develop in the confluence to the lee of the Rockies. Disturbances of the air by mountains can create a wave pattern much like that found in the wake of a ship. This may create zones of clear air turbulence that create problems for airplane pilots, or they may produce *lee waves* with beautiful lenticular (standing-wave) clouds.

Mountains also cause the forced ascent of air. When moist air blows perpendicular to a mountain range it is forced to rise; as it does it is cooled. Eventually the dew point is reached, condensation occurs as clouds, and precipitation results. For this reason, some of the rainiest places on earth are mountain slopes in the path of winds blowing off relatively warm oceans. For example, in the Pacific Ocean the precipitation around the Hawaiian Islands averages about 650 mm per annum, but at Mount Waialeale on Kauai the average annual total reaches no less than 12 344 mm! While such heavy precipitation may take place on the windward side of mountains, where the air is forced to ascend, the leeward side may receive considerably less precipitation because the air is no longer being lifted and much of the moisture has already been removed by precipitation on the windward side (figure 7.2). If the air is forced to descend on the lee side

it will become heated by compression, a process called *adiabatic heating*, and this will result in clear, dry conditions. The characteristics of some local winds, including the föhn and the Chinook, are associated with this phenomenon.

The quality of solar radiation received also changes with altitude. In particular, mountains receive a greater quantity of ultraviolet light, and this is thought to have numerous harmful effects, ranging from retardation of growth in tundra plants to cancer in humans. Certainly solar energy in the ultraviolet spectrum is mainly responsible for the deep tans of mountain dwellers, skiers and climbers.

The amount of solar radiation that is received in mountainous areas depends very substantially on slope angle and aspect. Most mountain slopes receive fewer hours of sunshine than level surfaces, although a slope directly facing the sun may receive more energy than a level surface (especially at higher latitudes). Level surfaces in the tropics usually receive a higher solar intensity than slopes because the sun is always high in the sky at those lower latitudes. Whatever the duration and intensity of the sunlight, the effects are generally clearly evident both in the local ecology and in human activities. In the Northern Hemisphere, south-facing slopes are warmer and drier than north-facing slopes, and the number and diversity of plants and animals are greater.

Figure 7.2 A cross-section from San Francisco on the Pacific coastline of California to Reno in the desert of Nevada, illustrating the relationship between precipitation and topography. Note the high levels of precipitation on the windward (western) side of the mountains at high altitudes, and the 'rain shadow' effect on the lee (eastern) side.

Timber-lines also tend to be higher on the south-facing slopes, and in the east-west valleys of the Alps in Europe most settlements are located on south-facing slopes. In spring north-facing slopes will tend to keep their snow cover longer; they therefore tend to be given over to forestry whereas south-facing slopes are used for high-altitude pastures. The French draw a distinction between the sunny (*adret*) and shady (*ubac*) slopes.

Relief conditions can also have marked effects on temperature by creating conditions for *temperature inversions* to form. While temperatures normally decrease with elevation, during a temperature inversion the lowest temperatures occur in the valley and increase upward along the mountain slope. An explanation for this is that cold air is denser than warm air so that, as slopes cool down at night, the colder air begins to move downward, displacing the warm air in the valley. This can happen on calm, clear nights when there is rapid radiation and loss of surface heat to space, and no wind to mix and equalise the temperatures. As a consequence, enclosed valleys can become filled with a pool of cold stagnant

air, which can give extremely low temperatures and severe frosts. Sensitive species of plants, whether crops or natural vegetation, may not grow in these hollows, although they may flourish at slightly higher altitudes on the slopes above.

The range of temperatures in mountains is another interesting feature of their climatology. The temperature difference between day and night and between winter and summer gradually decreases with elevation; for the higher and more isolated a mountain, the more its temperature will reflect that of the surrounding free air. Surface temperatures will vary much more than air temperatures, and even at high altitudes sunny soil surfaces may warm up in the middle of the day, though they cool down below air temperatures at night. Studies in the Karakoram Mountains in Pakistan, for example, at altitudes in excess of 4000 m indicated that diurnal rock surface temperature ranges were normally between 30 and 40° in summer, when those in air were between 6 to 16°.

The moisture content of the atmosphere

decreases quickly as altitude increases (figure 7.1(d)). At 2000 m it is only about 50 per cent of that at sea level, and at 8000 m (the height of some of the highest peaks in the Himalayas), the water vapour content of the air is less than 1 per cent of that at sea level. This decrease in water vapour with altitude might at first sight appear difficult to square with the well-known fact that precipitation may increase with altitude, but the reason for higher precipitation levels is that moist air from lower elevations has been forced upward into an area of lower temperature. In fact, at very high elevations aridity does prevail, and plants and animals may have evolved adaptations to survive the lack of moisture. Thick, corky bark and waxy leaves, rather like those of some desert plants, are common in alpine plants, while mountain sheep and goats, and beasts like the ibex and the chamois, are all able to live for prolonged periods on little moisture.

The presence of clouds in mountainous areas may increase precipitation levels. Water droplets from clouds may be caught by trees as *fog drip*. The tiny fog droplets are intercepted by the leaves and branches and grow by coalescence until they become heavy enough to fall to the ground. Many tropical and subtropical mountains sustain so-called cloud forests through the abundance of such moisture. Along the east coast of Mexico, for example, luxuriant cloud forests occur in the Sierra Madre Oriental between 1300 and 2400 m.

There is some dispute, brought about partly by a paucity of measurements and problems of maintaining instruments at high altitudes, as to whether precipitation always decreases above a certain altitude. In the tropics, however, this does seem to be established. In the Andes and Central America the zone of maximum precipitation lies at between 900 and 1600 m, in the Cameroon Mountains of West Africa at 1800 m, and in East Africa at 1500 m. The existence of a zone of maximum precipitation in mid-latitude mountains is being increasingly questioned; available information seems to suggest that precipitation continues to increase with altitude in middle latitudes at least up to 3000–3500 m. The difference between the low and middle latitudes in this respect may be due to the presence of the trade-wind inversion in the tropics (see section 6.2) and

Plate 7.1 Mountains create their own clouds and their own climate. In the Cape Peninsula of South Africa, Table Mountain and neighbouring peaks are often mantled in white clouds, which are locally called 'The Table Cloth'. Such clouds deposit much moisture in the form of fog drip.

the higher windspeeds of mid-latitudes which cause greater orographic lifting.

Mountainous areas are some of the windiest places on earth. The winds protrude into the high atmosphere, where there is less friction to retard wind movement, and may be compressed and channelled round peaks. Wind is a major en-

(a)

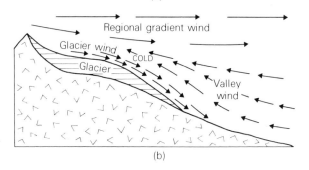

(b)

Figure 7.3 Miscellaneous types of mountain wind: (a) slope and valley winds; the view on the left is looking up valley at mid-day, while that on the right provides a vertical cross-section of the same situation viewed from the side; (b) a glacier wind.

vironmental stress for plants, so much alpine vegetation has a low-lying habit and often survives only in sheltered micro-habitats.

Mountains also create some of their own wind systems (figure 7.3). Winds are common that blow upslope and up valley during the day and in the reverse direction at night. The driving force of such winds is differential heating and cooling, which produces density differences between slopes and valleys and between mountains and plains. During the sunlight hours the slopes are warmed more than the air at the same elevation in the valleys, and the warm air, being less dense, moves upward as an *anabatic wind* along the slopes. At night when the air cools it moves downwards, creating a *katabatic wind* and causing a temperature inversion. An important variant on these thermal slope winds is the *glacier wind*, which arises as the air adjacent to an icy surface is cooled and moves downslope because of gravity. These may blow continuously, as the refrigeration source is always present, but they tend

to reach their greatest depth and intensity at mid-afternoon, when the thermal contrast is greatest.

In addition to thermal winds, there are winds caused by barrier effects. These are generally called *föhn winds*, though in some parts of the world they have their own names (e.g. Chinook in North America, and north-wester in New Zealand). They are characterised by a rapid rise in temperature and gustiness and an extreme dryness that puts stress on plants and animals and creates a fire hazard. A typical situation in which a föhn might develop consists of a ridge of high pressure on the windward side of the mountain range and a trough of low pressure on the leeward side, creating a steep pressure gradient across the range. Air is forced up the mountain slope and condensation begins. As the air continues to rise it cools at what is called the *wet adiabatic rate* (c.1.7°C per 300 m). This is a relatively slow rate of cooling because latent heat of condensation is being added to the air. On the lee side of the summit, precipitation ceases and the

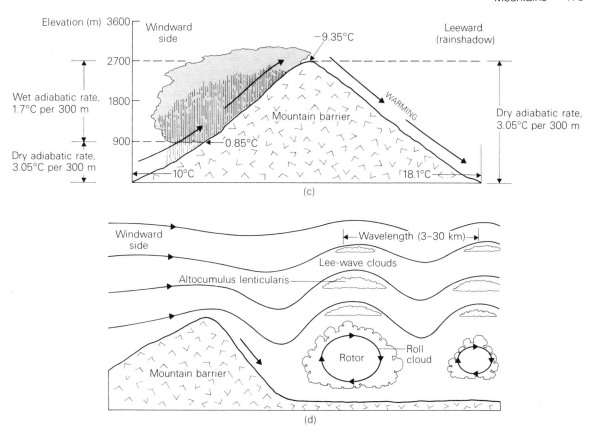

Figure 7.3 Miscellaneous types of mountain wind: (c) Föhn wind; (d) lee wave and rotors.

air starts to descend. It begins to warm as it descends, but does so at the relatively quick *dry adiabatic rate* of about 3.05°C per 300 m. Consequently the air has the potential for arriving at the valley or plain level on the leeward side much warmer and without much of its moisture, compared with its state at the same elevation on the windward side.

A further consequence of the barrier effect on winds is the creation of *lee waves* (figure 7.3(d)). When wind passes over an obstacle – in this case a mountain – its normal flow is disrupted and a train of waves may be created that extend downwind for considerable distances. Such lee waves may be associated with windspeeds exceeding 160 km h^{-1} and are often marked by lenticular clouds that form at the crest of waves. Lee waves may also have *rotors*, roll-like circulations that develop to the immediate lee of mountains, usually forming beneath the wave crests.

7.3   Snow and the snow-line

At higher elevations on mountains much of the precipitation falls as snow – snow which nourishes glaciers, snow banks and avalanches, provides the basis of winter sports, affects plants and animals, and provides water supplies to some of the world's great rivers.

On the highest peaks the snow may be permanent, in the sense that it persists on the ground throughout the year; whereas at lower levels it will be seasonal, and melt in the warmth of summer. The zone between permanent and seasonal snow is called the *snow-line*, though because it changes from year to year and from slope to slope it is often difficult to define with any precision. In general, the snow-line corresponds to the level where the average temperatures are 0°C or less during the warmest month of the year, but it is also related to the amount of precipitation

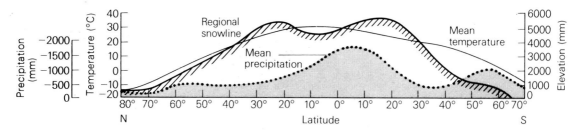

Figure 7.4   Generalised altitude of the snow-line on a transect across the world from north to south. Note the slightly lower snow-line elevation in the tropics as a result of the increased precipitation and cloudiness in these regions.

there is. If there is more snow, then the snow-line occurs at a lower altitude, because it requires more heat to cause large quantities of snow to melt.

The regional snow-line is lowest in the high latitudes (figure 7.4), where it may occur at sea level, and highest in the tropics, where it tends to occur between 5000 and 6000 m. The highest snow-lines are found in the drier parts of the Tibetan Plateau and the Andes, where they reach levels as high as 6500 m. Indeed, the greater cloudiness and precipitation of the equatorial belt means that the snow-line may be lower near the Equator than in those areas between 20° and 30° N and S, which are under the influence of the subtropical high-pressure cells. At any given latitude, however, the snow-line is generally lowest in areas of heavy precipitation, such as coastal locations, and highest in areas of low precipitation, such as are encountered in continental interiors. Because of the nature of the prevailing winds, there is also a tendency for snow-lines to rise in elevation towards the west in the tropics and the east in middle latitudes.

7.4 Mountain vegetation

At the end of the eighteenth century, Alexander von Humboldt, the great German scientist and geographer, visited South America and climbed some of the mountains in the tropical sector of the Andes. He recognised that both vegetation and climate changed in a vertical sequence, and he suggested that this vertical sequence from tropical rainforest at low altitudes to permanent snow at the highest elevations was a microcosm of similar zones with changing latitude from tropics to the poles. In a very broad sense there is some truth in this analogy, but in many impor-

tant respects the altitudinal pattern and the latitudinal pattern are very different. In particular, the only similarity between a high tropical mountain climate (the *tierra fria* of Humboldt) and a polar climate is that of the average annual temperature. In terms of length of day, diurnal fluctuations in temperature and seasonal variability, they are totally different, and plant life reflects these differences.

The primary characteristic of mountain vegetation is the presence of sequential plant communities with increasing altitude. There is a tendency towards smaller and less elaborate plants with slower growth rates, decreased productivity, lower diversity and less inter-species competition. Forests on the lower slopes are called *submontane* or *montane forests*; the higher forest comprises the *subalpine zone*, and the treeless area above is known as the *alpine zone*.

Northern Hemisphere mountain forests in middle and high latitudes are dominated by needle-leaf evergreen conifers – pine, spruce and fir. These species are closely related to those of the great belt of boreal forest (see section 4.7), which stretches south of the Arctic tundra across North America and Eurasia. On the lower and intermediate slopes of humid regions in the middle and lower-middle latitudes, broadleaf deciduous forests are the dominant vegetation type. Areas in which they occur include parts of western Europe, the eastern United States and eastern Asia. Dominant species include oak, maple, beach and chestnut. Southern Hemisphere mountain forests are composed primarily of broadleaf evergreen trees and may contain large numbers of tree ferns.

The generalised sequence encountered on the mountains of East Africa astride the Equator is shown in figure 7.5(a). At the lowest levels, below

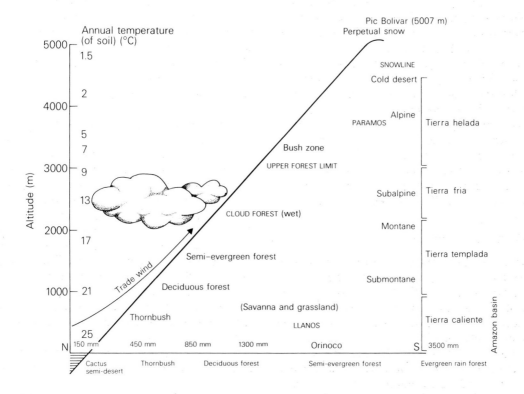

Figure 7.5 (a) Generalised representation of vegetation belts at different altitudes in the equatorial mountains of East Africa; (b) the zonation of vegetation with altitude in a north–south transect across Venezuela.

Plate 7.2 The high mountain peaks of East Africa have very distinctive vegetation. On the slopes of Mount Kenya there is a belt with various types of *senecio*. The tall plants are the giant tree groundsel (*Senecio keniodendron*), while the bushier plants are cabbage groundsel (*Senecio brassica*). These plants occur at around 4300 m, while the peaks in the background, with the Diamond Glacier in between, lie at just below 5200 m.

around 2000 m, there is normal lowland forest or savanna, according to whether the area is moist or dry. Above this is the montane forest belt, distinguished by an abundance of broadleaved hardwood trees with some conifers. In some of the wetter areas the montane forest may contain bamboo (*Arundinaria alpina*), especially in the higher parts of this belt. Above the montane forest belt there is the ericaceous belt, characterised by many small leaved trees and shrubs, especially members of the Ericaceae, including giant heathers of the genus *Philippia*. Between that belt

and the ice caps on the mountain summits is the Afroalpine belt, which includes various scrub, giant groundsel (*Senecia*) and grassland communities.

Figure 7.5(b) illustrates another low-latitude zonation of vegetation with altitude, based on a north-south transect across Venezuela. In that country, the vegetation communities at sea level range from semi-desert through a thorn bushland to deciduous, semi-evergreen and eventually evergreen rainforest in the Amazon Basin. With increasing altitude, the classic zones of Humboldt

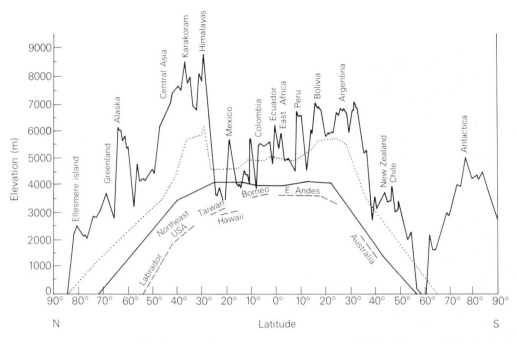

Figure 7.6 Schematic north–south view of the highest summits (top solid line) and the upper limit of vascular plants (dotted line). Timber-line altitudes are shown both for drier continental situations (lower solid line) and for the wetter marine situations (dashed line).

may be recognised: *tierra caliente*, *tierra templada*, *tierra fria* and *tierra helada*.

7.5 The timber-line

The transition from forest to treeless tundra on a mountain slope is often a dramatic one. Within a vertical distance of just a few tens of metres, trees disappear as a life form and are replaced by low shrubs, herbs and grasses. This rapid zone of transition is called the upper *timber-line*. In many semi-arid areas there is also a lower timber-line where the forest passes into steppe or desert at its lower edge, usually because of lack of moisture.

The upper timber-line, like the snow-line, is highest in the tropics and lowest in the polar regions (figure 7.6). It ranges from sea level in the polar regions to 4500 m in the dry subtropics and 3500–4000 m in the moist tropics. Timber-line trees are normally evergreens, suggesting that

Plate 7.3 At high altitudes, trees, like these *Pinus flexilis* in Colorado, USA may have their shapes deformed by wind, an example of krummholz.

these have some advantage over deciduous trees in the extreme environments of the upper timber-line. There are some areas, however, where broadleaf deciduous trees form the timber-line. Species of birch (*Betula*), for example, may occur at the timber-line in parts of the Himalayas. The timber-line vegetation of tropical mountains is dominated by the Ericaceae (the heath family). They grow as evergreen shrubs and trees with characteristically tough and leathery leaves.

At the upper timber-line the trees begin to become gnarled, stunted, prostrate and deformed – characteristics to which the Germans give the name *krummholz*. This is particularly true for trees in the middle and upper latitudes, which tend to attain greater heights on ridges, whereas in the tropics the trees reach their greater heights in the valleys. This is because middle and upper latitude timber-lines are strongly influenced by the duration and depth of the snow cover. As the snow is deeper and lasts longer in the valleys, trees tend to attain greater heights on the ridges, even though they are more exposed to high-velocity winds and poor, thin soils there. In the tropics, the valleys appear to be more favourable because they are less prone to dry out, they have less frost and they have deeper soils.

There is still no universally agreed explanation for why there should be such a dramatic cessation of tree growth at the upper timber-line. Various environmental factors may play a role. Too much snow, for example, can smother trees, and avalanches and snow creep can damage or destroy them. Late-lying snow reduces the effective growing season to the point where seedlings cannot establish themselves. Wind velocity also increases with altitude and may cause serious stress for trees, as is made evident by the *krummholz* types. Some scientists have proposed that the presence of increasing levels of ultraviolet light with elevation may play a role, while browsing and grazing by animals like the ibex may be another contributing factor. Probably the most important environmental factor is temperature, for if the growing season is too short and temperatures too low, tree shoots and buds cannot mature sufficiently to survive the winter months.

7.6 Alpine tundra

Above the tree-line there is a zone that is generally called *alpine tundra*. Immediately adjacent to the timber-line, the tundra consists of a fairly complete cover of low-lying shrubs, herbs and grasses, while higher up the number and diversity of species decreases until there is much bare ground with occasional mosses and lichens and some prostrate cushion plants. Some plants can even survive in favourable micro-habitats above the snow-line. The highest plants in the world occur at around 6100 m on Makalu in the Himalayas, where rocks, warmed by the sun, melt small snowdrifts.

The most striking characteristic of the plants of the alpine zone is their low growth form. This enables them to avoid the worst rigours of high winds, and permits them to make use of the higher temperatures immediately adjacent to the ground surface. In an area where low temperatures are limiting to life, the importance of the additional heat near the surface is crucial. The low growth form can also permit the plants to take advantage of the insulation provided by a winter snow cover. In the equatorial mountains the low growth form is less prevalent.

Another common characteristic of the alpine plants is that they tend to be perennials, rather than annuals. Alpine plants have to be able to make use of the limited growing season, and annuals find it difficult to germinate, flower and fruit in such a short period whereas perennials do not have to spend time in germination and initial growth processes. The perennials also have large and extensive root systems, like many desert plants. These roots are useful during droughts; they act as reserves of food, and provide nutrients to the plant for rapid initial growth in the spring.

7.7 Mountain hazards

Mountains have always been regarded with awe, but today their majestic scenery makes them prime country for recreation. More and more people visit them, and frequently they underestimate the hazards that the environment can pose. Mountain weather is often severe, and at high altitudes people can suffer from severe physiol-

Plate 7.4 Above the treeline is the alpine zone with low plants. This may provide summer pasture. In the last century glaciers almost reached to this meadow just above the village of Arolla in the Valais of Switzerland.

ogical conditions. In particular they may suffer from oxygen deficiency, which often reveals itself at about 2800–3000 m as a slight breathlessness and can produce *mountain sickness*, symptoms of which include headache, dizziness, nausea, lack of appetite and insomnia. A further health hazard is a pulmonary oedema, in which fluid accumulation in the lungs impairs oxygen transfer into the blood. Wind chill applies in cold, windy mountain areas as much as it does in the polar regions (see section 3.1), and frostbite and snow blindness are additional hazards. Rapid changes of weather, and the sudden appearance of fog and cloud, frequently take climbers unawares. Exposed ridges and summits may be especially prone to lightning strikes, and elsewhere snow avalanches can be a severe hazard (see section 3.14). Air pollution may occur in some mountain valleys as a result of topographically caused inversions, and on steep valley sides mass movements such as rockfalls may occur with some frequency

(see chapter 11). The high relief; oversteepening by glacial excavation; the presence of torrential streams at the base of slopes; the existence of rocks shattered by tectonic activity; the powerful operation of freeze-thaw processes; the existence of earthquakes and the frequent occurrence of high precipitation levels – all contribute to the instability of slopes in mountainous environments. Communication lines and settlements need to be located with care.

This is illustrated by a consideration of the Karakoram Highway, a strategic road which links China with Pakistan across the Karakoram Mountains at a height of 4604 m. Largely built with great loss of life in the 1970s it has had to contend with a formidable series of problems. Its course has been threatened by the rapidly fluctuating positions of the glacier snouts, bridges and stretches of the road have been washed away by capricious outwash streams, in the gorge of the Hunza River it has to face great flood waves caused by the collapse of natural landslide dams across the river, dust storms are whipped up from the glacial outwash plains, in the winter there are avalanches and deep snow falls, and because of the steep, unstable slopes, the road is frequently blocked by rock falls and debris flows. Teams of workmen labour continually to keep the road open.

8 Coasts

8.1 Coastlines

The world's coastlines, which have a length not far short of half a million kilometres, are an important habitat for man, for it has been estimated that around two thirds of the world's population lives within a few kilometres of a coast.

Coastlines show a tremendous diversity. This is the result of the climatic conditions under which they occur, their history of sea-level change, the geological structures that lie behind them, the sediments that are available to make their beaches and the nature of the waves, currents and tides that mould them. Even within the small compass of Britain, one can contrast the sinuous inlets of the south-west, the great sea lochs of Scotland, the low glacial coastline of East Anglia, the marshes of the Thames Estuary and the imposing chalk and limestone cliffs of the south coast.

Given this great variety, it is not surprising that there have been many attempts to classify coasts on the basis of numerous different criteria. One of the best known classifications was that of the American geomorphologist D. W. Johnson, who believed that the most important division was between those coasts that had a history dominated by emergence, and those that had been characterised by submergence. He also recognised 'neutral' coasts and 'compound' coasts. Coasts of submergence would include those in which rias and fiords were important, whereas emergent coasts would be characterised by barrier beaches like those of the Baltic (see section 8.3).

An American oceanographer, F. P. Shepard, believed that a useful distinction could be drawn between what he termed 'primary' (youthful) coasts, where non-marine forces were still in evidence as having moulded the landscape, and 'secondary' coasts, where marine action was more evident. Primary coasts would include those where land erosion was evident (e.g. rias, fiords, drowned karst), where subaerial deposition could be seen (e.g. deltas, – see section 14.9 – sand dunes, landslides, submerged glacial features), or where the effects of volcanism and tectonic movements could be traced. Secondary coasts would be those either where marine erosion had greatly modified the coast (e.g. wave-straightened coasts), or where marine deposition had occurred (e.g. barrier coasts, cuspate forelands, mud flats), or where the coasts had been built up by marine organisms like coral or mangrove.

More recent classifications have recognised the importance of the coast's position *vis à vis* plate tectonic boundaries (see section 1.8) and the amount of energy supplied to different coastlines by different types of wave attack (see section 8.2). It has also become increasingly evident in recent years that virtually all coastlines have undergone a very complex series of sea-level changes during the Pleistocene and Holocene, so that any simple division into emergent or submergent coasts must be fraught with difficulty, as must any attempt to explain modern beaches and coasts without references to their past history. The nature of world sea-level changes has been discussed in section 2.15, and the effects of ice caps and tectonics in sections 3.8 and 10.9, respectively.

8.2 Waves

Waves are crucial for an understanding of the geomorphology of beaches and coasts, because it is waves that bring most of the input of wave energy into the beach system. Many of the changes that one can observe result from waves of different characteristics – their height and wavelength – and the direction from which they come.

Waves obtain their energy from wind, and the wind may occur either quite near to the coast where the waves break, or at a vast distance from the coast. This is because, once large waves have been formed by the wind, they will travel across the oceans, slowly losing height (and therefore energy), until eventually they reach shallow coastal waters and break against the land. In this way, waves generated by strong, persistent winds in the southern Pacific Ocean may extend as far as the coast of Alaska.

Before we progress further, a few terms relating to waves should be introduced. *Wavelength* is the horizontal distance separating two wave crests or two wave troughs; the *velocity* is the distance travelled by the wave in a unit period of time; the *period* of wave is the length of time required for two crests or two troughs to pass a fixed point; and the *frequency* is the number of periods that occur within a set interval of time – say a minute.

It is important to remember, when we see a procession of waves coming in from the ocean, that it is the form of the wave that moves forward through the water and not the water itself. It is rather like the rippling motion that wind makes as it blows across a field of corn: waves follow one another across the stalks of wheat, and yet the wheat does not pile up in a heap on the far side of the field! Instead, the motion of the grain results from the nodding of the individual stalks each time a wave passes through them. Similarly, particles within a wave in the ocean do not move forward with the advancing wave itself but follow a circular orbit (figure 8.1).

If the wind that generates the waves is strong and reasonably constant, the waves will increase in size as long as the wind blows, and will gain their energy from the wind. In enclosed seas the limitation on the largest size of wave that can be produced is the distance of open water in a straight line, known as the *fetch*. High winds will generate waves related to fetch by the formula

$$H = 0.36 \sqrt{F}$$

where H is the wave height in metres, and F is the fetch in kilometres. For long fetches, H is general-

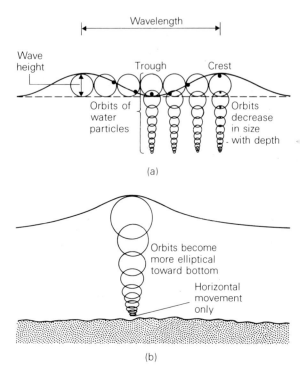

Figure 8.1 The motion of waves. (a) Wave forms are produced by the orbital motions of water particles – each water particle continues orbiting about the same position while the wave form travels. (b) Orbits of water particles become elliptical as they approach a shallow bottom; at the bottom, particles move back and forth only.

ly held to be proportional to U^2, where U is the wind speed:

$$H = 0.0024 \, U^2$$

Once again, H is the height in metres, and U is the wind speed in kilometres per hour.

There appears to be a finite limit to the size that waves can reach. In the open ocean they have occasionally been observed with a height of as much as 34 m, wavelengths of over 800 m, velocities over 120 km h^{-1} and periods of 22.5 s.

As they move shorewards, however, waves change in character. They lose energy abruptly when they arrive at the coast, for as they move into shallow water they suffer friction and distortion. This process, which eventually causes the wave to break, seems to start when the depth of water is equal to about half the wavelength. The waves become shortened and their height increases relatively, until the upper part of the wave

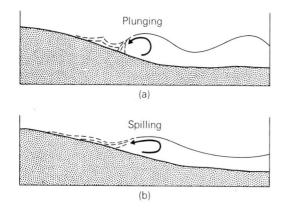

Figure 8.2 Two different types of wave which have great geomorphological significance: (a) destructive; (b) constructive.

topples over. The wave breaks at the *plunge line*, where the depth of water and the wave height are approximately equal. Above this line the water rushes shorewards as *swash*, carrying sand with it. On a sloping beach it will run back down as *backwash*.

The relationship between the shore profile and the waves breaking upon it determines the effect of the waves on beach materials, and hence on beach form. With small, long-wavelength waves and/or a shallow gradient shore profile, the wavefront steepens relatively gradually, and instead of breaking forcefully it spills over. As such waves move up the beach they rapidly lose volume and energy by percolating into the beach materials, and thus the backwash has much less energy to remove sediments down the beach. The backwash is also not sufficiently strong, in spite of having gravity on its side, to impede the following wave-break and swash. These waves therefore tend to be constructive and to be important in building up beaches (figure 8.2).

Destructive waves, by contrast, are those with short wavelengths and high crests occurring on a more steeply sloping shore. Such waves plunge rather than spill, causing erosion and generating a powerful backwash. They comb down the beach and move sand below low tide level. In temperate areas there is often a seasonal change between winter storm wave environments, which cut, and summer low-energy waves, which result in filling.

Beaches produced by short waves tend to be rather steep, whereas beaches formed under the influence of long swells tend to be wide and gentle. The reason for this contrast is related to the volume of water put on to the beach; the large volumes associated with long waves are capable of transporting sediment over a low slope, whereas the shorter waves have a much smaller water volume and hence need a steeper gradient if they are to transport the sediment.

Another important control of beach gradient is the grain size of the material involved. In general, the steepest beaches occur on the coarsest materials. This is because percolation rates increase as sediment becomes coarser, so steeper slopes are required before swash and the greatly diminished backwash are in equilibrium.

The backwash caused by the withdrawal of water carried shoreward by wave action may return down the beach either as *undertow* (sheet flow near the seabed, or in localised *rip currents* (figure 8.3). These are threads of water about 30 m wide, which flow through the breaker line at velocities of up to 8 km h^{-1} before dispersing seaward. A light or moderate swell produces numerous rip currents, while a heavy swell produces a few concentrated rips, fed by strong lateral currents in the surf zone. The currents and the rips themselves cut channels along the beach and through any sand bars that may be lying parallel to the shore.

The nature and importance of wave action varies in different environments, and R. A. Davies

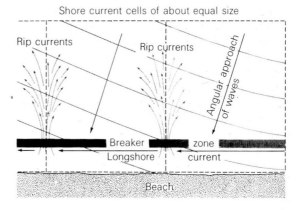

Figure 8.3 Rip currents flow out from the shore when, as a result of oblique wave attack, which forms the longshore current, the water tends to pile up; they break through the surf zone, fan out and dissipate.

has classified wave environments into four main types:

(a) storm wave environments
(b) west coast swell environments
(c) east coast swell environments
(d) protected sea environments.

Storm wave environments are those in which gales are frequent – namely the regions of cyclonic frontal activity in the higher mid-latitudes of both hemispheres. In the high polar regions and the tropical zones gales are infrequent, with the notable exception of tropical cyclones (hurricanes). The waves of this environment are short, high-energy waves of varying direction.

West coast swell environments have waves that are generated at some distance, generally by temperate latitude gales associated with the great belts of westerly winds. This westerly swell is particularly in evidence along such coasts as those of Peru and West Africa, where strong winds are few or offshore in direction so that there are not many locally produced waves of geomorphological importance. The waves are long and low and relatively consistent in frequency of occurrence and direction.

East coast swell environments are characterised by waves generated by the trade winds, and they are less subject to the regular swell generated in extra-tropical westerly wind belts. Superimposed on the swell, there may be important waves generated by the hurricanes that are such a feature of the east sides of the land masses in low latitudes. With the exception of the cyclone-generated waves, mean energy levels on such coasts are low to moderate, and are generally lower than those of the west coast swell environments.

Protected sea environments are coasts of seas in which there is little penetration of oceanic swell, either because they are enclosed (e.g. the Black Sea) or because they are protected by ice cover (e.g. parts of the Arctic Ocean).

Given variations in wave type and sediment character, it is obvious that there will be a wide range of different beach forms. However, it is worth discussing the form of an idealised beach (figure 8.4). This is composed of two main elements and sundry smaller ones. The first of the main elements is the *upper beach*, which is often composed of coarse materials such as pebbles and, being coarse, tends to have a slope of up to 10°–20°. The second is the *lower beach*, which, being generally formed of sand or even mud, has a low gradient (as low as 2° or less). On many though not all beaches there is quite a sharp break between these two elements. The minor elements that may be superimposed on this generalised section are:

(a) the storm beach – a well-defined and semi-permanent ridge standing above the level of highest spring tides;

Figure 8.4 The idealised features of a sand and shingle beach.

(b) beach ridges or *berms*, which are built up at successive levels below that of high spring tides by constructive waves;

(c) Beach *cusps* – small regular embayments developed on the face of the shingle or at the junction of the shingle and sand beaches;

(d) small channels – formed in the sand by water draining from the beach at low tide;

(e) ripples – developed on the sand by wave action or tidal currents;

(f) ridges and runnels – broad and gentle rises and depressions aligned parallel to the shoreline and found to the seaward side of the sand beach.

Waves do more than merely control (with the assistance of sediment size) the gradients and profiles of beaches. They are also extremely important in moving material along the shore. In an idealised situation, in which waves approach a completely straight coastline with their crests parallel to that line, a given wave will break at the same instant at all points and the swash will ride up the beach at right angles to the shoreline. The backwash will return along the same line. Consequently, particles of sand will move up and down

the beach slope along a fixed line. In the real world, however, such simplicity is seldom found, either because the shoreline is not completely straight, or because the waves approach the coast at an oblique angle, or because the depth of water offshore varies. As waves move towards the coast they are *refracted* as they are slowed down by the shallowing bottom. As the sections of a wave over the shallowest areas fall behind those still in deeper water the wave crests are distorted. This has an effect on the distribution of wave energy along the crest; for converging *orthogonals* (lines drawn at right angles to the wave crests) indicate a concentration of wave energy, and diverging orthogonals indicate areas of lower wave energy. Headlands will thus tend to be subjected to greater energy levels than the bays in between (figure 8.5).

Although wave refraction tends to cause wave crests to become curved in plan and to become more nearly parallel to the shoreline, the waves generally arrive in the breaker zone at an oblique approach. The swash therefore rides up the beach at an oblique angle, moving sediment with it. After the swash has spent its energy, the backwash flows down the slope of the beach under the influence of gravity, and so sediment moves back

Figure 8.5 Wave refraction. (a) The part of the wave that first encounters shallow water slows in speed, while that part of the wave still in deeper water continues to move with its original speed, making the wave change angle. (b) Because of the configuration of shallow and deep water around headlands and bays in a shoreline, wave energies are concentrated at projections and dispersed at indentations.

Plate 8.1 When waves approach the coastline they are refracted as they are slowed down by the shallowing bottom. This air photograph of Start Point in Devon shows the process clearly.

down the beach at a different angle to the shoreline from the one it went up. As a result, over a period of time the waves move sediment along the beach, by a process called *littoral* or *longshore drift*. Such littoral drift forms some important landforms (figure 8.6).

When a coastline possesses an embayment like an estuary or ria, littoral drift will tend to build a narrow beach across the embayment. Such a beach is called a *spit*. Because of wave refraction in the embayment across which the spit is growing, sediment is carried round the spit end and so a landward curvature develops. If the spit continues to grow it may eventually seal off the embayment, forming a *baymouth bar*. Another landform produced by the same process is the connection of an island to the mainland by the growth of a *tombolo* (figure 8.7). If the littoral drift converges from opposite directions upon

a given point on a shoreline, sediment may accumulate in the form of a *cuspate bar*, which may eventually expand to become a *cuspate foreland*.

8.3 Barrier beaches and related forms

The deposition of beach material offshore, or across the mouths of inlets or embayments, in such a way as to form barriers extending above the normal level of highest tides and partly or wholly enclosing lagoons is a widely distributed phenomenon. While some may form by the longshore growth of spits, others appear to develop offshore, especially where there is abundant sand to form the barrier, a suitably low gradient on which it can be formed and constructive waves associated with swell conditions. It has been estimated that barrier coasts comprise about 13 per

Figure 8.6 Some important examples of constructional features developed on the coastline of England and Wales.

cent of the world coastline. The longest stretches of barrier coastline are along the eastern coast of the United States and in the Gulf of Mexico (figure 8.8), but they are also common elsewhere, particularly on the shores of seas with a low tidal range, like the Mediterranean and the Baltic. They are less common in areas with high tidal range, and they become more fragmented as tidal range increases because of the action of tidal currents between the lagoon and the open sea.

Great Orme's Head

Carboniferous Limestone

Former Island

Llandudno   Little Orme

Tombolo

Mainland

Bridge

R. Conway

▦ Town

▣ Shingle and sand

Figure 8.7 (left) An example of a tombolo, which forms the land upon which the Welsh holiday resort of Llandudno is sited.

The exact mechanism by which the plentiful supply of sand is thrown up into a barrier and maintained above water level is the subject of considerable debate. At one time it was thought that a fall in sea level would expose a bar of sediment that had been formed beneath the waves as a breakpoint bar, but in most parts of the world sea level has generally been rising rather than falling over the last 10 000 years or so. An alternative explanation is that they are formed as a result of a rising sea level, such as has characterised the Flandrian Transgression (see section 2.15), which has partially submerged an old beach ridge capped by sand dunes. Other workers maintain that sea level change is not a *sine qua non* for their formation, and that submerged shoals can be built up so close to sea level that eventually the action of swash takes over and constructs them into an island or bar. Once the island is formed, sand may accumulate as dunes, and so the feature can be raised above water level.

8.4 Tides

Although waves are probably the most important process whereby coastlines are moulded, tides are also extremely important, for they help to control the height range over which wave action can operate.

Tides are regular movements of the ocean water arising from the gravitational attraction of the moon and, though to a lesser extent, the sun on the earth. This attraction causes the waters to be gathered as bulges at two opposite sides of the earth, so that on an earth wholly covered with water two areas of high water would be produced. These bulges are held fixed beneath the moon as the earth spins, giving high and low tides twice a day. The sun, though much farther away, has so much more mass than the moon that it too causes tides, though they are less than half the height of moon tides. The two sets of tides are not synchronous, those related to the sun coming every 24 hours. When the earth, moon and sun line up, the combined gravitational pull of the moon and sun reinforce each other and produce very high tides – the *spring tides*. The lowest tides – *neaps* – come when the sun and the moon are at right angles to each other with respect to the earth.

The above account describes what is termed the *equilibrium tide* – one that is calculated for a uniform globe. The earth's surface, of course, is, not uniform, so the heights of the actual tides are very different in different parts of the oceans. Because the oceans are of various shapes and sizes, tidal response is complicated. Their effect has been likened to connecting a great number of large and small pots and bowls in a complicated pattern and sloshing water back and forth between them.

In some constricted arms of the oceans like the Severn Estuary in Britain (maximum tidal range 13 m) and the Bay of Fundy in Canada (maximum tidal range 15–17 m), tidal ranges are high. On coasts facing the open ocean the range seldom exceeds 2 m, and in enclosed seas like the Mediterranean there is hardly any tidal range at all. In the Black Sea the range is no more than 10 cm. In the seas around the UK the complexity imposed by local factors becomes very apparent. After passing up the western coasts, the crest of a tidal wave swings around Scotland and into the North Sea, and then proceeds southwards. In passing northwards up the Irish Sea the Coriolis Force (see section 2.2) results in the tides being at least twice as high on the Welsh and English sides as on the Irish. The tides coming down the North Sea are higher in Britain than in Norway and Denmark, because the Coriolis Force drives the water towards the right. The tides running up the English Channel from the west are also forced to the right, giving the French coasts higher tides than the English. As one might imagine, where the tidal crests merge, as they do in the Straits of Dover and the southern North Sea, exceptional complexity arises.

The geomorphological consequences of tidal action are twofold: they create tidal currents, and they spread wave activity over varying height ranges.

Tidal currents are caused in two main situations. First, when there is a difference in the time of high tide between two ends of a strait, obviously a steep gradient is developed between the two ends. If the straits are narrow a strong current can develop. The second situation occurs even when there is no difference at either end of a

(a)

(b)

Figure 8.8 Barrier islands: (a) the outer banks of North Carolina, USA; (b) the offshore barrier island of the Texas coast; (c) a schematic representation of a barrier island, separated from the mainland by a wide lagoon; sediments gradually fill the lagoon, while dune ridges advance over the tidal flats.

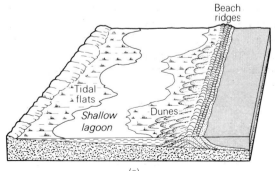

(c)

strait, and simply results from the canalisation of the tide within a narrow strait or estuary. Velocities in tidal currents can be high (up to 8 km h^{-1} in the Straits of Messina, 17–18 km h^{-1} between Alderney and the Cotentin Peninsula; and up to 25 km h^{-1} in the Moluccas), though the values given here are exceptional. Strong currents can cause erosion, while slower currents may be effective in moving silt and sand stirred into suspension by waves.

The tidal range of an area influences the relative importance of wave activity. Thus, if the tidal range is less than about 2 m, it can probably be assumed that wave action is the dominant coastal landforming process, with the result that such features as beaches, spits, and barrier islands are prominent. For example, if one looks at the English and Welsh coasts there are only three areas which experience tides with a range that is below c 3 m: the east Norfolk coast, the southern coast from Start Point to the Isle of Wight and part of the Welsh coast. This distribution coincides with the occurrence of spits along the coast (see figure 8.9).

Figure 8.10 Areas flooded by the great surge on the east coast of England in 1953.

8.5 Storm surges

Although waves and tides are the two main processes that mould coastlines, storm surges or storm tides may be of considerable importance in certain locations. These occur when water is piled up against the coast by very strong onshore winds and waves. In this way sea level may be raised by some metres, so that wave attack is lifted to unusually high, and often dangerous, levels. Both tropical cyclones and temperate frontal storms may generate surges, and they are especially severe in gulfs or gulf-like seas which are enclosed on all sides except that from which the big waves

Figure 8.9 The distribution of spits in England and Wales. The main concentrations occur where the tidal range is less than about 3 metres, though there are exceptions to this rule.

come. Areas that are known to be prone to them include the Gulf of Mexico, the Bay of Bengal, the Gulf of Tonkin and the southern part of the North Sea. Low-lying coasts such as the Netherlands and the Thames Estuary (figure 8.10) may be severely flooded if surges and high tides coincide, and are magnified in their influence by large flows coming down major rivers. It was this combination of circumstances that produced the serious floods around the southern North Sea in 1953 (see section 4.17).

8.6   Estuaries

Estuaries are the tidal mouths of great rivers. They are inlets of the sea reaching into river valleys as far as the upper limit of tidal rise. They are, however, very different from rivers *per se*, even though estuaries depend upon freshwater flow from upland rivers in order to maintain their characteristic processes. The two-way flow of estuarine water, the currents set up by the mixing of saline and fresh water, and the continuous variations which take place in both discharge and velocity during the course of a tidal cycle, mean that their processes are highly distinctive.

There are two large-scale flows in estuaries which serve to mould them: tidal currents caused by the movement of the tides up the inlet, and *residual currents* caused by the mixing of fresh and saline waters of different densities. These two types of current determine patterns of erosion and deposition of sediments within the inlets. Tidal range determines the tidal current and residual current velocities and therefore the amount and source of sediments. *Micro-tidal estuaries* occur where tidal range is less than 2 m and so are dominated by freshwater inflow upstream of the mouth and by wind-driven waves seaward of the mouth. They often contain a fluvial delta and spits and bars at the seaward margin. In *meso-tidal estuaries* (tidal range *c.*2–4 m) tidal currents are of greater importance but because of the still somewhat modest tidal range tidal flow does not extend very far upstream. Thus most meso-tidal estuaries are relatively stubby. In the case of *macro-tidal estuaries*, tidal ranges in excess of 4 m produce a situation where tidal influences extend far inland. Such estuaries have long, linear sand bars parallel to the tidal flow, but their most distinguishing characteristic is their trumpet-shaped flare. The Severn Estuary in Britain, the Delaware Estuary in the USA, and the Plate Estuary in Latin America are prime examples of this type.

Plate 8.2   The worst coastal flooding that has taken place in Britain in recent decades occurred in February 1953, when areas like Canvey Island were inundated by a storm surge. In this picture an amphibious DUKW vehicle churns up a muddy wake as it cruises down a Canvey Island street.

8.7 Coastal dunes

Inshore from the beach on many coasts there is a belt of sand dunes, though their presence and form depend on a combination of favourable circumstances. First, an abundant supply of sand of suitable grain size (generally about 0.25 mm diameter) is necessary for the dunes to build up. Rivers may be a major source of such sand, though substantial quantities may also have been provided during the Holocene rise in sea level (the Flandrian Transgression) which combed up sandy materials from the continental shelf and deposited them on beaches. Some sand may also be provided by the attrition of rock or coral debris. Second, given a supply of sand on the beach, it is necessary to have winds blowing onshore with sufficient frequency and velocity to transport the sand inland.

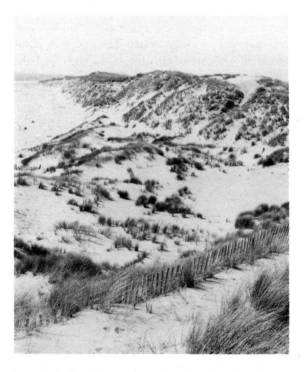

Plate 8.3 Coastal dunes at Braunton Burrows, Devon, England. Note the extensive cover of marram grass (*Ammophila arenaria*), a plant which colonizes the sand at an early stage of dune evolution, and helps to promote stabilization.

The overall importance of wind velocity in the evolution of large dune systems on coasts is attested by the preferential occurrence of dunes on temperate mid-latitude coasts where there is intense frontal activity. Large dunes occur on windward coasts as compared with leeward. Dunes are relatively rare in the doldrum zone of low latitudes, though wind velocity is probably only one of the factors involved here. In very wet areas the beach may be so damp for so long that the wind velocities required to entrain sand grains would need to be very high, and therefore sand movement is infrequent. Tidal range also seems to play a role, for beaches with a larger tidal range expose a larger sand expanse to wind action. A large tidal range also tends to produce a lower-gradient beach, and this favours sand movement because threshold velocities for sand movement increase with the steepness of the slope up which the sand is being moved.

Thus we can conclude that large coastal dune systems are more likely to occur where there is active sand supply, impeded littoral transport, strong onshore winds, low precipitation and humidity, high tidal ranges and low beach face angles. There also needs to be suitable topography behind the beach on which dunes can accumulate – beaches backed by high cliffs are most unlikely to have big dunes.

If colossal quantities of sand are available, or if the climate is so arid that there is no vegetation cover inland from the beach, one may encounter some of the classic dunes that are characteristic of the world's great deserts (see section 5.10). This is the case in parts of Washington and Oregon in the western United States, where there are no plant species capable of binding the sand very effectively, and along the hyper-arid desert coasts of the Namib and Morocco, among others. In such situations one may find large fields of free-moving barchans and transverse ridges. On most coasts, however, including those of Britain, vegetation is a major influence that affects the growth and form of dunes.

Parallel to many beaches there is a *frontal dune* or foredune. This is formed where sand is trapped on litter deposited by high tides or on vegetation. Dunes are initiated when sand accumulates round, or is colonised by, certain species of grass that tolerate sandy and salty conditions. In Britain the two main species are sea couch grass (*Agropyron junceiforme*) and marram grass (*Ammophila arenaria*). These grasses have extensive root systems, which hold the sand in place, and they trap further sand, with the result that individual small mounds grow and coalesce. Under favourable conditions the dunes will grow steadily in height, for their vigorous roots may grow fast enough to allow 50–60 cm of sand to accumulate in one year, and will give a continuous dune-line backing the sandy beach. If the dunes are breached by the sea because of a storm, or if the vegetation cover is disturbed by man or animals such as the rabbit, the exposed sand may be blown beyond the ridge, leaving behind a large gap or corridor in the foredune. A *blowout* has occurred, and sand may accumulate further inland of the gap as a hairpin-shaped dune called a *parabolic*. In this way sand may move inland.

In an area where the coast is building out, new foredunes may develop seaward of the original ridge. When this happens the inner dunes will start to decay, because they are cut off from their sand supply. They become degraded by rain, stabilised by an increasingly dense vegetation cover (including plants like heather, gorse and birch), and weathered so that a marked soil profile may develop. Such dunes are called *remanié* dunes. The low-lying areas between successive ridges are called *slacks*, which may be damp areas with their own plant assemblages. In some parts of the lower and middle latitudes, where the sands can be highly calcareous, the dunes may become *lithified* (cemented) as they get older to give a material that is sometimes hard enough to be used as a building stone. Such material is called *aeolianite*, and it has been extensively quarried around the Mediterranean Basin to build structures as different as Roman temples (as in Libya) or modern package tour hotels (as in Mallorca).

Sand dunes are important; they are a widespread type of landform, and they provide valuable habitats for a great diversity of interesting plants and animals. They are also a very good form of coastal defence. Finally, they are very beautiful. If they are abused by human activity they may march inland, overwhelming farmlands and buildings, or they may be degraded or breached. If, on the other hand, they are protected from overgrazing, deforestation, trampling and mining, they can prove an effective barrier against wave attack on low-lying coasts.

8.8 Salt marshes

In our discussion of the formation of coastal dunes we have seen the important role that vegetation plays. The same is true of another major coastal environmental type – the salt marsh.

In areas sheltered from wave action, as in estuaries or in the lee of spits and barriers, coastal accretion takes the form of mud flats which are subject to tidal flooding. The accretion is promoted by vegetation that is adapted to periodic inundation by salt water, whether it be the salt marsh vegetation of temperate regions or the mangrove swamp of low latitudes (see section 6.10). Sediment carried into marsh vegetation communities by the rising tide is filtered out by the vegetation and retained as the tide ebbs. In this way the level of the land is gradually built up, and vegetated marshland encroaches across the estuary or tidal flat. The rate of accretion is relatively slow at first because the vegetation cover is sporadic, but as the process goes on and the level of the land is raised, the vegetation cover becomes denser, and is therefore more efficient as a filter and stabiliser. Towards the end of the process the height of the marsh is such that the frequency of tidal inundation is reduced, and so the rate of accretion declines. Accretion tends to be uneven, so most marshes have well developed creek systems and small basins, called *pans*.

The sequence of vegetation colonisation as the accretion process goes on varies from area to area, but it does provide a good example of the early stages of a phenomenon called *vegetation succession* (see section 9.5). In southern England, in the early stages bare mud flats accumulate patches of green algae such as *Enteromorpha*. This allows some sediment accumulation, which permits the colonisation of muddy areas by some salt-tolerant plants (*halophytes*) such as *Salicornia* and *Suaeda maritima*. These plants are only annuals and so are of limited effectiveness for trapping silt for much of the year. None the less, they do in time permit sufficient accretion to take place so that other plants can come in that, although less tolerant of inundation and salinity,

Plate 8.4 Large areas of salt marsh have developed behind the coastal barrier of Scolt Head Island in Norfolk, England. In the foreground there are old shingle ridges formed by the growth of the barrier along the coast. Note the intricate creek system which will be flooded at high tide.

provide a denser, higher and longer-lasting vegetation cover. These include *Aster tripolium, Limonium vulgare* and *Puccinellia maritima.* Trapping of sediment by the often fleshy foliage is now greatly accelerated, and the marsh may grow at rates approaching 1 cm yr^{-1}. Creeks become established, and they are lined by a plant that likes the relatively well drained conditions on their banks, namely *Halimione portulacoides.* This plant is effective at trapping the silt and so may tend to stabilise the creeks and to cause the development of slight levées along their margins. Towards the end of the marsh-building phase plants such as *Juncus maritimus* become domi-

nant, and when the marsh is sufficiently high for inundation to be rare, freshwater sedges and reeds appear.

In Britain the speed of marsh accretion has been greatly accelerated in some areas by the introduction of a plant called *Spartina.* This has been a particularly effective salt marsh pioneer species since the vigorous hybrid *Spartina townsendii* originated in Southampton water as a cross between native British and American species in the 1870s. It perennial, tough spiky grass is very effective at trapping silt, and rates of accretion of 1–5 cm yr^{-1} may occur. It is very useful as a means of reclaiming land from the sea or for

Plate 8.5 As vegetation traps more silt, the general level of the salt marsh is raised, and creek systems develop. This creek, on the edge of Poole Harbour, Dorset, England, is lined by *Halimione portulacoides*. Creek systems on salt marshes differ from ordinary rivers in the way in which they rapidly flare out downstream.

stabilising mud flats, but unfortunately it also reduces the beauty and variety of the normal natural marshlands.

8.9 Coast erosion

The sea can be a potent agent of erosion. The destructive impact of waves against obstacles in their path can be substantial, and it has been calculated that the average pressure exerted by Atlantic waves in winter is not much under 10 000 kg m^{-2}, while in great storms it may exceed 30 000. Thus cliffs and man-made structures like sea walls are subjected to shocks of enormous intensity. Furthermore, water driven into cracks in the rock may compress the air that is already there, creating an explosive blast. This combination of bombardment and blasting is augmented by the impact of sediment thrown up by

the waves. In areas of susceptible rocks these mechanical processes may be assisted by weathering achieved by solution and by salt-laden spray. Furthermore, cliffs exposed to wave attack are at the same time exposed to the various subaerial processes of frost weathering and mass movements, and the sea is very effective, through the agency of longshore drift and tidal currents, at removing the debris supplied to the base of the cliff by these processes.

Erosion is most rapid in areas of friable, uncemented sediments and rocks. Glacial drifts, clays, Tertiary sands and gravels and volcanic ash are the sorts of materials that can be eroded very quickly; some rates of cliff retreat to which they are subjected are listed in table 8.1. In more resistant rocks, rates of cliff recession will be less, but even then, if wave action is marked and longshore drift active, the rates are measurable. The form of cliffs in resistant rocks will tend to be more complex than those in softer rocks, because wave action will eat out joints, fractures and faults. Caves, stacks, stumps, arches, blowholes and enlarged joints (called *geos*) are the sorts of features that may form (see figure 8.11). The joint pattern is also of considerable importance in controlling the nature of the cliff profile. If the beds dip fairly steeply towards the sea, there is a tendency for blocks of rock to break off at the joint planes, usually at right angles to the bedding, so that the cliff profile tends to be dominated by the dip of the beds. On the other hand, where the beds have an almost vertical or horizontal dip, joint blocks cannot so readily break off and slip down the bedding planes: the result is a tendency for cliffs to be more nearly vertical.

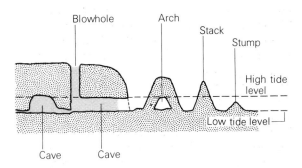

Figure 8.11 The formation of caves, blowholes, arches, stacks and stumps by marine erosion.

Table 8.1   Selected rates of cliff recession

Lithology	Location	Rate (m per 100 yrs)
Glacial drift	Holderness, E. England	175
Pleistocene deposits	Pakefield, E. Anglia	300
Volcanic ash	Krakatoa, E. Indies	3000
London clay	Isle of Sheppey	300
Pleistocene deposits	Dunwich, E. Anglia	400
Glacial drift	North Yorkshire	30
Chalk	Isle of Thanet, Kent	30
Chalk	Sussex	50
Lias shales	North Yorkshire	9

Plate 8.6 Cliffs are moulded both by direct marine influences and by sub-aerial processes. These cliffs in North Devon, England, appear to be largely inactive at present with respect to marine attack, and may be largely formed by frost weathering and soil creep.

Figure 8.12 The formation of a wave-cut platform by gradual cliff retreat.

Cliff forms will be more complex where rocks of differing character are exposed in the cliff face. If resistant rocks overlie rather weak rocks, the preferential attack of the sea on the weak rock will cause the undermining of the resistant upper beds, and major landslides may occur. A good example of this in England is the way in which the chalk has slipped over the weak Gault clay in Folkestone Warren, Kent.

As cliffs are worn back a *shore platform* (figure 8.12) is left in front, the upper part of which is visible as a rocky foreshore at low tide. The platform is caused partly by the abrasion of sand and shingle sweeping across it as the tide goes in and out, but in limestones, solution and other types of weathering may contribute to its development. In Britain spectacular examples of shore platforms, some a few hundred metres wide, occur on either side of the Bristol Channel, where they are associated with Liassic and Carboniferous limestones, but other fine examples can be found at low tide at the foot of some of the great chalk cliffs of the south coast of England as near Beachy Head. There is probably some limit to how wide these features can become, because as the wave platform becomes broader and broader an increasing proportion of wave energy will be expended by passage through the shallow water overlying the platform, and attack on the cliff base will become less intense.

Rock structures and character are also highly important in controlling the plan of a coastline. Where tectonic processes have created folding at right angles to the trend of the coast, a series of bays and headlands develops. South-west Ireland shows this type of *Atlantic coastline*. If, on the other hand, the general trend of the fold structures is parallel to the coast, as in Yugoslavia, a *Dalmatian coastline* is produced, with elongated islands and inlets running parallel to the coast.

8.10   The human impact on the coastline

Because of the concentration of so many settlements and human activities on the coastline, the pressures being placed on coastal environments are often acute, and the consequences of excessive erosion will be serious. We have already seen the importance of a plant that was introduced by man, *Spartina townsendii*, in altering the nature of salt marshes, and we have also seen that sand dunes can easily be affected by deforestation, trampling and other pressures so that their effectiveness as a coastal barrier is greatly reduced.

While most areas are subject to some degree of natural erosion and accretion, the balance can be upset by human activity in a variety of different ways. In general, the changes are the unexpected and unwelcome results of various economic activities, though perversely in some areas coastal erosion has been accelerated as a result of man's attempts to reduce it.

One of the best forms of coastal defence is a good beach. Thus, if material is removed from a beach to provide minerals of economic worth or aggregates for construction purposes, accelerated *cliff retreat* may take place. The classic example of this process was the mining of 660 000 tonnes of shingle from the beach at Hallsands in Devon in southern England in 1887 to provide material for the construction of the naval dockyards at Plymouth. The shingle proved to be undergoing very little natural replenishment, and in consequence the shore level was reduced by about 4 m, and the loss of protective shingle soon resulted in cliff erosion, which amounted to 6 m between 1907 and 1957. As a consequence the little village of Hallsands was cruelly attacked by waves and is now mostly abandoned and in ruins.

Plate 8.7   At Porthleven in Cornwall, western England, a wide shore platform occurs beneath a cliff line indented with caves. The large boulder in the foreground is an erratic that may have been dumped by a Pleistocene iceberg. Although such platforms are often described as being 'wave-cut', other processes, including frost and salt weathering, may play a role in their development.

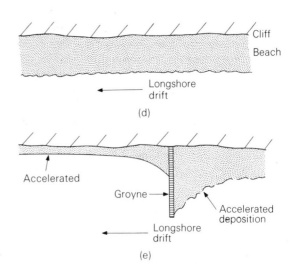

Figure 8.13 Human influences on coast erosion. (a) – (c) Sea walls and erosion: a broad high beach prevents storm waves from breaking against a sea wall and will persist, or erode only slowly; but where waves are reflected by the wall, scour is accelerated, and the beach is quickly removed and lowered. (d) – (e) Diagrammatic illustration of the effects of groyne construction on sedimentation on a beach.

Another common cause of beach and cliff erosion at one point is coast protection at another (figure 8.13). Engineers frequently try by constructing groynes, to create a broad beach to protect a cliff from erosion. Groynes will accelerate accumulation, but they may mean that sediment is not transported, as it was in the past, further along the shoreline by longshore drift. Thus protection by the groynes may cause serious beach depletion and erosion further along the coast.

Piers or breakwaters can have similar effects to groynes. This has occurred at various points along the British coast: erosion at Seaford in Sussex resulted from the Newhaven breakwater; erosion at Lowestoft resulted from the pier at Gorleston; and erosion at West Bay in Dorset followed the construction of a harbour mouth jetty.

One of the reasons why sediment mining from beaches and the construction of groynes, piers and breakwaters can be so serious is that in many parts of the world beaches are no longer being so actively replenished as they were in the past. There is now abundant evidence to indicate that much of the reservoir of sand and shingle that creates beaches is in some respects a relict feature.

Much of it was deposited on the continental shelf during the maximum of the last glaciation (around 18 000 years BP), when sea level was about 120–140 m below its present level. It was transported shorewards and incorporated in present-day beaches during the phase of rapidly rising postglacial sea levels that characterised the Flandrian Transgression until about 6000 years BP. Since that time world sea levels have been relatively stable, and as a consequence much less material is being added to beaches and shingle complexes.

In some parts of the world the sediments brought to the coastline by rivers are an important source of material for beach replenishment, for they become incorporated into beaches through the mechanism of longshore drift. Thus any change in the sediment load of such rivers may result in a change in the sediment budget of neighbouring beaches. On the one hand, accelerated soil erosion in their catchments may cause beach accretion and silting of estuaries, while on the other the building of dams may trap river sediments so that coastal erosion occurs.

In other parts of the world vegetation modification by man creates the potential for increased erosion. In low latitudes some small islands are, under natural conditions, covered by a dense thicket of vegetation that acts as a baffle against waves and as a means of trapping coral blocks and shingle thrown up by cyclonic storms. However, on many islands the natural vegetation has been replaced by coconut plantations: these have an open structure, shallow roots and little or no undergrowth, so they are impotent in the face of hurricane attack. Observations during Hurricane Hattie in Belize, Central America, showed that, where the natural vegetation had been replaced by coconuts, the heights of the small sandy islands (*cays*) was reduced by around 2 m; whereas, where natural sediments remained, banking of storm sediments against the vegetation thicket led to net vertical increases in height over 1 m.

In recent years a new human threat to world shorelines has emerged: accelerated sea-level rise. Over the last century or so, world sea levels appear to have risen by around 15 cm, and this has coincided with a general warming in global temperatures. The reason for this is that increased temperatures cause the world's ice sheets and glaciers to melt more quickly, and to deliver more water into the oceans. In addition, as the temperature of ocean water increases it also expands in volume. The human role in this relates to the probability that the burning of fossil fuels and the removal of large areas of forest in the humid tropics and elsewhere has caused the amount of carbon dioxide in the atmosphere to increase. As explained in section 6.7 increased carbon dioxide levels in the atmosphere lead to an increase in atmospheric temperatures as a result of the 'greenhouse effect'.

It has been projected that in the future atmspheric carbon dioxide levels will continue to rise, and so it is probable that global temperatures and global sea levels will also continue to rise. Predictions are surrounded by certain difficulties, so that precise estimates of what is likely to happen vary considerably, but it is probable that over the next century the average amount of rise will be

Plate 8.8   The ruined village of Hallsands in Devon, which was attacked by the sea when its beach was depleted by shingle removal for the construction of Plymouth dockyards in 1887.

somewhere between 25 and 150 cm. For communities living in low-lying coastal areas, particularly those which may also be suffering from subsidence caused by local tectonic activity, such rates may be a cause for considerable concern, for they are likely to cause accelerated flooding and accelerated erosion. Sandy beaches will probably erode by 1 m or more for every 1 cm-rise in sea level, and saline waters may advance for considerable distances up estuaries and tidal rivers, posing problems for drinking water supplies. In addition, many salt marshes will be flooded and coastal barriers may be overtopped with greater regularity.

Plate 8.9 At West Bay, Dorset, the construction of a breakwater for the harbour, has caused changes in the configuration of the beach. This sequence of photos shows the position of the beach in 1860, 1900 and 1976. While accretion is taking place in the foreground, severe coastal retreat has taken place on the far side of the breakwater, and coast protection has had to be adopted. Note how the beach in front of the cliff has narrowed.

PART IV

Landscapes and Ecosystems

9 Plants and Animals

9.1 Ecology and ecosystems

The study of the interactions between organisms (plants and animals) and their environment is called *ecology*, and the term *ecosystem* is used to describe any unit that involves the interactions, in a given area, of organisms with the physical environment, so that a flow of energy leads to an exchange of materials between living and non-living parts within the system. An ecosystem can be of any size, from a cowpat or a goldfish bowl to the Amazon rain forest or the world as a whole. Scientists who study the various relationships between the different components of an ecosystem are called *ecologists*.

The key features of an ecosystem are the transmissions of energy through its different components, and the source of this energy can be traced back to solar radiation. This provides both the energy of wind and rain and the energy used by plants in *photosynthesis*, a process that leads to the creation of plant tissue, the basic food for the animal population. The decaying plant and animal remains are incorporated into the soil, and the nutrients they release are taken up again by plants.

Let us start with a consideration of green plants. These contain the pigment chlorophyll, which can absorb energy derived from the sun and convert it into molecules containing carbon (i.e. organic molecules). This process, which is called photosynthesis, is the source of energy in living things and thus in all ecosystems. It converts radiant energy into chemical energy (although some lower organisms can convert energy in the absence of light), and fixes that energy in the form of organic compounds that do not spontaneously break down and can thus be stored until needed by the plant.

For photosynthesis to take place, light, water, carbon dioxide and heat are required. Basically, the elements of carbon dioxide and water are combined with light energy, which is absorbed by the chlorophyll of plant leaves. Molecular processes act on this combination to produce oxygen and organic compounds in the form of glucose and carbohydrates. The oxygen and water vapour are released into the atmosphere as respiration through the stomata of plants. Plants grow when photosynthesis produces plant materials (glucose and carbohydrates) in excess of the rate of utilisation of these materials by the biochemical processes of respiration. In other words, some of the sugar produced by photosynthesis is used as an energy source by the plants for respiration; this energy is degraded from the highly concentrated chemical form to a highly dispersed form as heat, which cannot be recycled into chemical energy but must be radiated out to the atmosphere and then to space and so is lost to the ecosystem.

The rate of organic material output by the plant cover is referred to as *production*, and it is equivalent to net photosynthesis:

$$\text{Net photosynthesis} = \text{total photosynthesis} - \text{respiration}.$$

Production is measured in terms of the weight of organic matter added to a ground area of unit size per unit time (e.g., $g\ m^{-2}\ d^{-1}$). The rate of production depends basically on heat, light, carbon dioxide and water. Under *the principle of limiting factors*, the highest rate of production

Opposite Large herbivores, in this case elephants in the Kidepo Valley National Park, Uganda, are an important component of savanna ecosystems, modifying vegetation through their trampling, pushing, feeding and nutrient recycling.

that can be obtained is controlled by the factor that is in shortest supply. So, for example, without enough heat to maintain a temperature above 10°C, photosynthesis will be minimal no matter how much light, water and carbon dioxide are available. Of the four essential factors, carbon dioxide is the least variable throughout the world, but the other three are highly variable over the planet, and in many regions are also variable from season to season.

Of all the major climatic regions, it is the low latitudes that receive the greatest combined total of heat, moisture and light. This is also the zone in which they are least variable. With such ample and dependable supplies of energy, it is understandable that plant productivity shoud be higher in the tropics than in any other major region. By contrast, in polar regions heat is insufficient to produce appreciable levels of biochemical activity for plant growth; light is severely limited in winter; and for much of the year water is frozen and so is largely unavailable for plant use. The same sort of trends can be seen in the seas (see section 9.3). The most productive environments are the tidal marshes, estuaries and coral reefs of tropical coastlines. In their shallow waters, light, heat and moisture are all present in profusion. By contrast, in the colder, darker waters offshore, production is very much less (say, 1 g m^{-2}d^{-1} compared with 25 g m^{-2}d^{-1}).

The fate of energy can be followed through a consideration of a simple energy transfer model, called a *food chain* (figure 9.1). Each stage in the chain is called a *trophic level*. Plants are the first level in the chain and are called *producers*. Normally, some of the plant material continues as storage in perennial plants, some is eaten by plant-eating animals (*herbivores*) and some dies to form a litter on the soil surface. These herbivorous animals are the second trophic level and are called *primary consumers*. They in turn are eaten by the carnivorous animals (*secondary consumers*) of the third trophic level. Plants and animals that die are chemically decomposed by soil fauna and flora (*decomposer organisms*), which help to recycle mineral nutrients into the system. At each trophic level a conversion to heat takes place, which means that less energy becomes biomass at the succeeding trophic level. No organism can convert the food it makes into an equal amount of stored energy.

Let us consider a simple plant-herbivore-carnivore food chain consisting of grass plants, mice and snakes. The mice obtain approximately 10 per cent of the energy absorbed by the grass plants, and the snakes that feed on the mice obtain approximately 10 per cent of the energy absorbed by the mice. Thus the snake receives only 1 per cent or so of the energy originally absorbed by the plants. The fraction of the original energy available to a succeeding carnivore stage – is still less. This explains why most food chains are limited to four or five trophic levels, and why the animals at the end of the food chain, for example lions, have to roam over large areas to obtain their food, because one small area cannot support many of them.

A food chain is seldom as simple as the fore-

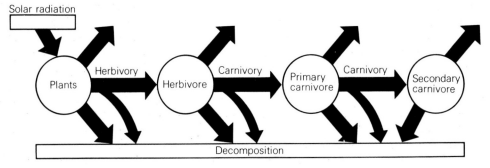

Figure 9.1 Energy flow through a food chain. At each stage some energy is available as food for the next trophic level, some is lost as excretory products, some as decay of dead organisms and some as respiration. Thus the quantity of energy decreases down the chain away from the plants; the number of secondary carnivores in a given area is therefore likely to be much smaller than that of plants. Much of the energy 'lost' to the chain ends up with the decomposer organisms, which in terrestrial ecosystems are in the top few centimetres of the soil.

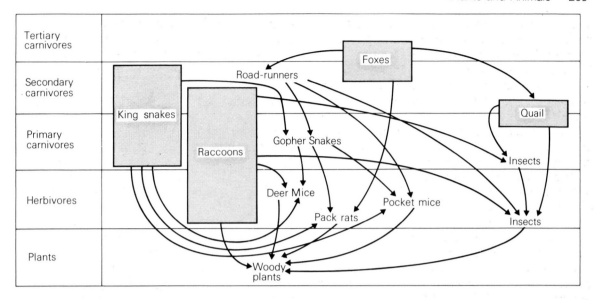

Figure 9.2 A simplified food web, showing some of the more complex linkages in an actual ecosystem – the chaparral scrub of California. The various trophic levels demarcate the animals of different groups and it is noticeable that not all animals are confined to one trophic level – raccoons, for instance, are both herbivores and carnivores. However, they are all ultimately dependent on the plants.

going discussion might imply. It is more realistic to think in terms of a *food web* (see figure 9.2), for the relationships between different organisms are often complex, and there are usually various different species of plants and animals at each trophic level, each animal having its own feeding patterns.

However, to understand how ecosystems function it is necessary to consider elements of the environment other than energy; for life is sustained by a number of chemical elements that enter ecosystems via the plants. Plants are fed by various mineral nutrients that come from the atmosphere and the rocks, and many of the important elements circulate between living organisms and non-living (abiotic) pools of various scales. These movements are generally cyclic, involving the use and re-use of nutrients, and are termed *biogeochemical cycles*.

Eighteen essential nutrients are required by plants to fulfil their growth requirements. These can be divided into the macro-nutrients (e.g. carbon, nitrogen, oxygen, phosphorus, potassium, sulphur and magnesium), and micro-nutrients (manganese, iron, silica, sodium, and chlorine,

and various trace elements such as zinc, molybdenum, boron and copper).

The general nature of a nutrient cycle is shown in figure 9.3 Nutrient inputs come from the weathering of rocks. Silica, aluminium, manganese, potassium and sodium may be made available as nutrients in this way. Another major source of nutrient inputs is the atmosphere, either in precipitation or by biological processes. Rainfall is never entirely pure water, for it contains various impurities, including salt spray and windblown dust. As far as biological processes are concerned, fauna obtains oxygen for respiration from the open atmosphere, and plants absorb nitrogen and carbon dioxide through their leaves. Bacteria and algae may fix nitrogen in the soil. Other nutrient inputs include those brought into an area by animals that have either migrated naturally or have been introduced by man, and fertilizer applied by farmers.

Nutrient outputs are achieved in a variety of ways. Soil erosion by wind and water can lead to the export of large amounts of nutrient material, especially if fertile topsoils are involved. Leaching is also a significant cause of nutrient loss, for

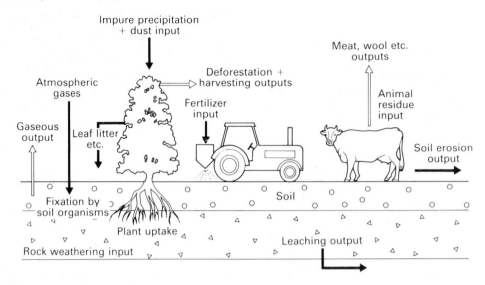

Figure 9.3 A simple model of biogeomechanical cycling within an ecosystem.

water percolating through the soil carries with it nutrients in solution, which may ultimately be carried into streams and rivers. Other losses may take place in the gaseous form by diffusion of gases from soil pores into the atmosphere or because of transpiration by plants. Increasingly, nutrient losses may result from human activities, including harvesting.

The energy within an ecosystem is more or less continuously renewable, but the same is not the case for the nutrients involved in the biogeochemical cycles. Although atmospheric inputs may be quite important in some areas, and for some elements, most nutrient's are derived from the weathering of rock and the creation of soil by the action of organisms. Such transformations are rather slow, with the result that, unless nutrients are constantly recycled within the ecosystem by the return of decaying plant and animal remains to the soil, there is a decline in fertility. In a mature, stable woodland, for example, there will be some loss of nutrients by erosion and leaching, but these will be more or less balanced by release of fresh minerals through weathering and by

additions from the atmosphere. In the great equatorial rainforests (see section 6.7) most of the nutrients are actually stored in the vegetation layer; many of the soils are relatively infertile, and under natural conditions there is very little loss of nutrients to drainage water. As a consequence, if deforestation takes place the great store of nutrients will be depleted, and the whole ecosystem will become greatly depleted in nutrients.

9.2   Plants and their habitats

The place where an organism or community of organisms lives is called its *habitat*. A habitat possesses various environmental conditions or factors that affect the growth of plants. In order to cope with these conditions, plants may have made certain physiological and morphological adaptations by selective evolution through time. Such adaptations are beneficial in that they permit the plant to live in a particular environment; but a plant, by being so specialised that it can withstand the factors in one environment only,

Plate 9.1 Plants that can withstand water shortages for long periods are termed xerophytes. Two of the most characteristic xerophytes of the deserts of the south west of the United States are the yucca and the ocotilla.

may lose its adaptability to changing factors. Over-specialisation can be the first step to extinction. Although we will now discuss some of the environmental factors in habitats individually, it should be remembered that factors are normally closely intermeshed and interrelated. For example, climate may affect other factors – soils, vegetation, the incidence of fire, the nature of landforms, etc. Moreover, although all factors are interrelated in a complex way, some are more independent than others. In particular, climate and geological factors tend to be independent, whereas, soil, vegetation and animals tend to be dependent on them.

Water is a most important factor in a habitat, for water carries nutrients, is a raw material of photosynthesis, is essential for chemical reactions within a plant, makes up a large proportion of the plant mass and helps to maintain a relatively equable soil climate because it can absorb much heat with relatively little temperature change.

According to their responses to the water environment, plants are classified into three main groups:

(a) *Xerophytes* These are plants that can withstand water shortages for long periods, either because the climate is dry or because the plants live on surfaces, like bare rock, that have a limited water-storing capacity. Xerophytes are of four main types:

   (i) annuals or ephemerals, which get through a drought in seed form;
   (ii) plants that tap groundwater by sending down deep roots (such plants are called *phreatophytes*);

(iii) succulents, which store water in their stems or leaves (e.g. cacti);

(iv) plants that withstand drought by having a great variety of structural adaptations such as large-spreading root systems to tap available soil water, bulbs and tubers to store water and nutrients, woody structures to withstand wilting, etc.

(b) *Mesophytes* These are plants that cannot inhabit water or saturated soil, yet cannot survive a prolonged water deficiency. Most plants of temperate regions come into this category.

(c) *Hydrophytes* These are plants that cannot withstand drought. Many of them, like mangroves and water lilies, have their roots permanently in water; others, like the ferns of the tropical rainforests, live in a permanently humid micro-climate.

Another major climatic factor is *temperature*. Different plants have different optimum temperatures for their growth, and different temperatures at which growth begins. Some plants cannot withstand freezing, some require rhythmic daily changes of temperature, some cannot withstand great heat and some require a cold season in which they can lie dormant. Likewise, *light* is an

Plate 9.2 Fire is a major control of certain vegetation types and is a habitat factor of some importance. In savanna areas fires may be of regular occurrence and sometimes huge, as is shown by this photograph of the Okavango Delta in Botswana by a Space Shuttle crew. The white plume is a belt of smoke crossing the Delta from east to west. The stripes on the left of the photo are fossil dunes (compare plate 2.6).

important factor, for light is required for photosynthesis. Some plants have developed notable adaptations that enable them to seek light (e.g. climbing plants), but if conditions are dark, as in the lower layers of the rainforest, vegetation growth will be limited, and the ground may remain bare until a break in the canopy improves lighting conditions. *Wind* is another climatic factor – it affects plants by increasing transpiration, by mechanical damage, and by scattering pollen and seeds. Deformed *krummholz* trees are a feature of the timber-line on mountains (see section 7.5) and some very exposed situations, such as high-latitude islands, may have only low-growing cushion plants and dwarf shrubs. This is the main reason why islands like the Falklands have such a limited tree cover.

Another major group of factors in habitats are those associated with soil conditions. These are called *edaphic* conditions. Plainly, soils with limited nutrients, a high salt content, very shallow depth, waterlogging or impermeable and impenetrable layers (like some laterites or podzols) will pose certain limitations on plant growth. For example, in many desert areas the presence of salt in the soil (see section 5.7) requires that if they are to survive plants will need to make adaptations that will enable them to overcome the effects of the salt. Such plants are called *halophytes*. Likewise, in some tropical areas (see section 6.9) it has been shown that, whereas the normal type of vegetation in an area is rainforest, there are patches of grassland (savanna) which occur because the trees cannot grow in soils that either are very highly leached of nutrients (as on old erosion surfaces underlain by chemically rather inert rocks like quartzites), or have a laterite horizon which limits root growth.

A factor of some importance which is rather difficult to place into any other category is *fire*. It is a factor that is plainly more prevalent in certain environments than others – e.g., where there is a long dry season, or where lightning is common – but it can also be important where fires are deliberately started (see section 4.9). In environments with a marked dry season, some shrubs have seeds that remain dormant until their hard pods are cracked open by fire and seedlings can emerge. Cork oaks, some pines and many savanna trees have barks that protect them from all but the hottest fires. Some of the great vegetation types – e.g. savanna grassland, prairie, and maquis – are a response to fire, while others require fire to open up the forest to enable new seedlings or new species to spread.

Finally, there are the *biotic* factors, for we must remember that no plant is independent of the activity of other organisms. The decomposers in the soil and litter layers are vital in nutrient cycling; insects cause pollination; birds and mammals disperse seeds; the grazing of herbivorous animals influences the plants on which they live; and one plant will compete with another for light, moisture and nutrients. Some plants are entirely dependent on others for providing support (e.g. lianas) or for providing their nutrients (e.g. parasites like the mistletoe).

9.3 Life in the oceans

We can investigate some of these themes further by a brief consideration of life in the oceans.

Marine life is diverse, and the range of size alone is very great: from microscopic one-celled plants to seaweeds over 30 m long, and from microscopic bacteria to the great blue whale, the largest animal ever to live on earth. None the less, species numbers are much greater on land than in the sea – one or two million species to the sea's hundreds of thousands. This is primarily because of the greater variety of habitats and environments on land.

Marine organisms occupy two major habitats: the *benthic* realm (the sea bottom), and the *pelagic* realm (the water above). Benthic organisms may live either *on* the bottom (*epibionts*) or *in* the bottom (*endobionts*). The *sessile* (immobile) types may, as in the case of barnacles, corals, etc., cement themselves to a hard substrate. Other epibionts, such as seaweed, attach themselves to the substrate by rootlike structures. Reclining epibionts, such as mature oysters, simply lie unattached on the bottom. Others crawl along the seabed or burrow beneath the surface.

Pelagic organisms may be classified into *nekton* (which actively swim and can make headway against normal currents) and *plankton*, which cannot swim against a normal current.

As on land, the organisms can be regarded in terms of their position in a food chain. At the first trophic level are the *phytoplankton*. The second trophic level constitutes the *herbivorous zooplankton*, and then at higher levels there are miscellaneous carnivores ranging from carnivorous zooplankton through plankton-eating fish and fish-eating fish:

Bacteria and biogenic detritus

↓

Phytoplankton

↓

Herbivorous zooplankton

↓

Carnivorous zooplankton

↓

Fish (*planktivores*)

↓

Fish (*piscivores*)

The production of these various organisms is surprisingly low when one considers the enormous volume of the world's oceans. As we have already seen, photosynthesis is powered by sunlight, and without photosynthesis production is of necessity very limited. In the oceans sunlight intensity diminishes very rapidly with depth. On average, at a depth of 10 m only 10 per cent of the light entering the sea is available for photosynthesis; at 100 m, only 1 per cent. In turbid coastal waters these values may be reduced even further.

Another highly important control of productivity is temperature. Over much of the ocean, temperatures lie below the temperature optimum for many species. Ocean water, especially at depth, is cold. Only 8 per cent of ocean water is warmer than 10°C, and more than one-half is colder than 2.3°C.

Although taken as a whole the oceans are unproductive with respect to their enormous volumes, there are some areas of high productivity – especially the continental shelves and areas in the open ocean where upwelling enriches the surface water in nutrients. The continental shelves are productive because, being shallow, they are warm and sunlit. Moreover, their productivity is enhanced where they receive nutrient-rich river discharge from the land. Areas of upwelling are productive because nutrients are continuously being brought up from depth to replenish stocks.

This process goes on most effectively in those areas in mid-latitudes on the west sides of continents, such as California, the coasts of Chile and Peru, south-west and north-west Africa, parts of north-west Australia, the coast of Somaliland, and southern Arabia. Because of this great productivity, particularly of small pelagic organisms, these areas can provide food to support large fish stocks. The key nutrient in such locations appears to be phosphorus, and it is a peculiarity that phosphates are more soluble in cold water than in warmer water, so that it occurs in larger quantities where cold upwelling waters prevail. At a more local scale estuaries and coral reefs may be amongst the most highly productive of all ecosystems, being equal to or sometimes greater than that of tropical rainforest, with mean net primary prouction being 1500 and 2500 respectively $(g\ m^{-2}\ yr^{-1})$.

Overall, however, the oceans are biological deserts, and the strong contrast between continental areas and marine areas of the earth's surface is brought out in table 9.1. The mean productivity and biomass are strikingly different. Thus although oceans cover about two thirds of the world's surface, they account for only about one third of its production.

9.4 Community

Within a given landscape, it is often apparent that the plants and animals are not distributed independently of one another but that similar combinations are often found living together in habitats that are characterized by similar combinations of environmental conditions. This is termed the *community*. Three types of interaction between the different members of the community can be identified. The first is *competition*, in which individual plants or animals are competing for a scarce environmental resource. Competition for light is particularly important; in the absence of any limiting factors, the most successful plant species are those that grow the fastest or the tallest, or that produce dense shade or large accumulations of litter. The second of these types of interaction is where species are *complementary* to one another, co-existing by occupying different niches rather than demanding the same environmental resources. This is well shown in the

Table 9.1 Productivity and biomass of continents and oceans

	Continents	Oceans	Difference
Area (10^6 km^2)	149	361	×0.4
Mean net primary productivity per unit area (g m^{-2} yr^{-1})	773	152	×5.1
World net primary production (10^9 t yr^{-1})	115	55	×2.1
Biomass per unit area (kg m^{-2})	12.3	0.01	×1230
Total world biomass (10^9 t)	1837	3.9	×471

Source: modified from data in R. H. Whittaker, Communities and Ecosystems (London: Collier–MacMillan 1975), table 5.2.

stratification of vegetation in a forest, where the plants occupying the lower strata are capable of surviving in the shade cast by the taller species. The third category of interaction is called *dependence*. Here a species can occur only through the presence of others, which provide either physical support or nutrients.

Within a plant community some species are called *dominants*. These are plants that occupy more space, absorb more nutrients and contribute more biomass than the rest. They are almost always the tallest plants in the community, and as such exert considerable influence on the environment within the community – by affecting the light regime beneath their canopy, by creating areas of protection from exposure, and by utilising a larger proportion of available nutrients. If one compares an oak forest with a beech forest one can see this significance. Oak tree leaves are so arranged that light can reach the lower layers of the woods, thereby permitting the development of rich shrub and herb vegetation. By contrast, beech leaves are so arranged that little light can penetrate, so that the ground layer is relatively impoverished with regard to species and cover. There is thus a tendency for beech to be more dominant in a beech wood than oak in an oak wood.

9.5 Succession

The habitats of plants change through time, and the plants change with them. Plants, in fact, are able themselves to change various aspects of the environments they inhabit. *Succession* occurs because altered environmental conditions favour certain species, which therefore can compete more successfully than before for nutrients, light, space, etc. As a result, populations of well-adapted species replace earlier ones now less well equipped to compete in the altered conditions. Thus, during the course of succession, individual species populations come and go, giving rise to a gradual progressive change in the community (figure 9.4).

The process of succession may start with bare ground. This might be produced by a mudflat being formed on a coast, by a sand dune developing behind a beach, by a glacier uncovering a rock surface as it melts, by a volcanic cone erupting, by a farmer clearing some land, or by fire destroying the previous vegetation cover. Over time, such bare ground becomes colonised by vegetation, and the vegetation in turn alters the nature of the environment. Eventually, in the mature stage of the succession process, the ecosystem becomes stable and relatively unchanging, and this stage is referred to as *climax*. Where this climax lasts for some hundreds or thousands of years and appears to be in equilibrium with environmental conditions it is sometimes called the *climatic climax*. The climax community represents a steady state between the plant cover and the physical environment. The whole group of plant communities that successively occupy the same site from the pioneer to the final stage of climax is called a *sere*, and the relatively transitory communities that occupy the site at a given time are *seral stages*. Seres can be classified according to environmental conditions: *hydroseres* are initiated in fresh water; *haloseres* are initiated in saline water; dry places give rise to *xeroseres*, of which *lithoseres* are initiated on bare rock and *psammoseres* on dry sand.

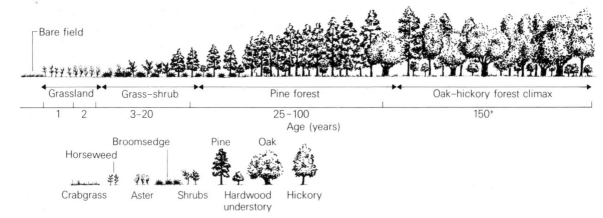

Figure 9.4 Succession from open land to a mid-latitude deciduous forest. Note how in the initial stages of the succession low, fast-growing grasses and shrubs dominate. Each stage alters the soil and micro-climate, enabling other species to establish themselves and become dominant. The final stage consists of high trees that overshade and force out some of the low shrubs of earlier stages.

Let us consider an example of succession. A glacier retreats and exposes a small lake. Initially only aquatic plants, such as water lilies and algae, and semi-aquatic plants, such as reeds and rushes, inhabit the water. As the plants grow and die their remains are deposited on the bottom, and after many years a thick organic layer may develop. In the shallow water near the shore, where plant productivity is highest, the organic layer gradually builds up to the water surface, where it provides new habitats for certain types of mosses, grasses and shrubs. These plants in turn both add organic matter to the habitat and help to stabilise the surface. Meanwhile inflowing streams are probably adding sediment to the organic mass. Little by little the community of plants encroaches on the open water and adds more and more organic matter. When the pond has completely filled, the aquatic and semi-aquatic plants no longer have anywhere to live because their original environment has been so greatly changed. Eventually the types of trees characteristic of that particular climatic zone colonise what had once been pond.

Another glacial example (this time from Glacier Bay, Alaska) will serve to demonstrate further the nature of succession. As the glacier melts and retreats, morainic material is deposited adjacent to the snout of the glacier. These morainic ridges can be dated, and so offer a means of studying how vegetation composition changes through time. On the youngest ridges, in close proximity to the glacier, lichens mosses and herbs colonise the bare moraine, and may be joined by some small trees like *Salix* and *Populus deltoides*. In the next stage alder (*Alnus*) becomes more important, and this, with some of the herbs from the previous stage (e.g. *Dryas*), increases the soil nitrogen content through nitrogen-fixing activities. This increase in soil nitrogen, together with a reduction of pH brought about by decomposition of the alder leaves, creates conditions suitable for spruce (*Picea*) and hemlock, which comprise the final woodland stage.

Other simple examples of succession described in this book include those on coastal sand dunes (see section 8.6) and those on salt marshes (see section 8.7).

A number of trends or progressive developments underlie most successional processes and sequences:

(a) There is a progressive development of the soil, with increasing depth, increasing organic content and the differentiation of soil horizons towards the mature soil of the climax community.

(b) The height of plants increases and strata become more evident.

(c) Productivity increases, as does biomass.

(d) Species diversity increases from the simple

communities of early succession to the richer communities of late succession.

(e) As height and density of above-ground plant cover increases, the micro-climate within the community is increasingly determined by characteristics of the community itself.

(f) Populations of different species rise and fall and replace one another, and the rate of this replacement tends to slow through the course of succession as smaller and shorter-lived species are replaced by larger and longer-lived ones.

(g) The final community is usually more stable than the earlier communities and there is a very tight cycling of nutrients.

The rate of succession varies according to how favourable environmental factors are. If a tundra area is denuded of its vegetation cover by human activity or by a natural agency it will take a very considerable period of time for full successional development to take place, whereas in an area in the humid tropics the various stages of succession may occur with great rapidity. For example, when the volcano of Krakatoa exploded in 1883, all life on the island was killed and smothered with a layer of fresh ash some 30 m in thickness. Yet only 50 years later, a rich and maturing tropical rainforest with over 250 component plant species and many epiphytes had re-established itself, together with 720 insect species and a few reptiles.

When he first proposed the concept of succession in 1916, F. E. Clements argued that for any major regional climatic zone only one type of *climax vegetation* could be expected, even though this might be derived from a wide variety of pioneer sites (dunes, marsh, pond, etc.). It is evident, however, that there may be some *arresting factors* (topographic, edaphic, biotic, etc.) that may halt the succession process and give rise to *subclimaxes*, in which plants are held in an apparently stable situation by non-climatic controls. Human activity may be one such arresting factor, and if its effects are permanent then a man-controlled *plagioclimax* community may be created (as in the case of many British heather moorlands). Some plant communities that were originally thought to be climatic climax types –

savannas and mid-latitude grasslands, for instance – are now recognised as being partly the result of human activities, with fire playing a major role. In general, it is now believed that, instead of having just one ultimate climax type in any one climatic zone (the *monoclimax* idea), a whole species of possible stable communities might develop according to the relative importance of the different types of environmental factors (the *polyclimax* idea).

9.6 Dispersal and migration of plants

In order for a newly exposed area of land to be colonised as a first stage in the process of succession, there needs to be a means whereby plants can enter the area. This brings us to the question of the ability of plants to disperse and migrate. *Dispersal* involves dissemination from the parent and distribution to a new place; *migration* involves successful dispersal and establishment.

Many plants are adapted to use the wind as an agent of dispersal. Trees like the sycamore, and flowers like the dandelion, have seeds that are specially adapted to wind transport, and many light seeds and spores are spread very effectively by this mechanism. Other plants may be distributed by water. Some mangroves have seedlings that float easily, for example, while coconuts have fibrous outer husks which favour their transport in the sea. Animals and man may also play a role in dispersal. Seeds may be carried adhering to the fur, hair, skin or feathers of beasts by hooks or sticky surfaces, or they may be carried internally. Since the development of long-distance transport, plant dispersal has been accelerated by man – sometimes deliberately and sometimes accidentally. Finally, dispersal may be achieved by mechanical means. Some plants have seed pods that explosively scatter their contents in the wind, while other plants send out runners and suckers over quite long distances.

In spite of the range of dispersal mechanisms that are available, plants are not evenly distributed over the face of the earth, for there are certain *barriers to dispersal*. These include sheets of water, deserts, high mountains, forests and other environmental factors. It is a characteristic of remoteness that the flora and fauna will be impoverished.

9.7   Dispersal and migration of animals

As we saw in chapter 2, the world can be divided into certain major regions or realms which have distinctive assemblages of animals. Australia, for example, has a very different fauna from Asia, and has certain distinctive characteristics like the presence of marsupials. Even quite small areas of land, like islands or mountains, may have species that are found only in those particular environments and nowhere else. Such unique species are described as being *endemic*. From this, it is evident that animals are faced by barriers to dispersal in much the same way that plants are, permitting different areas to acquire different species by the process of evolution.

Once again, *isolation* is an important consideration. Britain's fauna is impoverished in comparison with that of mainland Europe because Pleistocene glaciation drove out many types of animals and the postglacial rise in sea level cut the country off before they all could come back again. Being still further removed from the mainland, Ireland's fauna is even more impoverished, and Ireland today lacks certain beasts that are encountered in England and Wales: these include the poisonous adder, the mole, the common shrew, the weasel, the dormouse, the brown hare the yellow-necked field mouse and the English meadow mouse.

The importance of isolation is still more important in oceanic islands distant from major land masses. New Zealand, for instance, had a very limited fauna before certain species were introduced by Europeans over the last two centuries. The only mammals were two families of bats, though there were various flightless birds, including the kiwi, and the moa (now extinct). The latter were probably descended from flighted birds, but in the absence of predators they took to the ground.

9.8   The importance of area

In discussing the factors that affect the nature of plant and animal geography we have so far said very little about one extremely important factor: the areal size of the ecosystem. A substantial body of work has now shown that there is a rela-

tionship between the number of species in an area and the size of that area (figure 9.5). Throughout the world, larger islands support more species than smaller ones. Generally speaking, if the number of species in a given area is plotted against island area (both on log scales), a linear relationship results:

$$\log S = \log C + Z \log A$$

where S is the number of species, C is a constant giving the number of species when A has a value of 1, A is the area of the island, and Z is the slope of the regression line relating S and A. The value of C shows considerable variation from area to area and for different types of organisms, but Z is remarkably constant, with most values falling in the range 0.24–0.34.

(a)

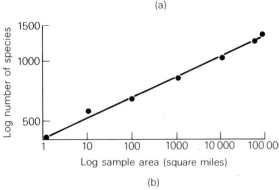

(b)

Figure 9.5 Two examples of the relationship between the area of an ecosystem and the number of species that it possesses: (a) the number of amphibian and reptile species living on West Indian islands of various sizes; Trinidad, joined to South America because of low sea levels as recently as 10 000 years BP, lies well above the area–species curve of the other islands; (b) the area–species curve for the number of species of flowering plants found in sample areas of England.

The reason for this extremely widespread and important relationship is the subject of some controversy. Some scientists believe that as area increases so does the range of topographical relief and habitat diversity. Other scientists argue that differences in area alone may be responsible for differences in species numbers. It is probable that habitat diversity is an important factor affecting species diversity, and that habitat diversity does tend to increase with island size, but there is also evidence that area in itself has some significance.

An explanation for the importance of area has been put forward in the influential *Equilibrium Theory* of R. H. MacArthur and E. O. Wilson. This is illustrated in figure 9.6. The model envisages the number of species on an island as a dynamic equilibrium resulting from a continuing immigration of new species to the island and the extinction of species already there. As the number of species present on the island increases, fewer of the immigrants are new, so the immigration rate of new species falls, reaching zero when all mainland species are present. Furthermore, as the number of species increases, the rate of extinction increases for two reasons. First, there is an increasing number of species to go extinct, and, second, each species may be rarer (because of

competition) when more species are present, so each may have an increased chance of extinction. At the point where the immigration and extinction curves cross, the two rates are equal, with new species arriving at the same rate as the old ones are becoming extinct.

Let us see how this explains the importance of area. Imagine two islands at the same distance from the mainland but one much larger than the other. Since they are equally accessible, they will enjoy similar immigration rates. However, the smaller island will usually support smaller populations of any species than will the larger one, and small populations are more likely to become extinct than large. Thus the smaller island will have a higher rate of extinction and will hold fewer species at equilibrium.

The relationship between species diversity and the area of an island is a concept that can be applied to isolated habitats on the continents: lakes, desert oases, sphagnum bogs, patches of woodland, mountain summits, etc. Similar relationships to those found for true oceanic islands have been found for habitat 'islands' on the continents. This has its own intrinsic biogeographical interest, but it is of interest also in terms of the design of nature reserves, for many such reserves may be small patches of a particular habitat preserved in what is otherwise an inhospitable environment. They too may be 'islands'. This implies very clearly that, since area is an important consideration, nature reserves should in general be as large as we can make them. A large reserve will support more species at equilibrium by allowing the existence of larger populations with lower extinction rates.

9.9   Human impact on plants and animals

As *Homo sapiens* has diffused over the face of the earth, as the world population has increased, and technological competence has developed, people have become more and more capable of having a significant impact on plants and animals. Our impacts are legion:

(a) *Genetic change* We have changed the genetics of plants and animals so that they are of greater use to us, and so that in many cases they cannot survive without human help. This is the process of *domes-*

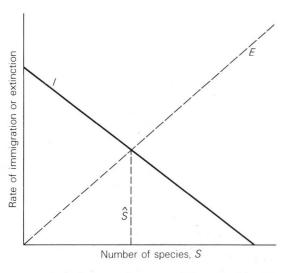

Figure 9.6 A diagrammatic representation of the Macarthur and Wilson model showing an island's extinction curve *E* and immigration curve *I* as functions of the number of species (*S*) on the island. The equilibrium number of species for the island is S, where the curves intersect.

tication. The effect of domestication is to replace the processes of natural selection by those of human selection. We have been domesticating plants and animals for at least 10 000 years.

(b) *Ecosystem change* We have altered habitats (e.g. by irrigation, forestry, ploughing, pollution, hunting) and modified the numbers of species, their distribution and their population sizes.

(c) *Protection, preservation* and *conservation* We have deliberately tried to counter the effects of (b) by creating reserves for animals and by protecting their habitats.

9.10   Domestication

In the last 10 000 or so years, we have sought to replace the processes of natural selection of species by human selection of species, with the aim of changing the genetics of the organism so that the new characteristics (which are regarded as

desirable) are passed down to succeeding generations. This process is called *domestication*. Our agricultural crops and our main domestic animals are the consequence of this form of environmental control, and different crops and animals have been domesticated at different times and in different places (figure 9.7). Barley may have been deliberately cultivated as long as 18 000 years BP, but one of the most active phases of domestication occurred in the Near East (modern Palestine, Iraq and Iran) after about 11 000 BP. From that area came such useful species as cattle, sheep, goats, barley, wheat, oats and rye. Rice and the chicken came from south-east Asia, and maize and various types of beans from Central America.

Domestication has been a most important stage in our cultural evolution, enabling us to produce much larger volumes of food from a much smaller area than was possible for most hunters and gatherers. This in turn has permitted the great population densities that we have today. The breeding of plants and animals has also had major

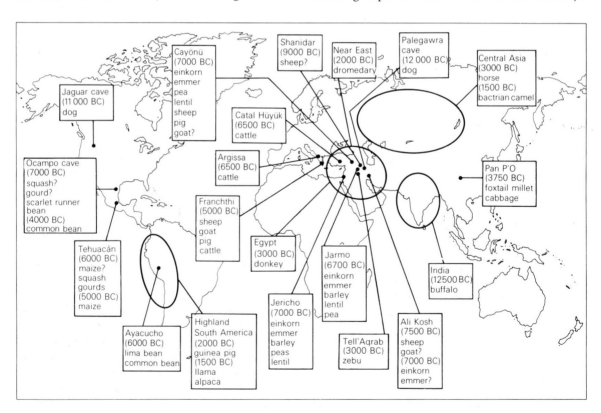

Figure 9.7   (a) The dates and locations of the earliest domestications of plants and animals.

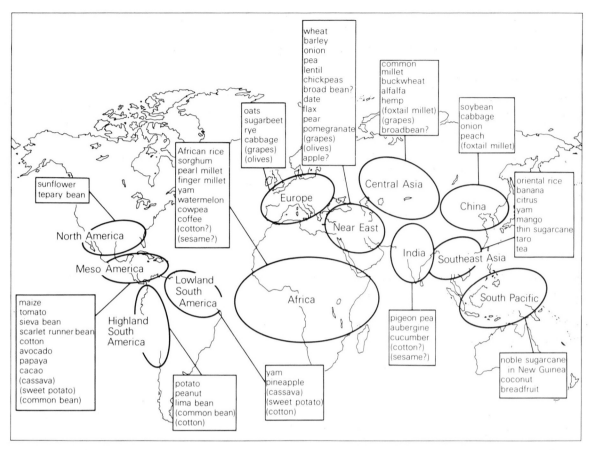

Figure 9.7 (b) The places where the major plant domestications occurred; some crops appear to have been domesticated independently in more than one major focal area, and these are given in brackets.

consequences of biogeographical significance. First, because of this breeding, the domesticated plant or animal is often reproductively isolated from its wild ancestors and so becomes effectively a new species. Second, domestic varieties show marked changes in shape and size; domesticated maize, for example, has a very large husk compared with its wild predecessors. Third, domesticated species often show very considerable variety. Consider, for instance, the extraordinary range in the characteristics of dogs, from the diminutive chihuahua to the spotted dalmatian, and from the shivering whippet to the robust mastiff.

9.11 Introductions

Another powerful way in which we have altered ecosystems is through the introduction of plants

and animals. We have crossed the oceans and other barriers and taken plants and animals with us (figure 9.8). Sometimes the introductions have been deliberate, supplying people with food, sport, ornament, or a means of combating local pests and predators. Frequently, however, the introductions have been accidental, as when seeds have been carried in ballast, or when rats have jumped ship in a foreign port.

Sometimes these introductions, whether deliberate or accidental, have found their new habitat so congenial, or free from competition, that they have undergone a major population explosion, have eventually become pests and have dramatically altered the environment. In Britain, for example, many elm trees died in the 1970s because of the accidental introduction of the Dutch elm disease fungus which arrived at cer-

Figure 9.8 The spread of the European starling (*Sternus vulgaris*) in North America following its release in 1891 in New York. Outside the 1926 isochrone, the dots are instances of early phases of colonisation. Less than a century after its release, the starling is now well established in most states and in Canada.

tain ports, notably Avonmouth and those in the Thames Estuary. Ocean islands have been particularly vulnerable. Their relatively simple eco-systems appear to be unstable, and introduced species often find that the comparative lack of competition enables them to broaden their ecological range more than they were able to do on the continents. Moreover, because many of the natural species inhabiting remote islands were selected primarily by their ability for dispersal, they were not necessarily dominant or even highly successful in their original continental setting. Therefore introduced species may prove more vigorous and effective than the indigenous ones. A clear illustration of this comes from the atoll of Laysan. Rabbits and hares were introduced there in 1903 in the hope of establishing a meat cannery. The number of native species on the island at that time was 25; by 1923 it had fallen to 4. At that point all the rabbits and hares were systematically exterminated to prevent the island from being turned into a desert by overgrazing. By 1961 there were 16 species on the island.

However, it is not only simple ecosystems that

are prone to disturbance by invaders. In South Africa, for example, there is an immensely species-rich and beautiful natural heath vegetation called *fynbos*, which occurs in the coastal regions of the Cape Province. Over large areas it has been displaced by various type of introduced Australian trees of the *Acacia* family, which, freed from the organisms which control them in their native continent, have spread explosively in their new homeland.

There are also many examples of the deliberate introduction of an organism to check the explosive invasion of a particular plant. One of the most spectacular examples of this involves the history of the prickly pear (*Opuntia*) in Australia. This plant came from the Americas and was introduced some time prior to 1839. By 1900, 4 million hectares had been invaded by it, and by 1925 more than 24 million hectares. Sometimes

Plate 9.3 Large cities and industrial areas produce substantial quantities of atmospheric pollutants, such as sulphur dioxide and ozone. These pollutants can affect plant growth. This picture shows a smog over Sydney, Australia.

the density of the cactus was such that other more useful plants were excluded. To combat this menace one of *Opuntia*'s natural enemies, a South American moth, *Cactoblastus*, was introduced to remarkable effect: by 1940 something like 95 per cent of the prickly pear had been eradicated.

Another introduction to Australia was the water buffalo. They were deliberately introduced into northern Australia, bringing their own blood-sucking fly with them. This fly breeds in cattle dung. Australia's native dung beetles, accustomed only to the small sheep-like pellets of the grazing marsupials (the natural fauna of Australia before the arrival of Europeans) could not tackle the large dung pats of the buffalo. Thus unconsumed pats abounded and the flies were able to breed undisturbed until African dung beetles were introduced to compete with the flies.

9.12 Pollution

One consequence of human activity that appears to be having an increasingly widespread effect on plants and animals is pollution. Some of the *air pollutants* that have been released into the atmosphere have had detrimental impacts on plants; for example sulphur dioxide, one of the pollutants resulting from the burning of fossil fuels, is toxic to plants. Experiments with growing lettuces in different parts of Leeds, northern England, as early as 1913 showed that the size and quality of lettuce leaves was very closely related to the amount of sulphate in the air in different parts of the city. Likewise, lichens are very sensitive to air pollutants and are rarely found in central areas of cities like Bonn, Helsinki, Stockholm, Paris and London. Overall, it has been calculated that over one-third of England and Wales, extending in a belt from the London area to Birmingham and broadening out to include the industrial Midlands, most of Lancashire and West Yorkshire and part of Tyneside, has lost nearly all of its epiphytic lichen flora, largely because of sulphur dioxide pollution.

Another form of air pollution that affects plant growth is *photochemical smog* (see section 15.2). In California, Ponderosa pines in the San Bernadino Mountains, as much as 120–130 km to the east of Los Angeles, have been extensively dam-

aged from smog coming from that metropolis. The gas that seems to be the culprit is ozone; in normal clean air it occurs in low concentrations of only 4 parts per hundred million (pphm), but during smog conditions in Los Angeles it can reach concentrations of 70 pphm. In summer months in Britain ozone concentrations produced by photochemical reactions can reach 17 pphm. Fumigation experiments in the laboratory suggest that damage to plants can occur if ozone concentrations stay above 5–6 pphm for any extended period – a figure not very much above the natural background levels.

One of the problems of air pollution is that it can have repercussions over very wide areas. If we return to the example of sulphur dioxide, this gas is pumped into the atmosphere in great quantities by manufacturing plants and power stations in industrial areas, and it can create a phenomenon called *acid rain*. Normally, water in the

Plate 9.4 The great metal smelter at Sudbury in Canada has one of the largest chimneys in the world and produces polluting fumes that extend over large areas. Trees in the immediate vicinity are badly affected.

atmosphere will have an acidity that is relatively small (pH of *c*.5.7). However, recently much stronger acids have been observed in snow and rain in the north-east United States and in Scotland, with pH values as low as 2.1–2.4 (the latter the acidic equivalent to vinegar). In much of the north-east United States and western Europe the sulphate pumped into the atmosphere causes average annual acidity values to be around pH 4. As a result, the rain feeding many rivers and lakes is much more acidic than it used to be, and these waters have become more acid. Many fish and other organisms inhabiting freshwaters are sensitive to this acidity, so the ecology of many lakes has changed considerably.

In addition high levels of soil and rain acidity appear to be injurious to trees, and acid rain probably contributes to the widely observed damage that has occurred to the forests of western and central Europe and various other parts of the world. It has been calculated that in 1986 approx-

Plate 9.5 An unpleasant manifestation of the importance of pollution for animal life: an oiled razorbill, fouled by an oil slick produced by the wrecking of the oil tanker *Torrey Canyon*.

imately 14 per cent of Europe's forests (covering an area equivalent to Austria and East Germany combined) exhibit signs of injury, especially to conifers: yellowing of needles, casting off of older needles, and damage to the fine roots through which these trees take up their nutrients.

Another example of the widespread implications of pollution is provided by the role of certain *pesticides* related to DDT. These were introduced on a world-wide basis after the Second World War and proved highly effective in the control of insects like malarial mosquitos. However, evidence soon accumulated to suggest that DDT was persistent, capable of wide dispersal, and prone to becoming concentrated at high levels in certain animals at the top trophic levels in a food chain or web. For example, a lake might be sprayed to kill gnats, introducing a small concentration of DDT into the lake water. Bacteria and algae might accumulate some of the insecticide in their tissues, and would then be eaten by fish, who would have slightly higher levels of DDT, and so on, until the fish-eating birds at the top trophic level would have very high concentrations indeed. Studies of birds like the osprey, the bald eagle and the peregrine falcon have showed that, as DDT levels have built up in them, so the thickness of their egg shells has been reduced, thereby impairing their success at reproduction. Some dramatic declines in the populations of such species have therefore occurred.

A final example of the effects of pollution on organisms is provided by a consideration of a process called *eutrophication*. This is the enrichment of waters by nutrients. The process occurs naturally during, for example, the slow ageing of lakes, which become enriched during the process of succession (see section 9.5) by the accumulation of organic material. However, water to which large quantities of sewage or fertiliser-derived nitrates and phosphorus have been added, becomes greatly enriched in some very important nutrients, so there can be a great increase in biological activity, leading sometimes to the spread of great blooms of algae. This is an increasingly serious problem for world fertilizer usage has skyrocketed in recent decades, increasing from just 14 million tons in 1950 to 131 million tons in 1986.

A topic of considerable recent importance is the effect that human activities may be having on the layer of ozone which screens all life on earth from the harmful effects of the Sun's ultraviolet radiation. Ozone is a gas which only ever occurs in low concentrations of a few parts per million, but which is relatively abundant 15 to 50 km above the earth's surface, in the layer known as the stratosphere. Recent studies have shown that it is becoming depleted over the Antarctic, producing the so-called 'ozone hole'. It is generally believed that the ozone is being decomposed by certain man-made compounds called Chlorofluorocarbons or CFCs. The CFCs come from aerosol sprays (where they from the pressurised propellant to produce a spray from the aerosol can nozzle), form refrigerating systems, and from the foam-blowing process used to produce fast-food take-away cartons. The possible consequences of depleted ozone levels have still to be fully explored, but one possibility is that changes in the amount of ultraviolet radiation received in the upper layers of the oceans will occur, and that this could have deleterious effects on small, single celled plants (phytoplankton) found in the sea. Such phytoplankton are vital in that they form the base of the food chain in the oceans.

9.13   Extinction

Extinction is a process in which human activity plays a role, but it is not a process caused only by man, for as an examination of the fossil record shows, extinction is a normal feature of evolution. What we have done is to accelerate the rate of extinction by a variety of acts: predation, as with hunting of animals, collecting of eggs and plants, etc.; by introducing alien animals and plants which compete with native species; by altering the food supply as by removing for human consumption the food of beasts which are higher up the food chain; by polluting air, water or soil with toxic substances; by introducing disease into the environment, either deliberately as with the myxomatosis which decimated rabbit stocks in Britain and Europe, or accidentally, as with the Dutch elm disease fungus which has severely depleted the elm trees of much of eastern North America and England; and, as we shall see in the next section, by changing or removing various types of natural habitat with which particular plants or animals are inextricably entwined for their existence.

Some species are more vulnerable than others to human pressures because of certain inherent characteristics which they possess. Some species require large areas to maintain themselves. This is particularly true of the large carnivores, which need expansive hunting territories to find enough prey. Slow reproducers, often large mammals or birds, represent another vulnerable group: their recovery from natural catastrophe or human exploitation is very slow. The Californian condor, a bird now down to fewer than ten individuals in the wild, does not breed until at least six years of age, lays only one egg, and fails to nest at all in some years. A pair of these birds on average requires some 10 to 15 years to replace themselves. Species that forage or breed in large groups are also susceptible to rapid extermination, as are species that have become very highly specialised. For example, island species, because they may have evolved in isolation and have not developed defences against certain types of pre-

Plate 9.6   One of the most famous examples of the process of extinction caused by human activities is provided by the hapless Dodo. This appealing bird disappeared from Mauritius c.1680.

dator, may be vulnerable if such predators are introduced. Other species are highly specialised in the sense that they have evolved in unique types of habitat or required highly specialised food supplies. If those habitats or supplies are removed, the species become extinct.

There is some evidence that a major wave of extinction occurred when man was still predominantly a hunter and gatherer. The date varies according to the level of stone tool technology achieved in different parts of the world, and according to the date that *Homo sapiens* arrived in an area. In North America, for example, many major animals disappeared rather quickly round about 11 000 years BP, and this has been attributed to the southward movement of tribes with sophisticated hunting techniques who had migrated across what is now the Bering Strait towards the end of Pleistocene times. Climatic changes may also have played a role, but this cannot be the explanation for the rapid extinctions of fauna that have taken place when man arrived at islands like Madagascar and those of the Pacific.

Extinctions are still proceeding at a fast rate, in spite of conservation efforts aimed at stemming the loss (see figure 9.9).

Before a state of complete extinction is attained, the geographical spread of particular organisms may become severely reduced. This is illustrated for the North American bison (*Bison bison*), or buffalo (figure 9.10). Prior to European colonisation this mammal was an essential element of the environment, thriving on rich summer herbage in the Prairies, and moving into forest or woodland in winter for warmth. Its range was huge, and the animals relied on their strength, size and numbers for protection against predators like wolves. In the nineteenth century hunters brought the once great herds to the point of extinction, but fortunately there are a few small areas where they were able to survive, including the Badlands of South Dakota.

9.14 Habitat change

Pollution is but one of the ways in which human beings have so changed the environment of other organisms that their distribution and well-being have been affected. Of very great importance have been changes in the nature of the habitats in which organisms live, and the area that is covered by such organisms.

Habitat destruction can take many forms, and

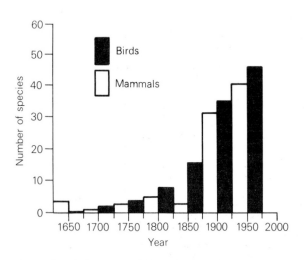

Figure 9.9   A histogram of the extinction of mammals and birds since 1600. As human population levels have grown exponentially and technology has become more sophisticated, so the rate of extinction has increased.

Figure 9.10   The changing range of the North American bison (*Bison bison*) under the influence of hunting pressures, especially in the nineteenth century.

they have been listed thus in the *World Conservation Strategy*:

(a) Replacement of the entire habitat by settlements and other human constructions.

(b) Replacement of the entire habitat by cropland, grazing land, plantations, etc.

(c) Replacement of the entire habitat by mines and quarries.

(d) The effects of dams, which drown certain habitats, block spawning migrations, and change water conditions (temperature, etc.)

(e) Drainage, channelization and flood control

(f) Chemical, nutrient and solid waste pollution

(g) Overexploitation of water, causing, for example, lakes to dry up

(h) Removal of materials, such as vegetation, soil, etc.

(i) Dredging and dumping

(j) Overgrazing and overbrowsing by domestic stock

(k) Erosion and siltation

(l) The introduction of invasive alien plants and animals. For example, the introduction of goats to the Galápagos Islands probably caused the extermination of at least four of the island races of the giant tortoise.

The effects of habitat change can be both beneficial and detrimental according to the nature of the species involved. For example, the spread of open country as a result of agricultural practices in Britain encouraged the spread of the rabbit,

Losses of the heritage of nature

Habitat
Lowland herb-rich hay meadows: 95% now lacking significant wildlife interest and only 3% left undamaged by agricultural intensification.

Lowland grasslands of sheep walks. On chalk and Jurassic limestone: 80% loss, largely by conversion to arable or improved grassland (mainly since 1940), but some scrubbed over through lack of grazing.

Lowland heaths on acidic soils: 40% loss, largely by conversion to arable or improved grassland, afforestation and building; some scrubbed over through lack of grazing.

Limestone pavements in northern England: 45% damaged or destroyed, largely by removal of weathered surfaces for sale as rockery stone, and only 3% left completely undamaged.

Ancient lowland woods composed of native, broad-leaved trees: 30–50% loss, by conversion to conifer plantation or grubbing out to provide more farmland.

Lowland fens, valley and basin mires: 50% loss or significant damage through drainage operations, reclamation for agriculture and chemical enrichment of drainage water.

Lowland raised mires: 60% loss or significant damage through afforestation, peat-winning, reclamation for agriculture or repeated burning.

Upland grasslands, heaths and blanket bogs: 30% loss or significant damage through coniferous afforestation, hill land improvement and reclamation, burning and over-grazing.

Species
The large blue butterfly became extinct in 1979, but ten more species are vulnerable or even seriously endangered, and out of a total British list of 55 resident breeding species of butterfly another 13 have declined and contracted in range substantially since 1960.

Three or four of our 43 species of dragonflies have become extinct since 1953, six are vulnerable or endangered, and five have decreased substantially.

Four of our 12 reptiles and amphibians are endangered.

At least 36 breeding species of bird have shown appreciable long-term decline during the last 35 years as a result of habitat loss or deterioration, 30 in the lowlands and six in the uplands.

The otter has become rare or has disappeared in many parts of England and Wales.

Bats in general have decreased and several of our 15 species, notably the greater horseshoe and mouse-eared bats are at risk of extinction. Others such as Bechstein's, Leisler's and the barbastelle are rare, and even the pipistrelle is no longer common. Problems are food supply, destruction of breeding and hibernation roosts and pollution.

There have been local increases and extensions of range in some vertebrate populations (e.g. wild cat and pine marten), but the overall balance of change is on the debit side.

Figure 9.11 Summary of current habitat and species changes in Britain.

and its success was further increased as a result of the decline in the number of its natural predators (such as hawks and foxes) brought about by game-guarding landlords. By the 1950s there were more than 60–100 million rabbits in England and it was only the introduction of a South American virus, *Myxomatosis*, which has kept their numbers under control.

For other species, however, agricultural change has caused adverse changes in their habitat. One of the most important habitat changes in Britain has been the removal of many of the hedgerows that are such a characteristic part of the landscape. They have been removed at a very fast rate to create larger fields (which are more efficient for large farm machines), to provide more usable space for crops and animals, because as farms become amalgamated many boundary hedges be-come redundant, and because as many farms become more specialized hedges are less necessary to divide farms up for different uses. Their removal is highly detrimental to many types of nesting bird. Figure 9.11 illustrates some of the major habitat changes that have been taking place in Britain in recent decades.

Possibly one of the most fundamental ways in which humans are causing changes in animal numbers and distribution is by reducing the *area* of natural habitat available to them. As we saw in section 9.8 many of the classic studies in island biogeography have shown that the number of species living at a particular location is related to area. Space is an important consideration, especially for those animals that require large expanses of territory, such as the great carnivores.

9.15   Conservation

As a result of all the pressures that we have been placing on plants and animals, there has arisen a desire to protect some species and some ecosystems from alteration, and to preserve them for posterity. This desire has a long history but was given a great boost by the work of George Perkins Marsh in the late nineteenth century.

The motives for the protection of species and landscapes are many:

(a) *Ethical*   It is asserted that wild species have a right to co-exist with us on our planet, and that we have no right to exterminate them.

(b) *Scientific*   It is asserted that we know very little about our environment, and that we should learn all we can before we destroy it.

(c) *Aesthetic*   Plants and animals are beautiful, and so enrich our lives.

(d) *The need to maintain genetic diversity*   By protecting species we maintain the species diversity upon which future plant and animal breeding work will depend. Once genes have been lost they cannot be replaced.

(e) *Environmental stability*   It is argued that in general the more diverse an ecosystem is, the more checks and balances there are to maintain stability. Thus environments that

Plate 9.7   In 1864 George Perkins Marsh wrote a book called *Man and Nature*, in which he put forward ideas that form the basis of the conservation ethic.

have been greatly simplified by human activity may be inherently unstable.

(f) *Recreational* Preserved habitats have great recreational value, and in the case of some game reserves they may have economic value as well (e.g. the safari industry in East Africa).

(g) *Economic* Many of the species in the world are still little known, and it is possible that they are great storehouses of food crops, medicinal plants, etc. which, when knowledge improves, will be a useful economic resource. At present we derive some 85 per cent of our food from no more than 20 species of plant, and there are doubtless many more plants that would be of great value to human welfare if we understood their properties.

10 Tectonic Features

10.1 Introduction

Tectonic activity, associated with movement of the plates that make up the earth's crust, is a most important part of the environment; for not only does it affect landscape evolution, but it also has certain implications in the shape of major natural hazards. We live in an active world, and areas that are affected by tectonic processes undergo variable rates of uplift or subsidence. It is useful to have some conception of the speed at which such vertical movements are occurring.

Regarding *uplift*, the *old shield areas* tend to be relatively highly stable and have rates of crustal movement that are generally less than 1 mm in each 1000 years. *Ancient mountain belts*, associated with earlier phases of plate collision and orogenic activity, may have slightly higher rates (up to 5 m in each 1000 years); *active block-faulted regions*, such as the basin and range province of the United States, may have higher rates still (up to 10 m in each 1000 year); but the highest rates of all (up to 20 m in each 1000 years) occur in the *major orogenic belts* undergoing current mountain-building. Even this maximum rate may not appear very fast, but it is important to remember that, if the rate persisted over a period of a million years, and if no erosion occurred in the meantime, the mountain range thereby created would be very much higher than any in existence today. A more general rate of uplift for an active mountain belt is probably around 3–5 metres per 1000 years, and allowing for a rate of erosion of about 0.5–2 m per 1000 years, it may be reasonable to postulate that an 8000 m mountain could form in around 2 to 8 million years.

The main areas of *subsidence* are probably the deltaic basins of some of the great rivers like the Rhine and the Mississippi, where the weight of sediments progressively depresses the crust. The Netherlands, for example, currently appear to be subsiding at a rate of up to 2.5 m in each 1000 years, thereby contributing to the flooding problems of that area.

Let us now move to a consideration of one of the most important classes of tectonic features: volcanoes.

10.2 Volcanoes

As we saw in chapter 1, volcanoes are not scattered randomly around the world. Indeed, one remarkable fact is that almost all the volcanoes in the world occur within a couple of hundred kilometres of the sea, and that only a few active volcanoes occur in the centres of the continents. Furthermore, if one plots their distribution on a world map, many of them appear to occur as a series of distinctive narrow chains. It is therefore evident that volcanoes occur in certain preferred locations, most of which can be related to the positions, types and movements of the world's major tectonic plates:

(a) *along the mid-ocean ridges*, where sea-floor spreading is taking place and where up-welling mantle creates lithosphere on a constructive plate margin;

(b) *in island arcs* that are created by the subduction of ocean crust, as in the Pacific Ocean;

(c) *in recent orogenic belts*, where at least one continental area is in collision with a subduction zone (e.g. the Andes);

(d) *at isolated places within the boundaries of*

plates, where rising plumes of material within the mantle create hot spots (as within the borders of the Pacific Plate);

(e) *along some of the great continental rift valleys and fractures*, notably in East Africa.

According to the type of volcano, there are differences in the composition of lava. Lava produced by upward movement of mantle material is *basaltic* and occurs in locations (a), (d) and (e). Lava that is produced by the process of subduction, either in island arcs or in association with Andean-type orogeny, is described as *andesitic.* Andesites, named after the Andes, where they make up almost all the major volcanoes, are very different from basalts because during the process of subduction a great deal of other material is added from the mantle and the continental crust. This affects the type of eruptions and volcanoes with which they are associated. Basalt is normally very free-flowing, with something like the consistency of syrup. Thus it forms bubbling lava lakes or fast-moving rivers of molten rock, andesite, by contrast, is much more viscous and moves more slowly, forming thicker but generally less extensive lava sheets. Moreover, andesite, being viscous, tends to trap gas until the pressure is sufficient to blow the lava apart, and so andesitic eruptions are often accompanied by a great deal of explosive activity, which shoots lava fragments (called *pyroclastic* material) into the air.

Pyroclastic materials

The word 'pyroclastic' means fire-broken. Pyroclastic materials are quite simply those materials that have been ejected from volcanoes in a solid but fragmentary form. The most straightforward types of pyroclastic deposits are made up of fragments that have been shot up into the air and fallen back down again as what are called *tephra* (pyroclastic fall deposits). They occur in a variety of sizes. including *ash* (very fine material less than 4 mm across), *lapilli* (little stones between 4 and 32 mm across), and *bombs* and *blocks* (which are much larger).

There is, however, another type of pyroclastic material – that produced by *pyroclastic flows*. The fragments may occur as mudflows or as avalanches down the side of the volcano, or they may roll away as a very hot, fast-moving cloud called *nuée ardente*. The heat, the gas and the blast associated with their movement makes them extremely dangerous. Some material produced by the frothing-over of a volcano is called *ignimbrite*.

Plate 10.1   Ol Doinyo Lengai (2879 m) is an active volcano which almost blocks the great rift valley in Tanzania. The western half of the rift is on the right hand side.

Types of volcanic eruption and volcanic landscape forms

The form that a volcanic eruption takes can be highly variable, and may be classified on the shape of the vent, on the nature of the eruption itself and on the nature of the deposits that it produces.

With regard to the nature of the vent, by far the most important division is between central and fissure eruptions. *Central vent eruptions* result when lava and other material are ejected from a hole in the ground, fed by a single pipe-like supply channel extending deep down below ground. Ejected material piles up around the vent as the eruption continues, producing a heap of material that is called a *volcano*. Central vent eruptions occur in all situations where volcanic activity can occur. This is in contrast to *fissure eruptions*, which occur only in those places where the earth's crust is being subjected to tensional forces, trying to pull it apart. Where this happens a long narrow series of deep cracks may form through which magma forces its way. Mid-ocean ridges, like that which Iceland is astride are favourite spots for this type of activity. If the material does not reach the surface a dyke is formed. If it does reach the surface then a fissure

Plate 10.2 An eruption of Mount Vesuvius, near Naples in Italy.

Plate 10.3 The Deccan Plateau in Central India is composed of thick layers of lava, and its margins are marked by stepped escarpments produced by erosion of beds of variable resistance.

eruption takes place and basalt lavas pour out over the surface. The volumes involved can be enormous in the case of *basaltic flood eruptions*.

It is not very easy to make a hard and fast line between these two main types. Volcanic cones may occur in lines, and some of the basalt flowing from volcanic cones may emerge from fissures. Lava does not always flow out of the central vent on a volcano and can be erupted from a vent or fissure on the flanks of the volcano.

Traditionally, vulcanologists have grouped eruptions into a sequence of progressively more violently explosive types (figure 10.1(a)). *Hawaiian eruptions* are the mildest of all, and tend to be typified by basalt flowing with great ease from a central vent. Slightly more explosive are *Strombolian eruptions*, named after a small volcanic island between Sicily and Italy. In this type gas escapes spasmodically, producing small explosions. In the case of *Vesuvian eruptions*, named after Mount Vesuvius, near Naples, there

are longish periods of inactivity during which gas pressure builds up behind the lavas that clog the vent. The blockage is removed by a substantial explosion, or series of explosions, during which large quantities of pyroclastic ash are blown out. When very large quantities of material are ejected by the gas blast there is said to be a *Plinian eruption*, and when the material that is ejected is in the form of one of those dangerous *nuée ardente* clouds the eruption is said to be *Peléean*.

The landforms produced by volcanic activity are the end result of two opposing forces – constructive and destructive. The constructive forces are those involving the deposition of lava and the ejection of pyroclastic material. The destructive forces may be the result either of the normal processes of erosion found in most environments (such as wind, water and mass movement) or of the volcano's own explosive activity. Since most volcanoes have long lives, they may, during their existence, go through several phases of construction, erosion and explosion.

Plate 10.4   A lava flow in the Galápagos Islands. This example is composed of pahoehoe, a type which produces festooned, ropey surface structures.

Basalt plateaus are formed by the eruption of fluid basalts through fissures rather than central vents. The voluminous flows may pile up one on top of another, drowning earlier relief, to produce flat plateaux like the Deccan of India (figure 10.1(b)) or the Columbia River plateau in North America. When they become dissected by erosion, as in the case of the Drakensbergs in South Africa, the seaward side of the Deccan behind

Bombay or parts of Ethiopia, thick piles of basalt lavas give rise to characteristic 'stepped' topography. There are some remnants of an ancient basalt plateau in Britain – northern Ireland, Skye, Mull, Rhum and many of the small islands of the Inner Hebrides contain fragments of a plateau that, about 60 million years ago, covered much of the area north of the Irish and west of the Scottish coasts which is now below the sea, and

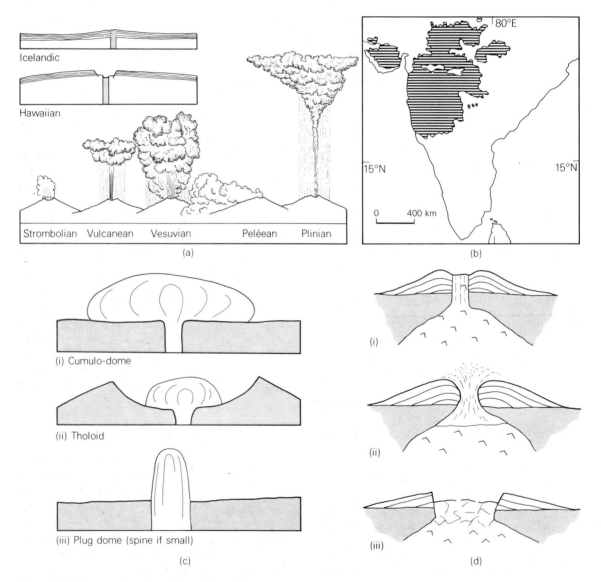

Figure 10.1 Some major volcanic landforms: (a) types of eruption; (b) a lava plateau – the Deccan of India; (c) acid lava (viscous) extrusion forms; (d) the stages in the formation of a caldera by collapse: (i) initial volcano, (ii) explosion, (iii) collapse.

which was once united with similar remnants in the Faroes, Iceland and Greenland. They are the result of eruptions associated with the plate movements flat led to the opening up of the North Atlantic.

If, rather than being erupted through a fissure, the lava erupts through a single central vent and flows easily in the fashion of the *Hawaiian* type of volcano, then a broad, convex-swelling volcano is produced, usually with a relatively small sunken crater or *caldera* on the crest of the swelling. These are called *shield volcanoes*. The slopes are gentle and are made up of many layers of lavas, but they can form large volcanoes. Mauna Kea and Mauna Loa in Hawaii both reach over 4000 m above sea level; if one allows for the fact that part of them is below sea level, they are the highest mountains on earth – over 9000 m high.

The classic shape for a volcano is *conical*, with smooth, symmetrical profiles. Lava and pyroclastic material occur as interleaved layers, and such volcanoes are usually, though not always, made of the relatively viscous andesitic lavas.

Among the destructive forces that mould volcanoes are the eruptive, explosive and subsidence forces that create craters. *Eruption craters* are the holes at the top of a volcanic cone, and when activity ceases the crater will become partially filled with debris. *Explosion craters* are produced when surface water percolating downwards comes into contact with hot magma and is converted into steam. The resulting explosion blasts up to the surface, blowing out a large hole in the ground in the process. Such craters are usually simple, circular depressions surrounded by low rims of ejected debris, and they may become occupied by a lake. Such lake-filled craters are often called *maars*. *Subsidence craters* may be either small, in which case they are called *pit craters* or *collapse craters*, or greater than *c.* 1 km in diameter, in which case they are called *calderas*. The latter are usually circular in outline, with broad bottoms and steep to precipitous walls (figure 10.1(d)). The largest known are some tens of km across. Explosive activity also may play some role in their development.

The shape of volcanoes and associated landforms is also affected by erosive processes (figure 10.2). On a classic conical cone, for example (figure 10.2(b)), gullies will cut down and will continue to develop until they are separated only from each other by sharp ridges. In this state the cone looks rather like a partly opened umbrella, and the pattern of alternating V-shaped ridges and gullies is known as *parasol ribbing*. As the erosive processes proceed, however, the cone will gradually become reduced to a rather shapeless hill – a process that may take some tens of millions of years. Pyroclastic deposits may also be intricately dissected by gullies to give badlands topography. Erosion will tend to etch out the weaker layers in a volcanic sequence, in some cases producing caverns; whereas elsewhere some resistant parts of the original volcano, such as the necks or feeder pipes of central-vent-type volcanoes, may stand up after most of the surrounding material has been eroded. The Puys of the Massif Central in France result from such differential erosion, as does Arthur's Seat in Edinburgh, the site of a large Carboniferous volcano.

If the lava that flows from a volcano is harder than the rocks that make up the valleys into which it flows, then relief inversion may occur (figure 10.2(a)).

Extremely viscous lavas of the acidic type, if they are not afflicted by an explosion, give rise to a number of distinctive landforms. The features formed include *cumulo-domes*, *tholoids* and *plug domes*, the last being produced when the lava is so viscous that it moves up like a piston, producing a roughly cylindrical body (figure 10.1(c)).

The permeability of lava flows may give a partial explanation of why valleys in basalts tend to be broad, flat-floored and steep-sided. They have a U-shaped cross-profile reminiscent in many ways of a glacial valley, and they also possess steep amphitheatric heads.

Volcanoes as hazards

Volcanoes pose many dangers (table 10.1). First, lava can flow at considerable speeds (as much as 48 km per hour) and cover considerable distances. The longest recorded flow of historic times was on Hawaii, when a flow from Mauna Loa ran downslope for 53 km before reaching the sea. Fissure eruptions can cover even wider areas. The Laki eruption on Iceland in 1783 covered an area the size of the Isle of Man, and in places the laval flow was 180 m thick.

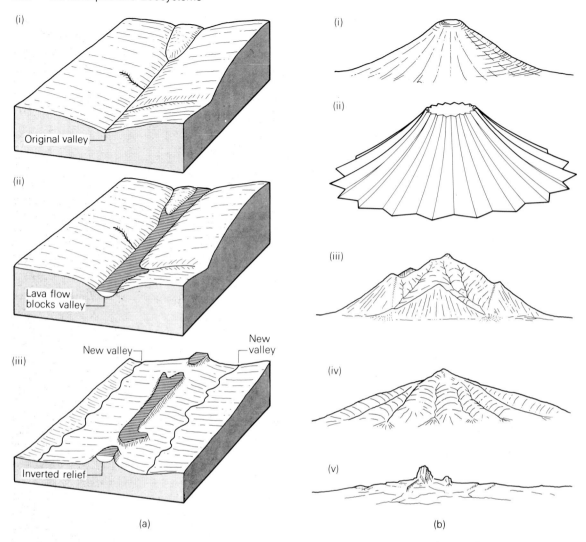

Figure 10.2 Post-eruption modifications of volcanic landscapes: (a) stages of relief inversion following a lava flow; (b) stages of the erosion of a volcano: (i) intact cone; (ii) parasol ribbing; (iii) planeze stage; (iv) residual volcano; (v) volcanic skeleton.

Falls of tephra also pose problems. Heavy ash falls will destroy vegetation (including crops), cause buildings to collapse, disrupt drainage, create suffocation, provide erodible material for subsequent mudflows and, if hot, cause fires. Pyroclastic flows, such as *nuées ardentes*, are especially serious. In 1902 Mont Pelée exploded on the Isle of Martinique in the Caribbean, and there were only two survivors out of a population of 28 000. Most of them were killed by the *nuées*

Table 10.1 Deaths resulting from some of the most severe volcanic eruptions this century

Year	Locality	Deaths
1902	Mt Pelée, Martinique	30 000
1902	La Soufrière, St Vincent	1565
1909	Kelut, Indonesia	5500
1951	Mt Lamington, Papua	3000
1963	Mt Agung, Bali, Indonesia	1500
1911	Taal, Philippines	1335
1965	Taal, Philippines	500
1980	Mt St Helens, Washington, USA	70

ardentes, which travelled at speeds of 33 m s^{-1} and had temperatures of as much as 1200°C.

If there is heavy rainfall during the course of an eruption and the rain mixes with volcanic ash on the steep slopes of a volcanic cone, then a great mudflow or *lahar* may result. The most disastrous mudflow of this type occurred on the Kelut Volcano in Japan in 1919, when 5500 people were killed. Other destructive mudflows are caused by the rupturing of crater lakes.

How serious are all these hazards? C. D. Ollier (1969) sums up the situation in a rather surprising way:

In the past 500 years volcanoes have probably killed, directly or indirectly, over 200,000 people, of whom half died in the eruptions of Tamboro, Krakatoa, and Mont Pelée. This toll is in fact very low when compared with those of earthquakes, floods, wars, or road accidents.

Plate 10.6 The eruption of Mount St Helens in 1980 produced severe damage in the north western parts of the United States, and waves of superheated dust and gas knocked down millions of trees.

Plate 10.5 A volcanic plug at Le Puy in the Massif Central, France, exposed by differential erosion of volcanic deposits.

On the credit side volcanoes provide fertile land, energy and materials for industry, and a livelihood for many people in the tourist trade. Even when activity has long ceased, most volcanic regions retain a great natural beauty, and frequently display most spectacular scenery. Such areas are often tourist attractions, and a large number of National Parks are located on volcanic centres. On balance volcanoes do more good than harm.

The scale of change that can be wrought by one volcanic eruption can be gauged by this account of the Mount St Helen's eruption that took place in 1980 (from J. E. Costa and V. R. Baker, 1981):

The northward blast of the lateral eruption reduced the mountain's elevation by 396 m. ...ash was blown 19 km into the atmosphere. Waves of superheated dust and gas knocked down millions of trees. Mudflows filled lakes, rivers and streams, destroying fish, roads and bridges.... Two earthquakes of magnitude 5.0 were recorded during the eruption. The blast left a crater 1.6 km across and 900 to 1500 m deep.... An estimated 4.2×10^9 m^3 of debris had been blown out of the volcano by the start of summer. ...the ash fall closed schools, factories, stores, officers, airports, and highways, and idled 370,000 workers in Washington State.... Damages from the eruption are estimated to be \$2.0 billion.... Shipping on the Columbia River ... was halted by the Coast Guard because of sediment and log jams. The harbor of Portland was reduced in depth from 12 to 4 m in places by sedimentation.... .

Prediction of volcanic eruptions

Observations of many volcanoes have led to the discovery of a number of phenomena that may be taken as warning signs of impending eruptions. It needs to be said, however, that these predictions can seldom be given with complete certainty.

The commonest form of eruption prediction is the measurement of earth tremors by seismic methods. As the ascent of magma causes tremors, there is usually a marked increase in the number and violence of local tremors with a focus at shallow depth just before an eruption. Another method is to undertake tilt measurements, because before an eruption a volcano is liable to swell as a result of lava pushing up inside it. Tiltmeters measure very accurately the tilt of the ground, and any change in tilt may be regarded as a warning. Likewise, the temperature of crater lakes, hot springs and *fumaroles* often shows a sharp increase before eruption, so that constant or regular readings of water temperatures may give some warning. The composition of gases erupted from craters or fumaroles may vary before eruption, so gas monitoring can be employed for predictive purposes. In addition, movements of lava at depth may cause changes in local gravity, and magnetic field measurements of these effects may give some way of predicting possible eruptions.

Once a volcano has made up its mind that it is going to erupt there is precious little that can be done to stop it. However, there are some ways of making sure that the effects are as small as possible. For instance, lava tends to flow down pre-existing drainage lines or depressions on a slope so these areas should be avoided. Given that lava flows relatively slowly this is often possible. The speed and direction of lava flows may also be influenced by bombing them, building diversion walls and spraying them with water. However, because mudflows and *nuées ardentes* travel so much faster than lava flows, and are so much less dense, they are much less easy to cope with.

Some environmental consequences of volcanic eruptions

Although the direct consequences of volcanic eruptions, such as ash falls, gas clouds, debris flows, explosions and the flow of lava, have serious consequences and may create serious hazards, there are a number of other consequences that are of potential significance.

A rather specialised consequence is the existence of *jökulhlaups*. When a volcano beneath an ice cap erupts, large amounts of ice above it will melt. But if there is insufficient heat to melt through the entire thickness of the ice cap, the ice sheet immediately over the volcano may collapse, forming an immense hole, and the water melted by the eruption will be ponded up. This ice-dammed water may sometimes burst out from the ice cap, causing enormous quantities of water and sediment to gush across the outwash plains around the ice cap. Individual flows have been known to exceed 400 000 m^3 s^{-1}, and a boulder 400 m^3 in size was carried 14 km by such a flow in Iceland in 1918. (For comparison, it is worth noting that the Amazon, which normally carries more discharge than any other river, has an estimated flow of about 200 000 m^3 s^{-1}).

A no less spectacular effect of some volcanic eruptions is the production of some 'tidal waves' called *tsunamis*. The explosion of the volcano Krakatoa in the East Indies in 1883 was so violent that great waves ravaged the shores of Java and Sumatra, killing over 36 000 people. The biggest wave is estimated to have been no less than 15 m in height at the shore, and where it washed up on to the land its momentum carried it even higher, to as much as 30 m! Some tsunamis can result from earthquake activity without volcanic eruptions taking place.

Volcanic eruptions also have an effect on world climate over various time scales. This is because some explosive eruptions can produce a dense dust-veil in the lower stratosphere which shuts out some of the incoming radiation from the sun, resulting in cooling. The ash emissions of Krakatoa were injected at a height of 32 km and produced a global decrease of solar radiation received at the earth's surface by 10–20 per cent. A series of cold, wet years followed in Europe; and many of the coldest and wettest summers in British history, including 1695, 1725, the 1760s, the 1840s, 1879, the 1880s, 1903 and 1912, occurred in conjunction with times of high volcanic dust inputs into the stratosphere and upper atmosphere. Moreover, the period of more or less world-wide warming of the 1920s, 1930s and 1940s coincides with a period when there were no major explosive eruptions in the Northern Hemisphere, suggesting that the absence of a volcanic dust pall in those decades was one factor in the warming process. Going back further, a study of the Byrd Ice Core that has been drilled through the ice of the Antarctic ice cap has produced evidence of particularly heavy and frequent volcanic dust falls at 20 000 to 16 000 years BP – the same time as the phase of maximum cold of the last glaciation of the Pleistocene.

10.3 Intrusive igneous rocks

Not all igneous rocks are extrusive in the sense that volcanic lavas are. Many are said to be *intrusive*, because, rather than being poured out on to the earth's surface, they have cooled and solidified within the earth's crust. Intrusive rocks occur in a great variety of forms. Some form enormous bodies as much as 1600 km × 160 km in size, while others may form a small dyke only a few centimetres wide. Some are relatively fine-grained while others are fairly coarse. Some have a very dense network of joints while others may have very few. Some are *concordant* into the structures into which they are intruded, while others cut across the structures and are said to be *discordant*. Bearing these sorts of considerations in mind, one can classify igneous rock masses as follows (see figure 10.3):

Major
    Concordant: lopoliths
    Discordant: batholiths with associated bosses and stocks, diapirs
Minor
    Concordant: sills, laccoliths, bysmaliths, phacoliths
    Discordant: dykes, ring complexes including cone sheets, ring dykes and cauldron subsidence

These different types of intrusion have different effects on relief. *Lopoliths* are intrusive complexes which have a saucer-like form and are basically concordant to the structures of the rocks into which they are intruded. They are of enormous size (the Bushveld igneous complex in South Africa covers some 55 000 km²), and are often layered so that there is a tendency towards the development of outward-facing scarps with variations in the resistance of the various layers. *Batholiths* are also large; they are nearly always formed of granite, they are common, and they are exposed at the surface by the erosion of the rocks into which they were intruded discordantly. These rocks are often altered (*metamorphosed*) by their contact with the magma that made up the batholith. This zone of alteration is called a *metamorphic aureole*. Examples of batholiths include the granite masses of the West Country in England and the uplands of Brittany. They are particularly widespread in the old Pre-cambrian shield areas, as in Zimbabwe. Batholith landscapes are often characterised by such landforms as tors and inselbergs, though their development depends very much on the nature of the jointing within the granite.

Sills are minor intrusions approximately concordant with the bedding planes of the rocks; they may be of any thickness and extend over large areas. In Britain the most striking example is the great Whin Sill of northern England. It is up to 70 m thick and forms a natural rampart, part of which was used by the Romans in locating Hadrian's Wall. One of Britain's finest waterfalls, High Force, occurs where the River Tees plunges over its resistant outcrop.

Rather more complex in form (see figure 10.3) are *laccoliths, bysmaliths* and *phacoliths*. If, as in the classic Henry Mountains of the United States the sediments surrounding the intrusions are removed, then almost perfect exhumation may reveal some striking relief forms. *Dykes* are thin, long discordant intrusions that may have a variety of relief effects according to how they weather and erode in comparison with the rock into

Figure 10.3 Some of the major types of igneous intrusion: (a) discordant; (b) concordant.

which they are intruded. Where they are harder than the surrounding rocks they project; where they are weaker than the surrounding rocks they form depressions; and where they are harder they may stand higher than the surrounding rocks but be surpassed in resistance and elevation by the baked margins of the country rocks. Dykes may occur in various configurations, thereby creating patterns in the landscape.

10.4 Earthquakes

Another major demonstration of the power of tectonic forces is provided by the existence of

Plate 10.7 Earthquakes are a major type of natural hazard, ranking third (after floods and cyclones) in terms of the total loss of life that they cause. In December 1972 the city of Managua in Nicaragua was severely damaged.

earthquakes. These are motions of the ground, ranging from a faint tremor to a wild motion capable of shaking buildings apart and causing gaping fissures and steps to open up in the ground. An earthquake can be likened to a form of wave motion in which energy is transmitted through the surface layer of the earth in widening circles from a point of sudden release – the *earthquake focus*. Like the ripples produced when a pebble is thrown into a pond, these *seismic waves* travel outwards in all directions, gradually losing energy.

Earthquakes are the results of earth movements, many of which are associated with the boundaries of the major plates. If stress is placed upon a section of rock by forces operating in opposite directions, the rock initially deforms, because it is to some extent elastic. If the stress is maintained long enough, this strain may exceed the elastic strength of the rock, so that fracture takes place along a line called a *fault* (see section 10.11). At the moment of fracture the rock regains its original shape but in a new position. The quaking and shaking takes place during the sudden movement of the rock back to its original shape, after the stress is released. The place at the ground surface above the point where the stress release occurred is called the *epicentre*.

There have been various attempts to define the degree of destructiveness (*intensity*) of earthquakes. Two of the most used scales are the Mercalli scale of intensity and the Richter scale of magnitude. An earthquake's intensity depends upon such things as magnitude, distance from epicentre, acceleration, duration, amplitude of waves, type of ground, water table and the nature and type of constructions affected. Its determination is based on interviews and observations, and is rated on a scale from I to XII (table 10.2). Magnitude is a more objective, instrumentally determined measure of the amount of energy released by an earthquake. The Richter scale is logarithmic, and the numbers are proportional to the amplitude of seismic waves measured 100 km from the earthquake's epicentre.

On a global basis, earthquakes can be ranked third in terms of the total loss of life that they cause. During the 20-year period 1947–67 over 56 000 people were killed by earthquakes throughout the world. These deaths comprise

12.7 per cent of the total lives lost to natural hazards during this period. Only floods and cyclones exceeded the toll of deaths caused by earthquakes during those two decades. Given that earthquakes are less predictable and less avoidable than the other two major hazards, and given that there is an increasing trend of urbansiation in many areas of seismic risk, the potential for earthquake damage and deaths may increase rapidly. Individual earthquake events have the potential to inflict the greatest loss of life and property of any geological hazard (table 10.3). Loss of life in an extreme earthquake can be more than ten times that of extreme volcanic eruptions.

The shocks produced by earthquakes can create *slope instability*. One of the most horrendous examples of this was the tragedy that afflicted the town of Yungay in Peru in May 1970. A strong earthquake triggered off a collapse of the summit ice cap of the lofty north peak of a mountain called Huascaran (6654 m). Thousands of tonnes of rock were dislodged by the falling ice, and a gigantic debris flow was generated, which travelled at speeds up to 320 km h^{-1}, collecting water and debris *en route*. Within minutes the debris had travelled about 15 km carrying individual blocks measuring 15 m^3 (bigger than an average house). It overwhelmed the town of Yungay and 25 000 people were killed.

One of the most important consequences of earthquake activity is that changes in the level of the ground surface may take place, thereby creating fault traces, changes in sea level, etc. The Alaska earthquake of 1964 produced ground displacement of 10–15 m, and displacements of the order of a few metres are not uncommon. Some seismic movements are more gradual, and occur by a process called *seismic creep*. Although their effects are less immediately dramatic, detailed surveys with precise levelling instruments in parts

Table 10.2 Scale of earthquake intensities with approximately corresponding magnitudes

	Mercalli intensity	Description of characteristic effects	Richter magnitude corresponding to highest intensity reached
I	Instrumental	Detected only by seismographs	
II	Feeble	Noticed only by sensitive people	3.5
III	Slight	Like the vibrations due to a passing lorry; felt by people at rest, especially on upper floors	to 4.2
IV	Moderate	Felt by people while walking; rocking of loose objects, including standing vehicles	4.3
V	Rather strong	Felt generally; most sleepers are awakened and bells ring	to 4.8
VI	Strong	Trees sway and all suspended objects swing; damage by overturning and falling of loose objects	4.9–5.4
VII	Very strong	General alarm; walls crack; plaster falls	5.5–6.1
VIII	Destructive	Car drivers seriously disturbed; masonry fissured; chimneys fall; poorly constructed buildings damaged	6.2
IX	Ruinous	Some houses collapse where ground begins to crack, and pipes break open	to 6.9
X	Disastrous	Ground cracks badly; many buildings destroyed and railway lines bent; landslides on steep slopes	7–7.3
XI	Very disastrous	Few buildings remain standing; bridges destroyed; all services (railways, pipes and cables) out of action; great landslides and floods	7.4–8.1
XII	Catastrophic	Total destruction; objects thrown into air; ground rises and falls in waves	>8.1 (maximum known, 8.9)

of California, where there are major faults like the Garlock and the San Andreas, reveal movements of 5–13 m in 1000 years.

The principal danger in an earthquake is construction failure, and the extent of *earthquake vibration damage* is controlled partly by the characteristics of the ground upon which the buildings are constructed. In unconsolidated surface materials, such as alluvium, artificial fill or swamp deposits, earthquake vibrations last longer and the wave amplitudes are greater, causing more shaking than on bedrock. Thus, the greatest damage during the San Francisco earthquake of 1906 occurred in areas of susceptible superficial materials, whereas buildings on bedrock received relatively little damage. Vibration, however, is not the only problem. When the ground shakes and vibrates during an earthquake, unconsolidated sediment becomes more compact, for the material assumes a more dense arrangement by particles moving together and decreasing the volume. As a consequence ground subsidence occurs, and this too can damage buildings. The ground locally subsided 0.6 m by compaction of sediment in the 1906 San Francisco earthquake, and by 1.8 m during the 1964 Alaska earthquake. The consequence of settlement will be especially severe if building foundations are built across deposits of varying physical properties, which would cause one part of the foundations to settle more than another.

In areas where unconsolidated material has a water table close to the surface, ground shaking may cause the sediment to be transformed from a solid to a liquid by a process called *liquefaction*. The liquified sediments may slide or flow, causing further damage, especially on slopes.

In many earthquakes fire is a major hazard, as stoves are overturned, gas mains are fractured and so on.

Tsunamis, which, we have already noted, sometimes result from great volcanic eruptions like that of Krakatoa, can also result from earthquakes and can cause great loss of life. The amount of damage they cause is related partly to the intensity of the earthquake that produced them but also to the nature of the coastline, and its distance from the epicentre. Broadly, gently sloping continental shelves allow tsunamis to build to great heights, whereas deep water ex-

Table 10.3 Deaths resulting from some severe earthquakes of the twentieth century

Year	Location	Magnitude (Richter scale)	Deaths (max. estimate)
1905	Kangra, India	8.6	20 000
1907	Afghanistan	8.1	12 000
1908	Messina, Italy	7.5	200 000
1915	Avezzano, Italy	7.5	30 000
1917	South Java	?	15 000
1918	South east China	7.3	10 000
1920	Kansu, China	8.5	180 000
1923	Tokyo–Yokohama, Japan	8.3	163 000
1927	Nansham, China	8.0–8.3	180 000
1933	North central China	7.4	10 000
1934	Bihar, Nepal	8.4	10 700
1935	Quetta, Pakistan	7.5–7.6	60 000
1939	Chillan, Chile	8.3	40 000
1939	Erzincan, Turkey	8.0	32 700
1948	Kagi, Formosa	7.3	19 800
1960	Agadir, Morocco	5.6–5.9	14 000
1962	Buyin-Zara, Iran	7.3	14 000
1968	Dasht-i-Bayaz, Iran	7.3–7.8	18 000
1970	Chimbote, Peru	7.8–7.9	67 000
1974	West central China	6.8	20 000
1975	Haicheng, China	7.3–7.4	10 000
1976	Guatemala	7.5	23 000
1976	Tangshan, China	7.8–8.1	750 000
1978	Tabas, Iran	7.7–7.8	25 000

Source: data in *Open Earth* no. 15, pp. 50–1.

tending close to the shore minimises bottom friction and wave size. Narrow V-shaped bays and harbours that concentrate the wave energy are thought to provide conditions favouring maximum wave heights. Tsunamis are especially common in the Pacific, averaging more than two per year, but most are small and not destructive. They are more rare in the Atlantic because it is not ringed by active plate boundaries, but major tsunamis were caused by the great Lisbon earthquake in 1755; they killed 25 000 people in the eastern Atlantic and caused 3.5–4.5 m waves as far away as the West Indies.

10.5 Man-made seismic activity

Although we can do relatively little to predict or stop earthquakes an increasing amount of evidence suggests that human activity is capable of triggering off seismic events, some of which can have unfortunate consequences.

In Denver, Colorado, in the early 1960s nerve gas waste was disposed of in a well at a great depth in the hope of avoiding contamination of useful groundwater supplies. The waste was pumped in at high pressures and triggered off a series of earthquakes, the timing of which corresponded very closely to the timing of water disposal into the well. It appears that the increased fluid pressure reduced the frictional force across the contact surface of a fault, thereby allowing slippage to occur, which created the earthquake. The significance of this 'accident' has now been verified experimentally at an oil field in Colorado, where variations in seismicity have been produced by deliberately controlled variations in the fluid pressure in a zone that is seismically active.

However, perhaps the most important seismic-

Plate 10.8 As this contemporary print demonstrates, the great Lisbon earthquake of 1755 generated devastating tsunamis or tidal waves. Their effects were felt as far away as the West Indies.

ity induced by human activity results from the impoundment of great volumes of water in reservoirs behind dams. With the ever-increasing number and size of reservoirs, this threat increases. Detailed monitoring has shown that earthquake clusters occur in the vicinity of some dams after their reservoirs have been filled, whereas prior to construction seismic activity was less clustered and less frequent. It has even been found that the seismic activity varies as the level of water in the reservoir changes with the seasons. Some of these earthquakes can eventually damage the dam, thereby causing flooding and loss of life.

Miscellaneous other human activities appear to affect seismic activity. In the gold mining area of South Africa, for example, and also in the coal mining area of Staffordshire, England, excavation and blasting associated with underground mining have produced small tremors. There are also cases where seismicity and faulting can be attributed to fluid extraction, as in the oil fields of Texas and California and the gas fields of the Po Valley in Italy.

10.6 Faults

A major consequence of tectonic activity is the formation of *faults*. These are breaks in the surface rocks of the earth's crust as a result of sudden yielding under unequal stresses. Faulting is accompanied by a displacement along a fault plane, and since faults are often of great horizontal extent they can often be followed along a fault line for many kilometres. In some places clearly recognisable layers of rocks can be seen offset on opposite sides of a fault, and the amount of displacement can be measured.

Faults take various forms that can be classified according to the angle of inclination and the relative direction of displacement (figure 10.4). A *normal fault* has a steep or nearly vertical fault plane, and movement is predominantly in a vertical direction, with one side being raised (or upthrown) relative to the other (which is downthrown). In a *reverse fault* the beds on one side of a fault are thrust over those on the other side as a result of compressive forces. With *transcurrent faults*, which are also called tear, strike-slip and wrench faults, the displacement is horizontal along the line of the fault. The Great Glen in Scotland is such a fault, where the horizontal displacement is about 100 km. Elsewhere faulting can be associated with slumping and twisting, while a *low-angle overthrust fault* involves movement that is predominantly in a horizontal direction, with the fault plane also in a more or less horizontal position. One slice of rock rides over the adjacent ground surface.

In general, faults occur in groups. Regions that are divided by a series of normal faults into relatively elevated or depressed blocks are said to be *block-faulted*. Upstanding fault blocks, bounded by striking fault scarps, are called *horsts*, and examples of these include the Vosges, the Black Forest and the Harz Mountains (figure 10.5). Fault blocks depressed below their surroundings are called *fault troughs*, and long fault troughs between approximately parallel fault scarps are known as *rift valleys* or *graben*. Between the horsts of the Black Forest and the Vosges the Rhine flows through such a graben. An example of a very large graben produced by continental rifting is the Red Sea, separating the Arabian Peninsula from Africa.

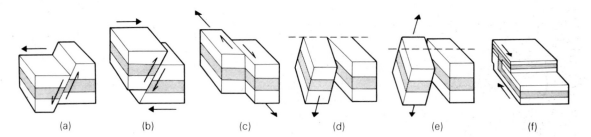

Figure 10.4 Different types of fault: (a) a normal fault produced by stretching; (b) a reversed fault caused by compression; (c) a strike-slip (transcurrent) fault produced by shearing; (d) a hinge fault produced by slumping; (e) a rotational fault produced by twisting; (f) a low-angle overthrust fault.

Plate 10.9 An earthquake produced this fault which disrupted the regular rows of garlic in a California field.

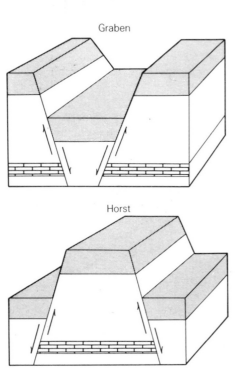

Faults and fractures influence relief in three main ways: by the tectonic displacements that they create (see section 10.1), by the modification of the rocks in their vicinity (crush zones, breccias and mineral veins), and by the juxtaposition of rocks of differing weathering qualities along fault lines. Among the landforms produced are fault scarps with distinctive facets, rivers with disrupted courses, cave systems with marked changes of course and many alluvial fans.

10.7 Folding

One way in which the rocks of the earth's crust respond to stresses set up by tectonic activity is to deform by crumpling – a process called *folding*. Folds vary in size from a few millimetres to hundreds of kilometres across.

Figure 10.5 (left) The development of horst and graben. When faulting causes one block to be lower than those on either side, a graben is formed, and where one is raised a horst is formed.

Figure 10.6 Different types of folds: (a) an open symmetrical anticline and syncline: (i) because of erosion the oldest rocks will be found in the core of an anticline and the youngest in the core of a syncline; ((ii) and (iii)) symmetrical folds before and after erosion; ((iv) and (v)) symmetrical plunging folds before and after erosion; (b) different types of anticlinal folds showing in each case the relation of the axial plane and the axis to the geometry of the fold: (i) asymmetrical fold; (ii) recumbent fold; (iii) symmetrical fold; (iv) overturned fold.

Upfolds or arches of layered rocks are called *anticlines*, and downfolds or troughs are called *synclines*. A steplike bend in an otherwise gently dipping or horizontal bed is a *monocline*. Anticlines that lack a well-defined elongation and plunge from a point nearly equally in all directions are called *domes*, and the corresponding synclinal structures are called *basins*. As figure 10.6 shows, there are various subdivisions of the main types of fold caused by differences in asymmetry, angles etc.

Because folding creates patterns in rocks of different character, it is a process that has an important effect on landscape. During the building of the Alps in Europe, for example, some of the Cretaceous sedimentary rocks of southern England were deformed. In the Weald (figure 10.7) a great dome was formed on which were superimposed some smaller anticlines, giving a corrugated effect. This was subsequently eroded to produce a landscape dominated by escarpments and vales, according to the different resist-

Plate 10.10 Contorted strata in sedimentary rocks at Stair Hole, Lulworth, Dorset, England. Folding has created anticlinal and synclinal structures.

Figure 10.7   Drainage pattern, rock type and relief in the Weald of south-east England.

Plate 10.11   A great escarpment formed in gently dipping sandstones in the Brecon Beacons, South Wales.

ances of the rocks exposed as the dome was dissected by rivers.

The precise form of the escarpments will depend in part on the angle at which the rocks lie after they have been deformed. Moderately dipping strata tend to form a typical *cuesta scarpland* like that of the Cotswolds in the West Midlands of England, a *cuesta* being a ridge or upland with a steep scarp slope and a gentle back or dip slope. Horizontal strata will tend to produce plateau-like relief, whereas if the dip is very steep the result is a ridge with deep slopes on both sides, called a *hogback* (figure 10.8).

During the early stages of erosion anticlines are identical with mountains or ridges, and synclines with valleys, but frequently the anticlines may be rendered less resistant to erosion because of the presence of many joints caused in the process of flexuring. As time passes, therefore, relief inversion sometimes occurs so that the anticline becomes a valley and the syncline a hill.

Another way in which streams may gradually adjust to structures is by *river capture*. In areas of variable lithology, streams may be able to expand their networks preferentially in areas of less resistant rocks. This is evident in the north-east of England, where the North Tyne (figure 10.9) has cut back through the relatively unresistant Scremerston Coal Series rocks, beheading the Wansbeck and Blyth Rivers. A distinct change in direction occurs at the point of capture, creating what is called the *elbow of capture*.

Although in general drainage lines become adapted to the arrangement of rocks of different resistance caused by folding, there are cases where there appears to be a striking lack of adjustment. Such maladjustment is brought about in two main ways: by the development of structures across drainage lines, and by the lowering of drainage lines on to a new set of structures (figure 10.10).

Figure 10.8 refers to the left diagrams:

Plateau — Caprock
Horizontal strata
(a)

Cuesta
Back or dip slope — Scarp
Moderate dip
(b)

Hogback
Steep dip
(c)

Figure 10.8 Three different ways in which landforms result from differences in the dip of strata in areas of tilted sedimentary rocks: (a) a plateau in horizontal strata; (b) a cuesta in gently dipping strata; (c) a hogback ridge in male deeply dipping strata.

E = elbow of capture
- - - - former river courses
///// Scremerston Coal Series

Figure 10.9 The courses of some rivers in northern England which have been affected by river capture. The North Tyne, by cutting back along the weak Scremerston Coal Series, has beheaded the Blyth and the Wansbeck. River capture is also sometimes called 'stream piracy'

The first of these two situations results when a fold rises across the line of a stream, but sufficiently slowly that the stream, by continuing to cut down, can persist across the axis of folding. Drainage that cuts across structures in this way is termed *antecedent*. One of the most spectacular examples of this is provided from the great fold mountains of the Himalayas. The Indus, the Ganga and the Brahmaputra persist in their southward escape from the rising Himalayas as the Indian and Eurasian Plates collide at a rate of 3 cm per year, even though the Brahmaputra in particular flows for 1300 km along the direction of the mountain axis.

The second of these two mechanisms produces drainage that is said to be *superimposed*. Such drainage arises if a stream network, however well adapted to the structure within which it is developed, is let down on to a completely different set of structures. It is then thrown completely out of adjustment. This is what happens when streams cut through a cover of folded sedimentary rocks on to some older rocks beneath that have a markedly different arrangement of structures.

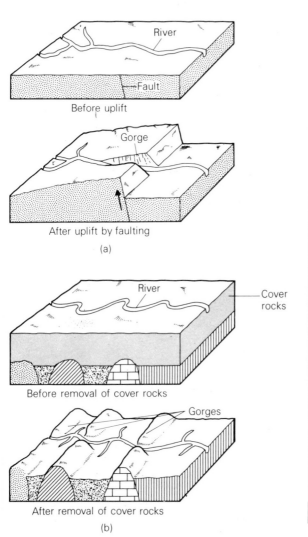

Figure 10.10 Examples of the way in which rivers may become unadjusted to structures: (a) antecedence; (b) superimposition.

Plate 10.12 The Avon Gorge in Bristol, England, is an example of a river that cuts across geological structures, either because of superimposition or because of antecedence.

11 Slopes

11.1 Mass movements

Mass movement is a term that covers the movement of material on slopes under the influence of gravity without the benefit of a contributing force such as flowing water, wind or ice. In reality, however, there is a continuum between a river, where there is a great dominance of water over debris, and rockfalls, where there is a great abundance of debris and very little water. Because we are dealing with a continuum, and because some mass movement events may include more than one type of mass movement, any classification is bound to be arbitrary to a certain extent. However, a very useful classification is that of M. A. Carson and M. J. Kirkby (1972), in which a triangular diagram (figure 11.1) can be used a classify the main types of movement according to mechanism (heave, slide and flow) and moisture content.

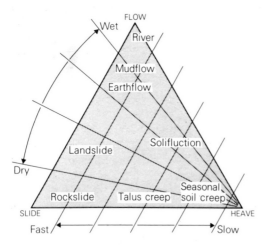

Figure 11.1 A classification of mass movement processes on slopes.

Slides

The simplest type of movement is a fall (figure 11.2(a)). *Falls* are generated on the steepest hill-

Plate 11.1 A debris fall taking place in glacial debris in the Karakoram Mountains, Pakistan, 1980. The jeep tracks give an idea of scale. The debris is falling into the Hunza River thereby contributing to its enormous load.

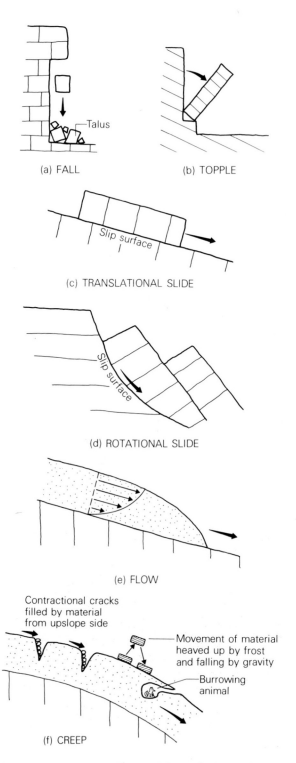

(a) FALL

(b) TOPPLE

(c) TRANSLATIONAL SLIDE

(d) ROTATIONAL SLIDE

(e) FLOW

Contractional cracks filled by material from upslope side

Movement of material heaved up by frost and falling by gravity

Burrowing animal

(f) CREEP

Figure 11.2 Examples of some of the major types of mass movement.

slope faces and occur where there are discontinuities such as joints or bedding planes along which weathering can occur. The debris falls from the cliff face through the air and accumulates at the base as a cone of talus (scree). Weathering, especially frost action, and heavy snow and rainfall can cause the fall to occur. Related to falls are *topples* (figure 11.2(b)), which are forward movements about some pivot point.

Landslides and *rockslides* involve the movement of material as a mass over a discrete surface or plane, and there are two main types. *Rotational slides* (figure 11.2(d)) have a curved surface of rupture along which sliding occurs and they produce slumps by their backward rotational movement. *Translational slides* (figure 11.2(c)) have a relatively flat, planar surface of movement along one or several surfaces.

Flows

The distinction between debris slides and debris flows is usually difficult to make. Frequently the saturation of soil on a slope by a cloudburst will initiate failure as a debris slide; however, as motion increases the water-soaked mass will begin to flow.

Flow movements (figure 11.2(e)) occur in a wide variety of forms. Materials involved vary from huge blocks of rock to clay; the water content ranges from fairly dry to very wet; and velocities range from little more than creep to hundreds of metres per second (figure 11.3). *Debris flows* involve the relatively rapid movement of fairly coarse material. They are characteristic of mountain fronts in arid regions, for the mountain slopes are often covered with a debris layer that is unstabilised by vegetation, so that when a severe storm occurs the water mobilises the debris into a slurry; movement then resembles the flow of wet concrete and occurs as a series of pulsations or surges. Flow can take place for quite long distances into the plains, and helps to form alluvial fans. It tends to take place along pre-existing channels. Debris flows characteristically move at velocities of 3 to 10 m s^{-1}; they carry blocks of rock that are often 2–8 m across, have water contents of around 20 per cent, and may flow for many kilometres. They can carry away cars, tractors and houses, and they can rapidly and easily block culverts and bridges on roads and railways.

Solifluction, which literally means soil flowage, occurs widely in periglacial areas, though it is by no means restricted to them. It comprises two main processes: the flow of water-soaked debris, and the creep of surface material by freeze-thaw action. The water-soaked debris occurs as a result of thawing of permafrost or seasonally frozen ground in the active layer (see section 3.9), assisted by snow melt. In addition, the presence of permafrost just below the surface creates a relatively impermeable layer that helps to maintain water saturation in the near-surface material. Creep is caused by freezing and thawing, which causes changes in the volume of the surface layers and so makes them potentially unstable for the soil flow processes to operate. Solifluction is also favoured by the presence of silty soils, which can hold a great deal of moisture, by a moderate slope, and by a limited amount of binding vegetation.

Soil creep itself is a general term, applied to the slow downhill movement of soil and related material such as talus (figure 11.2(f)). A number of processes, each capable of producing only very slight movements, combine to cause it. Rainwash and raindrop impact may move small particles downslope, and may remove fine material from the downslope side of large stones, thus facilitating the movement of the stones. The swaying of vegetation and the treading of animals, both wild and domestic, also tend to give a slight downslope movement to the weathered material on a slope. Ploughing also may contribute to such movement. However, the two prime causes of soil

Plate 11.2 The Alport Castles in the Peak District of England are a major landslide complex. The masses in the left of the picture have slipped down from the escarpment to the right. The cause of the instability is the presence of well-jointed millstone grit overlying weak and impermeable shales.

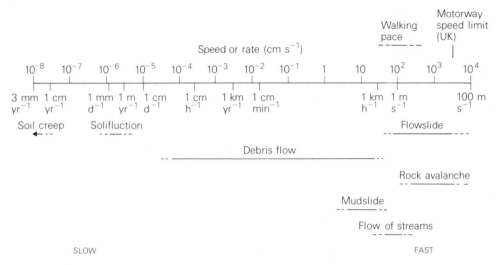

Figure 11.3 The rate of movement of various mass movement processes.

Plate 11.3 Debris flows in the Karakoram Mountains, Pakistan, are generated on steep, unvegetated scree slopes. Debris has crossed irrigated fields and plunged into the Hunza River.

creep are expansion and contraction, caused either by seasonal wetting and drying, or by seasonal and diurnal freeze-thaw processes. In the case of freeze-thaw, for example, frost heaving, arising from the growth of ice crystals and needle ice beneath particles, lifts those particles up at right angles to the slope, but they fall back perpendicularly under the influence of gravity. Equally, as a soil dries out a crack may form as a result of contraction. When it rains again this crack will fill with material from upslope and so a net movement of material downslope will have taken place.

Various techniques have now been developed to measure rates of soil creep. On moderately steep slopes in humid temperate areas soil layers commonly creep downhill at a mean rate of about 1 to 2 mm yr^{-1}. In the moist tropics the rates may be 3 to 6 mm yr^{-1}, and in semi-arid regions with cold winters they may be 5 to 10 mm yr^{-1}. Thus, although this is rather an unspectacular process in comparison with some of the more violent types of mass movement, over a period of years soil creep may achieve a considerable amount of geomorphological work.

11.2   Slope instability

Many types of mass movement occur sporadically, and it is very often their sporadic behaviour that creates hazards. There is seldom only one cause for such instability; usually it results from a sequence of events that ends with downhill movement. The causes, however, can be divided into those that are disturbing forces and those that result from a weakening in the strength of the materials upon which the disturbing forces operate. The sort of factors that lead to increases and decreases in the power of the disturbing forces are listed in table 11.1.

The presence of water in slope materials is an important cause of their stability or instability, for water creates various forces in the soil (see figure 11.4(a)). If the soil's pore spaces are not completely filled with water (i.e. if the soil is unsaturated), then a suction force is exerted which tends to draw the soil grains more closely together. This suction is caused by a process called *capillary tension* – the force that enables sand castles to be made of wet sand but not of dry

sand. However, if the soil pore spaces are completely filled with water, then the soil is said to be saturated. In this state the water exerts a pressure within the pore spaces that tends to produce forces that push the grains apart. Therefore, when *pore water pressures* reach high levels in slope materials these materials may become unstable. Such conditions could be caused by extremely heavy rainfalls, the blocking of drains, the seepage of irrigation water, or slope saturation arising from the impounding of a reservoir behind a dam.

A few examples will illustrate why slope instability occurs and can be hazardous. In 1963, in the Italian Alps, a huge rockslide (240×10^6 m^3) fell into the large reservoir impounded behind the Vaiont Dam. The slide was 2 km long, 1.6 km wide and over 150 m thick. As it collapsed into the reservoir it displaced so much water that the dam was overtopped and a flood wave 70 m high poured down valley from the dam, killing as many as 3000 people. There were certain factors that made this slope potentially unstable: the rocks in the area are alternating bands of clays and limestones which have been heavily folded, so that they have a steep dip and rapid changes in their permeability to seeping water; the valley has been greatly steepened, first by glacial scour and then by postglacial fluvial incision; and because of the severe tectonic stresses in the area and the opening of joints associated with the erosion caused by glaciers, the rocks were deeply split up by joints. What actually triggered the rockslide was the water in the reservoir, for this led to the saturation of the lower part of the potentially unstable slope, increased the pore water pressure in the rock, and thereby reduced its strength below a critical threshold.

Some of the most severe examples of accelerated slope instability occur on coasts. A classic example is provided by Folkestone Warren, southern England, where a large landslide complex developed where a thick bed of Chalk overlies impermeable Gault Clay. The complex lies to the east of Folkestone Harbour and the direction of littoral drift of sediment is from the west. Thus the construction of large harbour breakwaters at Folkestone in the nineteenth century blocked the eastward movement of coastal shingle so that the Warren became depleted in beach material. This

Table 11.1 Factors involved in slope failure

Factors leading to an increase in shear stress

Removal of lateral or underlying support
Undercutting by water (e.g. river, waves) or glacier ice
Weathering of weaker strata at the toe of the slope
Washing out of granular material by seepage erosion
Man-made cuts and excavations, draining of lakes or reservoirs[a]

Increased disturbing forces
Natural accumulations of water, snow, talus
Man-made pressures (e.g. stockpiles of ore, tip-heaps, rubbish dumps or buildings)

Transitory earth stresses
Earthquakes
Continual passing of heavy traffic

Increased internal pressure
Build-up of pore-water pressures (e.g. in joints and cracks, especially in the tension crack zone at the rear of the slide)

Factors leading to a decrease in shearing resistance

Materials
Beds that decrease in shear strength if water content increases (clays, shale, mica, schist, talc, serpentine) (e.g. *when local water table is artificially increased in height by reservoir construction*, or as a result of stress release (vertical and/or horizontal) following slope formation
Low internal cohesion (e.g. consolidated clays, sands, porous organic matter)
In bedrock: faults, bedding planes, joints, foliation in schists, cleavage, brecciated zones and pre-existing shears

Weathering changes
Weathering reduces effective cohesion, and to a lesser extent the angle of shearing resistance
Absorption of water leading to changes in the fabric of clays (e.g. loss of bonds between particles or the formation of fissures)

Pore-water pressure increase
High groundwater table as a result of increased precipitation *or as a result of human interference (e.g. dam construction)*

[a] Human influences are italicised.
Source: modified after R. U. Cooke and J. C. Doornkamp, *Geomorphology in Environmental Management* (Oxford: Clarendon Press, 1974), p. 131.

made it more susceptible to undercutting and oversteepening by wave attack. A series of failures occurred, with a major slip in 1915 disrupting the Folkestone-Dover railway line. Remedial action, such as weighting and protecting the toe of the slip with masses of concrete, has been employed to make the area less unstable.

In parts of Canada and Scandinavia there is a type of landslide caused by the failure of materials called *quick clays*. These clays are highly deceptive, for in their natural undisturbed state they seem to be strong, and are often seen to be supporting steep stream banks. However, for reasons that are not fully understood, they sometimes change into a liquid state of negligible strength. Failures come without warning and may be disastrous. One theory, which may well apply to the Canadian examples, is that during the Ice Age some fine-grained sediments were deposited in marine coastal areas. The clays were coagulated by the electrolytes in the sea water and settled quickly. Some of the chemical constituents from the seawater, such as sodium (Na^+), helped to bind the clays together and give them strength. However, postglacial isostatic uplift elevated these deposits high above present sea levels, and subsequently fresh rain water leached the sodium 'glue' from the clays, leaving them with a very unstable structure. Upon shaking, this structure collapses, expelling the interstitial water, liquefy-

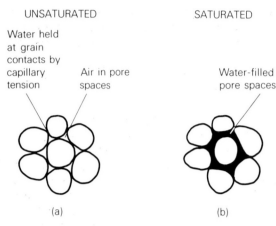

Figure 11.4 The effect of water on the stability of slope materials. In the case of unsaturated grains suction forces draw the grains together; in the case of saturated grains high pore water pressures tend to push grains apart.

ing the clay and allowing it to flow on gentle slopes. The shaking may be caused by earthquakes. Thus we have a combination of factors that make certain parts of the St Lawrence Valley area prone to slope failures: glacial action has provided the right material, postglacial uplift has provided the right setting, and earthquakes provide the trigger.

The incidence of debris flows and mudflows can be accelerated by human activity. The removal of vegetation, perhaps by fire or in the process of converting forested land to agricultural use, can expose potentially unstable materials to the effects of massive storms. However, catastrophic rainfalls can lead to debris flows in steep, humid terrain, even without human intervention.

Whatever the exact combination of forces that causes them, major mass movements can cause great loss of life (see table 11.2), and they play an important role in moulding the forms of slopes.

11.3 Other processes operating on slopes

The various forms of mass movement described above are not the only ones that operate on slopes and mould their form. Weathering is extremely important, since it attacks bare rock faces, creates a layer of weathered material (regolith) and affects the strength of the slope by forming materials like clays. Solution is also extremely important in removing material from slopes.

A third highly important process is *surface wash* (figure 11.5). This is the downslope transport of regolith across the ground surface through the action of water. There are two distinct processes involved: the impact of raindrops on the ground surface (*raindrop impact*), and the flow of water across it (*surface flow*). Surface wash probably has its greatest effect in areas with limited vegetation cover, poorly structured soils and occasional storms of high energy. For these reasons it may attain its optimum impact in semi-

Table 11.2 Major mass movement disasters of the twentieth century

Year	Location	Nature	Deaths
1920	Kansu, China	Earthquake-triggered flow and slide in loess	200 000
1936	Loen, Norway	Rockfall into fjord, causing tsunami-like flood-wave	73
1941	Huaraz, Peru	Avalanche and mudflow	7000
1956	Santos, Brazil	Landslides	100+
1959	Montana, USA	Earthquake-triggered landslide	26
1962	Mt Huascaran, Peru	Ice avalanche and mudflow	c.4000
1963	Vaiont Dam, Italy	Landslide-created flood	c.3000
1966	Rio de Janeiro, Brazil	Landslides in shanty towns	279
1966	Hong Kong	Landslides on steep tropical slopes after heavy rain	64
1966	Aberfan, Wales	Debris flow from colliery waste tip	144
1970	Mt Huascaran, Peru	Earthquake-triggered ice and rockfall and debris flow	25 000
1971	Quebec, Canada	Landslides in quickclay	31
1971	Romania	Mudslide in mining village	45
1972	West Virginia, USA	Landslide and mudflow in mining tip waste	400
1974	Mayunmarca, Peru	Rockslide and debris flow	450
1976	Pahire-Phedi, Nepal	Landslide	150
1976	Hong Kong	Landslide	22
1978	Myoko Kogen Machi, Japan	Mudflow, overwhelming ski resort	12

arid areas, though it also operates effectively in tropical rainforests, where there is often only very limited litter on the ground surface, and where torrential tropical storms manage to produce large raindrops that fall from the drip tips of the very tall trees (section 6.7).

There are also some subsurface transport processes that may be of importance. In soils with the right sort of structure, water may move laterally as *throughflow* (see section 13.6), and in doing so it may transport fine particles through the regolith by a process called *lateral eluviation*. Lateral movement of soil water may also take place in concentrated lines of seepage or' flow, and tunnelling or piping may occur by mechanical corrasion. Sometimes such tunnelling causes ground subsidence, and may also initiate the formation of gullies, which create gashes in many eroded hillsides.

Slopes are going to be further affected by such processes as river erosion at their bases; and by the removal of weathered material by fluvial, aeolian and other processes.

11.4 Slope forms

It is essentially the balance between the power of all these different processes and the nature of the material on which they operate that explain the evolution of slope forms. Three main types of slope may occur. The first is a *denudation slope*, which is one on which ground loss is occurring.

The second is a *transportation slope*, which is one that undergoes neither ground loss nor ground gain, because at each point the material brought in from upslope is equal to that carried away downslope. The third type of slope is an *accumulation slope*, one on which ground gain is occurring.

In the case of denudation slopes, there is an important distinction to be made between those that are controlled by weathering and those that are controlled by erosion, or *removal*. On the former, the potential rate at which weathered material can be removed from the slope exceeds the rate of weathering; hence weathered material is removed shortly after it is formed, and the rate at which denudation occurs is thus limited by the rate of weathering. Control by removal occurs where the potential rate at which weathering produces debris exceeds the rate at which the debris can be removed; ground loss is then dependent on the efficiency of the removal processes. In the case of a weathering-controlled slope, the relative resistance of different rocks to weathering controls the slope form, whereas in the case of a removal-controlled slope, the slope form is very much influenced by the nature of the regolith that is produced.

Strictly speaking, these terms should be applied only to a point on a slope, for slopes need not be subject to the same type of control throughout their length. A typical slope profile may well possess, for example, a weathering-controlled cliff, a

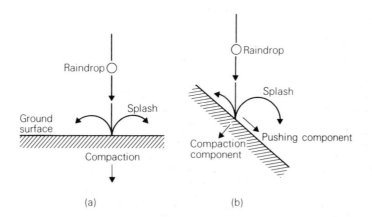

Figure 11.5 The effect of rainsplash on slopes (a) On a flat surface the net effect of splashing and pushing of grains is equal in all directions and no net erosion takes place. (b) On a slope, the splash trajectories are much longer downslope than they are upslope and grains will be pushed downslope more easily; as a result, erosion increases with slope angle.

basal concavity that is essentially a transportation slope, and a talus cone where accumulation is dominant. Some of the different forms of debris accumulation that occur on slopes are illustrated in figure 11.6, and include debris cones, alluvial fans (see also section 5.11) and rock avalanche tongues.

There are basically three fundamental slope forms that may exist in various combinations on any one slope profile (figure 11.7). A *straight slope* is a section of a profile on which the mean angle does not change with distance; a cliff or *free face* is a special form of straight slope. A *convexity* is a section of a profile on which slope angle increases downslope, while a *concavity* is a section of a profile on which slope angle decreases downslope.

Let us now consider the circumstances that might produce each of these fundamental types.

A *straight slope* may develop in a number of ways. For example, if a slope is undercut by a river or by very active weathering at its base, it may be oversteepened and then fail; the resulting slope will then rest at an angle that is related to the strength of the material and the water that it contains. In general, straight slopes, or the straight parts of slopes, are to be expected where rapid types of mass movement operate as a major slope-forming process. For instance, if weathering attacks a cliff face, boulders will be detached and these will accumulate at their angle of repose (generally, 32°–38°) as rockfall screes. Scree slopes tend to have a straight upper segment and a concave lower segment. The straightness of the cliff itself may be controlled by joints in the bedrock.

Straight slopes are controlled by threshold conditions; when the threshold is reached as a result

Plate 11.4 Enormous debris cones produced by severe frost weathering in the Karakoram Mountains, Pakistan.

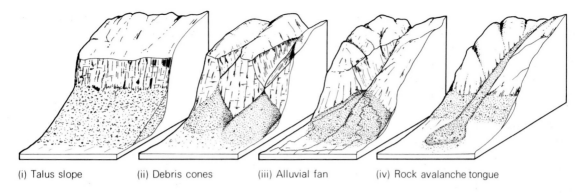

(i) Talus slope   (ii) Debris cones   (iii) Alluvial fan   (iv) Rock avalanche tongue

Figure 11.6   The four main forms of debris accumulation that may occur below rock slopes.

of attack from below, or because of weathering attack on joints, or because of a build-up in pore water pressure, the slope adjusts rapidly to an angle that is related to its material properties. By contrast, on curved slopes there is usually a slow evolution towards a characteristic form involving a variety of processes.

Convexities tend to occur on the upper portions of slopes, though in some humid tropical areas they may exceed 90 per cent of the total slope profile length, and in locations where stream undercutting occurs convexities may also occur at the base of a slope. Rainsplash and soil creep are the two processes most responsible for

the development of the upper convexity, though weathering will tend to round off exposed right-angles of bare rock, and on slopes where a resistant caprock overlies weak clays rounding may occur as a result of a process called *cambering*. The mechanism whereby soil creep can produce rounding was postulated by G. K. Gilbert in 1909 (figure 11.8). The two parallel lines represent the position of the ground surface at two points in time. If one assumes uniform soil depth, and no change of soil depth through time at any one point, the volume of soil between A and B will have passed point B and the volume between A and C will have passed point C for this amount

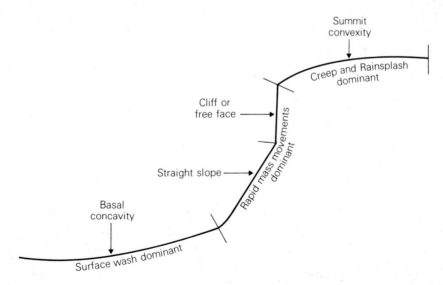

Figure 11.7   The three fundamental slope forms (straight, convex and concave) shown in an idealised four-segment profile, with some suggestions for the dominant types of process acting on each segment type.

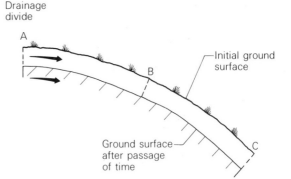

Figure 11.8   G. K. Gilbert's model of slope top convexity through soil creep processes. For explanation see text.

of lowering to have occurred. Thus, the volume of soil passing a position progressively further down the slope increases commensurately with position from the drainage divide. If the transport rates for the creep process are proportional to slope angle, then clearly the slope angle must also increase with distance from the divide in order that the sediment can be transported from the slope. This is one explanation for slope-top convexity.

Slope concavity, which tends to occur towards the base of a profile, but which may be a very lengthy part of the profile on pediment slopes in arid regions and elsewhere, tends to occur where rapid downcutting is not taking place at the base of the slope. It also tends to be associated with surface wash processes, and therefore may be most common on slopes composed of soils with low infiltration capacities. The normal explanation for the association of surface wash with

slope concavity is much the same as the explanation given for most river long profiles being concave (see section 14.3): namely, as one moves downslope, discharge tends to increase because the contributing area to the process also increases. As discharge increases, so the transporting ability of the flow grows greater, and as flow depth increases velocity can be maintained on lower slope angles. Moreover, because of abrasion and sorting processes, particle size decreases downslope and any given flow can carry a greater load of fine material than of coarse material. This combination of factors and tendencies combines to produce an excess transporting capacity in the flow so that slope can be reduced while the power to transport load is maintained. The steepest concavities occur in the coarsest materials, and the gentlest concavities in the finest.

11.5   Slope development through time

One of the most controversial subjects in geomorphology is the question of the way in which slope form evolves through time. Basically there have been three main theories of slope evolution: slope decline (an idea associated with the name of W. M. Davis), slope replacement (an idea associated with the name of W. Penck) and parallel retreat (an idea associated with L. C. King). These three main ideas are illustrated in figure 11.9.

In the case of *slope decline* the steepest part of the slope progressively decreases in angle, accompanied by the development of a convexity in the upper portion and a concavity in the lower por-

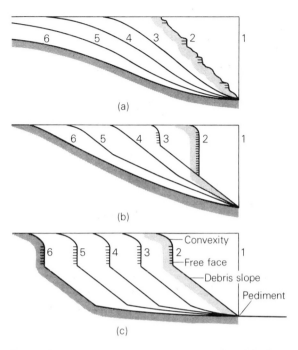

(a)

(b)

Convexity
Free face
Debris slope
Pediment

(c)

Figure 11.9 Three models of slope evolution: (a) slope decline; (b) slope replacement; (c) parallel retreat. 1 represents the same initial cliff form, and 2–6 represent subsequent stages in development of the slopes.

tions of the slope. In the case of *slope replacement* the maximum angle decreases through replacement from below by gentler slopes, causing the greater part of the profile to become occupied by the concavity, which may be either smoothly curved or segmented. In the case of *parallel retreat* the maximum angle remains constant, the absolute lengths of all parts of the slope except the basal concavity remain constant, and the concavity increases in length.

The ideas of W. M. Davis on slope decline (figure 11.9(a)) were first formulated towards the end of the nineteenth century, and they were presented as his *Cycle of Normal Erosion*. In this extraordinarily influential model, Davis envisaged that a mass of land would be quickly uplifted from beneath the sea by tectonic movements. He made the assumption that, because the rate of uplift was so rapid, the processes of denudation were able to act almost from the start on what was, in effect, a stable mass. In the stage of youth, under a humid environment a system of rivers would quickly develop, and they would cut

down rapidly, producing steep valley side slopes. However, as time progressed the rate of deepening of these V-shaped valleys would decrease, for the rivers would have lowered their channels nearer and nearer to *the base level of erosion* (which in most cases is the level of the sea into which the rivers flow). In this stage of maturity, with the retardation of down cutting, lateral erosion would become more significant. Weathering, soil creep and rainwash would gradually cause the retreat of the valley sides and the lowering of the areas between the valleys, called the *interfluves*. By the end of the mature stage, Davis envisaged that slope angles in general would have been considerably reduced by the process of divide wasting, and smoothly curving slope profiles, with no major breaks, would dominate the landscape. A decrease in the vertical height separating interfluve summits and valley floors would occur. In the third stage – that of old age – processes would have slowed down, for the reduction of river gradients would have led to a

Plate 11.6 A great contemporary of G. K. Gilbert was the American geomorphologist W. M. Davis, who produced a model of slope evolution called the Cycle of Normal Erosion, in which slope angles were thought to decline through time.

decline in stream energy, and slopes would have been degraded by slope processes. Rivers would, however, still broaden their valleys by meandering, and broad flood plains would develop. By the end of this stage, the land surface would assume the form of a very gently undulating plain, which Davis called a *peneplain*. This would stand only a little above the base level of erosion.

The cycle of erosion postulated by L. C. King (figure 11.9(c)) was different from that of Davis, possibly because, whereas Davis initially formulated his ideas in the humid temperate landscapes of Appalachia in the United States, King formulated his ideas in South Africa, where there are broad plains above which stand some steep-sided island-like hills, called inselbergs or *kopjes*. King's examination of the African landscape led him to conclude that it was made up of two basic elements: gently concave lower slopes, called *pediments*, and steep slopes, or *scarps*, bounding upland blocks. The former have angles that

Plate 11.7 The German geomorphologist Walther Penck believed that slope evolution was more complex than had been envisaged by Davis, and stressed how the nature of tectonic processes would affect the changing form of slope profiles through time.

generally range from $0.25°-7°$, while the latter tend to have angles of $15°-30°$. King believed that the landscape evolved as a result of the extension of pediments (pedimentation) and by the backwearing or parallel retreat of scarps. In its stage of youth the cycle is initiated by uplift of a previously formed plain. Rivers cut down rapidly towards base level, exploiting joints, and cliff-like slopes are very important. Once these have reached a stable angle of repose related to the characteristics of the material of which they are made, King envisages them retreating, parallel to each other, away from the drainage lines, leaving continually expanding pediments between the slopes and the drainage lines. The residuals on these *pediplains* will become progressively smaller in area, until they are left as small, steep-sided, isolated hills.

Unlike Davis or King, W. Penck worked in areas such as the Alps and the Andes, where tectonic processes were extremely active, and as a result he believed that the nature of uplift was vital, as it controlled the rate of river erosion, which in turn affected the evolution of valley side slopes. In his theory of slope replacement he rejected the simple Davisian assumption of rapid uplift followed by a period of stability, and attempted to establish a relationship between the nature of a slope and the tectonic history of a region: convex slopes were formed in periods of accelerated uplift, straight slopes in periods of constant uplift, and concave slopes in periods of decreasing uplift or stability. He saw the rate of retreat of a slope as being determined by gradient. Thus a steep slope would undergo more rapid weathering and debris movement than a gentle slope, on which the more slowly moving weathered layer would tend to persist and thereby cushion the rock from atmospheric agencies. As a result, a steep slope beneath a gentle slope will weather back so quickly that in due course the gentle upper slope will be destroyed. In addition, rapid retreat will destroy the steeper slopes on either side of a drainage divide, and these will be replaced by gentler slopes developing at their bases (figure 11.9(b)).

No one of these three models of slope evolution is universally correct. They are all ideal models that simplify the complexity of the real world, and it is unlikely that the retreat of any natural slope corresponds to any one of them absolutely. The extent to which it does correspond depends to a large extent on the structure of an area, and on the comparative rates of operation of different slope processes as influenced by climate. Indeed, under certain circumstances slopes may evolve in ways other than the three discussed above. In some rainforest areas, for example, slopes are dominated by long convexities and may even tend to become steepened through time.

Because of the great length of time that it takes for most slopes to evolve, their evolution can scarcely be checked in one lifetime; but if one is able to locate landforms of similar material quality under the same climatic conditions, but which are known to have different ages, then it may be possible to see which slope evolution model is most appropriate in any particular set of environmental conditions. For example, geomorphologists have used clifflines that have been abandoned by the sea at different times, lake shorelines exposed as a lake progressively dries up, moraines that have been deposited by a gradually retreating glacier, and slag heaps of known initial form but of different age.

Plate 11.8 The slopes in Monument Valley, Arizona, illustrate how slope retreat through time can lead to the development of steep-sided residuals.

12 Soils and Weathering

12.1 Factors of soil formation

Soil is the support of vegetable life, and thus plays the most fundamental of roles in providing sustenance for all living things. It can be defined as 'a natural body of animal, mineral and organic constituents differentiated into horizons that comprise a profile of variable depth which differs from the material below in morphology, physical make-up, chemical properties and composition, and biological characteristics.'

The decay of rock by weathering processes plays a fundamental role in the formation of most soils. But soil is far more complex than simply decayed rock: it is the product of a wide range of different factors. The study of soils is called *pedology*.

A pedologist called H. Jenny attempted to summarise the various factors involved in soil formation by the following expression:

$$S = f(cl, o, r, p, t, \ldots)$$

where S denotes any soil property, cl the regional climate, o the biota (comprising plants and animals), r the topography, p the parent material, t the time (or period) of soil formation, and the dots represent additional unspecified factors. These factors are often closely interrelated. Regional climate, for example, will affect both the nature of the biota and the form of the topography, and certain types of parent material may be a feature of certain climatic zones (e.g. boulder clay in glacial regions, and aeolian sand in desert areas).

Climate

Because the nature of weathering, of erosion and of organic activity are so closely controlled by climatic conditions, climate is a vital factor in soil formation. As we saw in chapter 2, world soil types show a broad correspondence to world climatic zones. There are considerable differences between tropical soils (see section 6.12), arid zone soils (see section 5.7), and tundra soils (see section 3.13).

The biota

Soil is more than simply weathered rock, because its organic component is also important. The vegetation cover of an area provides partially de-cayed organic matter, called *humus*, and a cycling of plant nutrients takes place between plants and soils (see section 9.1), aided by the role of 'decomposing' micro-organisms such as bacteria, actinomycetes and fungi. Some macro-organisms, including worms and termites, mix up the soil and thereby affect its character. Charles Darwin, for example, observed that English garden worms can turn over up to 6.5 tonnes of soil per hectare, per year.

Increasingly, human activity is becoming an important component of the biotic factor in soil development. Indeed, as table 12.1 shows, humans can have both beneficial and detrimental effects on all five of the classic factors of soil formation. Of particular importance are their effects on soil salinity (section 5.7), laterite formation (section 6.12) and soil erosion (section 12.6).

Topography (relief)

Relief conditions in an area are a most significant control of soil formation and character, especially at the local scale. Slope steepness, for example,

Table 12.1   Suggested effects of the influence of man on five classic factors of soil formation

Factors of soil formation	Type of effect	Nature of effect
Climate	Beneficial	Adding water by irrigation; rainmaking by seeding clouds; removing water by drainage; diverting winds, etc.
	Detrimental	Subjecting soil to excessive insolation, to extended frost action, to wind, etc.
Organisms	Beneficial	Introducing and controlling populations of plants and animals; adding organic matter including 'nightsoil'; loosening soil by ploughing to admit more oxygen; fallowing; removing pathogenic organisms as by controlled burning
	Detrimental	Removing plants and animals; reducing organic matter content of soil through burning, ploughing, over-grazing, harvesting, etc; adding or fostering pathogenic organisms; adding radioactive substances
Topography	Beneficial	Checking erosion through surface roughening, land forming and structure-building; raising land level by accumulation of material; land levelling
	Detrimental	Causing subsidence by drainage of wetlands and by mining; accelerating erosion; excavating
Parent material	Beneficial	Adding mineral fertilisers; accumulating shells and bones; accumulating ash locally; removing excess amounts of substances such as salts
	Detrimental	Removing, through harvest, more plant and animal nutrients than are replaced; adding materials in amounts toxic to plants or animals; altering soil constituents in a way to depress plant growth
Time	Beneficial	Rejuvenating the soil through adding of fresh parent material or through exposure of local parent material by soil erosion; reclaiming land from under water
	Detrimental	Degrading the soil by accelerated removal of nutrients from soil and vegetation cover; burying soil under solid fill or water

Source: modified from O. W. Bidwell and F. D. Hole, Man as a factor of soil formation, *Soil Science* 99, (1965), 65–72.

affects soil moisture conditions and the rate of mass movement and erosive processes. Thus, if a slope is steep the runoff is rapid, erosion removes the soil as fast as it forms, little water enters the soil and the soil profiles are thin and poorly developed. On more level terrain runoff is inhibited, and more water enters the terrain to weather minerals and to redistribute the soluble components of the soil profile. Erosion is less rapid, so that thicker profiles may occur, and waterlogging may be an influence on soil form. Thus soils and landforms may be related in a topo-sequence or *catena*. The catena concept (figure 12.1) was originally put forward by a soil scientist called G. Milne, who worked in East Africa in the 1930s. He originally defined a catena as: 'a unit of mapping convenience ... a grouping of soils which while they fall wide apart in a natural system of classification on account of fundamental and morphological differences, are yet linked in their occurrence by conditions of topography and are repeated in the same relationships to each other wherever the same conditions are met with'.

Parent material

When a soil forms directly from underlying rock or sediment, the soil minerals and type may bear a direct relationship to the original material. Weathering processes may mean that the balance of ions in the soil is different from that in the parent material, but none the less the nature of such *residual soils* owes much to the nature of the parent material. However, in a second category of soil, known as *transported soil*, the soil may be largely independent of the underlying solid rock because the parent material has been transported from somewhere else. Soils derived from glacial drift, alluvium or windblown dust (loess) come into this category.

Time

Whether a soil is deep or shallow, it requires a period of time to form. One would expect soils that have developed on old, stable, flat land surfaces, such as some of the great pediplains of

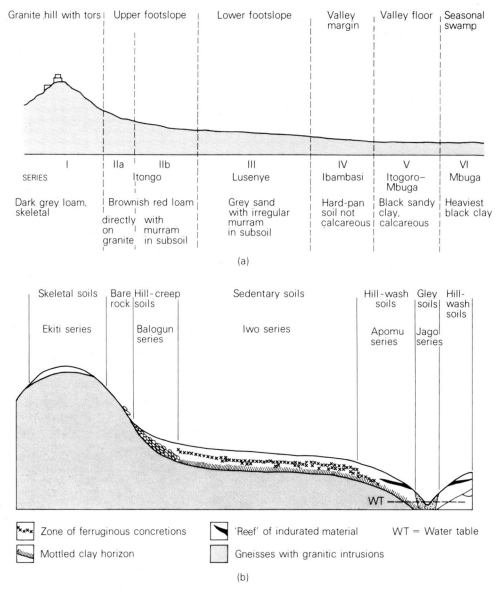

Figure 12.1 Examples of two catenas in Africa: (a) the Ukiriguru catena from Tanzania as proposed by Milne; (b) the Iwo catena, western Nigeria.

Africa, to be very highly weathered. By contrast, soils developed on recently formed glacial moraine or sand dunes might be expected to show only very limited development.

Together these five factors account for the character of the four main constituents that make up a soil: mineral matter, organic matter, air and water. The mineral matter includes all those minerals, such as clays, weathered from the parent material as well as those formed in the soil by recombination from substances in the soil solution. The organic matter (which includes material like humus) is derived mostly from decaying vegetation which is decomposed with the assistance of the many different forms of animal life that live in the soil. Air and water occupy the spaces between the structures of the soil. If the soil is well drained its pores and fissures will be open to the penetration of the atmosphere; if it is saturated with water most of the air will be driven out, and the soil is then said to be *anaerobic*.

The mineral portion of the soil is derived from the parent material by the various weathering processes described later in this chapter. Different soils will have very different textures according to the relative proportions of materials of different sizes. At the one extreme there are soils composed largely of coarse rock fragments (these are often termed *skeletal soils*), while at the other there are soils formed of very fine materials, called clays, which have a particle size that is less than 0.002 mm. Particle size is an important consideration, because it affects the erodibility of the soil, its tillability, its moisture and its warmth. Sandy soils, for example, will tend to be freely drained and easy to cultivate, but on the other hand in a dry year they will suffer from drought and may be susceptible to wind erosion.

Clay minerals are probably the most important mineral constituents of the soil, and they result from chemical weathering of parent material. They consist of minute platy-structured mineral fragments which can be identified only by sophisticated microscopic and chemical methods. They are members of a group of minerals that are characterised by a layered, crystalline structure, and they are built up from layers of silica and aluminium atoms with their attendant oxygen atoms arranged like a sandwich. Three major groups of aluminosilicate clay minerals may be distinguished: the *kaolinite*, the *montmorillonite* (or smectite) and the *hydrous mica groups*. They differ in crystal structure, surface electrical charges and resulting mechanical properties, though intermediate forms frequently occur. Most weathered rock material contains a mixed assemblage of the different clay minerals, and it is difficult to generalise about the factors that produce one particular assemblage rather than another. In the early stages of weathering, parent material type may be important, with granite, for example, tending to alter to kaolinite and basic igneous rocks to montmorillonite. But other factors also play a role. Acid soil conditions are conducive to the production of kaolinite, while alkaline conditions favour the evolution of montmorillonite. In the United States kaolinite is particularly abundant in the warm, wet, southeastern parts of the country, the hydrous mica group becomes increasingly prominent in the cooler north-east, while montmorillonite reaches its fullest development in the drier west.

Clay minerals may make the soil poorly drained, cold and hard when dry. They are also prone to shrink and swell according to their moisture content, which may create problems for buildings constructed upon them. On the other hand, they tend to retain moisture longer in dry years and being cohesive, tend to be resistant to wind erosion.

Additional minerals are formed in the soil itself, for weathering releases elements from the parent material's minerals, and these may precipitate elsewhere in the soil profile. Lime concretions may occur in dry areas, for example, while iron and manganese concretions may develop in poorly drained soils.

Soil organic matter also can take on a variety of forms: peat, mull, moder and mor. Under wet, ill-drained anerobic conditions organic accumulations may be in the form of layers more than 40 cm thick. This is *peat. Mor* tends to develop under acidic conditions associated with heathland or coniferous plant communities, in which the role of soil fauna is limited. *Mull* forms in freely drained, base-rich soils with good aeration. Plant growth is good and provides much litter, but there is also a rich soil fauna, including earthworms. The organic matter is broken down and well mixed into the mineral components of the soil. *Moder* is a form of organic matter intermediate between mor and mull, because it has a higher soil fauna level.

Organic matter decomposes to form humus, and this humus, together with clay minerals, plays an important role in absorbing ions released by chemical weathering of rock or dead tissue. The clay-humus complex acts as an invaluable reservoir of soil nutrients and serves as a buffer against rapid loss of nutrients by leading away in soil water. The nature and amount of clay and humus in a soil are therefore highly significant in terms of fertility.

12.2 Soil profiles

The vertical succession down through the soil is called a *profile*, and recognition of the differences between the profiles of different soils is the basis of schemes of soil classification. The soil profile is separated into various bands, which result from the balance between inputs and outputs into the soil system, and the redistribution of, and chemical changes in, the soil constituents. These bands are called *horizons*, and some of the major processes involved are as follows.

(a) *Organic accumulation*: takes place mainly at the ground surface owing to accumulation of decaying vegetable matter
(b) *Eluviation*: the mechanical translocation of clay or other fine particles down the profile
(c) *Leaching*: the removal of material from a horizon in solution, and its movement down (and possibly out of) the profile
(d) *Illuviation*: the accumulation in the lower part of the profile of material eluviated (washed down) from above
(e) *Precipitation*: the formation of solid matter, sometimes in the form of nodules or concretions, in the subsoil from solutions leached from above or derived by capillary rise from groundwater
(f) *Cheluviation*: the downward movement of material, akin to leaching, but under the influence of organic chelating agents
(g) *Organic sorting*: the separation of material, usually of differing grain sizes, by organic activity (e.g. the churning action of worms and termites).

The *inputs* into the soil system include:

(a) water from the atmosphere;
(b) gases from the atmosphere and from the respiration of soil fauna;
(c) organic matter from decaying vegetation and animals;
(d) excretions from plant roots;
(e) chemicals (nutrients) from weathered parent materials.

The *outputs* from the soil system include:

(a) losses of soil material by soil erosion and soil creep;
(b) nutrient losses into water percolating through the soil;
(c) nutrients taken up by plants growing in the soil;
(d) evaporation.

The soil system is not only influenced by simple inputs and outputs: some *recycling* may occur. For example, some of the chemicals or plant nutrients lost as an output (output c) may well return in leaf litter at a later time (input c). Man may modify the nature of these inputs and outputs in many ways, for example by adding artificial nutrients in the form of fertilisers, by accelerating or slowing the rates at which soil erosion takes place (see section 12.6), by changing the amount of water movement in the soil through drainage activities, or by modifying the nature of the vegetation cover.

Traditionally, three soil horizons were recognised. The uppermost, the A horizon, consists of thoroughly weathered rock material and humus. It is a band that has been strongly affected by the washing out, or leaching, of soluble materials and by the downward dispersion, or eluviation, of clay particles. Beneath this is the B horizon, which consists of less thoroughly weathered parent material, a minor proportion of organic matter and materials carried down, or illuviated, from above. The C horizon consists dominantly of still less weathered parent material, affected little or not at all by organic action, eluviation or illuviation.

This three-fold division is extremely useful, but rather oversimplified. For this reason various schemes of elaboration have been developed. Each uses number or letter systems in addition to A, B and C. For instance, the surface layer of plant litter at the top of the A horizon can be subclassified as L, F or H according to the dominance of litter proper (L), fermented organic material (F) or humus (H). Part of the A horizon can be subclassified Aa, Ah or Ae according to whether it is bleached (a = *a*shy), *h*umus-rich or *e*luviated. Likewise, if the B horizon has an *iron*-pan caused by the accumulation of iron leached down from above, this can be labelled Bir. If the B or C horizons have an accumulation of *ca*lcium carbonate, they can be labelled Bca or Cca. If the soil is subjected to waterlogging in the lower part of the profile, a *gley horizon* results: this is the product of an oxygen shortage, which produces grey-coloured iron compounds. A well-developed gley horizon (depicted by G) is uniformly pale, but where the soil dries out from time to time the pale grey colouration becomes mottled with yellows, reds and purples. Such moderate *gleying* is connoted by a small g.

12.3   Types of weathering

Most rocks and sediments in the top few metres of the earth's crust are exposed to physical, chemical and biological conditions much different from those prevailing at the time the rocks were formed. Because of the interaction of these conditions, the rock or sediment gradually changes into soil-like material. These changes are collectively called *weathering*, but two main types are recognised:

(a) Processes of disintegration (physical or mechanical weathering)

   (i) Crystallisation
         Salt weathering (by crystallisation, hydration and thermal expansion)
         Frost weathering
   (ii) Temperature changes
         Insolation weathering (heating and cooling)
         Fire
         Expansion of dirt in cracks
   (iii) Wetting and drying (especially of shales)
   (iv) Pressure release by erosion of overburden
   (v) Organic processes (e.g. root-wedging),

(b) Processes of decomposition (chemical weathering)

   (i) Hydration and hydrolysis
   (ii) Oxidation and reduction
   (iii) Solution and carbonation
   (iv) Chelation
   (v) Biological-chemical changes (organic weathering)

Mechanical weathering involves the breakdown or *disintegration* of rock without any substantial degree of chemical change taking place in the minerals that make up the rock mass. *Chemical weathering* involves the *decomposition* or decay of such minerals. In most parts of the world both types of weathering tend to operate together, though in differing proportions, and the one may accelerate the other. For example, the mechanical disintegration of a rock will greatly increase the surface area that is then exposed to chemical attack.

12.4   Mechanical weathering

Mechanical weathering can be brought about by a variety of processes: freeze-thaw action (section 3.13), heating and cooling (insolation) (section 5.8), the growth of salt crystals (section 5.8), the prizing effect of tree roots and unloading or pressure release.

This last process is the reason why in many parts of the world the rock close to the surface is cut by joints that more or less parallel the surface. The term *exfoliation* is used for the sheeting that explains this onion-layered appearance of many rock outcrops. The cause is the upward expansion of rock as an overlying or confining burden is removed, as for instance by intense glacial erosion (section 3.6). At depth the rock is under high confining pressure equivalent to the weight of the overlying mass; as erosion removes the overlying rock – say, a sedimentary cover from above a granite batholith – the remaining rock can expand, usually either upward or towards valley walls. The release of pressure results in joints that are oriented at right angles to the direction of the release – hence they usually parallel the land surface. When men dig mines or excavate quarries they can trigger the same effect as erosion, and the pressure release may occur as violent rock bursts.

12.5   Chemical weathering

Solution

Solution is one of the simplest chemical weathering processes to visualise, for some rocks may literally dissolve, rather like sugar in a drink or salt in a saucepan of water. Limestone, which is composed of calcium carbonate, is especially prone to weathering in this way, for it is readily

Plate 12.1 As a consequence of pressure release resulting from the erosion of overlying material, this granite near Kyle ir Zimbabwe is being broken up into a series of sheets which parallel the land surface. Such sheeting is called exfoliation.

attacked by carbonic acid. This acid is produced by the union of water and carbon dioxide, the latter coming either from the atmosphere or, in larger concentrations, from the soil:

$$H_2O + \quad CO_2 \quad \rightarrow \quad H_2CO_3$$
Water   carbon dioxide   carbonic acid

Thus the formula which expresses the dissolution of calcium carbonate in the presence of water and carbon dioxide can be written as follows:

$$CaCO_3 \ + \ CO_2 \ + H_2O$$

calcium   carbon   water
carbonate   dioxide

$$\rightarrow \quad \boxed{Ca^{2+}} \quad + \quad \boxed{2HCO_3^-}$$

calcium in   hydrogen carbonate
solution   in solution

Water enriched in CO_2 attacks many silicate minerals. Olivine, for example, which is found in some igneous rocks, can be dissolved almost completely in a sequence of reactions represented in a very simplified form in the formula:

$$MgSiO_4 + 2H_2O + \quad 4CO_2$$
Olivine   water   carbon dioxide

$$\rightarrow \quad 2Mg \ C(CHO_3)_2 \quad + \quad SiO_2$$
magnesium bicarbonate   soluble silica

Hydrolysis

The common rock-forming minerals weather by a process called hydrolysis, a class of chemical reactions with water involving the action of H and OH ions. This produces as a by-product a substance that is very different in character from the minerals of which the rock was initially composed. For instance, the weathering of feldspar (an aluminium silicate mineral that is found in igneous rocks like granite) can lead to the formation of clays, as shown by the following equation:

$$K_2O.Al_2O_3.6SiO_2 + 11H_2O$$
orthoclase feldspar   water

$$\rightarrow Al_2O_3.2SiO_2.2H_2O + 4H_4SiO$$
kaolinite   silicic acid
                                    in solution

$$+ \quad 20H^- \quad + \quad 2K^+$$
hydroxyl   potassium in solution

Kaolinite is one type of clay mineral. The silicic acid and the potassium may go into solution and be leached away, leaving only the clay mineral behind.

Hydration

Hydration occurs when minerals incorporate water into their molecular structure. This includes some of the minerals commonly found in igneous rocks, together with some of the constituents of sedimentary rocks, as well as many of the silicate clay minerals. Hydration often causes swelling, and it is believed to be a major cause of the crumbling of coarse-grained igneous rocks which are disrupted by the progressive expansion of their hydrated minerals.

Oxidation

Rusting is a process familiar to most of us. Iron objects exposed to moisture are soon affected. Most rocks contain iron-bearing minerals, and these change in the presence of moisture and oxygen. This process is responsible for the first visible signs of chemical weathering in many rocks – their discolouration to red and yellowish-brown colours.

Mineral composition and weathering

The mineral composition of a rock is an important control of the rate at which weathering may occur, for some minerals are more susceptible to chemical change than others. For example, igneous rocks show great variety in the minerals they contain, and it is possible to rank them in order according to their susceptibility following the *Goldich System* (table 12.2). Granite is composed primarily of quartz, orthoclase, muscovite and biotite, which are four of the least susceptible minerals in the series. Thus granite would tend to be less prone to chemical attack, and to be more resistant than an igneous rock such as a gabbro, which is composed primarily of two more susceptible minerals, augite and lime-soda plagioclase. Mineral composition is not the only factor influencing the rate of rock decay – factors such as crystal size and the way in which the crystals interlock may be of equal importance.

Chemical composition is also important in affecting the weathering of sedimentary rocks. These have four common cement types: silica, calcium carbonate, iron oxides and clay. If silica is the cement, the rock will tend to be relatively resistant. Thus, silica-cemented quartz sandstone is one of the most durable rock types, for neither the cement nor the cemented grains succumb easily to chemical attack. On the other hand, calcium carbonate cement may be prone to solutional processes, and an iron oxide cement to oxidation processes, both of which may weaken the rock. Clay cements tend to be especially weak, and physical weathering processes, such as freeze-thaw may cause rapid weathering of the rock.

The importance of joints in chemical weathering

Water is the prime control of the intensity of chemical weathering of all the types discussed above. Thus the presence of joints and other discontinuities in a rock mass are highly important, since they help to control the rate at which water can move within the rock, and also control the surface area for the weathering processes to operate on. Other things being equal, a densely jointed rock will tend to weather more quickly than a rock with just a few joints. This is thought to be particularly important when considering the development of landforms in igneous rocks, including tors and inselbergs. For example, a major hypothesis of tor formation is that deep chemical weathering penetrates a rock mass unevenly according to the spacing of the joints. As weathering proceeds, zones of relatively sound rock remain where the joints are widely spaced;

Table 12.2   The Goldich System

	Dark-coloured minerals	Light-coloured minerals	
Least stable	Olivine		Most susceptible
		Lime plagioclase	
	Augite		
		Lime-soda plagioclase	
	Hornblende	Soda-lime plagioclase	
		Soda plagioclase	
	Biotite		
		Orthoclase	
		Muscovite	
Most stable		Quartz	Least susceptible

whereas a thick regolith, containing much clay produced by the chemical weathering of feldspar minerals, occurs where the joints are close together. Subsequent erosional stripping will remove the regolith, exposing the sounder rock as a series of upstanding tors and piles of boulders (core-stones). The formation of tors is explained at greater length in section 4.16.

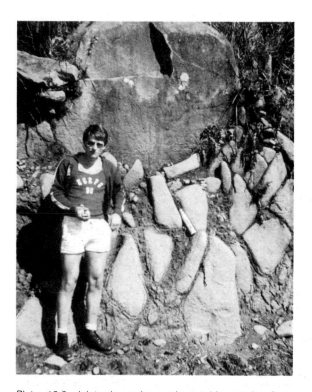

Plate 12.2 Joints in rocks such as this granite from Swaziland provide avenues along which weathering can proceed. Cores of relatively sound rock are becoming surrounded by the products of rock decomposition.

Organic weathering

The action of carbonic acid is probably supplemented in many cases by the action of other acids, especially those derived from the decomposition of vegetable matter, which are termed *humic acids*. Moreover, bacterial action and the respiration of plant roots tend to raise carbon dioxide levels in the soil atmosphere, and thereby help to accelerate solutional processes. Bacteria can also contribute to a process called *reduction*, for some of them obtain part of their oxygen requirement by reducing iron from the ferric to the ferrous form. Some of these ferrous compounds tend to be markedly more soluble in water than the original ferric ones, so that they can relatively easily be mobilised and removed from the soil. *Chelation* is another important weathering reaction. The word 'chelate' means 'clawlike', and refers to the tight chemical bonds that hydro molecules may impose on metallic cations. The process occurs because plant roots are surrounded by a concentration of hydrogen ions which can exchange with the cations in adjacent minerals; the metallic cations are then absorbed into the plant. Through this process, otherwise relatively insoluble elements such as aluminium can be mobilised.

The weathering of limestones

Limestones are a type of rock in which the effects of chemical weathering, especially solutional attack, are particularly evident. But limestones are extremely variable in their composition, hardness, jointing, etc., so that their response to

Plate 12.3 Some limestone pavements are flat expanses of bare rock, while others, like this example from The Burren of western Ireland, are dissected by solution working along closely spaced vertical joints.

Plate 12.4 Lapiés (karren) produced by limestone solution in Mallorca.

solutional modification is very varied. Thus the Cretaceous chalk of southern England is a relatively soft, pure limestone with many joints and bedding planes, and it results in a very different scenery from some of the harder, denser, more crystalline, widely jointed Carboniferous limestones that form some of the classic limestone terrain of areas such as South Wales, the Mendips and the Ingleborough district of Yorkshire. Areas where the limestone is thick, massive and extensive, and where the water table is at depth, may develop characteristic solutional features which in extreme cases produce a type of landscape called *karst*.

Within an area of karst relief it is possible to distinguish three main types of relief features:

(a) *Surface solutional forms* These are termed *clints* and *grikes* in northern England, *lapiés* in France and *karren* in Germany. They tend to be small features which are given a bewildering range of names; some characteristic forms are illustrated in figure 12.2. They are of often especially well developed on limestone surfaces that have been stripped of their cover of soil or superficial debris by glacial action. Such surfaces are termed *limestone pavements* (see section 3.6).

(b) *Closed depressions and individual hills* In most karstic areas the ground surface is pocked by a series of closed depressions of variable size and steepness. Some of the largest forms, called *poljes*, may owe at least part of their form to faulting rather than solution, but the smaller types of depression, called *dolines*, tend to be the result either of solutional enlargement of joints or of the collapse of the ground surface into a cavern produced by underground solution (figure 12.3). Surface drainage may disappear down such holes (termed *swallow holes* in many British limestone areas), as is the case with the famous example of Gaping Ghyll in Yorkshire. In the tropics the landscape may be composed of a succession of cone-like hills alternating with enclosed polygonal depressions or 'cockpits'. Alternatively, landscapes may be characterised by wide plains

Figure 12.2 Surface solutional forms from limestone areas. Some of the minor solutional forms (karren or lapiés) that develop on limestone surfaces. Rinnenkarren are small scale flutes that occur on steep surfaces, rillenkarren are sharp-edged rills that occur on bare surfaces, rundkarren are rounded runnels that tend to occur beneath a soil cover, meanders develop on slightly sloping surfaces, while step karren resemble miniature cirques cut into a sloping limestone surface. In Northern England, where such features are widespread on glacially-stripped limestone pavements, the flat areas between grooves are called clints, while the deep grooves that break them up are called grikes.

from which tall, isolated hills, called *towers*, arise.

(c) *Underground features, including caves and caverns* Much of the water in karstic areas flows underground in cave passages and along joints. Surface drainage tends, therefore, to be relatively ill-developed. The caves are formed by the solutional enlargement of major joints in the limestone, aided by the corrasional activity of the streams that may flow in them. Some caves, especially those marked by a tube-like cross-section, may develop beneath the water table (*phreatic caves*), while many develop above the water table (*vadose caves*). In the past, when climatic conditions were different, or before weathering processes had rendered the rock permeable by solutional widening of joints, surface drainage may have occurred in limestone regions; these are represented in the landscape today by dry valley systems (see section 4.15).

Figure 12.3 Five different types of limestone solution hollow (doline): (a) solution doline produced by widening of joints; (b) collapse doline produced by a cave roof falling in; (c) subsidence doline produced by removal of unconsolidated sediment down a fissure or joint; (d) subjacent karst collapse doline; (e) cockpits (intersecting star-shaped dolines), typical of tropical areas.

Rates of chemical denudation

By measuring the amount of water being discharged from an area of known size by springs or streams, and by determining the amount of soluble material present in the water, it is possible over a period of years to make an estimate of the rate at which limestone weathering takes place. Some early studies, notably by a French geomorphologist called J. Corbel, indicated that perhaps some of the highest rates occurred in cold areas (possibly because carbon dioxide is more soluble in water at low temperatures), thereby producing waters rendered more acidic with carbonic acid. Other investigators, however, have argued that, as there is more carbon dioxide and humic acid generated in the soils of wet tropical areas, and as the rate of chemical reactions increases with temperature, rates of limestone denudation should be highest in the low-latitude humid areas. However, as figure 12.4 shows, the main control of the rate of limestone denudation appears to be not temperature so much as the availability of water to cause solution to occur. Thus, the highest rates of limestone denudation appear to be in the wettest areas. Cold dry tundra areas such as the far north of Canada may have rates similar to hot areas like the margins of the Sahara (both having rates of less than 5 mm of vertical lowering per 1000 years), while cold wet areas such as western Norway may have rates similar to the rainforest-clad slopes of the East Indies (both having rates of several hundreds of millimetres of vertical lowering per 1000 years).

Comparable studies can be taken for other rock types with a view to assessing the relative susceptibility of different rock types to chemical

Plate 12.5 In limestone areas that have been glaciated bare limestone surfaces, called pavements, occur. At Newbiggin Crags in northern England the sloping pavement has been weathered by solutional processes to give clints and grikes.

Plate 12.6 In the tropics, as this air photograph of Jamaica shows, one of the characteristic forms of karst consists of a succession of cone-like hills alternating with enclosed polygonal depressions – cockpits. The roads and buildings give an indication of scale.

decay. Many studies have shown that rock type has an important affect on stream water composition; this is brought out in table 12.3, which shows some data for streams in Bohemia. The Cretaceous sedimentary rocks produce much higher solute concentrations in rivers than do the ancient igneous rocks like granite. Figure 12.5 presents comparable data for the Sangre de Cristo Mountains in New Mexico. As might be expected, the quartzites show very low rates of denudation, because they are composed of relatively inert silica grains cemented with a silica matrix; whereas the younger sedimentary rocks (sandstone, shale and limestone) show much higher rates of denudation (up to 11 times those of the quartzite). One should also note that in this area the rates of denudation on all three main rock groups increase as the annual runoff levels increase. The higher annual runoff levels in turn reflect higher precipitation levels and lower evapo-transpiration losses.

Plate 12.7 In China, and some other parts of the low latitudes, a typical limestone landscape consists of tower karst, in which tall, isolated hills rise above wide plains.

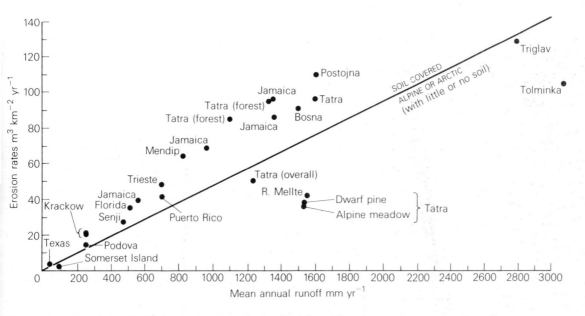

Figure 12.4 The relationship between mean annual rate of solution of limestone and mean annual runoff.

Table 12.3 The influence of rock type on the chemical composition of stream water in Bohemia

Rock type	Ion concentration (mg l⁻¹)							
	Ca	Mg	Na	K	HCO₃	SO₄	Cl	Total
Phyllite	5.7	2.4	5.4	2.1	35.1	3.1	4.9	58.7
Granite	7.7	2.3	6.9	3.7	40.3	9.2	4.2	74.3
Mica schist	9.3	3.8	8.0	3.1	48.3	9.5	5.4	87.4
Basalt	68.3	19.8	21.3	11.0	326.7	27.2	5.7	480.0
Cretaceous	133.4	31.9	20.7	16.4	404.8	167.0	17.3	791.5

Source: modified after data in K. J. Gregory and D. Walling, *Drainage Basin Form and Process* (London: Edward Arnold, 1973), p. 321.

Figure 12.5 The rate of chemical denudation for different rock types in the Sangre de Cristo Mountains, New Mexico, USA. This graph illustrates two main points: first, that the rate of chemical denudation of quartzites is very low; and second, that rates of chemical denudation increase with increasing amounts of river discharge.

12.6   Accelerated soil erosion

Although it becomes clear from this consideration of rates of weathering that, given time, soil and weathering profiles will develop to an advanced stage, especially on susceptible rock types, this cannot happen if the rates of erosion exceed those of weathering. Soils are a resource that generally form slowly, whereas erosion can occur with great rapidity, especially when human activity accelerates its operation. It has been estimated that in the United States soil erosion on agricultural land operates at a rate of about 30 t ha⁻¹ yr⁻¹, which is approximately eight times more quickly than topsoil is formed.

The main cause of *accelerated erosion* is the replacement of natural forest cover by agricultural land. Forest protects the underlying soil from the direct effects of rainfall; runoff is greatly re-duced, tree roots bind the soil, and the litter layer protects the ground from rainsplash. The rates of erosion that will result when forest is removed will be particularly high if the ground is left bare, whereas under crops the increase will be less marked. Furthermore, the method of ploughing, the time of planting, the nature of the crop and the size of fields will have an influence on the severity of the erosion.

Soil erosion resulting from deforestation and agricultural practice is especially serious in tropical and semi-arid areas (see section 6.7 and 5.11). However, recent measurements in the English East Midlands near Bedford indicate that, even there, rates of soil loss under bare soil on steep slopes can reach 17.7 t ha⁻¹ yr⁻¹, compared with 0.7 under grass and virtually nothing under woodland (see table 12.4). This erosion is caused primarily by processes like rainsplash, but elsewhere in eastern England wind is also an active process. Ever since the 1920s dust storms have been recorded in the Fenlands, the Brecklands, Lincolnshire and East Yorkshire, and they appear to be occurring with increased frequency. This results from changing agricultural practices, including the substitution of artificial fertilisers for farmyard manure, a reduction in the process of 'claying', whereby clay was added to peaty soils to stabilise them, the removal of hedgerows to facilitate the use of bigger farm machinery and, perhaps most importantly, the increased cultivation of sugarbeet. This crop requires a fine tilth and tends to leave the soil relatively bare in the early summer.

Another type of severe soil erosion in Britain is peat erosion. Deposits of blanket peat in upland areas like the Pennines are heavily degraded, producing pool and hummock topography, areas of

Plate 12.8 Limestone areas may have numerous underground caves and caverns. Some of the largest and most spectacular examples occur in the Mulu area of Sarawak.

Plate 12.9 This bizarre landscape, which has a relief of about 4 m, is an example of severe soil erosion caused by gully extension in Swaziland.

Table 12.4 Annual rates of soil loss under different land use types in eastern England (t ha⁻¹)

Plot	Splash	Overland flow	Rill	Total
Bare soil				
Top slope	0.33	6.67	0.10	7.10
Mid-slope	0.82	16.48	0.39	17.69
Lower slope	0.62	14.34	0.06	15.02
Bare soil				
Top slope	0.60	1.11	—	1.71
Mid-slope	0.43	7.78	—	8.21
Lower slope	0.37	3.01	—	3.38
Grass				
Top slope	0.09	0.09	—	0.18
Mid-slope	0.09	0.57	—	0.68
Lower slope	0.12	0.05	—	0.17
Woodland				
Top slope	—	—	—	0.00
Mid-slope	—	—	—	0.012
Lower slope	—	0.012	—	0.008

Source: from R. P. C. Morgan, Soil erosion in the United Kingdom: field studies in the Silsoe area, 1973–75, *National College of Agricultural Engineering, Occasional Paper,* 4 (1977).

bare peat, and incised gullies. River waters draining the moors are rendered brown and turbid by the eroded peat particles which they contain. Some of the peat erosion may be an essentially natural process, for the high water content and low cohesion of undrained peat makes the bogs inherently unstable, especially if a severe rainstorm occurs. However, there is evidence to suggest that the natural rate has been accelerated in the last 200 to 300 years as a result of a variety of human pressures: heavy sheep grazing, burning, peat cutting, military manouevres, the incision of pack horse trails, increased hiking and rambling, and severe air pollution from the factories of northern England.

Because of the adverse effects of soil erosion, a whole array of techniques has now been widely adopted to conserve soil resources:

(a) Revegetation
    (i) Deliberate planting
    (ii) Suppression of fire, grazing, etc., to allow regeneration
(b) Measures to stop stream bank erosion

Plate 12.10 Deforestation and overgrazing near St Michael's Mission in Zimbabwe has led to the development of this gully system in a once flat valley floor. Note the exposure of the tree roots.

(c) Measures to stop gully enlargement
  (i) Planting of trailing plants, etc.
  (ii) Weirs, dams, gabions, etc.
(d) Crop management
  (i) Maintaining cover at critical times of year
  (ii) Rotation
  (iii) Cover crops
(e) Slope runoff control
  (i) Terracing
  (ii) Deep tillage and application of humus
  (iii) Transverse hillside ditches to interrupt runoff
  (iv) Contour ploughing
  (v) Preservation of vegetation strips (to limit field width)

(f) Prevention of erosion from point sources like roads, feedlots
  (i) Intelligent geomorphic location
  (ii) Channelling of drainage water to non-susceptible areas
  (iii) Covering of banks, cuttings, etc., with vegetation
(g) Suppression of wind erosion
  (i) Soil moisture preservation
  (ii) Increase in surface roughness through ploughing up clods or by planting windbreaks

The implementation of such methods is vital if this basic, but only slowly renewable, resource is to remain productive to feed the world's rapidly growing human population.

13 The Hydrological Cycle

13.1 Introduction

Water occurs in three states: as crystalline ice (the solid state), as water (the liquid state), and as water vapour (the gaseous state). Water may pass from the solid to the liquid state by melting, and from the liquid to the solid state by freezing. It may pass from the gaseous to the liquid state by condensation, and from the liquid to the gaseous state by evaporation. If temperatures are below freezing point, molecules can pass directly from the gaseous to the solid state by sublimation.

When water changes state there are exchanges of heat energy that have considerable meteorological importance. When water evaporates, for example, *sensible heat*, which we can feel and measure by thermometer, passes into a hidden form held by the water vapour and known as the *latent heat of vaporisation*. This change results in a drop in temperature of the remaining liquid, as when evaporation of sweat causes cooling of the skin. Likewise, when the reverse process of condensation occurs an equal amount of energy is released to become sensible heat and the temperature rises correspondingly. Similarly, when water freezes heat energy is released, whereas melting absorbs an equal quantity of heat, called the *latent heat of fusion*.

Water is present in the air in varying amounts; the measure of it is referred to as *humidity*. The humidity varies according to the nature of the surface that the air is in contact with and according to the temperature. At any specified temperature the quantity of moisture that can be held by the air has a definite limit, with warm air being able to hold more than cold. The proportion of water vapour present at a given temperature relative to the maximum quantity that could be present is the *relative humidity*. If a parcel of air is warmed, therefore, its relative humidity would fall, and if it were cooled the relative humidity would rise. If the cooling proceeds beyond a critical point – the *dew point* – the air becomes saturated and the excess vapour condenses into a liquid or solid state.

Although relative humidity is a very important concept, and gives an important indication of the state of water vapour in the air, it is only a statement of the quantity of water vapour present compared with a saturation quantity. The actual quantity of moisture present is known as the *specific humidity*; this is defined as the mass of water vapour in grams contained in a kilogram of air. Warm air, like that at the Equator, has a very high potential specific humidity, whereas cold air has a very low potential specific humidity. For this reason warm air can provide a very large amount of precipitation in comparison with cold air.

Clouds (figure 13.1) form when the dew point is reached, with some of the water vapour in the air condensing into minute water droplets or ice crystals. These clouds, being extremely small and light, float in the air, and occur either as layers or as heaps. The most extensive *layer clouds* (stratus) form along fronts and near lows and troughs where converging air streams in the lower atmosphere force air to rise. These are rather featureless clouds and tend to produce overcast skies. For example, *nimbostratus* is a grey, dark, heavy opaque rain cloud. Heap or *convective clouds* tend to be less extensive, but have considerable vertical development; they are formed by pockets of warm, unstable air rising. The most common type is the *cumulus* cloud. The third type of cloud, *cirrus*, is high, white and thin, and consists of delicate veil-like patches of feathery appearance. There are ten main cloud genera:

CLOUD TYPES

Figure 13.1   The major types of clouds and the typical altitudes at which they occur.

(a) *Cirrus (Ci)* Small clouds in the form of white, sometimes silky, patches or bands. Often occur as feathery filaments with their ends swept into hooks by wind shear.

(b) *Cirrostratus (Cs)* Transparent white veil: smooth and uniform or fibrous. Commonly produces haloes.

(c) *Cirrocumulus (Cc)* Thin layer, which is either continuous or in patches that are made up of small elements. Commonly forms a 'Mackerel sky'.

(d) *Altostratus (As)* Grey, featureless layer cloud that can be fibrous or uniform. The sun may penetrate weakly, but this type of cloud does not produce optical phenomena.

(e) *Altocumulus (Ac)* Very variable in form – can be continuous or patchy. As it is usually waved or in rolls, lumps or laminae, it is better known as *lenticular* or *crenellate*.

(f) *Nimbostratus (Ns)* A grey, dark, heavy, opaque raincloud.

(g) *Stratus (St)* Forms a grey uniform layer that may be continuous or patchy and often produces rain, or snow.

(h) *Stratocumulus (Sc)* Grey or white layer with dark areas. Usually in rolls, undula-

tions and rounded masses but not fibrous. Elements often in a regular pattern.

(i) *Cumulus (Cs)* Separate dense white clouds with a well-defined form and strong vertical development. Flat base, upper parts brilliant white and cauliflower-like.

(j) *Cumulonimbus (Cb)* Extreme vertical development of a cumulus cloud. It has a huge tower, is dark at the base and is often associated with precipitation and thunder. Top smooth, occasionally fibrous and pulled out laterally.

13.2 Precipitation

Understanding the different states of water gives us the key to understanding the nature of rainfall and other types of precipitation such as fog, snow and hail; for only where large masses of air experience a steady drop in temperature to below the dew point can precipitation occur in appreciable amounts. Such a cooling normally results from a parcel of air rising to higher altitudes.

Rising air experiences a drop in temperature even though no heat energy is lost to the outside. This is a consequence of the decrease in air pressure that occurs at higher altitudes, which permits rising air to expand. The expansion means that individual molecules of the gas are more widely diffused and do not move so fast, so that the sensible temperature of the expanding gas is lowered. Parcels of air that descend undergo the opposite, with compression leading to warming.

The rate at which the air cools with altitude is termed the *adiabatic lapse rate*. For dry air it is about 10°C per 1000 m of vertical rise. However, if the air contains moisture and uplift takes place, the cooling produces condensation when the dew point is passed, and this condensation releases latent heat, so that as a result the adiabatic lapse rate is reduced to around 3–6°C per 100 m. This lower rate is termed the *wet adiabatic lapse rate*.

During the rapid ascent of a parcel of air in the saturated state, clouds form. The clouds contain water particles that may progressively coalesce to form first drizzle and then rain. In the warm clouds of the low latitudes rain forms directly by liquid condensation and droplet coalescence.

This *collison – coalescence process* was proposed by an American physicist called I. Langmuir, and operates as follows. Cloud droplets are most-

ly very light and remain suspended in the air, but a few have sufficient weight to start falling slowly through the cloud. As they fall so they collide with other droplets and thus grow even bigger. The deeper the cloud, the bigger the drops grow and the faster they fall (figure 13.2(a)).

In middle and high latitudes, however, another mechanism operates, called the *Bergeron-Findeisen* process (figure 13.2(b)). This theory is based on the observation that many clouds extend so high into the atmosphere that the temperature may be as low as −20 to −40°C. Clouds at such levels are made up of a mixture of ice crystals, supercooled water droplets and water vapour. At these low temperatures, if air is saturated with respect to water then it is supersaturated with respect to ice. This means that, in terms of the ice crystals, there is too much vapour in the air. Thus some of the vapour freezes on to the ice, so that the crystals become enlarged. But this process reduces the amount of water vapour in the air, making it unsaturated with respect to water. Some droplets therefore evaporate to redress the balance, and by this process there is a

Plate 13.1 A cumulonimbus cloud, illustrating its great vertical development and an upper 'anvil' of fibrous clouds.

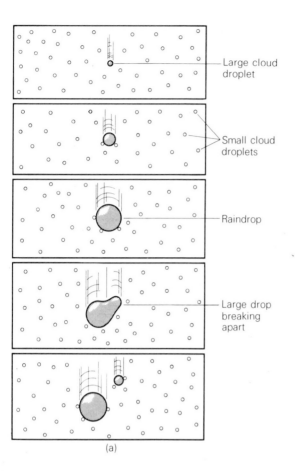

Large cloud droplet

Small cloud droplets

Raindrop

Large drop breaking apart

(a)

Water molecule   Cloud droplet

Ice crystal

(b)

Figure 13.2 Two mechanisms for rain formation: (a) the collision–coalescence process: because large cloud droplets fall more rapidly than smaller droplets, they are able to sweep up the smaller ones in their path and grow; (b) the Bergeron–Findeisen process: ice particles grow at the expense of cloud droplets until they are large enough to fall. Note that the size of these particles has been greatly exaggerated in this diagram.

continuous transfer of moisture through vapour to ice, and the ice particles grow rapidly. Such particles eventually become large enough to fall as snow, and as they move to lower altitudes they may be converted into rain. This theory forms the basis of many rain-making experiments, where the growth of large ice crystals is stimulated by introducing dry ice or similar crystals into clouds of supercooled water droplets.

The next question to ponder is what causes a parcel of air to rise. There would appear to be two main mechanisms: the spontaneous rise of moist air, and the forced rise of moist air.

Spontaneous rise is associated with convection, a form of atmospheric motion consisting of strong updraughts taking place within a convection cell. A major cause of such updraughts is the heating of a parcel of air by heat radiating from the earth's surface. The warm air produced is less dense than the surrounding air and thus rises. As the air rises it is cooled adiabatically so that eventually it is cooled beyond its dew point and condensation occurs. Heat is then liberated by the condensation process, and this serves to fuel the convection cell further. Unequal ground heating under conditions of high temperature and humidity are thus the sorts of circumstance that favour the production of the unstable air that produces this type of convectional rain.

Precipitation can also be caused by *forced ascent* of moist air. For example, when prevailing winds encounter a mountain barrier, the air is forced to rise to surmount the range. This type of relief-produced precipitation is termed *orographic*. A layer of dense cold air may operate in rather a similar way to a mountain range. Being dense it will tend to remain close to the ground, acting as a barrier to the movement of the lighter warm air. The warm air may therefore be forced to rise over the cold air, as is the case with frontal precipitation of the type found in mid-latitudes (see section 4.2).

In addition to rain there are other types of precipitation. The nature of some of the main types is described in Table 13.1. As Figure 13.3 indicates, the nature of the precipitation that actually reaches the ground depends on the conditions that exist between the cloud and the ground. One of these is *fog*, a substance made up of tiny droplets of liquid water that forms when air is cooled below its dew point so that some of the invisible water vapour it contains condenses to form small water droplets. It differs from cloud only in that, whereas clouds form when air rises and is cooled, fog is formed when air cools near the ground surface. *Radiation fog* develops when relatively warm air is cooled by contact with a cool land surface, as on clear nights when calm conditions exist. If warm air flows over an area of cold sea, as for example where upwelling takes

Table 13.1 Major types of or precipitation

Precipitation type	Description	Normal clouds from which precipitation can fall and reach the ground
Rain	Drops with diameter >0.5 mm (0.02 in) but smaller drops are still called rain if they are widely scattered	Ns, As, Sc, Ac castellanus, Cu congestus
Drizzle	Fine drops with diameter <0.5 mm (0.02 in) and very close to one another	St, Sc
Freezing rain (or drizzle)	Rain (or drizzle), the drops of which freeze on impact with the ground	The same clouds as for rain or drizzle
Snowflakes	Loose aggregates of ice crystals, most of which are branched	Ns, As, Sc, Cb
Sleet	In Britain, partly melted snowflakes, or rain and snow falling together	The same clouds as snowflakes
Snow pellets (also known as soft hail and graupel)	While opaque grains of ice, spherical, or sometimes conical with diameter about 2–5 mm (0.1–0.2 in)	Cb in cold weather
Snow grains (also known as granular snow and graupel)	Very small, white, opaque grains of ice. Flat or elongated with diameter generally <1 mm (0.04 in)	Sc or St in cold weather
Ice pellets	Transparent or translucent pellets of ice, spherical or irregular, with diameter <5 mm (0.2 in). There are two types: (a) frozen rain or drizzle drops, or largely melted and then refrozen snowflakes. (b) snow pellets encased in a thin layer of ice (also known as small hail)	Ns, As, Cb Cb
Hail	Small balls or pieces of ice with diameters 5–50 mm (0.2–2.0 in) or sometimes more	Cb
Ice prisms	Unbranched ice crystals in the form of needles, columns or plates.	St, Ns, Sc (sometimes falls from clean air, when it is just an advanced stage of ice fog)

place along the west coasts of some land masses (e.g. California and Namibia), then *sea fogs* may develop. In coastal Arctic regions *steam fog* is produced when cold air comes into contact with warm water. In areas where fogs are frequent and there are trees on which the droplets may impinge, *fog water* may be a significant component of the hydrological cycle.

Another important type of precipitation is *snow*. The conditions necessary for snow to fall are exactly the same as for rain except that temperatures at ground level are lower. Once again, the fundamental requirement is an upward movement of air produced by an area of low pressure, by the convergence of air streams or by the physical barrier of a range of mountains. As warm air holds more moisture than cold, the heaviest snowfalls tend to occur when the temperature is close to freezing rather than at much lower temperatures. The snowiest place in the world for which we have records is a place called Paradise in the Mount Rainier area of the north-west United States, where in the winter of 1971–72 a total of 31 metres of snowfall was recorded.

Hail, consisting of spherical lumps of ice from 5 mm in diameter upwards, forms in vigorous cumulonimbus clouds in which the upcurrents are strong enough to carry the weight of the stones as they grow. The hailstones originate as pellets of snow or frozen raindrops which rise and fall in the violent air currents of a storm cloud, growing by accretion as cloud droplets freeze on to them. Hail is relatively rare in cold areas because convectional activity is not sufficiently severe, and also in very warm areas because any stones that do form are likely to melt before reaching the ground. It therefore tends to be a feature of areas like the central plains of North America and of subtropical areas like South Africa. The record weight for a hailstone is of a specimen weighing 766 g and having a diameter of 44 cm which fell in Kansas in 1970. Hailstorms can cause great damage, especially to crops; the damage caused each year in the United States exceeds $500 million.

13.3 Interception

Under most conditions, rain and snow do not fall directly on the ground surface but are *intercepted* by the branches and foliage of plants (figure 13.4). They can then take three possible routes to the ground surface: (a) dropping off the plant leaves (a process known as *throughfall*), (b) undergoing secondary interception by plants at lower levels, or (c) flowing down stems and trunks (a process termed *stemflow*). But not all intercepted moisture finds its way to the ground. Some is lost from plant leaves by evaporation back to the atmosphere. This amount will vary greatly with the nature of the vegetation and the nature of the rainfall. For light falls of rain it can be substantial (as much as 60 per cent), but for heavier storms it tends to even out at about 15 per cent.

In winter deciduous trees are capable of relatively little interception, as they have lost their leaves. This does not apply to coniferous trees, and even in summer there is evidence that coniferous trees intercept more than deciduous because drops of water appear to find it easier to cling to individual needles. Some leaves of trees in the equatorial forests may have drip tips that tend to shed raindrops easily. In general, however, tropical evergreen forests, with their closed crown covers and several layers of vegetation, are quite effective at preventing intercepted rainfall from reaching the ground and are thought to have interception losses of about 30 per cent. An average

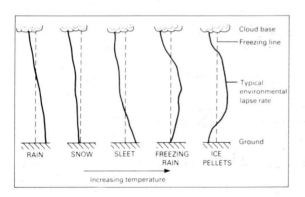

Figure 13.3 The type of precipitation that reaches the ground depends on the temperature structure of the air layer between the cloud base and the ground. In the situations illustrated, precipitation falls from a mixed cloud. The resultant precipitation type depends on the relation between the environmental lapse rate and the freezing temperature. In all cases typical profiles are shown and temperature increases from left to right.

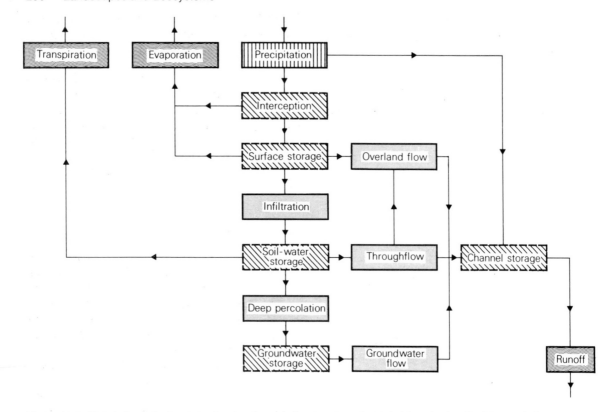

Figure 13.4 The drainage-basin cycle showing the main inputs, stores (bounded by a broken line), transmission processes and outputs.

figure for the interception loss under a grass cover is about 20 per cent of the total precipitation.

13.4 Evaporation

When one compares the amount of water that comes into a drainage basin in rainfall with the amount that leaves the basin as river discharge, it becomes apparent that there is a very substantial loss within the system. If we take the case of south-east England, the stream output from an area is only about 30 per cent of the input, and in desert areas the loss is even greater. This large difference between the input and the output values is predominantly because of *evapotranspiration*.

There are two components to evapotranspiration. One of these is *evaporation*, which is the direct loss of water to the atmosphere from water, soil and other surfaces as a result of physical processes. The other is *transpiration*, which is the

biological process of evaporation of water from the leaves of plants through openings known as stomata. Transpiration rates vary markedly during the growing season and with the nature and amount of the vegetation cover. Evaporation rates vary markedly according to temperature, wind speeds, atmospheric turbulence, humidity, number of sunshine hours, etc. Climatologists distinguish between *potential evapotranspiration* (E_p) (the amount of water loss that would occur if sufficient moisture were always available for the needs of vegetation that covers the area), and *actual evapotranspiration* (E_a) (the real quantity of moisture that is lost given that sometimes there is no moisture available).

If we take an idealized model (figure 13.5(a)), in which we assume that precipitation inputs are uniformly distributed throughout the year, we can see the importance of this difference between E_p and E_a; for, while the precipitation is constant during the year, E_p shows a strong annual cycle because of higher summer temperatures and rapid vegetation growth. During the period when precipitation (P) is greater than E_p there is a water surplus, and so runoff (R) can be generated. However, when, as in the summer months, E_p exceeds P, then moisture is lost from the soil as plants draw upon soil moisture. Under these conditions of *soil moisture deficiency*, E_a is less than E_p. Once the period of soil moisture deficiency

has ended because P once again exceeds E_p, there follows a period of soil moisture recharge in which soil moisture is restored to the field capacity – the amount of water that is held when a soil has first been saturated and then allowed to drain under gravity until no more water moves downward. When this recharge of soil moisture is complete a period of water surplus will exist and R can once again occur. This idealised model compares reasonably well with a real water-balance diagram for a station in Yorkshire, England (figure 13.5(b)).

(a)

(b)

Figure 13.5 Soil moisture budgets: (a) an idealised representation of the annual soil moisture budget for a mid-latitude location in the Northern Hemisphere; for explanation see text; (b) an annual soil water balance diagram for Huddersfield Oakes, Yorkshire, England.

13.5 Infiltration

Once it has passed through the vegetation layer, rainfall hits the soil surface. Depending on the nature of the soil, some of it will run off the surface, and some of it will enter the soil by a process called *infiltration*. There is a maximum rate at which the soil in a given condition can absorb water, and this upper limit is called the *infiltration capacity* of the soil. If rainfall intensity is less than this capacity, then the infiltration rate will be equal to the rainfall rate. If rainfall intensity exceeds the ability of the soil to absorb moisture, infiltration will occur at the capacity rate; the excess of rainfall over infiltration will cause water to accumulate on the ground surface, and *runoff* will commence.

Water that enters the soil by infiltration has to move through small cracks and pore spaces in the soil. Hence its rate of movement is low – lower than the rate at which water will run off the surface. The soil therefore plays a major part in determining the volume of storm runoff, its timing and its peak rate of flow.

Water is drawn into the soil by forces of gravity and capillary attraction. The rate of infiltration declines rapidly during the early part of a storm and reaches an approximately constant value after one or two hours of rain. There are several factors that account for this. First, the filling of fine soil pores with water reduces capillary forces drawing water into pores and fills the storage potential of the soil. Second, as they are moistened, soil clay particles swell and reduce the size of pores. Third, the impact of raindrops during rainsplash breaks up soil aggregates, splashing fine particles over the surface and washing them into pores where they impede the entry of water.

Many factors influence the nature of the infiltration capacity curve over time. Long, intense rainfall packs down the loose soil surface, disperses fine soil particles and causes them to plug soil pores. It also causes clay minerals to swell. Soil properties are also vitally important, for coarse-textured soils with a sandy texture have large pores down which water can easily drain, while the exceedingly fine pores in clay retard drainage. Likewise, if the soil particles are held together as aggregates by organic matter, and have a good, friable crumb structure, then that will permit rapid infiltration and drainage. The depth of the soil profile and its initial moisture content are important determinants of how much water can be stored in the soil before it is saturated and overland flow can occur. Similarly, vegetation plays a role. Vegetation and litter help to prevent soil from packing by raindrop impact and provide the necessary humus for binding soil particles together in open aggregates. Soil fauna that live on the organic material assist in this process by churning together the mineral particles and the organic material.

The infiltration capacity of surfaces can be changed by human activity. Overgrazing by domestic animals may trample and puddle the soil so that its structure is destroyed; the removal of forests will reduce the protection against rainsplash and will decrease the soil's organic content; and the building of cities may lead to the extension of large areas of impermeable concrete, tarmac and roof tiles over the ground surface (see section 15.3). The first part of table 13.2 gives a qualitative impression of how infiltration rates vary with different types of land use, while the second part indicates how different the infiltration rates are on heavily grazed land compared with ungrazed land: on the heavily grazed land the mean rate is only 31.3 mm h^{-1} compared with 77.5 on ungrazed land.

13.6 Surface runoff

Traditionally, it has been assumed that surface runoff is the result of rainfall intensities being in excess of the infiltration capacity of the soil, and indeed many observations that have been made,

during heavy storms, of water standing on or flowing over the ground surface of many river basins. In 1935 an American hydrologist, R. E. Horton, presented a highly influential *model of overland flow* (figure 13.6(a)). It predicts that prolonged rain falling on the slopes of a drainage basin possessing relatively uniform infiltration capacity will, if the rainfall intensity is greater than the infiltration capacity, produce overland flow over all the basin more or less simultaneously. Horton believed that such overland flow was the prime contribution to the rapid rise of river flow levels during storms, and that it was a major cause of slope erosion. He maintained that, according to the intensity of the storm and the nature of the surface materials, there would be a critical distance downslope from the drainage divide where the depth of overland flow would become sufficient to generate a shear stress competent to entrain the surface soil particles and to erode rills. Above that critical line Horton believed there was a zone called *the belt of no*

Table 13.2 The influence of land use on infiltration rates

A qualitative ranking of the influence of land use on the minimum rate of infiltration

Highest infiltration	Woods, good
	Meadows
	Woods, fair
	Pasture, good
	Woods, poor
	Pasture, fair,
	Small grain crops with good rotation
	Small grain crops with poor rotation
	Legumes after row crops
	Pasture, poor
	Row crops with good rotation
	Row crops with poor rotation (one-quarter or less in hay or sod)
Lowest infiltration	Fallow

Rates of infiltration on grazed and ungrazed lands in the United States (mm h^{-1})

State	Ungrazed	Heavily grazed
Montana	34.4	10.2
Oklahoma	222.3	62.2
Colorado	62.2	25.4
Montana	147.3	58.4
Wyoming	34.3	24.2
Louisiana	45.7	17.8
Kansas	33.0	20.3
Arizona	40.6	30.5
MEAN	77.5	31.1

erosion where slope top convexity was the norm, associated with the effects of rainsplash and soil creep (see section 11.4). Below that line there would be active surface erosion by overland flow, and slopes would thus tend towards concavity.

The sequence of events that takes place in the Horton scheme can thus be summarised as follows.

(a) Rainfall intensity exceeds the soil's infiltration capacity.
(b) A thin water layer forms on the surface and downslope surface flow is initiated.
(c) The flowing water accumulates in surface depressions.
(d) When full, these depressions begin to overflow.
(e) Overland flow enters small rills, which coalesce to form rivulets, which discharge into gullies, which discharge into channels and produce a rapid rise in stream level.

Horton overland flow occurs in areas with high-intensity rains, in areas devoid of vegetation and in areas with thin soils of low-infiltration capacity. Semi-arid areas and cultivated fields in areas with high rainfall are the sorts of places where the process can be observed. It can also be seen where the soil has been compacted by vehicles or animals.

However, two pieces of evidence suggest that Horton's model in its simple form may not have very wide applicability. First, on some slopes where surface water has been observed in storms, measured infiltration rates are very high. Rainfall intensities in the United Kingdom, for example, rarely exceed 20 mm in an hour for any prolonged period, even in flood-causing storms, and

Plate 13.2 In desert areas, Hortonian overland flow can occur. Silty soils have low infiltration capacities, and when a storm occurs little wadis on the island of Bahrain can rapidly fill with storm runoff.

(a)

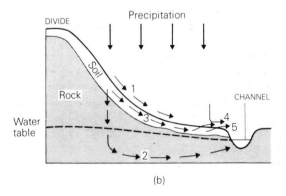

(b)

Figure 13.6 Water movement into channels from hillslopes: (a) the classic model of R. E. Horton; (b) the more complex throughflow and saturation overland flow model: 1, infiltration excess Horton-type overland flow; 2, groundwater flow; 3, shallow subsurface stormflow; 4, saturation overland flow composed of direct precipitation; 5, return flow.

yet the infiltration capacities of the soils may exceed 200 mm h^{-1}. Second, it has been noted that runoff is not generated from all over the catchment in the way envisaged in Horton's model, but that it is restricted to certain specific parts of a basin.

The explanation for these two pieces of evidence lies in a consideration of a process called throughflow, for it has now become evident that the downslope movement of water within the soil layers is more important than overland flow. Most soils occur on sloping land and so soil water movement will be towards the base of the slope. The vertical component of this movement is called *percolation*, and the horizontal component is called *throughflow*. Unless there is a storm of extremely high intensity, or unless the soil is very dry, all the effective rainfall will infiltrate into the soil, filling up empty soil pore spaces and establishing a zone of higher water content near the surface. The leading edge of the newly penetrating water is called the *wetting front*: this separates a zone of high permeability above from one with drier soil and a low permeability below. If the storm is of sufficiently long duration, the wetting front eventually reaches the base of the soil profile and all storage is filled. Thereafter water moves downslope by throughflow. However, soil adjacent to the stream channels, or soil at the base of a slope, may already be saturated and will expand as throughflow water reaches it (figure 13.7), and water falling on this saturated area will not be able to infiltrate into the soil so overland flow will occur. This will cause river level to rise and will be a major cause of any rapid rise in stream level, but some water will enter the sides of river channels directly from throughflow. The lateral movement of throughflow in the soil may produce small pipes or tunnels (figure 13.8), and these can transmit water downslope to channels at some speed, thereby contributing to a rapid rise in stream levels during a storm. Water that percolates slowly through the soil matrix rather than in pipes travels much more slowly (table 13.3).

The sequence of events that takes place in the thoughflow and saturated overlandflow model can be summarised thus (see figure 13.6(b)).

(a) Early in the storm there is a small wedge of saturated ground near the stream channel (point 1 in the figure). The saturated area in the soil is close to the surface and throughflow or subsurface storm flow (SSSF) (point 3) has just begun.

(b) As the storm proceeds the saturated area intersects the ground surface over the lower part of the slope and water seeps over the surface as something called return flow (RF) (point 5).

(c) This type of overland flow is augmented by direct precipitation (DPS) on to the saturated area and on to the water surface in the channel (point 4).

(d) As the storm goes on the saturated wedge migrates upslope, so that the contributing area for runoff in the basin increases.

(e) When the storm ceases there is a very sudden drop in DPS, and RF also decreases very rapidly. However, SSSF continues for a long time, with flow through the soil matrix being rather slow and that in pipes rather faster.

The importance of throughflow processes in small British catchments can be established by empirical studies of stream hydrographs. In various studies it has been found that following a period of high intensity rainfall there are two distinct peaks in the hydrograph (Figure 13.9). The first seems to occur fairly shortly after the peak of the storm, sometimes with a lag of only an hour, and reflects rapid runoff from rain that has fallen directly on the channel, on roads, or on highly compacted surfaces. The second hydrograph peak occurs some hours after the first, and is related to slower throughflow processes, sometimes assisted by the presence of tile drains.

13.7   Groundwater

Precipitation that succeeds in passing from the soil layer downwards into the underlying bedrock (figure 13.6(b), point 2) will at some point meet a zone of saturation – the *groundwater zone*. The top of this zone is generally called the *water table*. Normally the shape of the water table is a subdued image of the surface topography. Groundwater tends to flow towards a low point, and this is often represented by the river channel.

The classic model of the rate of groundwater motion is *Darcy's Law*, named after a mid-nineteenth-century engineer from Dijon in France. Darcy said that, for a given aquifer, the rate of water flow from one place to another is directly proportional to the drop in vertical elevation between the two places and inversely proportional to the horizontal distance the water travels. The relation between the horizontal and vertical distances can be seen to be akin to the angle of an inclined plane; it is, in fact, the force of gravity that makes water run 'downhill' underground, just as a ball rolls with varying speeds down planes of different slopes. Darcy also found

Contour interval 10 feet

N

Summer

Immediately after snowmelt period

Autumn

Saturated area at start of storm

Saturated area at end of storm

0   100   200   300   400 ft

(a)

(b)

Figure 13.7 The area of saturated ground in a river basin is a major control of the nature of runoff, and it varies both seasonally and during the course of one event; (a) the seasonal variation of the pre-storm saturated area in a small, steep-sided, well drained hillside with a narrow valley floor in Vermont, USA; (b) the saturated areas as they expand during a single rainstorm of 46 mm; (c) The effect of a rainstorm on a catchment is to cause stream expansion, and the extension of the saturated zone adjacent to stream channels. The soil thickness has been exaggerated for clarity.

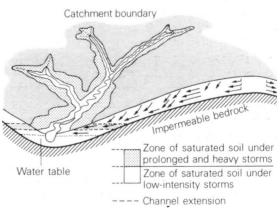

Catchment boundary

Impermeable bedrock

Water table

Zone of saturated soil under prolonged and heavy storms

Zone of saturated soil under low-intensity storms

– – – – Channel extension

(c)

Pipe

Crescentic slip

Ground level (m)

Rushes

N

0   100 m

Figure 13.8 Pipe network in the lower Nant Gerig Valley, central Wales.

Table 13.3 Estimated flow velocity of various hydrologic processes

Flow type	Velocity range (m h^{-1})
Open channel	300–10 000
Overland flow	50–500
Pipeflow	50–500
Soil matrix throughflow	0.005–0.3
Groundwater flow:	
Sandstone	0.001–10
Shale	0.00000001–1
Jointed limestone	10–500

Source: adapted from D. Weyman, *Runoff Processes and Streamflow Modelling* (Oxford: Oxford University Press), 1975.

that the greater the permeability of the rock, the faster the flow.

It is important to note, however, that there is a difference between porosity and permeability. The former is a measure of how much water can be stored in a rock or sediment, whereas permeability measures the properties of a rock or sediment which determine how fast water can flow through it.

Primary permeability (or *porosity*) results from the open texture, coarse-grained constituents and loose cementation of rocks. *Secondary permeability* (or *perviousness*) is the result of the presence of joints, cracks and fissures through which water can flow. Typical groundwater velocities lie in the range 1.0 to 0.001 m d^{-1}. Coarse-grained sedimentary rocks (gravel, conglomerate, sandstone) show the highest permeabilities, and fine-grained sedimentaries (e.g. clays), or igneous rocks (including granite) the lowest. For unconsolidated sediments, the coarser varieties (sand and gravels) are more permeable than the finer-grained varieties (silts and clays), even though they are in general less porous. The reasons for this are twofold. The angular and platy shape of many clay particles means that they have a tendency to interlock and thus isolate the spaces between them. This inhibits water movement through the sediment. More importantly, the smaller grain sizes in silt and clay result in a greater surface area of particles relative to volume which means that water tends to be held in the pores by surface tension effects.

Some rocks may have a very high secondary permeability along joints and bedding planes which have either been enlarged by solution (as in the case of limestone) or along cooling joints (as in the case of basaltic lavas). Groundwater tends to seep out where a rock of high permeability (the *aquifer*) is underlain by less permeable material; for example, if a limestone overlies a clay, groundwater may be discharged through springs.

Groundwater occurs in two main forms which are related to geological structure and topography. When it is not overlain by relatively impermeable materials it is said to be *unconfined*. In many places a zone of unconfined water may exist near the surface of the ground where downward movement of percolating water is impeded by the presence of an underlying impermeable

Figure 13.9   A stream hydrograph (i.e. a plot of discharge against time) for a small drainage basin in the Mendip Hills, south west England. The bedrock consists of impermeable Devonian Old Red Sandstone, and this is overlaid by deep, permeable brown earth soils. Note the two peaks in the hydrograph.

stratum called an *aquiclude.* A body of water that is isolated in this way from other groundwater is termed a *perched water table* (figure 13.10(a)).

The second main mode of groundwater occurrence is in the *confined* state. Such water is also called *artesian*. Artesian water is confined beneath a relatively impermeable stratum such that, if a well penetrates the confined zone, water will rise into the well to an elevation above the land surface (figure 13.10(b)).

The low velocities and high storage capacities of some groundwater systems, especially in rocks like sandstones, mean that the outflow of groundwater at springs and into the river channel can maintain river flows over long periods without rainfall. Groundwater flow is therefore a major component, along with some of the slower forms of deep throughflow, of what is called *base flow*.

13.8   Streamflow and the hydrograph

If one measures the amount of runoff flowing in a stream continuously, one can then plot a graph of flow as a function of time. This is called a discharge *hydrograph*, and it expresses the sequence of relationships that occur between runoff and the other components of the basin water balance, together with their adjustments to the physical characteristics of the basin.

When a storm occurs the flow rises relatively rapidly; this portion of the hydrograph is called the *rising limb*. A point is reached, called the 'peak' or 'crest', when the quantity of water passing the gauging position has reached a maximum. Thereafter a 'recession' occurs, and the shape of the *recession limb* is controlled by the amount of water stored in the basin and the way

Plate 13.3 Groundwater is a major resource in many arid areas. This satellite image shows some fields in Libya which are irrigated by pumping groundwater up from great depths and then distributing it over the ground by means of a rotating sprinkler arm – the centre-pivot irrigation technique.

Plate 13.4 Centre-pivot irrigation technology, employed here in the High Plains of the United States, can produce large crops in otherwise dry areas, but excessive pumping can cause rapid groundwater depletion.

Plate 13.5 One of the most famous artesian basins is that of Australia. This is an artesian bore at Moree in New South Wales.

Figure 13.10 (a) A perched water-table. In an area of gently dipping sedimentary rocks some layers will have high porosities and permeabilities (e.g. sandstones) while others (e.g. shale) will not. The sandstone could act as an underground storage reservoir for groundwater – an *aquifer*. By contrast, a shale bed, by dint of its lower permeability, would virtually preclude groundwater flow. Such a bed is called an *aquiclude*. In this example, a thin impermeable layer has blocked downward percolation of water to the main water table, and so a perched water table has developed. Where the perched water table meets the valley side a seep or spring can occur. (b) An artesian spring and well. The water table in the confined aquifer lies near the top of the dipping layers. The upper well drilled through the top impervious layer is not artesian, since the head of hydrostatic pressure is not sufficient to force water to the surface. The top of the artesian well, lower down the slope, lies below the level of the head of hydrostatic pressure, and so water can flow out at the surface. The artesian spring arises where a fault has occurred in the strata, which provides a route along which water, under sufficient hydrostatic pressure, can move.

in which it is held in the soil and the bedrock. Further rain during the recession can cause two or more peaks to occur, but if there is no further rain, discharge decreases until the extra water in storage arising from the recent rain has been depleted and the flow approaches its original volume. This original volume, which may depend to a large degree on a contribution from groundwater, is the *base flow* of the hydrograph.

The shape and size of the hydrograph are controlled by two sets of factors: those that are permanent and those that can be classed as transient. In general, the permanent factors are those involving the character of the basin, while the transient ones are associated with climate and related features (see figure 13.11). It should be remembered, however, that many of the factors are interdependent rather than independent, and that virtually all the controls are related to one another in some way.

Let us then consider some of the more important controls of the shape of the flood peak

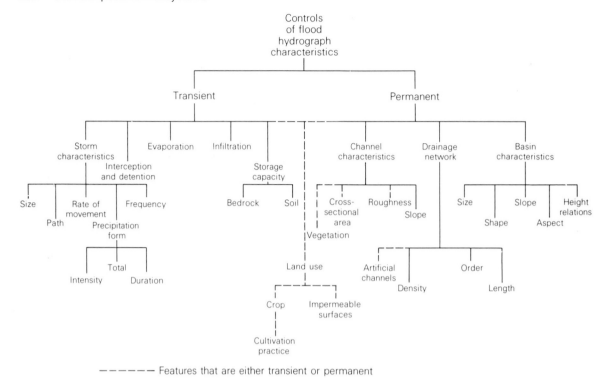

Figure 13.11   Controls of flood hydrograph characteristics.

shown on a stream hydrograph. First, other things being equal, basin area affects the size of the flood peak because this controls the amount of rainfall. Large basins receive more rain than small basins, and so have larger flood runoff discharges. However, this may not be a very simple relationship; large basins, for instance, tend not to have such steep slopes as smaller ones, and slope angle may control the nature of surface runoff rates.

Shape of basin is another important factor (figure 13.12(a)). In general, a round basin will generate a more peaked flood hydrograph than a long thin one with the same area, because when a storm occurs over the basin the distances from the edges of the round basin to the gauging station are broadly comparable, whereas in a thin basin the water from the far end will take longer to reach the gauging station than will water from nearer to the gauging station. For the same sorts of reason basins of very complex shape may have rather complex hydrograph shapes.

Basin slope is an obvious control of peak dis-

charge (figure 13.12(b)); for, other things being equal, channel flow will be faster down a steep slope than down a gentle slope, and the same probably applies to throughflow in pipes and to surface runoff.

Several characteristics of the flood hydrograph hinge on the efficiency of a basin's drainage network (figure 13.12(c)). For example, given that channel flow is quicker than overland flow or throughflow, the less distance water has to travel to reach a channel the faster it will reach the gauging station. Thus if there is a dense network of stream channels, the rising limb of the hydrograph may be steep (figure 13.12(d)).

The geology of a catchment area will also exert a fundamental influence on runoff. Especially important are the types of rock into which the basin has been eroded, and the main structural features of the area. Rock type affects the nature of the soil, the texture of the stream network, the nature of groundwater and its speed of movement. Rock structure is largely important as a factor guiding the movement of groundwater towards the

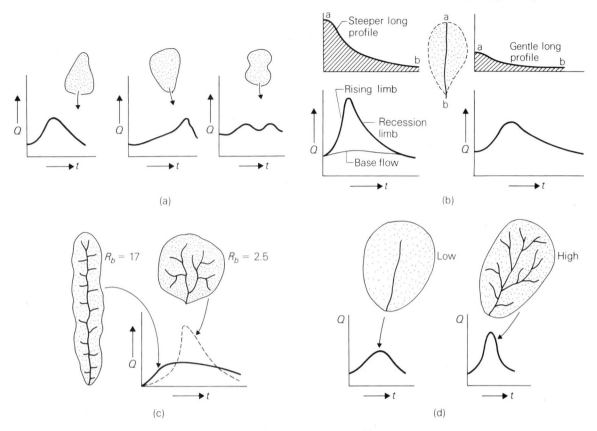

Figure 13.12 Diagrams to illustrate probable hydrograph shape in relation to some permanent characteristics of the drainage basin (Q is discharge, and t is time): (a) the shape of the basin; (b) the nature and steepness of the stream long profile; (c) the network characteristics. The long thin basin has a high bifurcation ratio (R_b) in comparison with the rounder basin; (d) the drainage density.

streams. Thus it is probable that the time lag between the rainfall and groundwater runoff peaks will be smaller in the case of a synclinal catchment, where the rocks dip towards the channel, than in the case of a catchment with horizontally bedded strata (figure 13.13).

Soil type, through its influence on infiltration rates and the speed of throughflow, is plainly very important. So is vegetation cover; the amount of vegetation affects the transpiration rate, the amount of interception, the ease with which water can flow across a slope, the soil structure and so on. It is through our influence on vegetation and soil that we may greatly modify the natural runoff characteristics of a catchment.

With regard to the more transient factors, meteorological conditions are of great significance. For example, if the precipitation in a catchment falls as snow rather than rain, the hydrograph will be modified. A blanket of snow has a storage effect, so for some parts of the year its presence will lead to relatively low discharges given the amount of precipitation, whereas in the season of spring melt water will be released very rapidly into the streams. Moreover, if a blanket of snow is present and a rainstorm occurs, the snow may absorb the rain, only to release it when melting occurs. The intensity of rainfall is one of the most important factors in determining the proportions of the rainfall that go to surface and groundwater runoff. Thus heavy rain may exceed the infiltration capacity of the soil, so that it runs off rapidly, while rain falling at lower intensities will be largely absorbed by the soil, so that its

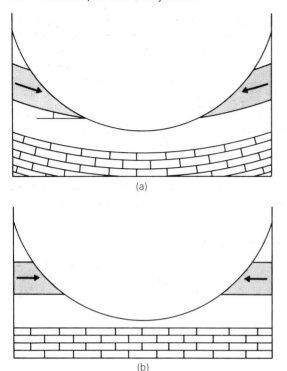

Figure 13.13   Groundwater will tend to move more speedily in synclinal strata (a) than in horizontally bedded strata (b).

addition to streamflow will probably be much delayed. The duration of rainfall is also important, for the infiltration capacity of a soil often decreases through time, while the size of the saturated wedge may increase in time. Therefore, the longer the rain continues, the smaller the infiltration capacity will become and the larger the contributing portion of the basin.

Land use changes

That land use changes could affect the nature of streamflow has been known for centuries. Studies of the torrents of the French and Austrian Alps in the late eighteenth and early nineteenth centuries showed that the increase in flooding was the result of wholesale felling of forests. The first experimental study in which planned land-use change was executed to enable observation of the effects of streamflow began at Wagon Wheel Gap, Colorado, in 1910. Here streamflow from two similar watersheds of about 80 ha each were

compared for eight years. One valley was then clear-felled and the records were continued. After the clear-felling the annual water yield was increased by 17 per cent above that predicted from the flows of the unchanged control valley.

As regeneration of vegetation takes place after forest has been cut or burned, so streamflow tends to revert towards normal, though the process may take some decades. This is illustrated in figure 13.14, which shows the dramatic effects produced on the Coweeta catchments in North Carolina by two spasms of clear-felling together with the gradual return to normality in between. The substitution of one forest type for another may also have affects on streamflow. This can be exemplified from the same Coweeta catchments. Two experimental catchments were converted from a mature deciduous hardwood forest cover to a cover of white pine (*Pinus strobus*). Fifteen years after the conversion took place annual streamflow was found to be reduced by about 20 per cent. The reason for this notable change is that the interception and subsequent evaporation of rainfall is greater for pine than it is for hardwoods during the dormant season.

Changes in river bank vegetation may have a particularly strong influence on river flow. In the south-western United States, for instance, many streams are lined by the salt cedar (*Tamarix pentandra*). The roots of this shrub abstract large quantities of water from the water table or the

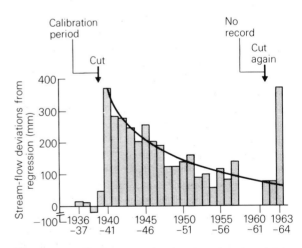

Figure 13.14   The increase of water yield after clear-felling a forest: a unique confirmation from the Coweeta catchment in North Carolina.

capillary fringe just above. It was introduced by man to help combat bank erosion, but it spread unexpectedly explosively, and in the Upper Rio Grande valley in New Mexico it came to consume approximately 45 per cent of the area's total available water.

At present, *field drainage* is spreading to wide areas of Britain and Europe to increase crop productivity. Ditches are dug and tile drains are installed. This process may well affect runoff, though the exact nature and direction of the effect has been the subject of some debate. On the one hand, the installation of ditches increases the drainage density in any area, which should facilitate rapid runoff for the reason explained in section 13.6. On the other hand, effective drainage may greatly reduce the area of saturated land in a catchment, thereby reducing the amount of runoff generated by return flow and saturation overland flow.

13.9   Annual river regimes

In the above section we have seen why the flow of streams varies in response to individual precipitation events. It is also, however, possible to consider why the annual regimes of rivers vary in different parts of the world (figure 13.15).

Some rivers have *simple regimes* because climate provides one major peak of flow. One such environment is the glacial environment, where maximum flow occurs in the summer when glacial ablation is at a maximum. Low flows occur in winter because most of the winter precipitation is in the form of snow. Another simple regime is that of some tropical rivers, which are influenced by one relatively short summer wet season. The Blue Nile is such an example. In areas with a Mediterranean climate the regime may also be simple but will be the reverse of that just described, for most of the precipitation occurs in the winter months, so that there is very little flow in the hot, dry summers.

Other rivers, however, have more *complex regimes*. For example, in some Mediterranean areas there is an autumn maximum associated with the start of the rainy season, and then a spring maximum associated with snowmelt from the higher areas of the catchment. In some equatorial regions there are two peaks associated with two

peaks of rainfall. Another cause of complex regimes is a river being so large that it has tributaries coming from a variety of different climatic zones. The Nile, for example, crosses several climatic zones – the equatorial lands of central Africa, the monsoonal lands of Ethiopia, the extreme desert of the Sahara and the Mediterranean climate of the Egyptian coastal zone. Furthermore, the timing of the peaks of flow in the Nile are affected by the role that the East African lakes play in regulating the flow of the White Nile, and the role that the great Sudd swamps play in delaying the progress of the flood through the Sudan.

13.10   Lakes

As has just been suggested, in many parts of the world, such as East Africa, the hydrological cycle is complicated by the presence of lakes, which act

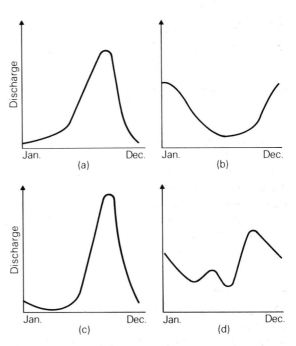

Figure 13.15 Characteristic runoff regimes of some major world zones in the Northern Hemisphere: (a) a regime dominated by snow and ice melt, as would occur in an area of high altitude or in high latitudes; (b) the mid-latitude oceanic regime with low summer discharge levels caused by high rates of evapotranspiration; (c) the tropical monsoonal type of regime dominated by high rainfall inputs during the summer and a long winter dry season; (d) the complex regime of an equatorial river, with rainfall throughout the year, but with two clear peaks.

Plate 13.6 A classic area for identifying pluvial lake basins is Utah, in the United States. The benches on the hillside between the school and the I on the hillside were cut by waves when the great expanse of Lake Bonneville occurred in the late Pleistocene.

as stores within the system which may regulate peaks in discharge. They may also provide surfaces from which substantial evaporation can occur. Some lakes provide the base level for a drainage basin instead of the sea. This is particularly the case in some arid areas where large depressions like Death Valley (California), the Dead Sea and the Caspian Sea lie below sea level.

The basins occupied by lakes show not only a wide range of dimensions but also a wide range of origins. Some of these origins are listed in table 13.4.

Table 13.4 The origins of lake basins

Mechanism	Example
Tectonic activity	Rift Valley lakes in East Africa
Volcanic	Valleys blocked by lava flows, or crater and caldera lakes (e.g. the Eifel region, Germany)
Mass movements	Valleys blocked by landslides
Solution of limestone and other susceptible rocks	Many of the lakes of Florida, the Breckland meres of East Anglia and the flashes of the Cheshire salt areas
Fluvial	Oxbow lakes, etc.
Glacial action	Basins created by glacial excavation or blocked by morainic debris (e.g. the tarns of the English Lake District, or the Italian lakes)
Shoreline processes	Lakes formed behind barrier beaches, etc.
Wind action	Basins created by deflational activity or by the blockage of river systems by dune movement (e.g. the pans of South Africa, the playas of the High Plains in the USA and the lakes in the Sandhills of Nebraska)
Organic processes	Basins dammed by such processes as beaver activity
Meteorite showers	Impact craters (e.g. Lonar Lake, India).
Man-made	Reservoirs

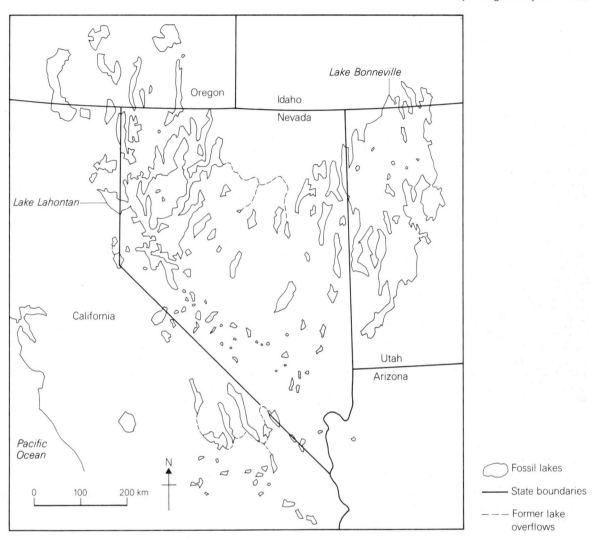

Figure 13.16 The great pluvial lake basins of the south-west USA. Compare this map with a map of present-day lakes in the area from your atlas.

Most lake basins are transient features of the landscape. Excessive sedimentation will fill in the basins, or erosion of their outlets will gradually cause them to be drained. They also respond very greatly to climatic change, and many of the great basins of the south-western United States, which are now dry or saline, were, in pluvial epochs, full of relatively fresh water (figure 13.16). Some of these, which are today closed sumps, were then linked up into a series of interconnecting basins.

14 Rivers

14.1 Introduction

Rivers are a most important component both our environment and of the landscape, as sources of water, transporters of sediment, causes of erosion and flooding and routeways for navigation. In this chapter we will first of all examine the form of river basins, the nature of river long profiles and the main feature of channel cross-sectional forms and patterns. We will then consider certain particular river environments – floodplains, terraces and deltas – before turning to the two aspects of river basins of special significance for people: the transport of sediment and the problem of floods.

14.2 Morphometry of drainage basins

Morphometry is the measurement of shape, and it is one of the most important types of quantification in hydrology and geomorphology. The great virtue of measuring shape as opposed to simply describing it in words is the precision that can be gained; one can compare and contrast different river basins, undertake correlations between different variables in the drainage basin and identify basins that are different from the norm. This was appreciated by one of the founders of modern morphometric studies in geomorphology, R. E. Horton.

One of the first aims of fluvial morphometry was to establish a hierarchy of streams ranked according to *order*. Many systems have been developed, but that of one of Horton's followers, A. N. Strahler, is objective and straightforward. According to Strahler's system, fingertip tributaries at the head of a stream system are designated as first-order streams, two first-order streams join

to form a second-order stream, two second-order streams form a third-order stream, and so on (figure 14.1(a)). It takes at least two streams of

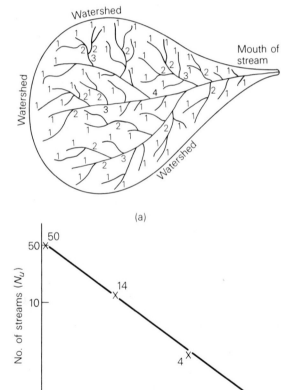

(a)

(b)

Figure 14.1 Drainage basin morphometry: (a) the Strahler system of stream ordering applied to a small drainage basin; (b) the relationship between the numbers of streams of different orders as determined for the basin above.

any given order to form a stream of the next higher order.

Using stream ordering systems of this type, it became apparent to Horton that there was an orderly arrangement of streams of different orders within a drainage basin, and this led him to propose a group of *laws of drainage composition*. He noted, for example, that in most basins the number of streams of different orders decreases with increasing order in a regular way. Thus if one plots the logarithm of the number of streams of a given order against the order, the points lie on a straight line. This is known as the *law of stream numbers* (figure 14.1(b)). Similarly, if the logarithms of the mean lengths of the stream segments of different orders are plotted against stream order, the result is usually a more or less straight line. This is the *law of stream lengths*. The *law of basin areas* follows the same general pattern. In a drainage network the mean basin areas of the orders approximate to a direct geometric sequence in which the first term is the average length of a first-order basin.

In addition to stream ordering, various aspects of drainage network form have been found to be useful. For example, *drainage density*, which is a measure of the length of stream channel per unit area of basin, gives a useful quantitative measure of landscape dissection. This measurement shows a very great range in different areas, and although some of this may be due to the differences in portrayal of streams on maps of different scales, much of it is real, and can be accounted for by varying conditions in different catchments. On highly permeable surfaces with very little potential for the generation of runoff, drainage densities may be less than 1 km km^{-2}. At the other extreme, in areas of severe erosion on impermeable but weak rocks – badlands – densities of over 700 km km^{-2} have been reported. In Britain most drainage densities are around 2 to 4 km km^{-2}, but there is considerable variation according to climatic condition and rock type. In addition to the nature of the rocks and soils in a basin, precipitation characteristics are an important control of drainage density, as they affect the extent of the vegetation cover, and thus the erodibility of the ground surface. Figure 14.3(b) and (c) suggests that the highest drainage densities are in areas where effective precipitation is low.

14.3   Drainage basin patterns

Although drainage density is one of the significant determinants of the nature of a river basin, it is also important to remember that the pattern of the drainage network may also be subject to considerable variety. Some characteristic examples are shown in figure 14.2

The least regular patterns are called *deranged* and are found in areas where the drainage net-

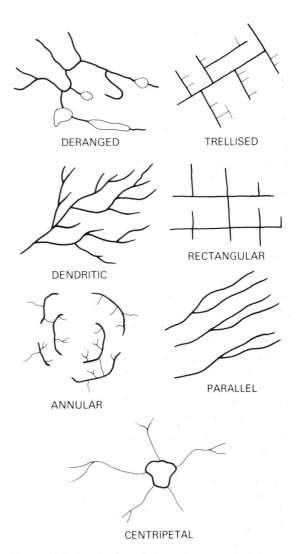

Figure 14.2 A selection of the main types of drainage pattern.

work has been modified by processes like glacial erosion and deposition. A look at a map of large parts of Finland will demonstrate this type. Most drainage patterns are said to be *dendritic*, and such systems are characteristic of well-adjusted rivers which have developed on relatively uniform materials. Departures from this 'normal' type occur where there is strict structural control. For example, *annular* patterns may develop on domes

or anticlines, *trellised* patterns may develop where a gently sloping surface cuts across rocks of different type, and *rectangular* patterns evolve where faults or joints guide stream channels. Slope may be another important control. For instance, on very steep slopes (as for example, on the side of an escarpment, the side of a mine spoil tip, or the side of a deep tidal creek) *parallel* patterns may develop. Finally, although most drainage systems

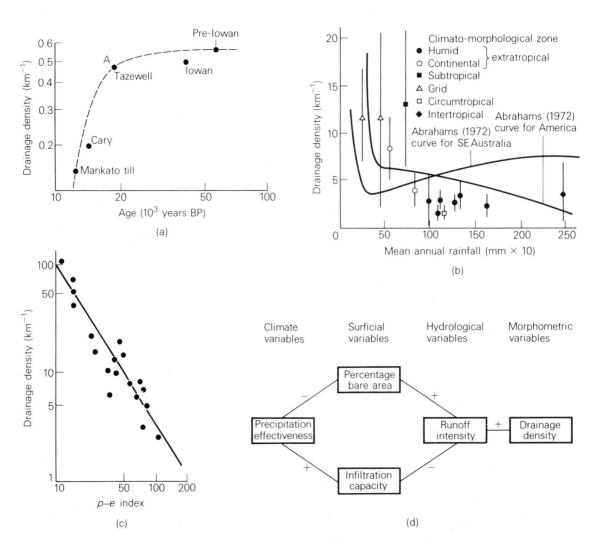

Figure 14.3 Drainage density and its controls. (a) Drainage density is greater on surfaces of greater age, as inferred from measurement on tills of varying age from North America, but an equilibrium value appears to be attained after about 20 000 years. (b) Global variation of mean annual precipitation, with each line representing the range of values represented by a particular data source. (c) Drainage density as a function of precipitation effectiveness, derived by subtracting evapotranspiration losses (*e*) from precipitation (*p*). (d) A correlation structure relating climatic, superficial, hydrological and morphological variables.

flow into the oceans or into each other, *endoreic* or *centripetal* systems develop in certain arid areas, because of such processes as deflation and dune blocking.

It also needs to be appreciated that drainage patterns may be influenced by their long-term evolutionary history. This is particularly the case where there appears to be a striking lack of correspondence between drainage pattern and fedofical structures. As we saw in section 10.7 antecedence and superimposition may be the cause of such anomalies.

14.4   Concave long profiles

The great majority of rivers have concave long profiles (figure 14.4), and through time their trend seems to be towards a removal of irregularities and the adoption of a smooth long profile with a gradient that becomes progressively less as one moves downstream. There are various factors, that, working in combination, serve to explain this general tendency.

First, the *calibre* of a stream's load tends to decrease downstream, partly because it is the finest materials that can be moved furthest, and partly because material becomes ground down by abrasion or attrition the further it travels. The coarse material of the upper tracts of a stream gradually gives way to finer material downstream, and the river can transport such finer material over a progressively gentler slope. In its upper tract, it can be argued, the gradient is steep in order to maintain the velocity and competence to move the coarse debris that is supplied to it there, while downstream the river can flatten its gradient and still transport the load.

Second, although the total amount of load to be transported increases in a downstream direction, the river discharge itself increases steadily as its catchment area is increased by the entrance of more and more tributaries. The cross-sectional area of the channel therefore grows larger, and the *hydraulic radius* (the area of water per unit of channel-water contact) will also increase. Thus the river becomes more efficient, and as a result has greater 'spare' energy to devote to load transport. Therefore, although the overall amount of load to be carried increases downstream, it can

be transported by an ever more efficient stream across gentler and gentler slopes towards the mouth. Moreover, contrary to what one might expect if one looked at the turbulent streams of the upper tract in comparison with the smoother streams of the lower tract, the mean velocity of streams tends either to remain constant or to increase slightly downstream. This is because the

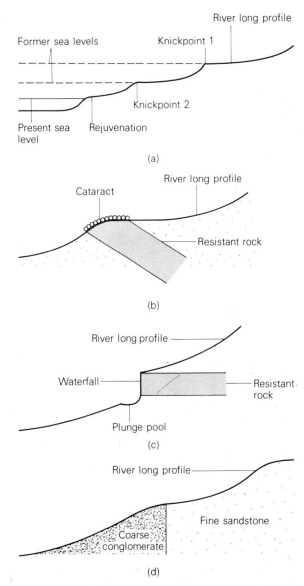

Figure 14.4   Various reasons why river long profiles may show irregularities. For explanation see text.

roughness of the bed decreases downstream as the bed material becomes finer, and once again the increasing depth of water makes the channel less prone to the effects of bed roughness.

The smooth concave curve of a river's long profile may not always exist (figure 14.4). For example, although there may be a general tendency for the grain size of bed material in a stream to decrease downstream, if the stream cuts across a particularly resistant rock in its lower course it may be loaded with some coarse debris, so that its long profile then steepens (figure 14.4(d)). The same resistant bedrock may cause a waterfall or cataract to form by limiting stream incision (figure 14.4(c)). Some rivers may contain insufficient abrasive material in their bed load to be able to cut down into underlying rocks, and this has been suggested as one of the reasons why some of the great tropical rivers have long profiles with great falls and cataracts (figure 14.4(b)). Extreme weathering under tropical conditions has furnished the rivers with bedload only of silt and clay size. Alternatively, some rivers may have irregularities in their long profiles because of changes in the base level to which they have to cut down. So, for example, if sea level falls (figure 14.4(a)), a river may cut down to adjust to the new level. This rejuvenation will, it is argued, first affect the mouth of the stream, so that the steep new lower section will undergo headward recession as a *knickpoint*.

14.5 Channel cross-section and hydraulic geometry

The size and shape of a river's cross-section varies according to a large range of factors. One of the prime controls is discharge, and studies of streams by American geologists like L. B. Leopold and T. Maddock have established some of the relationships between channel width and depth and discharge and velocity levels. Width, depth and velocity all increase with increasing discharge levels, though in geneal width seems to change more rapidly than depth in a downstream direction.

The material of which the river's banks are composed is also highly significant. If the banks are composed of unstable, non-cohesive coarse material, the stream will tend to be wide relative to its width; whereas banks with a high content of silt and clay are cohesive and thus tend to resist erosion, promoting the development of deeper and narrower cross-sections.

The investigation of the geometric relationships of channel cross-sections pioneered by Leopold and Maddock is known as *hydraulic geometry*. They were able to show the interrelationships, both in time and space, between width, depth, velocity, channel roughness, channel curvature and discharge.

If you plot the mean depth of a stream against its discharge for several different times at a point in the channel, you will find that there will be an increasing depth with increasing discharge. Stream width and velocity will also rise. If the data for these three variables are plotted on logarithmic graph paper, the points are found to lie close to a straight line, indicating that each tends to be a power function of discharge. One may therefore write three equations:

$$w = aQ^b$$
$$d = cQ^f$$
$$v = kQ^m$$

where Q is discharge, w is width, d is mean depth and v is mean velocity. The other terms a, b, c, f, k and m, are empirical constants.

It is important to understand channel shape in order to be able to identify the controls of water flow in channels. The rate at which water flows in any particular channel is influenced by three main factors: channel shape in cross-section, channel slope, and the roughness of the channel's bed and sides. Channel shape is best described by a term we have already mentioned – the hydraulic radius, the area of the channel cross-section divided by the length of its wetted perimeter. Where the river has a large wetted perimeter in relation to its cross-sectional area, there will be much friction and its velocity will be relatively reduced. None the less, the larger the cross-sectional area of the channel, the greater the flow that it will be able to carry. The roughness of the materials that make up the channel walls will depend on their shape and size and the presence of obstructions within or protruding into the flow, such as fallen trees, aquatic plants or roots. With a very rough bed there will be considerable resistance to flow.

However, roughness is very difficult to quantify, though one measure of it, called Manning's roughness coefficient, may be estimated visually (table 14.1).

These three factors are related to the mean velocity of flow in metres per second by the Manning equation:

$$\bar{v} = \frac{R^{0.67} \, S^{0.5}}{n}$$

where $\bar{v}$ is the mean velocity of flow in m s^{-1}, S is the channel slope in m m^{-1}, R is the hydraulic radius in m and n is the boundary roughness.

14.6   Channel patterns

The patterns that river channels take fall into one of three categories: braided, when a channel divides into several parts; meandering, when the channel twists; and, least frequently, straight. Any one river may take each of these three patterns at various points along its channel, and sometimes it may be difficult to separate one pattern from another. A meandering river may, for example, have straight and braided reaches. Definitions are also likely to be arbitrary, though generally a river is said to be straight if the reach is straight for at least ten times the width of the channel along that reach; and it is said to meander if the distance from a point A along its channel to a point B further down the channel is equal to, or more than, 1.5 times the distance from A to B measured along the valley. The ratio of channel distance to valley distance is known as the *sinuosity ratio*.

Rivers are seldom absolutely straight. Moreover, many *straight channels* prove to be unstable, both in the laboratory and in nature. If we take the deepest points along a stream channel and join them with a line, we have marked what is called the *thalweg* of the channel. It has frequently been noticed that, although a stream may have straight banks, the thalweg winds its way from side to side within the channel. In addition, the profile of a straight stretch shows a series of *pools* and *riffles* (deeps and shallows). These tend to be spaced about five to six bed widths apart, and once a pool-and-riffle sequence has been established, many channels develop a side-to-side swing. Alternate pools migrate to opposite sides, and riffles remain at the crossings between bends. There thus seems to be a propensity for water to flow in a sinuous course. A straight reach may therefore be abnormal and unstable, and can, for example, result from the river flowing along a feature like a fracture zone or a fault, which controls its natural tendency to wander in a wave-like manner.

Braided streams have received less attention than meandering channels, but have none the less been recognised in a wide variety of different environments, including semi-arid areas of low relief which receive their discharge from mountain areas, glacial outwash plains, periglacial areas underlain by permafrost and highland areas in all climates. The distinctive features of braided

Table 14.1   Estimation of Manning's Channel Roughness Coefficient

Bed profile	Vegetation (tree roots, aquatic weeds, etc.)	Manning's Coefficient values for bed-material size		
		Sand and gravel	Coarse gravels	Boulders
Uniform	None	0.020	0.030	0.050
Undulating[a]	None	0.030	0.040	0.055
Uniform	Some	0.040	0.050	0.060
Undulating[a]	Some	0.050	0.060	0.070
Highly irregular	None	0.055	0.070	0.080
Highly irregular	Extensive	0.080	0.090	0.100

[a]Undulating = pools and riffles well developed.
Source: modified after G. E. Petts, *Rivers* (London: Butterworth, 1983) table 3.4.

Plate 14.1 An aerial view of the braided course of the Rakaia River near Canterbury, New Zealand. Note the wide, shallow bed choked with sand bars, and the multi-thread channel.

Plate 14.2 Braided rivers are a common feature of areas with glacial outwash. They tend to occur, as in this example from the Valais of Switzerland, where there are steep slopes, a high sediment load, and variable discharge.

channels include a wide, shallow bed choked with sand bars, together with rapid shifts of sand banks and channels. In general, they appear to develop in coarser deposits than those that support meanders, and are initiated as short submerged bars which are pointed downstream. Once initiated, these accrete rapidly as finer material is trapped, allowing downstream extension; and their existence, by reducing channel width, can encourage bank erosion. The sorts of environmental conditions that favour braiding are the provision of large quantities of coarse bedload (as by glacial outwash, or on alluvial fans), the presence of non-cohesive banks, rapidly fluctuating discharges and steep slopes. This last factor is made evident by a consideration of figure 14.5. It is apparent that, immediately channel gradient exceeds a critical value compared with channel discharge ($S = 0.012Q^{-0.44}$), shown by the regresion line, the channel changes from a meandering to a braided one.

The problem of why *meanders* develop is a difficult one. The old and simple idea that chance initial irregularities in the configuration of the land, or the occurrence of hard rock outcrops – either of which could cause a deflection of the stream that subsequently would grow into a shapely, well developed meander – could be the explanation are quite inadequate. Laboratory and field observations show that the reverse tends to be the case – the best meanders are developed in homogeneous material like alluvium, in which they are free to move both downstream and to the side. The sideways movement is accomplished by erosion along the outside of the bend, where the current is strongest, and by deposition of a curved bar on the inside off the bend, called a *point bar*, where the current is weakest. As the meanders move sideways and downstream, so do the point bars, building up an accumulation of sand and silt that covers the part of the valley floor over which the channel has migrated. This, as we shall see, assists in the development of flood plains. As meanders move, they may progress unevenly so that loops become so close to each other that the river cuts through the land in between, shortening its course and leaving the abandoned bend behind as an *oxbow lake* (figure 14.6).

The proportions of meanders do not vary much. It is unusual to find meander wavelength less than eight times or more than twelve times bed width. The reason for this is that very tight bends (with a wavelength–width ratio of around 5) and very open bends (with a wavelength–width ratio of, say, 20) would increase resistance to flow round the bend.

Human activity has caused changes in the nature of river channel patterns, both deliberately and accidentally. For example, for purposes of navigation and flood control many river channels have been deliberately straightened. Removing meanders helps to reduce flooding because the shortened course that the river then follows increases both the gradient and the velocity, so that water runs away more quickly. One of the most impressive examples of this change is the Mississippi River, where 16 cutoffs have reduced the length of the river between Memphis and Baton Rouge by 270 km over a distance of 600 km. Non-deliberate channel changes may result from accidental side-effects of human activity on the amount of sediment and discharge in a channel (table 14.2).

14.7 Floodplains

The area of relatively flat land that borders the river channel and is inundated at time of high river flow is described as the *floodplain*. The features of floodplains are of two main types: those due to lateral accretion, and those due to overbank deposition (figure 14.7).

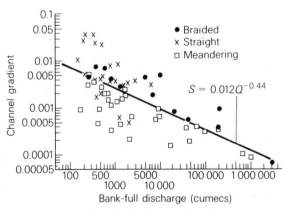

Figure 14.5 The relationship of discharge to gradient in straight, braided and meandering rivers.

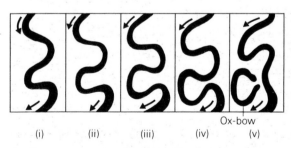

Figure 14.6 Successive stages in the development of meanders, showing the formation of an oxbow lake by a cut-off.

Plate 14.3   A satellite image (Landsat) of the Indus plain in Pakistan shows the numerous meanders, cut-offs and ox-bows. The light coloured areas are sand dunes and bare outcrops of limestone. The dark areas are the irrigated fields of the floodplain.

Table 14.2   Accidental channel changes caused by man

Phenomenon	Cause
Channel incision	'Clear-water erosion' below dams caused by sediment removal
Channel aggradation	Reduction in peak flows below dams; addition of sediment to streams by mining, agriculture, etc.
Channel enlargement	Increase in discharge level produced by urbanisation
Channel diminution	Discharge decrease following water abstraction or flood control
Channel diminution	Trapping and stabilising of sediment by artificially introduced plants

The *lateral accretion* materials are deposited as rivers cut and fill and meander laterally. Point bar accretion, which we encountered in our discussion of meanders, is perhaps the main agent of lateral accretion in some areas, though accumulation may also take place in oxbow lakes and the like. Studies in America suggest that possibly 80–90 per cent of floodplain deposits consist of lateral accretion and channel deposits. However,

Plate 14.4   The river Cuckmere in Sussex, England, has a floodplain which is traversed by an especially fine series of meanders.

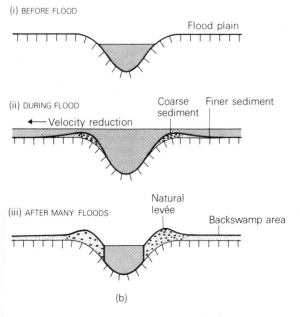

Figure 14.7 River floodplains: (a) some of the major characteristics of a floodplain indicated diagrammatically; (b) the formation of natural levées by river floods. As a river flood stage overflows its banks, it rapidly decreases in velocity away from the channel and drops most of its load, with the coarser material close by and the finer silts and clays across the floodplain.

when rivers overtop their banks, as normally happens once every one to three years, various overbank deposits can form. Of these, some of the most important are natural *levées*.

During floods, when a river overflows its banks the velocity of flow of sediment-laden water rapidly decreases as it spreads out over the floodplain. Along the strip where the decrease is particularly rapid, i.e. along the river banks, much coarse sediment is deposited; lesser amounts of fine sediment are distributed more widely over the plain. In this way successive floods build up ridges on both sides of a river channel to form features called natural levées. These confine the river within its banks between flood stages, but some levées have been built up so many metres above the surrounding plain that the plain may be lower than the river surface. If a river then breaks through its levée and water escapes, a series of distributary channels may deposit areas of coarser sediments, called *crevasse splays*, over the finer-grained materials of the backswamp areas.

14.8 Terraces

If for any reason a floodplain is cut into by the river that formed it, then alluvial terraces, or in some cases rock-cut terraces, will be formed. Most rivers have terrace remnants along their courses, and sometimes they may occur at a whole range of different heights, which may be either at the same height on either side of the valley, in which case they are termed 'paired', or at different heights, in which case they are said to be 'unpaired' (figure 14.8(a)).

Further complexity in terrace type can be introduced by the nature of their development (figure 14.8(b)), according to whether the river has cut down into one age of floodplain fill or into several.

The major question is, why does the river sometimes cut down and sometimes cease to cut down and begin to build up a floodplain? As with so many geomorphological features, there is a wide range of possible explanations, including changes in base level, climate, land use and vegetation cover (table 14.3).

In the case of the terraces of the upper Thames,

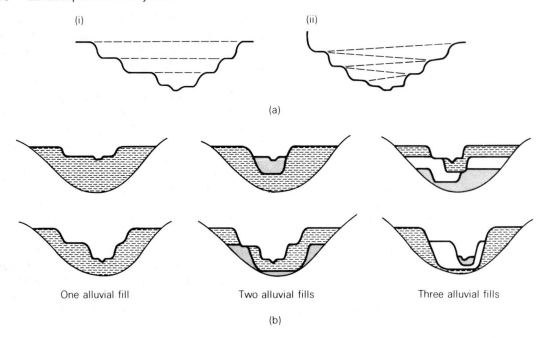

Figure 14.8 River terraces: (a) (1) paired and (ii) unpaired terraces; (b) valley cross-sections showing some possible terrace and alluvial fill combinations: (i) one terrace; (ii) two terraces.

of which there are four, they all appear to have developed in the Pleistocene; and studies of the sub-Arctic mollusca and pollen they contain, together with the presence of fossil ice-wedge casts (indicative of permafrost) in their rather short-travelled gravels, suggest that the majority of these terraces were caused by the rivers of the Cotswolds being heavily laden with coarse debris provided during cold phases by intense frost weathering and solifluction. During warmer interglacial conditions the rivers had very little load, because of the well vegetated nature of the terrain and the limited operation of mass movement processes, and so the rivers tended to cut down. In its lower course, however, the Thames may have been influenced much more by the rises

Table 14.3 Some possible explanations of why rivers sometimes cut down (incise) and why they sometimes build up (aggrade)

Incision	Aggradation

Lack of load to deposit
    Increased vegetation cover
    Decrease in mass movements
    Decrease in frost weathering
    Absence of inputs from wind
    No input of glacial drift
    Sediment trapped by dam
	Too much sediment for the river to cope with
	
	More erosion, weathering and mass
	    movements on slopes

Change in base level
    Land rises owing to tectonics, isostatic adjustment, etc.
    Sea-level falls owing to subsidence, water being ponded up
in ice caps, etc.
	Change in base level
	    Land sinks or sea-level rises

Change in velocity of flow (increase)
    Change of slope
    Change in climate
	Decrease in velocity of flow

Change in amount of discharge	Change in amount of discharge

and falls of sea level in response to the waxing and waning of the great ice sheets of the Pleistocene. When sea levels are low, rivers will tend to cut down into their floodplains, whereas when they are high they will tend to aggrade (figure 14.9).

14.9 Deltas

When a river enters a lake or the sea, its velocity rapidly diminishes and it deposits its load of sediment. If conditions are favourable this sediment will build up a distinctively shaped depositional landform called a *delta*. The simplest deltas are formed by streams entering freshwater lakes. Because the density of the entering river water is the same as that of the surrounding lake water, the river's current mixes in all directions in a cone-like pattern and rapidly slows to a halt. The coarsest material is inevitably dropped first, followed by medium and fine materials further out. Where the lake bed slopes away at a greater angle than the floor of the river channel, the coarse material builds up a kind of depositional platform (figure 14.10(a)). *Foreset beds*, inclined downcurrent from the delta front, are covered by thin, horizontal *topset beds* and are preceded

on the lake floor by thin, horizontal *bottomset beds*. Deltas formed in the sea are, broadly speaking, much the same, except that they are stretched out more in the horizontal direction (figure 14.10(b)). The reason for this is that there is a difference in the density of seawater and freshwater; the lighter river water tends to 'float' on the denser sea water, and consequently vertical mixing is more limited than in a lake. A lower mixing rate means that the current dissipates more slowly, so that the river sediments spread out along a much longer distance. As a consequence, the slope of foreset beds on large marine deltas may be only a few degrees. If the river branches where it enters the sea to form distributaries, the distributaries will build outwards as long sand fingers, called *bar-finger sands*; whereas the finer muds and silts get washed by currents and waves into the still water in between the distributaries, so that they gradually fill up with mud and swamp deposits.

The form of deltas is extremely varied (figure 14.11), and much of this variation can be attributed to the varying balance between stream discharge and wave power. As coastal processes become progressively dominant, the delta becomes progressively less irregular at the shoreline, and

Figure 14.9 A model of terrace formation in relation to the sea level and climatic changes of the Pleistocene.

may, as with the Senegal Delta on the exposed west coast of Africa, create only a slight protuberance. At the other extreme, if the discharge of the river is high, its sediment load is considerable and it occurs in a relatively sheltered environment, then a complex bird's foot form of delta, like that of the Mississippi, may form. Such *bird's foot deltas* also tend to develop where the river's load is predominantly fine-grained, whereas the arcuate form (of which the Niger is a classic

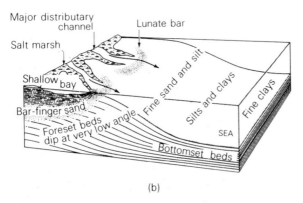

(a)

(b)

Figure 14.10 River deltas: (a) a typical freshwater delta, formed in a lake, and characterised by well defined topset, foreset and bottomset beds, of the type described from pluvial Lake Bonneville by G. K. Gilbert. Note that the slope of the delta front may be fairly steep (up to 25°); (b) a typical marine delta. The foreset beds are fine-grained and are deposited at very low angles (generally less than 5°); crescent-shaped sand accumulations called lunate bars form at the distributary mouths, where the current velocity suddenly decreases.

example) tends to be deposited by streams that carry coarser material as bedload.

Not all rivers have deltas, for conditions may not always be favourable to their development. Among conditions favouring deltaic accumulation are:

(a) a river with a large sediment load, for it can add more sediment at its mouth than can be removed by waves and currents. Rivers draining rapidly eroding mountains (e.g. the Indus) or highly erodible sediments like loess (e.g. some of the great Chinese rivers) have large deltas, other factors being equal;

(b) a river with a large discharge, for plainly a small river entering a large ocean will make relatively little impact, especially if waves and currents disperse its sediment load;

(c) reasonably shallow water offshore, so that the sediments can accumulate, rather than disappearing into a submarine canyon or an ocean trench;

(d) a relatively sheltered coast, on which wave and current action is inhibited. The development of deltas is more likely in seas such as the Gulf of Mexico, the Mediterranean and those inland from the island arcs of the western side of the Pacific, than on exposed coasts;

(e) a low tidal range: this factor reduces tidal scour, though it has to be noted that some deltas do occur in areas with quite substantial tidal range (e.g. the Ganga and Irrawaddy).

14.10   Stream transport

One of the main reasons why streams are of such geomorphological importance is that they carry a sediment load, transporting material from one part of a basin and depositing it elsewhere. The sediment load can be divided into three main types: dissolved load, suspended load, and bedload. *Dissolved load* is that portion of the stream's load that is in soluble form; it is derived primarily from the chemical weathering of rocks within its catchment and, normally to a lesser extent, from atmospheric inputs – rainwater is never completely pure. In areas of soluble rocks,

Figure 14.11 Some examples of river delta morphology in relation to the relative importance of fluvial, wave and tidal processes.

such as limestone, the dissolved load may be the most important component of a river's load.

Elsewhere the most important contribution comes from the *suspended load*. Fine particles of clay and silt are held up in the water by the upward elements of flow in turbulent eddies in the stream; as fine particles settle only very slowly once they are in suspension, they can travel long distances in this state.

The third component of a river's load is the *bedload*. This moves along the channel floor by rolling or sliding and with an occasional jump (called *saltation*). Most of the bedload is composed of material that is too coarse to be lifted into suspension, such as gravel, cobbles and boulders. Coarse material needs high velocities to move it, and at low flow many streams do not have the competence to move much bedload. *Competence*, the maximum particle weight that can be moved at a particular velocity, tends to vary according to the sixth power of this velocity. In other words, if the velocity of a stream is

increased by a factor of 4, the weight of individual boulders it can move is increased something like 4^6 or 4096 times. This explains to a considerable degree how rivers can achieve a great deal of their work during rare events of high magnitude.

A related concept is that of *capacity*. It has been estimated that the capacity of a stream (that is, its ability to move total bedload) varies according to the third power of the velocity; in other words, if stream velocity is doubled, capacity is increased 2^3 or 8 times. Capacity depends upon stream gradient, discharge and the calibre of the load.

Suspended sediment concentrations tend to increase markedly with discharge levels at any point on a stream. If one plots discharge against suspended load carried in tons per day (see figure 14.12(a)) on log-log paper the result is a straight line relationship. In the example given, for a discharge of 4 cubic metres per second (cumecs) the suspended sediment concentration is around 4

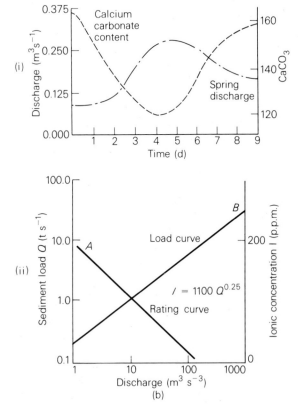

Figure 14.12 Water quality in rivers in relation to discharge levels: (a) the relationship of suspended sediments and solutes to discharge for the River Avon in Wiltshire, England; (b) dissolved load in relation to discharge: (i) Calcium carbonate concentration through a flood hydrograph for a Mendip limestone spring, England; (ii) An example of a solute rating curve for the Mekong River, south-east Asia.

mg l^{-1}, while at 100 cumecs the suspended sediment concentration has shot up to 1000 mg l^{-1}. Given that flow has increased by 25 times and the suspended sediment concentration by 250 times, the quantity of material carried as suspended sediment load at bank-full conditions in that particular channel (corresponding to c.100 cumecs) is over 6000 times greater than at low flow!

Unlike suspended sediment concentrations, *solute concentrations* tend to decline with increasing discharge (figure 14.12(b)), probably because at lower flows most of the river's discharge is derived from water that has been in contact with rock and soil for an extended period and has thereby picked up ions released by chemical weathering. The decrease may be attributed to the dilution of the groundwater and deep throughflow water by near-surface flow or overland flow during storms. However, although dissolved load contents may be reduced in their concentrations as discharge increases, in many rivers it has been found that something like a ten-fold increase in discharge causes only a halving of the solute concentrations. Consequently, solute load, which is the product of discharge and concentration, still continues to increase with discharge.

When one considers rivers in general, it is difficult to obtain any precise information on the relative importance of these three modes of material transport in rivers. A particularly severe problem is to assess the role of *bedload transport*, for this is especially difficult to estimate. For lowland rivers it is unusual for bedload to be more than about 10 per cent of the total load, and it is generally much less than this. For solutes the picture is clearer, and on a global basis they seem to make up about 38 per cent of the total load of the world's rivers. Thus, if one wants a rough rule of thumb, suspended load, solute load and bedload occur in the ratio 5:4:1. It should be pointed out, however, that for individual streams the ratios may be widely different from this. For example, an area with soluble rocks and a soil cover well protected by vegetation may have a high proportion of its total load made up by solutes, whereas an area of highly erodible sediments with a limited vegetation cover and much disturbance of the ground surface by human activities like ploughing will have a relatively high proportion of its total load made up by suspended sediment. In Britain the mean ratio of suspended sediment load to solute load based on a study of 35 catchments is 1.09, indicating that these two modes of transport are more or less equal.

In recent decades human activity has had an increased influence on the quantity and quality of material carried in rivers. For example, it is estimated that about 500 million tonnes of dissolved salts reach the oceans each year as a result of our activities. These inputs have increased by more than 30 per cent the natural values for sodium, chloride and sulphate, and have created an overall global augmentation of river solute loads of about 12 per cent. Some of the inputs are the products of industrial and municipal waste production (e.g. sewage), others are the result of the application of fertilisers to soils and pesticides and herbicides to crops, while others are the result of land-use changes. For example, the cutting or burning of a forest may release a great deal of nutrients into rivers.

Of even greater significance is the addition of suspended material to rivers as a consequence of soil erosion. Urbanisation (and especially construction activity), mining, over-grazing, deforestation and ploughing have caused severe soil erosion (see sections 12.6 and 15.5) and have thereby introduced increasingly large amounts of sediments into rivers. Such sediment makes rivers turbid, to the detriment of fauna and flora, and can also cause deposition downstream. For example, in a classic study in the Sierra Nevada Mountains of California the American geomorphologist G. K. Gilbert demonstrated the serious effects that gold mining could have. During the gold rush days in the second half of the last century gold was recovered by a process called hydraulic mining, which led to the addition of great quantities of sediments into the river valleys. This in itself raised their bed levels, changed their channel configurations and thereby caused flooding of lands that had previously been immune. Of even greater significance was the fact that the rivers transported increased quantities of debris into the estuarine waters of San Francisco Bay, causing extensive shoaling.

An illustration of how dams can catch suspended sediment and thereby reduce a river's sediment load is provided by the great Aswan High Dam on the Nile. Before the dam was built the average August silt concentration was over 2700 parts per million, while after its completion most of the sediment accumulated in Lake Nasser, so that downstream of the dam silt concentrations were a mere 45 parts per million (a sixty-fold reduction).

14.11   Rates of fluvial denudation

By long-term monitoring of the discharge levels of rivers, together with their loads of dissolved, suspended and bedload materials, it is possible to calculate the amount of material that is being removed per unit area of the land's surface in tonnes per square kilometre per year (table 14.4(a)). This figure can also be expressed as an overall rate of surface lowering in millimetres per 1000 years. Such figures indicate the rate at which rivers are denuding the face of the earth. Sometimes rates of denudation can be calculated

by other means, such as by examining the rates at which sediments accumulate in lakes or man-made reservoirs of known age (table 14.4(b)). Data are now available for a large number of catchments, and this has encouraged many scientists to ascertain how the rates may be controlled by different environmental factors. However, the situation is complex, for there are a large number of factors that might promote a high rate of denudation in a particular river basin:

(a) limited vegetation cover to protect ground surface from rainsplash etc.;
(b) intense rainfall;
(c) highly seasonal rainfall (e.g. dry tropical, monsoonal, 'Mediterranean');
(d) rapid mass movements and weathering (to feed the river with sediment);
(e) rapid tectonic uplift;
(f) large store of erodible materials (e.g. loess, unconsolidated glacial outwash);
(g) the presence of glaciers in the catchment;

Table 14.4   Sediment yields

(a) Suspended sediment yields for selected major river basins

River	Country	Annual sediment yield ($t\ km^{-2}yr^{-1}$)
Ganga	Bangladesh	1568
Yangtze	China	549
Indus	Pakistan	510
Meking	Thailand	486
Colorado	USA	424
Missouri	USA	178
Mississippi	USA	109
Amazon	Brazil	67
Nile	Egypt	39
Danube	USSR	27
Congo	Zaire	18
Rhine	Netherlands	3.5
St Lawrence	Canada	3.1

(b) Estimates of long-term sediment yield obtained from selected surveys of reservoir sedimentation in Britain

River	Reservoir	Annual sediment yield ($t\ km^{-2}yr^{-1}$)
Rede	Catcleugh	43.1
Bradgate	Cropston	45.6
Loxley	Strines	49.7
N. Esk	N. Esk	26.0
N. Tyne	Hopes	25.0
Churret	Deep Hayes	6.7
Wyre	Abbeystead	34.8
Mean	—	33.0

Source: modified from data of D. E. Walling and B. J. Webb in J. Lewin (ed.) *British Rivers* (London: Allen & Unwin, 1981) figure 5.12.

Table 14.5 Different interpretations of where maximum fluvial denudation rates occur

Investigators	Zone
Corbel	Mountainous relief (×2 to ×5 that of plainlands)
	Glaciated catchments
Fournier	Tropical monsoon and savanna regions
Strakhov	Tropical mountainous regions
Langbein and Schumm	Semi-arid regions
Walling and Kleo	Seasonal climates (Mediterranean, semi-arid, tropical monsoonal)

(h) steep slopes and long slopes;
(i) large amount of relief;
(j) disturbance of the ground surface (e.g. by grazing animals, ploughing, construction etc.);
(k) lack of conservation measures.

When we try to establish the zones where rates are highest, it becomes evident that over the years there has been a wide range of opinions about this (table 14.5). The most detailed analysis of available data has recently been made by D. Walling and A. H. A. Kleo and can be taken as the best available information (figure 14.13). They recognise three zones where rates may be especially high; the seasonal climatic zones of the 'Mediterranean', the monsoonal and the semi-arid areas. The zones with the highest rates have values of between around 600 and 1000 t km^{-2} yr^{-1}, whereas the mean value for British rivers tends to be between 10 and 200 t km^{-2} yr^{-1}.

14.12 Floods

As far as people are concerned, one of the most important aspects of the study of rivers is that connected with the main hazard that they pose – floods. Floods can be defined as the stage or height of water above some given datum such as the banks of the normal channel. In this sense, a flood occurs whenever a river overflows its banks. To the inhabitants of a floodplain, however, a flood occurs whenever water rises sufficiently so that life and property are damaged or threatened. There is a good deal of evidence that this threat is becoming increasingly serious in many parts of the world, for a number of reasons:

(a) Climatic changes
    (i) More frequent occurrence of storms of high intensity
    (ii) Heavier snowfalls
(b) Changes in landuse
    (i) Urbanisation
    (ii) Deforestation of basin slopes
    (iii) Drainage
(c) Ground subsidence
    (i) Natural seismic activity
    (ii) Man-made subsidence (arising from mining, oil abstraction, draining of peat, pumping of groundwater)
(d) Increasing population levels
(e) Development of new floodplain areas

Figure 14.13 Relationship between mean annual sediment yield and mean annual precipitation.

Plate 14.5 One contributing factor to the great Lynmouth Flood of August 1952 was the very deeply dissected and steeply sloping terrain of the Lyn catchments.

Plate 14.6 Floods result from a variety of different causes. The flood which destroyed this road bridge in Swaziland, in January 1984, resulted from an Indian Ocean cyclone which deposited an average of around 450 mm rainfall in less than three days. The waters of the Usutu river overtopped the bridge by as much as 7 m.

Since 1968 the average annual death toll from floods has risen to about 200 in the United States. This is double the rate of the 1960s and more than triple the rate of the 1940s. The total annual economic and social costs of floods in the United States now averages about $4000 billion. In probably the worst river flood in the last 100 years, which afflicted the Hwang-ho River in China in 1887, there were 800 000 deaths.

The cause of floods are legion and include:

(a) excessive levels of precipitation;
(b) melting snow;
(c) failure of man-made dams;
(d) failure of natural and man-made levées;
(e) rupture of a glacial lake or release of sub-glacial water;
(f) ponding up of rivers behind natural dams caused by glacial advance, mass movements, etc.

In addition to *causes*, we must also remember that there may be various flood-intensifying conditions, for example the degree of urbanisation, lack of vegetation cover, presence of impermeable soils, existence of steep slopes and so on. And as we saw in section 13.8, some basins, because of their various transient and permanent characteristics (figure 13.7), are prone to having a rather peaked flood hydrograph with a very steep rising limb.

The most common type of river flood is that caused by excessive levels of precipitation – a phenomenon normally associated with depressions, hurricanes, thunderstorms and other low-pressure systems. This was the cause of the flood of August 1952 which caused disaster in Lynmouth, on the margins of Exmoor in north Devon. During the first two weeks of the month the area had already received the total average precipitation for August, so the moorland soils were saturated when there followed a torrential downpour of as much as 386 mm in 36 hours. Slopes in the area are high, river gradients are steep, and bridges and debris jams caused temporary dams

that eventually broke. These factors aggravated the effects of high rainfall levels. In all, 34 people were killed and 200 000 tons of boulders were moved into the little town.

A second major catagory of river floods is that associated with snowmelt. If over the winter months snow falls in large quantities and then melts, particularly if it melts very quickly, rivers may be rapidly swollen as the thaw takes place. Another important contributory factor relates to the state of the ground during the melting phase, for if the ground is frozen to a great depth it will be rendered impermeable so that there will be little percolation of the meltwater to groundwater. An example of snowmelt floods in the UK is provided by the events of 1947, when the spring thaw caused by the movement of a warm air mass from the Atlantic ended one of the worst winters that has been experienced in living memory. Flooding was extremely widespread right across the country, from Wales and the West Country to Yorkshire and the East Anglian Fens.

Of the other causes of river floods, reference can only be made to a few examples. If dams fail (perhaps because they are badly made or are ruptured by an earthquake) the water from the reservoir may cause inundation in the valley downstream. A dambust flood resulted in 2209 drownings in Pennsylvania in 1889, and the rupture of the Bradfield Reservoir near Sheffield in Yorkshire in 1864 caused 250 deaths. Likewise, if a river breaks through its natural levées or man-made embankments along its sides, wide areas of the floodplain may be inundated. In some mountainous areas major landslides, glacier surges or mudflows may cause rivers to be blocked behind a natural dam. The water level will rise up behind this dam, and when it eventually ruptures, a flood-wave may pass downstream. The classic area for such behaviour is in the Karakoram Mountains in Pakistan, where the great tributaries of the mighty Indus River rise in the snow-clad hills of some of the steepest terrain on earth.

15 Cities

15.1 The climates of cities

Large cities, which form the home for an ever-increasing proportion of the world's population, have their own climatic conditions. In terms of their effect on climate, urban areas have been likened to volcanoes, deserts and irregular forests: they generate dust, they give out heat, they are relatively lacking in vegetation cover, and they have large structures that affect the frictional characteristics of the ground surface. The changes they bring about in the natural climatic conditions of an area can be significant; some of the most important effects are listed in table 15.1.

In comparison with the rural areas across which they sprawl, city surfaces absorb appreciably more solar radiation, because a higher prop-

Table 15.1   Average changes in climatic elements caused by cities

Element	Parameter	Urban compared with rural (− less; + more)
Radiation	On horizontal surface	−15%
	Ultraviolet	−30% (winter); −5% (summer)
Temperature	Annual mean	+ 0.7 deg
	Winter maximum	+ 1.5 deg
	Length of freeze-free season	+ 2–3 weeks (possible)
Wind speed	Annual mean	−20 to −30%
	Extreme gusts	−10 to −20%
	Frequency of calms	+5 to 20%
Relative humidity	Annual mean	−6%
	Seasonal mean	−2% (winter) −8% (summer)
Cloudiness	Cloud frequency + amount	+5 to 10%
	Fogs	+100% (winter) + 30% (summer)
Precipitation	Amounts	+5 to 10%
	Days	+10%
	Snow-days	−14%

Phenomenon	Consequence
Heat production (the heat island)	Rainfall + Temperature +
Retention of reflected radiation by high walls and dark-coloured roofs	Temperature +
Surface roughness increase	Wind − Eddying +
Dust increase (the dust dome)	Fog + Rainfall +(?)

Source: after H. Landsberg in J. F. Griffiths, *Applied Climatology: an introduction* (Oxford: Oxford University Press, 1976), p. 108.

ortion of the reflected radiation is retained by the high walls and dark-coloured roofs and roads of city streets. The concreted and tarmacked city surfaces have both great thermal capacity and good conductivity, so that heat tends to be stored during the day and released at night. By contrast, the plant cover of rural areas acts very much like an insulating blanket, so rural areas tend to experience relatively lower temperatures by day and night, an effect that is enhanced by the evaporation and transpiration that take place. A further thermal change is achieved because cities produce a great deal of artificial heat as a result of the activities of industrial, commercial and domestic energy users. Climatologists therefore talk about cities as being *urban heat islands*.

Generally speaking, the highest temperature anomalies between town and country occur in the densely built-up area near the city centre, and decrease markedly at the city perimeter. Observations in some large Canadian cities suggest temperature gradients of as much as 4 deg per kilometre between the urban centre and the urban edge. Temperature differences also tend to be greatest during the night. If we again consider the metropolis as a heat 'island', protruding distinctly out of the cool 'sea' of the surrounding landscape, we can say that the rural-urban boundary exhibits a steep temperature gradient or 'cliff' to the island, while much of the rest of the urban area appears as a 'plateau' of warm air with a steady but weaker horizontal gradient of increasing temperature towards the city centre. The urban core may be a 'peak' where the urban maximum temperature is found. The difference between this value (u) and the background rural temperature (r) defines the *urban heat island intensity* (ΔT_{u-r}).

The average annual urban-rural temperature differences for various large cities are listed in table 15.2, and it can be seen that the values range from 0.6 to 1.3°C. In general, larger cities have a greater urban heat island intensity, with ΔT_{u-r} being proportional to the log of the city's population. None the less, sizeable nocturnal temperature differences have been found even in relatively small cities. Factors such as building density, population density and the nature of the economic activities may be at least as important as city size, and cities that occur in areas with

very high wind velocities will tend to have smaller temperature differences than those that occur in areas of lesser wind velocity. Strong winds tend to lessen the heat build-up of the urban heat island.

The existence of the urban heat island has a number of implications. Snow may lie for a shorter period; frosts may be less frequent; more air conditioning may be necessary in summer; temperatures may prove oppressive for humans; some animals will be attracted to the thermally more favourable urban habitat; and plants may bud and bloom earlier than they do in the countryside.

The urban heat island effects are relatively straightforward to comprehend: it is much harder to measure and explain the urban-industrial effects on clouds, rain, snowfall and associated weather hazards. However, certain changes can be anticipated. For example, the thermal increase of the city would tend to promote upward movement of air; there might also be increased vertical movements caused by the presence of high buildings; pollution from industries might provide nuclei for cloud and raindrop formation; and industries might emit considerable quantities of water vapour.

Table 15.3 illustrates the difference in summer rainfall, thunderstorms and hailstorms between various rural and urban areas in the United States. These data indicate that rainfall increased by 9–27 per cent, that the incidence of thunderstorms increased by 10–42 per cent and that hailstorms increased by 67–430 per cent.

Table 15.2 Annual mean urban–rural temperature differences of cities

City	Temperature difference (deg)
Chicago	0.6
Washington D.C.	0.6
Los Angeles	0.7
Paris	0.7
Moscow	0.7
Philadelphia	0.8
Berlin	1.0
New York City	1.1
London	1.3

Source: from data in J. T. Peterson, in T. R. Detwyler (ed.), *Man's Impact on Environment* (New York, McGraw Hill, 1971), table 11.2, p. 136 and other sources.

Table 15.3   Areas of maximum increases (urban–rural difference) in summer rainfall and severe weather events for eight American cities

City	Rainfall		Thunderstorms		Hailstorms	
	Percentage	Location[a]	Percentage	Location[a]	Percentage	Location[a]
St Louis	+15	B	+25	B	+276	C
Chicago	+17	C	+38	A,B,C	+246	C
Cleveland	+27	C	+42	A,B	+ 90	C
Indianapolis	0	—	0	—	0	—
Washington DC	+ 9	C	+36	A,B	+ 67	B
Houston	+ 9	A	+10	A,B	+430	B
New Orleans	+10	A	+27	A	+350	A,B
Tulsa	0	—	0	—	0	—

[a]A, within city perimeter; B, 8–24 km downwind; C, 24–64 km downwind.
Source: after S. A. Changnon, Atmospheric alterations from man-made biospheric changes, in Sewell, W.R.D. (ed.) *Modifying the Weather: a social assessment* (Victoria, BC: University of Victoria Press, 1973) figure 1.5, p. 144.

An interesting example of the effects of a major conurbation is provided by the London area. It is believed that in this city the mechanical effect of the buildings has been an important factor affecting weather conditions, by creating an obstacle to air flow and by causing frictional convergence of airflow. A long-term analysis of thunderstorm records in south-east England is highly suggestive, indicating the higher frequencies of thunderstorms over the conurbation compared with elsewhere. The similarity between the conurbation and the area in the south-east having the highest frequency of thunderstorms is striking. Moreover, the historical analysis of weather records for the capital shows a steadily increasing number of thunderstorms as the city has grown.

One of the most celebrated examples of the effect of a city and industrial complex on local precipitation is provided by the Chicago area of the American mid-west. At La Porte, Indiana, some 48 km downwind of a large industrial complex between Chicago and Gary, the amount of precipitation and the number of days with thunderstorms and hail have increased markedly since 1925. There has been a 30–40 per cent increase in precipitation, and this seems to parallel the curve of increase in atmospheric pollution associated with the increasing production of the Chicago iron and steel complex. Moreover, peaks in steel production have been seen to be associated with highs in the La Porte precipitation curve.

Cities also affect wind velocities. As we have already seen, buildings of the high-rise type exert a powerful frictional drag on air moving over and around them. This creates turbulence, with characteristically rapid temporal and spatial changes in both speed and direction, though the average speed of the winds tends to be lower in built-up areas than in rural areas. The overall annual reduction of wind speed in central London is about 6 per cent but for the higher-velocity winds the reduction is more than doubled. The heat island effect also effects wind characteristics. In some English cities, such as Leicester and London, observations have shown that, on calm, clear nights when the urban heat island effect is at a maximum, there is a surface inflow of cool air towards the zones of highest temperatures. These so-called 'country breezes' have low velocities and become quickly decelerated by intense surface friction in the suburban areas.

15.2   Air pollution and its problems

Even 500 or 600 years ago, the growth of cities such as London was beginning to reduce the quality of the air. In medieval London the pollution from coal burning was regarded as such a serious matter that a commission was set up to investigate the problem in 1285, and by 1306 offenders were being punished by *grievous ransoms*, which probably included fines and confiscations. Lime furnaces appear to have been a particular cause of offence.

With the rapid increase in the size of urban areas and their degree of industrialization in the last two centuries, the pollution problem has accelerated in importance. This is made apparent by a consideration of the data for the number of days with fog in London (figure 15.1). Prior to 1750 there would appear to have been about 18–20 days of fog each year; by the end of the nineteenth century this figure had risen to over 50 days. A comparable situation is evident when one considers some of the data for cities in the Illinois industrial area in the United States (figure 15.2). Chicago, the biggest city in the group, was the first one to show a sizeable increase in the number of days with smoke haze conditions. Moderately industrialised cities like Moline, Peoria and Springfield also show sizeable increases beginning in the 1930s; but Cairo, a non-industrial city with minimal twentieth-century growth, has shown no marked upward trend in smoke haze conditions.

In general, it has been found that the average number of particles present over urban areas is ten times greater than over rural areas, and that the degree of pollution increases with city size. These particles, besides creating haze, may also act as condensation nuclei and thereby encourage fog formation. However, smoke control legislation, such as the British Clean Air Acts, can lead to a very considerable reduction in particle amounts, and in London, as a result of legislation, emissions of smoke had by 1970 been reduced to one-tenth of what they were in 1956. This legislation, has also succeeded in increasing the number of hours of sunshine recorded in city centres. In Manchester, over the same period the number of hours of sunshine recorded in the winter months of November–January increased from around 70 to about 110.

The sulphurous yellow 'pea-souper' fogs or smogs produced by coal-burning are only one of the types of fog that occur in urban areas. There is a second widespread type called *photochemical smog*. The name originates from the fact that most of the less desirable properties of such fog result from the chemical reactions induced by sunlight. Smog appears 'cleaner' than fog produced by the burning of coal in the sense that it does not contain the very large particles of soot. However, the eye irritation and damage to plant leaves that it produces still make it unpleasant. Photochemical smog occurs particularly where there is large-scale combustion of petroleum products, as in cities dominated by the motor car, such as Los Angeles. A portion of the exhaust emissions is converted into harmful substances like ozone by the effects of sunlight. However, such smogs are fortunately not universal. Because sunlight is a crucial factor in their development, they are most common in the tropics or during seasons of strong sunlight. Their especial notoriety in Los Angeles is due to a meteorological setting dominated for long spells by subtropical anticyclones with weak winds, clear skies and a subsidence inversion, combined with the general

Figure 15.2 Annual number of days with smoke-haze conditions in Illinois cities as based on a three-year moving average.

Figure 15.1 Number of fogs in London per year based on decadal means.

topographic situation partially bounded by hills and the enormous vehicle density of that affluent city.

The difference between the quality of air in cities and that of surrounding areas is brought out in a consideration of sulphur dioxide contents (table 15.4). Average values for sulphur dioxide in rural areas tends to be less than 2 μm m^{-3}, but in cities may reach over 100. The same picture emerges in the case of the amount of suspended particulate matter (SPM): background rural levels tend to have less than 10μg m^{-3} but in heavily polluted cities like Calcutta may approach 400.

15.3   Urbanisation and river flow

As we have already seen in connection with urban climatic modification, city surfaces are very different from rural surfaces. One of the most important consequences of this is that city surfaces respond in a very different manner to storms, so that the runoff they produce is different in quantity and timing, with obvious implications for flooding.

Research in both the United States and Britain has shown that, because urbanisation leads to an extension of impermeable surfaces of tarmac, tiles and concrete, the infiltration capacity of the surface is reduced. This means that there is a tendency for flood runoff to increase in comparison with rural sites (figure 15.3). Furthermore, the installation of sewers and storm drains further accelerates runoff; in general, the greater the area that is sewered, the greater is the discharge for a particular storm intensity. Some additional runoff may

be generated in urban areas because low vegetation densities mean that losses from evapotranspiration are limited.

However, in many cases the effect of urbanisation is greater for small floods, and as the size of the flood and its recurrence interval increase, so the effect of urbanisation diminishes. A probable explanation for this is that, during a severe and prolonged storm, a non-urbanised catchment may become so saturated and its channel network so extended that it will begin to behave hydrologically as if it were an impervious catchment with a dense surface-water drain network. Hence, under these conditions a rural catchment produces floods of a type and size similar to those of its urban counterpart. Moreover, in an urban catchment it seems probable that at very high discharges some throttling of flow may take place in surface-water drains and sewers, thereby damping down the peak of the flood. None the less, a study in Jackson, Mississippi, found that the 50-year flood for an urbanised catchment was three times higher than for a rural one.

River flow in urban areas may be modified in one further way. Cities import much water for industrial and municipal purposes, and such *inter-basin water transfers* are having an increasing impact on river regimes. Under dry weather flow conditions, streamflow in urban catchments in the Midlands and south-east England is now mainly imported water discharged from factories, etc. This is illustrated by the River Tame (figure 15.4), which contains about 90 per cent effluent in its 95 per cent duration flow. This proportion is increasing as more water is imported.

Table 15.4   Average concentrations of suspended particulate matter (SPM) and sulphur dioxide (SO$_2$) for selected cities (amounts in μgm^{-3})[a]

City	Commercial		Residential		Industrial	
	SPM	SO$_2$	SPM	SO$_2$	SPM	SO$_2$
Brussels	24	87	20	71	18	91
Calcutta	397	14	392	18	298	7
London	24	126	23	75	29	69
Madrid	170	116	44	47	214	112
Prague	170	108	112	100	133	49
Tokyo	43	68	47	42	52	77
Zagreb	147	117	112	40	144	49

[a]In rural areas, typical values for SPM are less than 10; for SO$_2$ less than 2.
Source: WHO Chronicle, 34, p. 147.

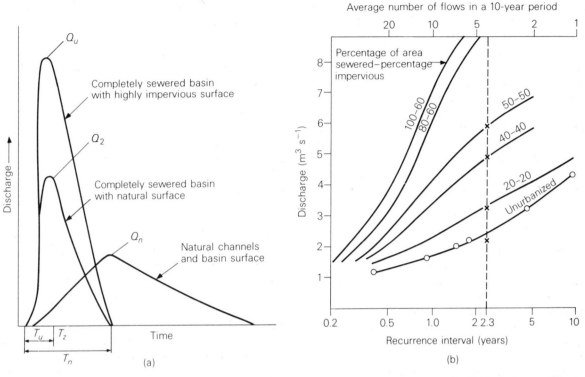

Figure 15.3   The effect of cities on floods. (a) The effect of urban development on flood hydrographs. Peak discharges (Q) are higher and occur sooner after runoff starts (T) in basins after they have been developed or sewered. (b) Flood frequency curves for a 1 square mile basin in various stages of urbanisation.

Figure 15.4   Trends in 25-month moving averages as a percentage of 25-month moving averages of rainfall for the River Tame, Lee Marston, England, 1957–74. The trend reflects increasing amounts of imported runoff.

15.4   Thermal pollution of river water

The pollution of water by increasing temperature is termed *thermal pollution*. As many river fauna are directly affected by temperature, this particu-lar environmental impact has some significance. In industrial countries probably the main source of thermal pollution is from power stations, which release large quantities of condenser cool-ing water into rivers. Water discharged from power stations has been heated on average by some 6–9°C, but usually has a temperature less than 30°C.

The extent to which such water affects river temperatures depends very much on the state of flow. For example, below the Iron Bridge power station in England, the River Severn undergoes a temperature increase of only 0.5°C during floods, compared with an 8°C increase at times of low flow. As electricity generation expands this problem will also expand, though as power stations become more efficient the amount of thermal pollution per unit of electricity produced will probably decline.

Thermal pollution may also follow directly from urbanisation. This results from various sources: changes in the temperature regimes of streams brought about by reservoirs: changes produced by the urban heat island affect; changes in the configuration of urban channels (e.g. their width–depth ratio); changes in the degree of shading of the channel, either by covering it over or by removing the natural vegetation cover; changes in the volume of storm runoff; and changes in the groundwater contribution. Studies in New York City have shown that the basic effect of the city on water temperature was to raise it in summer by as much as 5–8°C and to lower it in winter by as much as 1.5–3°C.

15.5   Soil erosion and sediment yield associated with construction and urbanisation

In the process of building a city the ground surface becomes greatly disturbed as the vegetation is removed, ditches are dug, excavations and fillings are made and construction vehicles churn up the surface. This can cause very high rates of erosion and sediment yield to occur, rates that in the course of a year may be equivalent to many decades of natural or even agricultural erosion. Studies in Maryland, in the United States, showed that, during the construction phases of urban development, sediment yields reached 55 000 t $km^{-2}yr^{-1}$, 80–200 t $km^{-2}yr^{-1}$. Likewise, studies in Devon have shown that suspended sediment concentrations in streams draining construction areas were ×2 to ×10 (occasionally up to ×100) those from undisturbed areas, while studies in Virginia showed that the rates during construc-

tion were ×10 those from agricultural land, ×200 those from grassland and ×2000 those from forest in the same area.

However, construction does not go on for ever, and once the disturbance ceases, roads are surfaced and gardens and lawns are created, the rates of erosion go down and may be of the same order as those under natural or pre-agricultural conditions.

15.6   Animals in cities

The growth of cities has often been detrimental to wildlife, but there are many examples of animals that have benefited from, and adapted to, the changes wrought by man, to the extent that they have become very closely linked to him. Such animals are called *synanthropes*. Pigeons and sparrows, for instance, now form permanent and numerous populations in almost all of the world's large cities; human food supplies are the food supplies for many synanthropic rodents such as rats and mice; a once shy forest bird, the blackbird, has in the course of a few generations become a regular and bold inhabitant of many gardens; and the grey squirrel in many places now occurs more frequently in parks than in forests. The marked increase in many species of gulls over recent decades in temperate regions is largely attributable to the increasing availability of food scraps on urban refuse tips. It may seem incongruous that the niches of scavenging birds that exploit rubbish tips should have been filled by seabirds, but the gulls have proved to be ideal replacements for the kites which men had removed, as they have the same ability to watch out for likely food sources from aloft and then to hover and plunge when they spy suitable morsels for sustenance.

Animals that can tolerate disturbance, are adaptable, utilise patches of open or woodland-edge habitat, creep about inside buildings, tap human food surreptitiously, avoid recognisable competition with man or attract human appreciation and esteem may increase in the urban milieu. For these sorts of reasons the north-east megalopolis of the United States hosts thriving populations of squirrels, rabbits, raccoons, skunks and opossums, while some African cities are now fre-

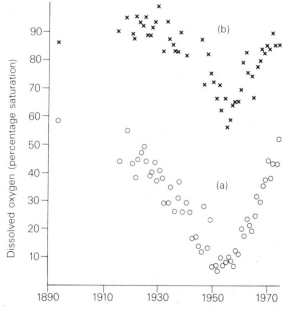

Figure 15.5 The average dissolved-oxygen content of the River Thames in England at half-tide in the July–September quarter since 1890. (a) 79 km below Teddington weir; (b) 95 km below Teddington weir.

Plate 15.1 Many wild animals are now adapting in various ways to city life. This fox patrols the streets of Oxford during the night hours, seeking appropriate food in the form of garbage or domestic animals.

quently blessed with the scavenging attention of hyenas.

Many species have suffered from the air and water pollution associated with cities. As industrialisation and municipal waste production proceeded, for example, the quality of the River Thames declined to such an extent that it contained virtually no fish (figure 15.5). The amount of dissolved oxygen in its waters declined dramatically until about 1950, when, because of more efficient controls on effluent discharge, the downward trend in quality has been reversed, and many fish, long absent from the Thames in London, are now returning.

PART V

Conclusion

16 Nature, Man and the Environment

16.1 Introduction

The purpose of this final chapter is to try to extract some of the key themes that have arisen throughout the book and are fundamental to an understanding of the field of physical geography. They can be summarised as follows.

(a) The environment of man is complex, and to understand the evolution and character of an area or landscape that many factors are involved.

(b) These factors should not be seen as discrete entities, for they interact with each other.

(c) The importance of different factors may vary according to the scale of the investigation.

(d) Man is an important factor in the environment – he both modifies it through his actions, and has his actions modified by the environment.

(e) The environment is always changing. This is partly because of human activity, but there are also natural environmental changes.

(f) It is often difficult to ascertain whether any particular change is the result of purely natural changes, or whether man has contributed.

(g) The problems of explanation are heightened by the fact that different processes can lead to similar end-forms – this is the *principal of equifinality.*

(h) Physical geographers because of their subject matter, attitudes and approaches, undertake studies that are of direct relevance to man.

16.2 Environmental complexity

The factors that can influence the nature of an area or cause a change in the environment are numerous. In general, therefore, it is not appropriate to seek single-cause explanations for phenomena. For example, there is a prima facie case for believing that a major vegetation type such as savanna is unlikely to be the result of merely one influence, such as climate; as we saw in section 6.9, other influences may also play a role, including soil quality, fires, evironmental history and topographic position. Likewise, as was demonstrated in chapter 12, the nature of a soil profile is influenced by numerous factors, including the regional climate, the biota, the topography, the nature of the parent materials, the period over which soil formation has taken place and human activities.

16.3 Environmental interactions

Having recognised that the environment is complex, the next stage in understanding is to appreciate that the factors with which one is concerned do not exist as discrete entities, but interact with each other in a variety of ways. The whole concept of *systems* involves a consideration of inputs, throughputs and outputs interacting until some sort of equilibrium state is reached. Likewise, the study of *ecosystems* involves an investigation of the relationships between organisms and their environments – relationships that may involve all sorts of feedback loops. Within ecosystems, the *cycling* of materials is important (see chapter 9), as is the transference of energy.

Opposite In 1988 many seals died in the North Sea (this photograph was taken on the beach near King's Lynn. Norfolk, in September 1988); there was considerable discussion as to whether pollution had lowered the animals' resistance to a viral infection.

Organisms interact with each other, through such processes as competition and dependence (section 9.4). Not only do they modify their environment, but as we saw in the concept of succession (section 9.5), this very act of modification may so change the nature of the environment that certain species may benefit while others will be disadvantaged.

16.4 The importance of scale

The relative importance of these many different and interacting processes varies according to the scale with which one is concerned. Scale has been an important consideration in this book, from global scale to the local scale exemplified by environments like cities and river catchments. For example, at a global scale the main influence on the pattern of soils will be climate, with the great soil orders (section 2.8) such as aridisols, alfisols and oxisols, broadly corresponding to major climatic belts. On the other hand, within a local area such as a river valley climate may be fairly uniform; there, the main influence on the nature of the soils will be relief (section 12.1), with soils and landforms being related in a toposequence or catena. Likewise, the broad pattern of a vegetational type like the savanna may be accounted for by the presence of a seasonal water deficit in the tropics (see section 6.9), but within this broad zone in which climate is a predisposing factor for savanna development, the precise character, distribution and boundaries may be caused by the presence of such local factors as human settlements or lateritic hardpans.

16.5 The influence of environment on man

Although the power of man to change his environment is increasing, owing to both exponential population growth and rapid technological change, his activities cannot be seen as being immune to the influence of his physical environment. As we saw in chapter 4, even a country such as Britain, which has a highly urbanised population with a considerable degree of technological skill, has to face the effects of a wide range of environmental hazards. In some environments the hazards are much greater; this has been stressed for periglacial (section 3.15), arid (section 5.16), humid tropical (section 6.14), mountainous (section 7.8) and coastal (section 8.10) situations. As population levels continue to rise over the next decades, placing greater pressure on marginal areas and on limited resources, the significance of some of these hazards and problems may increase. The basic knowledge acquired by physical geographers and those in related fields about the operation of environmental systems may help to reduce these threats.

16.6 Man's role and the human impact

Although during much of the nineteenth century and the first half of the twentieth many geographers were concerned with *environmental determinism* – the effect that the environment had on the actions and character of people and their societies – it has become more apparent in recent decades that man himself is an extremely important environmental influence. Among the important consequences of human activities that have been described in this book are:

The dispersal of animal species (sections 2.12 and 9.11)
Thermokarst development in periglacial areas (section 3.11)
Origin of mid-latitude grasslands (section 4.9)
Development of Mediterranean scrub (section 4.10)
Land subsidence (sections 4.17 and 5.13)
Increases in runoff and sediment yield (section 5.11)
Groundwater depletion (section 5.13)
Sediment trapping by dams (section 5.14)
Expansion of deserts (desertification) (section 5.15)
Tropical soil infertility and erosion (section 6.7)
The 'greenhouse effect' caused by high CO_2 levels (section 6.7)
Secondary rainforest formation (section 6.8)
Savanna origins (section 6.9)
Introduction of *Spartina* to British salt marshes (section 8.8)
Sea level change (section 8.10)
Coast erosion acceleration (section 8.10)
Domestication of plants and animals (section 9.10)

Atmospheric pollution (acid rain, etc.) (sections 9.12 and 15.2)
Eutrophication of lakes (section 9.12)
Extinction of animals (section 9.13)
Depletion of the ozone layer (section 9.12)
Conservation of species (section 9.15)
Habitat removal (section 9.14)
Initiation of mass movements on slopes (section 11.2)
Soil modification (section 12.1)
Soil erosion (sections 12.6 and 15.5)
Infiltration rates in soil (section 13.5)
Streamflow (section 13.8)
River channel changes (section 14.6)
River sediment type (section 14.10)
River flooding (sections 14.12 and 15.3)
Urban heat islands (section 15.1)

From this list it is apparent that the range of man's activities and their environmental effects is substantial. Some of the effects may be *deliberate*, such as the modification of stream discharge by the construction of a dam or the reduction of coastal erosion by the construction of a groyne; but some may be *inadvertent*, such as the salinisation that may accompany the introduction of an irrigation system, or the accelerated erosion that a groyne may cause down the coast from where it was emplaced.

16.7   The ever-changing environment

Our environment is in a state of constant flux because of a combination of natural and anthropogenic forces. The revolution in the earth sciences, involving the concept of plate tectonics (section 1.8), has caused a recent re-evaluation of the importance of tectonic activities in moulding the face of the earth. The plates, and their associated volcanism, earthquakes and land level changes, are fundamental to an understanding of broad-scale landscapes. Likewise, the discovery of a lengthy climatic record from the sediments in deep sea cores (section 2.13) and from other sources has demonstrated that the other great control of our environment is also prone to frequent and major changes over a very wide range of time scales, from the catastrophic individual event (such as a hurricane) to a long-continued event (such as the Ice Age of the Pleistocene).

Other highly important changes in our environment result from the passage of time. Important concepts here include the ideas of long-term slope evolution proposed by workers like W. M. Davis (section 11.5), and the ideas of plant succession in ecology (section 9.5). Thus, to understand the environment it is important to appreciate the significance of both time and history. In particular, we must remember that the present may be atypical, that in the present landscape there may be many relict features (see, for example, sections 4.13–4.16), and that we must undertake long-term monitoring of natural phenomena to comprehend their range of variability through time.

16.8   Man or nature?

In many cases of environmental change it is not possible to state, without risk of contradiction, that it is man rather than nature that is responsible. Most systems are complex and man is but one component of them, so that many of our actions can lead to end-products that are intrinsically similar to those that may be produced by natural forces (table 16.1). It is one example of the equifinality problem which we shall investigate in the next section. The determination of cause is often a ticklish problem, given the intricate interdependence of different components of ecosystems, the varying relaxation times that different ecosystem components may have when subjected to a new impulse, and the frequency and complexity of environmental changes. Obviously, the problem does not apply to the same extent to changes that have been brought about deliberately and knowingly by man, but it does apply to the many cases in which we may have initiated change inadvertently and non-deliberately.

We have been living on the earth and modifying it to different degrees for several millions of years, so it is problematical to reconstruct the environment before our intervention. We seldom have any completely clear baseline against which to measure man-made changes. Moreover, even without our intervention, the environment would be in a perpetual state of flux at a great many different time scales. In addition, there are spatial and temporal discontinuities between cause and effect. For example, erosion in one locality may

Table 16.1   Man or nature? Some examples

	Some possible causes	
Nature of the change	Anthropogenic	Natural
Desertification in a semi-arid area	Overgrazing, wood collection, etc.	Drought and climatic change
Gully development in a valley bottom	Runoff from a new road, removal of protective vegetation, etc.	Change in climate or base level
Increasing coast erosion	Effect of groynes up the coast, or of a reduced sediment supply because of the damming of rivers	More frequent storms or an increase in the height of sea level
Greater river flood intensity	Removal of natural vegetation, urbanisation, installation of field drains	Higher-intensity rainfall
Early twentieth-century climatic warming	The CO_2-generated 'greenhouse effect'	Changes in solar emission and the amount of volcanic dust in the atmosphere

lead to deposition in another, while destruction of one small but key element of an animal's habitat may lead to population declines throughout its range. Likewise, in a time context, a considerable interval may elapse before the full implications of an activity are apparent. For instance, changes in a soil profile caused by man-induced soil erosion may lead to changes in the vegetation cover, which in turn may trigger changes in the quality of stream water, which may eventually modify the habitat of fishes in a lake. Likewise, it is conceivable that erosion in a mountainous area will deposit silt in a river that will eventually reach the sea and therefore modify the sediment budget of a beach, setting off a phase of coastal progradation that may in turn modify the drainage conditions of a coastal marsh area. The ultimate impact will be removed a considerable distance from the initial cause, both in terms of space and time. Primary impacts give rise to a myriad of successive repercussions throughout ecosystems which it may be impracticable to trace and monitor.

16.9   Equifinality

The problems of explanation in physical geography caused by the number of factors involved and their interaction, by the difficulties of scale, by the frequency of change and by the problem of deciphering the role of man as against that of nature are heightened by the fact that different processes can lead to similar end-forms – the problem of equifinality. When seeking an explanation for a particular phenomenon it is important to remember that, although certain phenomena appear to be broadly similar in type, their form may be an inadequate guide to their origin. One should not be dogmatic as to the origins of many natural phenomena. Space has not allowed the development of this theme to its full extent, but the arguments that were put forward in section 4.15 for the development of dry valleys and mis-fit streams provide a striking illustration of this problem. Many landforms, including stone pavements (section 5.7), desert crusts (section 5.7), pediments (section 5.11), linear dunes (section 5.10), inselbergs (section 6.13) and patterned ground (section 3.12), have been explained in a variety of different ways, and such explanations may neither be mutually exclusive nor invalid. When conducting one's own fields investigations, therefore, it is necessary to adopt the principal of *multiple working hypotheses*, seeking to formulate and test as many explanations as possible.

16.10   The relevance and application of physical geography

Man cannot be seen in isolation from his environment, and thus the study of our environment and our interactions with it, has intrinsic importance. Physical geography is just such a study, and it should not be seen as divorced from human geography. The understanding of the environment and its complexity, the appreciation that it changes frequently and rapidly, the recognition that the environment both influences and is influenced by man and the concern with certain major problems facing the human race (pollution, conservation, extinction, erosion, etc.) ensure that physical geography is an important field of study that has great relevance and application to human problems.

A consideration of the role of the *applied geomorphologist* may illustrate these points further, and demonstrate some of the skills of the physical geographer. These include:

(a) mapping landforms, and describing what they are like;
(b) using landforms as indicators of other distributions (such as soils);
(c) identifying change through (i) monitoring and (ii) historical analysis;
(d) analysing the causes of change and hazards;
(e) assessing what happens when man intervenes in the system accidently;
(f) deciding what to do to prevent or control the undesirable consequences of such changes.

In the first instance the applied geomorphologist will attempt to map the distribution of phenomena that have been identified. Both the identification and the mapping are skills, and they depend partly on having 'an eye for country'. So, for example, if a road is to be built through a desert area, a map of landforms will help to determine the best alignment (e.g. the avoidance of shifting sand dunes, areas prone to flash floods, and locations where salt weathering may be extremely detrimental to a road's foundations). It will also help in determining suitable materials for the construction of the road; for certain landforms, especially depositional ones, may be composed of materials with particularly desirable or undesirable properties. Thus land forms can both be resources and hazards. Indeed, the general description of a particular terrain type may provide the engineer with some important information. For example, an alluvial fan (see section 5.11) is a depositional surface across which streams are prone to wander, where there may be alternations of cutting and filling, where the cause of deposition is often a mudflow charged with coarse debris and possessing considerable transportational power when confronted with a man-made structure. All these characteristics – instability, cut-

and-fill, coarse debris and the activities of mass movements – need to be considered if an alluvial fan environment is to be safely and successfully exploited.

Second, the applied geomophologist may use the fact that certain types of landform are especially distinctive on air photos to map the distribution of other phenomena that are less easily determined but are closely related in their distribution to the presence of the more distinct forms. For example, using the principle of the catena concept (section 12.1), the mapping of particular slope forms may enable a map to be made showing the boundaries of the main types of soil in an area. The boundaries can then be checked by field sampling and modified where necessary.

In addition to mapping, the applied geomorphologist is concerned with processes, changes and hazards in our ever-changing environment. It is important to know, for example, the rates at which geomorphological changes are taking place – how fast a coast is retreating towards a town or housing estate, how quickly a sand dune is encroaching on an irrigation canal, how stable the snout of a glacier near a new motorway may be, how active faults are in the vicinity of a nuclear plant, how much the sea level is changing in a flood-prone low-lying area, and whether a landslide near the site of a new dam is active or relict. The use of cartographic sources, historical records and air photos may help in this endeavour, as will the instrumentation and direct monitoring of such processes. The increasing concern of geomorphology with such processes over the last few decades has enabled an increasingly important contribution to be made in this field.

Fourth, having identified the changes taking place in the landscape and the environment, it is necessary to be aware of the causes of these changes. As has been mentioned, the causes of change are complex, involving many human and natural factors. In order to take the appropriate action to ameliorate the threat of any particular change, it is vital that the real cause or causes of change be identified.

Fifth, if the decision is made to intervene in the environment to remove or reduce the threat, then it is important to recognise that the intervention itself may have all sorts of repercussions through the environment. For example, as engineers have learnt to their cost, you cannot stop coast erosion at one point by the simple expedient of building a groyne without considering the possibility that this will increase the rate of erosion further down the coast, because the sediment supply to replenish the beach will have been retained upcoast by the groyne. Each engineering scheme needs to be seen in the context of not only the individual location, but also the wider area. In many countries all major construction schemes have to be preceded by an environmental impact statement or assessment, in which all the possible ramifications of a particular design and location are considered before construction can proceed. The physical geographer is able to appreciate the complex interactions within the environment at a variety of scales and so can assist in this task.

Thus, not only does the physical geographer have the pleasure of investigating the variety and beauty of the world's landscapes, but at the same time he or she can contribute to the welfare of society.

Appendix 1
Questions and Practicals

Chapter 1

1 (a) Explain the meaning of the term 'plate tectonics' and describe some of the evidence which supports this theory.

(b) With reference to detailed examples, describe and explain the landforms, both above and below sea level, associated with plate margins.

2 With reference to ONE large land mass of continental proportions:

(a) Describe its major physical divisions.

(b) Discuss how far these divisions are a result of both geological structure and processes at work in the past.

3 Account for the global distribution of earthquakes.

4 How is the formation of the three major types of rock related to the theory of plate tectonics?

Practical

Give a regional example of a rock formed during each of the geological periods shown in table 1.1 (p. 22).

Chapter 2

1 Give an explanatory account of EACH of the following:

(a) The relationship between atmospheric humidity and air temperature.

(b) The processes which result in the formation of snow and rain.

(c) The nature and importance of condensation nuclei in the atmosphere.

(d) The causes of atmospheric pollution.

2 (a) Describe and explain the principles upon which any ONE system of climate classification is based.

(b) Draw and label a sketch map to illustrate the subdivision of any ONE continent into climatic regions, based on the classification you have used in (a).

3 How does human activity affect the main components of the hydrological cycle?

4 What sort of changes has the world's climate undergone during the Quaternary period? How have these changes affected the environment?

5 How closely is the global distribution of vegetation types related to global climatic zones?

Practical

Using the weather maps and reports from a newspaper over one week, describe and explain how the weather changes with the passing of a depression.

Chapter 3

1 (a) Explain the term 'permafrost' and give an account of the factors which encourage its development.

(b) Give an explanatory account of the geomorphological processes operating in permafrost conditions, and show how they have contributed to the development of the landforms characteristic of such areas.

(c) Discuss how economic development in

Table A.1 Corries

	Hill mass 1			Hill mass 2	
Corrie no.	Height (metres)	Orientation (degrees from true N)	Corrie no.	Height (metres)	Orientation (degrees from true N)
1	266	310	1	316	10
2	383	330	2	333	30
3	283	120	3	466	240
4	400	140	4	633	310
5	383	70	5	416	20
6	333	340	6	833	40
7	333	345	7	750	5
8	366	85	8	933	80
9	416	155	9	666	85
10	300	345	10	466	70

tundra environments is affected by the existence of permafrost.

2 (a) (i) Explain the term 'régime of a glacier'.
   (ii) Discuss the factors which cause glaciers to advance or retreat.
   (b) How do landforms produced during the advance of a glacier differ from those developed when glaciers retreat?

Practical (A)

Under the headings 'Erosional features' and 'Depositional features', make a list of the major glacial landforms, giving regional examples.

Practical (B)

Study the data in table A.1 and figure A.1, showing the distribution of corries on two adjacent hill masses, and drumlins in a glaciated valley.

Figure A.1 Corries.

(a) (i) Plot TWO histograms to show how the corries vary in altitude *within and between* the two hill masses. Use a common scale. Use ONE side of graph paper only.
   (ii) Calculate the mean, median and modal class of the corries in each of the hill masses. Write your answer next to each histogram.
   (iii) Construct a SINGLE diagram to show the importance of ASPECT in the distribution of all corries in this region.
(b) In table A.2 plot the length, width, orientation and length:width ratio of each of the drumlins shown in figure A.1.
(c) Comment on the results of all your analyses.

Chapter 4

1 (a) Describe the characteristics of the profiles of podsols and prairie soils. You may use diagrams to illustrate your answer.
   (b) Explain why the characteristics of these two soil types are different.
   (c) Discuss the measures taken to increase or conserve the fertility of these two soil types.
2 With reference to any ONE area found in the mid-latitudes, examine the ways in which lithology and geological structure have influenced the development of its landforms and drainage pattern.
3 (a) Outline the world distribution of temperate grasslands.

Table A.2

Drumlin reference number	Length (metres)	Width (metres)	Orientation (degrees from true N)	Length: width ratio
1				
2				
3				
4				
5				
6				
7				
8				
9				
10				

(b) Describe the 'natural' vegetation of such areas, and discuss how climate, edaphic conditions, and the activities of people and animals, have influenced this vegetation.

Practical

Keep a record of natural hazards and their consequences as reported in your national newspaper.

Chapter 5

1 (a) Contrast the significance of wind and water in the development of landforms characteristic of arid areas.

(b) Outline the evidence which supports the theory that such areas have, in the past, experienced more humid conditions than those which exist to-day.

2 (a) Explain the term 'arid climate'.

(b) Choose ONE area in the world which has an arid climate and explain its temperature régime and the causes of its aridity.

(c) Show how the natural vegetation of your chosen area has adapted to the prevailing conditions.

Practical

Using an atlas of the world, classify the world's deserts according to the major causes of each one's aridity.

Chapter 6

1 (a) With reference to tropical rainforest areas, discuss the interrelationships which exist between climatic conditions, soils and vegetation.

(b) How far have humans been responsible for the degradation of climatic climax vegetation communities and soils in parts of the tropical rainforest?

2 Describe and explain the conditions which lead to the development and the associated weather conditions of tropical cyclones and monsoonal winds.

3 How and why do tropical disturbances differ from mid-latitude depressions?

4 What are the environmental consequences of large-scale tropical deforestation?

5 Explain the development of *inselbergs*. Are these features typical of tropical landscapes?

Chapter 7

1 Plant communities change with increasing altitude. With reference to ONE such example on a local or regional scale, describe and account for the changes which occur with altitude in the composition and structure of the natural vegetation.

2 Choose ONE mountainous area which you have studied.

(a) By means of sketch maps, cross-sections or profiles ONLY, illustrate the distribution of geomorphological features in the area.

(b) Discuss the ways in which the distribution and form of these features have been influenced by:

(i) Rock type and structure.
(ii) Man's activities.
(iii) Processes of denudation.

3 'Mountain barriers represent a strong influence on local climate.' Discuss.

4 It has been suggested that the altitudinal vegetation zones of tropical mountains closely resemble the global latitudinal zoning of vegetation. How far do you agree with this suggestion?

5 What contribution can the applied physical geographer make to the successful use of mountain environments?

Chapter 8

1 (a) With reference to specific examples, describe and explain how rock type and structure may influence the morphology of coasts.

(b) Discuss the geomorphological processes which operate during storm conditions on coastal cliffs and beaches.

2 (a) Explain the terms 'isostatic' and 'eustatic' changes.

(b) With reference to examples, describe and account for the effects of such changes on the morphology of coastlines.

3 Using specific examples, distinguish between erosional and depositional coastal features.

4 In what ways do humans influence coastal erosion?

5 'Since the coast is the interface between land and sea, it is not just marine processes that dictate the nature of coastal landforms.' Discuss.

Practical (A)

Under the headings 'Higher sea level' and 'Lower sea level', draw up a table of the sorts of coastal features you would look for as evidence for sea-level change.

Practical (B)

A fieldwork investigation was undertaken by a group of Sixth Form students on a beach along the Norfolk coast. The data in the table below were collected at a series of randomly selected points.

(a) (i) Using the data, employ the Spearman Rank method of calculating correlation coefficients to obtain a measure of the degree of correlation between distance along the beach and the mean shingle diameter. Set out your working in the spaces provided in the table.

(ii) Use the graph provided (see figure A.2) of the statistical significance of the coefficient and then interpret the results of your analysis. Comment on the trends and how far they might be expected, and suggest reasons for any anomalies.

The coefficient is derived from the formula:

$$R = 1 - \frac{6 \Sigma d^2}{N^3 - N}$$

where R is the Spearman Rank Correlation Coefficient; d^2 is the sum of the squares of the difference in rank of the variables; N is the number of samples taken.

(b) Describe appropriate sampling techniques which may be used to collect data of this nature.

Table A.3

Section line sampling point	Distance (metres) from SE end of beach	Rank	Mean shingle diameter (cm)	Rank	Difference	Difference
1	60		8.4			
2	310		8.1			
3	760		5.8			
4	900		7.1			
5	600		5.9			
6	120		8.3			
7	430		8.0			
8	560		6.1			
9	1200		5.0			
10	1000		5.6			

d^2 _____

Unable to reject H₀ at significance levels above 5%. Hence 5% level of significance is known as the Rejection Level

Figure A.2 Significance table.

Chapter 9

1 (a) (i) Explain the meaning of the term 'ecosystem'.
       (ii) Describe ONE specific ecosystem which you have studied.
    (b) Referring in your answer to specific examples, show how humankind may have upset the balance existing within ecosystems.
2 With reference to any TWO morphogenetic regions,
       (i) Describe the characteristics of the natural vegetation and show how these have been influenced by climatic and soil conditions.
       (ii) Discuss the changes in vegetation resulting from human activities in your chosen regions.
3 'To understand the workings of any ecosystem we must understand the energy flows through it.' Discuss.
4 What do you understand by the term 'succession'? How does human action affect the process?

Practical

Identify an area in your region that you consider to be worth conserving. Draw up a plan of the arguments you would use to convince the local inhabitants and the local community of your convictions. What sort of problems do you envisage in trying to get your plans to become reality?

Chapter 10

1 (a) Describe the landforms which result from both intrusive and extrusive vulcanicity.
    (b) How does an understanding of vulcanicity help to explain the formation of the world's major land masses?
2 (a) (i) Explain why earthquakes occur.
       (ii) Describe the variety of landforms which result from folding and faulting.
    (b) How far does the theory of plate tectonics aid in our understanding of the world pattern of earthquake zones?
3 'On balance volcanoes do more good than harm.' Critically examine this view of the volcanic hazard.
4 Do different types of volcanic eruption produce different types of volcanic landform?

Practical

Following a volcanic eruption in 1980, some of the products from the eruption were analysed and the results given in table A.4. The products were taken at 10 sampling sites at varying distances from the explosive vent of the volcano.

    (a) Choose ONE diagrammatic technique to show the variations with distance from the explosive vent in the percentages of gravel, sand, and silt/clay at the 10 sampling sites. Use one side of graph paper for your diagram/s.
    (b) On ONE side of graph paper, construct THREE scatter diagrams to show the relationship between each of the products of the eruption and distance from the explosive vent.
       Insert a best fit trend line on EACH scatter diagram, and number each of the sampling sites, and ring any points which deviate considerably from the line of best fit.
    (c) Using the table and your diagrams, comment on the results of the investigation.

Chapter 11

1 With reference to areas with tropical, arid and temperate humid climates, explain how the morphology of hillslopes varies with:

Table A.4

Site no.:	Distance from explosive vent (km)	% of sample taken		
		Gravel	Sand	Silt/Clay
1	4	27.8	69.2	3.0
2	12	9.5	82.5	8.0
3	14	4.0	85.0	11.0
4	19	2.7	85.5	11.8
5	25	2.6	82.4	15.0
6	29	3.6	81.8	14.6
7	37	3.3	79.1	17.6
8	46	2.5	78.7	18.8
9	51	2.1	76.1	21.8
10	53	2.0	75.0	23.0

    (a) Geomorphological processes.

    (b) Lithology and structure.

2 (a) (i) Describe and explain the physical processes by which weathered materials may be moved downslope.

      (ii) Show how these processes have contributed to the form and surface characteristics of slopes.

    (b) Discuss the influence of human activities on the downslope movement of weathered materials.

3 What factors might you use to make a classification of mass movements?

4 How and why do different slopes develop in different ways through time?

Practical

Using a topographical map of your area, construct five different slope profiles. Describe and explain why the slopes vary in form.

Chapter 12

1 (a) Describe and account for the factors which influence the rate of rock weathering.

    (b) With reference to any TWO major morphogenetic regions, discuss the importance of weathering in the formation of their characteristic landforms.

2 (a) With the aid of TWO clearly labelled soil profile diagrams, explain how the characteristics of their profiles are related to the climatic and vegetation conditions.

    (b) Discuss how humankind may have been responsible for both upgrading and/or degrading soils.

Practical

Collect some small specimens of sedimentary rock (all about the same size); make sure they are dry, and then weigh each and record the weights. In the laboratory immerse each in a solution of one of the following salts for around one hour (sodium carbonate – washing soda, sodium sulphate – glauber's salt; magnesium sulphate – Epsom salts). Remove sample from salt and dry in an oven. Repeat the procedure each day. What changes in the rock samples do you note? Explain them.

Chapter 13

1 (a) Draw a fully labelled diagram to illustrate the interrelationships which exist between the components of the hydrological cycle.

    (b) With reference to ONE drainage basin which you have studied:

      (i) Describe its discharge characteristics.

      (ii) Show how human activities may have influenced the discharge.

2 (a) Define the following terms used with reference to drainage basins:

      Overland flow;
      Soil throughflow;
      Base flow;
      Peak discharge.

    (b) Explain how and why the time lag may vary on the same flood hydrograph on different occasions.

    (c) With reference to specific examples, describe the range of measures taken by humans to prevent flooding.

Chapter 14

1　With reference to examples, discuss the extent to which lithology and structure are significant in forming different drainage patterns.

2　(a)　(i) Discuss the factors which affect the amount and type of load carried by a river.

　　(ii) Describe the conditions under which river deposition occurs.

　(b) Outline the variety of features resulting from river deposition, referring in your answer to their form, location and composition.

3　Why do rivers flood? How do floods affect human activities?

Practical (A)

　(a) Describe the practical techniques which may be used in carrying out TWO of the following fieldwork investigations.

　　(i) A study of the relative importance of different methods of sediment transportation within a catchment area.

　　(ii) Measuring variations in the discharge of a stream.

　　(iii) A study of the superficial deposits of a formerly glaciated area.

　　(iv) The soils, vegetation and land-use along a hillslope transect.

　　(v) Variations of weather across a valley.

　(b) Comment critically on the possible conclusions to your investigations.

Practical (B)

Study the map below (figure A.3) showing the drainage network within an upland catchment area in northern England.

　(a)　(i) Using the superimposed grid, calculate the area of the drainage basin.

　　(ii) Measure the total length of stream channel within the basin and calculate the drainage density. Write your answers in the table.

　(b)　(i) Using the Strahler system of stream ordering, order the network. Write the results on the map itself and in the table below.

　　(ii) Calculate the bifurcation ratios and write the results in the table below.

　(c) Comment on the morphometric characteristics of this drainage basin, and how these might be expected to change following afforestation in the area.

Morphometric characteristics of drainage basin	
Area of drainage basin (km^2)	
Total stream length (km)	
Number of streams in each order　N_1 (first order)	_____
N_2 (second order)	_____
N_3 (third order)	_____
N_4 (fourth order)	_____
Bifurcation ratios　$\dfrac{N_1}{N_2}$	
$\dfrac{N_2}{N_3}$	
$\dfrac{N_3}{N_4}$	

－－－－ Watershed

⌒ Stream

0　1
km

Figure A.3 Drainage network.

Chapter 15

1   Describe and account for the differences in climate which occur:

   (a) In large urban areas.
   (b) Between such areas and their rural surroundings.

2   Is it fair to say that cities warrant treatment as a special kind of physical environment?
3   'Climate affects cities more than cities affect climate.' Discuss.
4   Examine the ways in which cities affect the hydrological cycle.

Chapter 16

1   Using appropriate examples, explain why it is sensible to adopt multiple working hypotheses when conducting field investigations.
2   Evaluate the role of the physical geographer in combatting the natural hazards of any one major world physical environment.
3   Evaluate the contribution of systems theory to our understanding of the physical environment.

Practical

Devise a research project that would aim to settle one of the outstanding questions in table 16.1 on p. 340.

Appendix 2
Guide to Further Reading

Periodicals

These include much that will be of value to anyone wishing to pursue some of the themes described in this book:

The Geography Review
The Geographical Magazine
Geography
Progress in Physical Geography
Physical Geography
Earth Surface Processes and Landforms
Zeitschrift für Geomorphologie (many articles are in English)
Journal of Climatology
Weather
Journal of Meteorology
Quarterly Journal of the Royal Meteorological Society
Journal of Biogeography
Journal of Ecology
Journal of Arid Environments
Arctic and Alpine Research
Journal of Glaciology
Teaching Geography

From time to time some of these journals have carried series of articles or special numbers that may be of particular interest.

Detailed discussion of terminology, together with a further bibliographic guide, are in Goudie, A. S. (ed.) *The encyclopaedic dictionary of physical geography*. Oxford: Basil Blackwell.

Books

The following books cover some of the themes discussed in this volume

General

Briggs, D. and Smithson, P. (1985) *Fundamentals of physical geography*. London: Hutchinson.
Brunsden, D. & Doornkamp, J. (eds) (1973) *The unquiet landscape*. Newton Abbott: David & Charles.
Cooke, R. U. and Doornkamp, J. C. (1974) *Geomorphology in environmental management*. Oxford: Clarendon Press.
Dury, G. H. (1981) *An introduction to environmental systems*. London: Heinemann.
Goudie, A. S. (1986) *The human impact: on the environment*. Oxford: Basil Blackwell.
Hart, M. G. (1986) *Geomorphology: pure and applied*. London: Allen and Unwin.
Moore, D. M. (ed.) (1982) *Green planet: the story of plant life on Earth*. Cambridge: Cambridge University Press.
Press, F. and Siever, R. (1978) *Earth*. San Francisco: W. H. Freeman.
Smith, D. G. (ed.) (1982) *The Cambridge Encyclopedia of Earth Sciences*. Cambridge: Cambridge University Press.
Smith, P. J. (ed.) (1986) *Encyclopedia of the Earth*. London: Hutchinson.
White, I. D., Mottershead, D. N. and Harrison, S. J. (1984) *Environmental systems: an introductory text*. London: Allen and Unwin.

For practical work in physical geography

Goudie, A. S. (ed.) (1981) *Geomorphological techniques*. London: Allen & Unwin.
Hanwell, J. D. and Newson, M. D. (1973) *Techniques in physical geography*. London: Macmillan.

King, C. A. M. (1980) *Physical geography*. Oxford: Basil Blackwell.

Lenon, B. J. and Cleaves, P. G. (1983) *Techniques and fieldwork in Geography*. London: University Tutorial Press.

Newson, M. D. and Hanwell, J. D. (1982) *Systematic physical geography*. London: Macmillan.

The following books provide additional reading for individual chapters. Those starred are especially useful as simple introductions:

Chapter 1   Global Geological Background

Gass, I. G., Smith, P. J. and Wilson, R. C. L. (1972) *Understanding the earth*. Horsham: Open University Press.

Selby, M. J. (1985) *Earth's changing surface: an introduction to geomorphology*. Oxford: Clarendon Press.

*Tarling, D. H. and Tarling, M. P. (1977) *Continental drift: a study of the earth's moving surface*. Harmondsworth: Penguin Books.

Wyllie, P. J. (1971) *The dynamic earth: textbook in geosciences*. New York: John Wiley.

Wyllie, P. J. (1976) *The way the earth works: an introduction to the new global geology and its revolutionary development*. New York: John Wiley.

Chapter 2   Global Climatic Background

*Barry, R. G. and Chorley, R. J. (1982) *Atmosphere, weather and climate*. London: Methuen.

Boucher, K. (1975) *Global climate*. London: English Universities Press.

*Bridges, E. M. (1970) *World soils*. Cambridge: Cambridge University Press.

Crowe, P. R. (1971) *Concepts in climatology*. London: Longman.

Goudie, A. S. (1983) *Environmental change*. Oxford: Clarendon Press.

Hanwell, J. (1980) *Atmospheric processes*. London: Allen & Unwin.

Illies, J. (1974) *Introduction to zoogeography*. London: Macmillan.

Lockwood, J. G. (1974) *World climatology*. London: Edward Arnold.

Lockwood, J. R. (1979) *Causes of climate*. London: Edward Arnold.

Oliver, J. E. (1973) *Climate and man's environment*. New York: John Wiley.

Trewartha, G. T. and Horn, L. H. (1980) *An introduction to climate*. New York: McGraw Hill.

Chapter 3   Polar Regions

Andrews, J. T. (1975) *Glacial systems*. North Scituate, Mass.: Duxbury Press.

Davies, J. L. (1969) *Landforms of cold climates*. Cambridge, Mass.: MIT Press.

Drewry, D. (1986) *Glacial geologic processes*. London: Arnold.

Embleton, C. and King, C. A. M. (1975) *Glacial geomorphology*. London: Edward Arnold.

Embleton, C. and King, C. A. M. (1975) *Periglacial geomorphology*. London: Edward Arnold.

French, H. M. (1976) *The periglacial environment*. London: Longman.

*Price, L. W. (1972) *The periglacial environment: permafrost and man*. Washington: Association of American Geographers.

Price, R. J. (1973) *Glacial and fluvioglacial landforms*. Edinburgh: Oliver & Boyd.

*Sugden, D. E. and John B. S. (1976) *Glaciers and landscape*. London: Edward Arnold.

Sugden, D. E. (1982; paperback 1984) *Arctic and Antarctic: A modern geographical synthesis*. Oxford: Basil Blackwell.

Tricart, J. (1970) *Geomorphology of cold environments*. London: Macmillan.

Washburn, A. L. (1979) *Geocryology*. London: Edward Arnold.

Chapter 4   The Mid-latitudes

Chandler, T. J. and Gregory, S. (eds) (1976) *The climate of the British Isles*. London: Longman.

Goudie, A. S. and Gardner, R. A. M. (1985) *Discovering landscape in England and Wales*. London: Allen and Unwin.

*Perry, A. H. (1981) *Environmental hazards in the British Isles*. London: Allen & Unwin.

Chapter 5   Deserts

Cooke, R. U. and Warren, A. (1973) *Geomorphology in deserts*. London: Batsford.

*Goudie, A. S. and Watson, A. (1980) *Desert geomorphology*. London: Macmillan.

*Goudie, A. S. and Wilkinson, J. C. (1977) *The warm desert environment*. Cambridge: Cambridge University Press.

Louw, G. N. and Seely, M. K. (1982) *Ecology of desert organisms*. London: Longman.

Chapter 6   The Tropics

Gourou, P. (1961) *The tropical world*. London: Longman.

Harris, D. R. (ed.) (1980) *Human ecology in savanna environments*. London: Academic Press.

Jackson, I. J. (1977) *Climate, water and agriculture in the tropics*. London: Longman.

Lockwood, J. G. (1976) *The physical geography of the tropics: an introduction*. Kuala Lumpur: Oxford University Press.

Longman, K. A. and Jenic, J. (1974) *Tropical forest and its environment*. London: Longman.

Nieuwolt, S. (1977) *Tropical climatology*. London: John Wiley.

Thomas, M. F. (1974) *Tropical geomorphology*. London: Macmillan.

Tricart, J. (1972) *The landforms of the humid tropics, forests and savannas*. London: Longman.

Williams, C. N. and Joseph, K. T. (1970) *Climate, soil and crop production in the humid tropics*. Kuala Lumpur: Oxford University Press.

Chapter 7   Mountains

Barry, R. G. (1981) *Mountain weather and climate*. London: Methuen.

*Price, L. W. (1981) *Mountains and man: a study of process and environment*. Berkeley: University of California Press.

Chapter 8   Coasts

Barnes, R. S. K. (1977) *The coastline*. London: John Wiley.

Bird, E. C. F. (1969) *Coasts*. Cambridge, Mass.: MIT Press.

Brunsden, D. and Goudie, A. (1981) *Classic coastal landforms of Dorset*. Sheffield: Geographical Association.

Castleden, R. (1982) *Classic landforms of the Sussex coast*. Sheffield: Geographical Association.

*Clayton, K. M. (1979) *Coastal geomorphology*. London: Macmillan.

Davies, J. L. (1972) *Geographical variation in coastal development*. Edinburgh: Oliver & Boyd.

Davis, R. A. (ed.) (1978) *Coastal sedimentary environments*. New York: Springer Verlag.

Pethick, J. (1984) *Introduction to coastal geomorphology*. London: Arnold.

Steers, J. A. (1964) *The coastline of England and Wales*. Cambridge: Cambridge University Press.

Steers, J. A. (1973) *The coastline of Scotland*. Cambridge: Cambridge University Press.

Chapter 9   Plants and Animals

Begon, M., Harper, J. L. and Townsend, C. R. (1986) *Ecology: individuals, populations and communities*. Oxford: Blackwell Scientific.

Collinson, A. S. (1977) *Introduction to world vegetation*. London: Allen & Unwin.

Cox, C. B. and Moore, P. D. (1980) *Biogeography: an ecological and evolutionary approach*. Oxford: Blackwell Scientific.

Eyre, S. R. (1963) *Vegetation and soils: a world picture*. London: Edward Arnold.

Fitter, R. (1986) *Wildlife for man*. London: Collins.

Golley, F. B. (ed.) (1977) *Ecological succession*. Stroudsburg: Dowden.

*Gorman, M. (1979) *Island ecology*. London: Edward Arnold.

Kellman, M.C. (1975) *Plant geography*. London: Methuen.

Odum, E. P. (1975) *Ecology*. New York: Holt, Rinehart & Winston.

Simmons, I. G. (1979) *Biogeography: natural and cultural*. London: Edward Arnold.

*Simmons, I. G. (1982) *Biogeographical processes*. London: Allen & Unwin.

Viles, H. A. (1988) *Biogeomorphology*. Oxford: Basil Blackwell.

Chapter 10 Tectonic Features

Costa, J. E. and Baker, V. R. (1981) *Surficial geology: building with the earth.* New York: John Wiley.

*Francis, P. (1976) *Volcanoes.* Harmondsworth: Penguin Books.

Hallam, A. (1973) *A revolution in the earth sciences.* Oxford: Clarendon Press.

Ollier, C. D. (1988) *Volcanoes.* Oxford: Basil Blackwell.

Ollier, C. D. (1981) *Tectonics and landforms.* London: Longman.

Rice, R. J. (1987) *Fundamentals of geomorphology.* London: Longman.

Sparks, B. W. (1971) *Rocks and relief.* London: Longman.

*Weyman, D. (1981) *Tectonic processes.* London: Allen & Unwin.

Chapter 11 Slopes

Carson, M. A. and Kirkby, M. J. (1972) *Hillslope form and process.* Cambridge: Cambridge University Press.

Chorley, R. J., Schumm, S. A. and Sugden, D. E. (1984) *Geomorphology.* London: Methuen.

Selby, M. J. (1982) *Hillslope materials and processes.* Oxford: Oxford University Press.

Small, R. J. (1970) *The study of landforms.* Cambridge: Cambridge University Press.

*Weyman, D. and Weyman, J. (1977) *Landscape processes: an introduction to geomorphology.* London: Allen & Unwin.

Young, A. (1972) *Slopes.* Edinburgh: Oliver & Boyd.

Chapter 12 Soils and Weathering

Birkeland, P. W. (1984) *Soils and geomorphology.* New York: Oxford University Press.

*Briggs, D. (1977) *Soils.* London: Butterworth.

Fenwick, I. M. and Knapp, B. J. (1982) *Soil process and response.* London: Duckworth.

Courtney, F. M. and Trudgill, S. T. (1976) *The soil: an introduction to soil study in Britain.* London: Edward Arnold.

Jennings, J. N. (1985) *Karst geomorphology.* Oxford: Basil Blackwell.

Ollier, C. D. (1974) *Weathering and landforms.* London: Macmillan.

Ollier, C. D. (1984) *Weathering.* London: Longman.

Paton, T. R. (1978) *The formation of soil material.* London: Allen & Unwin.

Sweeting, M. M. (1972) *Karst landforms.* London: Macmillan.

Chapter 13 The Hydrological Cycle

Chorley, R. J. (1969) *Water, earth and man.* London: Methuen.

Dunne, T. and Leopold, L. B. (1978) *Water in environmental planning.* San Francisco: W. H. Freeman.

Henderson-Sellers, A. and Robinson, P. J. (1986) *Contemporary climatology.* London: Longman.

*Knapp, B. J. (1979) *Elements of geographical hydrology.* London: Allen & Unwin.

Leopold, L. B. (1974) *Water: a primer.* San Francisco: W. H. Freeman.

*Newson, M. D. (1975) *Flooding and flood hazard in the United Kingdom.* Oxford: Oxford University Press.

Pereira, H. C. (1973) *Land use and water resources.* Cambridge: Cambridge University Press.

Rodda, J. C., Downing, R. A. and Law, F. M. (1976) *Systematic hydrology.* London: Newnes-Butterworth.

Ward, R. C. (1975) *Principles of hydrology.* London: McGraw Hill.

Weyman, D. (1975) *Runoff processes and streamflow modelling.* Oxford: Oxford University Press.

Chapter 14 Rivers

Gregory, K. J. and Walling, D. E. (1973) *Drainage basin form and process.* London: Edward Arnold.

Leopold, L. B., Wolman, M. G. and Miller, J. P. (1964) *Fluvial processes in geomorphology.* San Francisco: W. H. Freeman.

Lewin, J. (ed.) (1981) *British rivers.* London: Allen & Unwin.

*Morisawa, M. (1968) *Streams: their dynamics and morphology.* New York: McGraw Hill.

Petts, G. E. (1983) *Rivers*. London: Butterworth.

Richards, K. S. (1982) *Rivers: form and process in alluvial channels*. London: Methuen.

*Smith, D. I. and Stopp, P. (1978) *The river basin*. Cambridge: Cambridge University Press.

Thornes, J. (1979) *River channels*. London: Macmillan.

Ward, R. C. (1978) *Floods: a geographical perspective*. London: Macmillan.

Chapter 15   Cities

Berry, B. J. (1974) *Land use, urban form and environmental quality*. Chicago: University of Chicago Press.

Chandler, T. J. (1965) *The climate of London*. London: Hutchinson.

Detwyler, T. R. and Marcus, M. G. (eds) (1972) *Urbanization and environment: the physical geography of the city*. Belmont: Duxbury.

Douglas, I. (1983) *The urban environment*. London: Edward Arnold.

Goudie, A. S. (1986) *The human impact on the environment*. Oxford: Basil Blackwell.

Oke, T. R. (1978) *Boundary layer climates*. London: Methuen.

Index